WRONGS AND RIGHTS COME APART

WRONGS AND RIGHTS COME APART

Nicolas Cornell

Harvard University Press

CAMBRIDGE, MASSACHUSETTS · LONDON, ENGLAND

2025

Copyright © 2025 by the President and Fellows of Harvard College

All rights reserved

Printed in the United States of America

First printing

Publication of this book has been supported through the generous provisions
of the Maurice and Lula Bradley Smith Memorial Fund.

LIBRARY OF CONGRESS CATALOGING-IN-PUBLICATION DATA

Names: Cornell, Nicolas, 1981– author.

Title: Wrongs and rights come apart / Nicolas Cornell.

Description: Cambridge : Harvard University Press, 2025. | Includes index.

Identifiers: LCCN 2024005628 | ISBN 9780674244979 (cloth)

Subjects: LCSH: Torts—Philosophy. | Liability (Law)—Philosophy. |
Interpersonal relations—Moral and ethical aspects.

Classification: LCC K923 .C67 2025 |
DDC 346.0301—dc23 / eng / 20240409

LC record available at https://lccn.loc.gov/2024005628

For my father

Contents

1	Two Ways of Relating	1
2	Third Parties	26
3	Shaping Action	67
4	Repair	94
5	The Unclaimable	115
6	The Complaintless	133
7	Preemptive Forgiving	157
8	Exploitation	181
9	Relational Dualism	202
	NOTES	229
	ACKNOWLEDGMENTS	281
	INDEX	285

WRONGS AND RIGHTS COME APART

I

Two Ways of Relating

1.1 Two Stories

On August 24, 1924, Helen Palsgraf was standing on a railroad platform, waiting to catch a train to Rockaway Beach. A different train was just pulling out from the station, and two men ran to catch it. One of them carried a small, paper-wrapped package. As these men struggled to board the moving train, two Long Island Railroad Company employees tried to help them. A guard on the train reached out to pull the man with the package aboard, and another guard on the platform pushed him from behind. The package fell from the man's arms onto the tracks.

Although it bore nothing on the outside to indicate it, the package contained fireworks. They exploded upon impact with the track. Mrs. Palsgraf, standing on the platform, was struck by metal scales, which were knocked over either by the explosion itself or by the ensuing tumult. She suffered head injuries, developing a stammer and eventually going altogether mute. Mrs. Palsgraf sued the railroad company, winning before both a jury and an appellate court. But she would receive no legal remedy. Instead, her story became the canonical backdrop to a foundational idea about the relationship between rights and wrongs.

In a famous opinion from New York's highest court, Benjamin Cardozo—one of the great American jurists and soon-to-be Supreme Court justice—dismissed Mrs. Palsgraf's lawsuit.[1] The crucial premise of Cardozo's opinion was that, to have been wronged, Mrs. Palsgraf must have held some right that was violated. Cardozo reasoned that, even supposing that the railroad breached some duties by being negligent in handling the package and its owner, the railroad did not breach any duty *owed to Mrs. Palsgraf*. She therefore could assert no legal wrong. The fulcrum of Cardozo's opinion, in other words, is that a wrong requires the violation of a right of the injured person. As he expressed it,

> Negligence is not actionable unless it involves the invasion of a legally protected interest, the violation of a right. . . . What the plaintiff must show is "a wrong" to herself, i.e., a violation of her own right, and not merely a wrong to some one else, nor conduct "wrongful" because unsocial, but not "a wrong" to any one. . . . The commission of a wrong imports the violation of a right. . . . One who seeks redress at law . . . must show that the act as to him had possibilities of danger so many and apparent *as to entitle him* to be protected against the doing of it though the harm was unintended. Affront to personality is still the keynote of the wrong.[2]

According to Cardozo, in order to assert a grievance, Mrs. Palsgraf must have been able to point to some right of her own against the conduct. She must have been entitled to contrary conduct; the railroad company must have owed a duty *to her* not to act as it did. In this case, however, whatever duties might have been breached were owed not to Mrs. Palsgraf but to the passenger with the package. So there could be no liability to Mrs. Palsgraf.

Cardozo's famous opinion thus turns on a conceptual claim: an agent X (here, the Long Island Railroad Company) wrongs Y (here, Mrs. Palsgraf) *only if* X violates Y's right—that is, *only if* X breaches a duty owed to Y. To reject this proposition, Cardozo tells us, "will involve us, and swiftly too, in a maze of contradictions."[3] A contrary view would require that "life will have to be made over, and human nature transformed."[4] It is, in short, a point about the structure of our basic moral concepts.[5] It is axiomatic that wrongs are tied to rights. To think otherwise would be a contradiction or a radical transformation of life and human nature. Many readers, especially those trained in law or moral philosophy, may be inclined to endorse Cardozo's axiom.

Now consider a second story. In *War and Peace,* Prince Andrei Bolkonsky, a wealthy, thirty-one-year-old widower, falls in love with Natasha Rostova, a vivacious girl who has just come out in society. Prince Andrei proposes to Natasha, and she joyfully accepts. Their love seems real. But

Prince Andrei's father disapproves of his son remarrying, and it is agreed that the marriage will be delayed for a full year. Prince Andrei declares to his young lover, "It will give you time to be sure of yourself. I ask you to make me happy in a year, but you are free: our engagement shall remain a secret, and should you find that you do not love me, or should you come to love . . ."[6] At this point, Natasha cuts him off, but Tolstoy informs the reader,

> No betrothal ceremony took place and Natasha's engagement to [Prince Andrei] was not announced; Prince Andrei insisted on that. He said that as he was responsible for the delay he ought to bear the whole burden of it; that he had given his word and bound himself forever, but that he did not wish to bind Natasha and gave her perfect freedom. If after six months she felt that she did not love him she would have full right to reject him. Naturally neither Natasha nor her parents wished to hear of this, but Prince Andrei was firm.[7]

Prince Andrei, it is quite explicit, had no right to Natasha's hand or to her continuing love.

A few months later, Natasha attempts to elope with an unworthy adventurer, who, unbeknownst to Natasha, already has an abandoned wife in Poland and is simply set on seducing her. In the midst of her misguided passion, Natasha calls off her engagement with Prince Andrei. But the plans to elope are foiled by Natasha's cousin, and Natasha quickly comes to see her error in judgment.

Tolstoy's novel turns on the fact that Natasha and Prince Andrei are, from that point forward, united as one who has wronged and one who has been wronged. Natasha experiences it this way, declaring, "I'm . . . tormented by the wrong I have done him. Tell him only that I beg him to forgive . . . me for everything."[8] And Prince Andrei likewise takes himself to be aggrieved, remarking to a friend, "I said that a fallen woman should be forgiven, but I didn't say I could forgive her. I can't."[9] It is at the heart of Natasha and Prince Andrei's tragic story—as it unfolds over the course of the novel—that she has wronged him in a way that can never be fully repaired.

What of Cardozo's axiom? Here is a wrong at the center of one of the great novels of all time, but it is unnatural to speak of a right to another's

WRONGS AND RIGHTS COME APART

love, and even if one could, Prince Andrei explicitly and firmly disavowed any rights.[10] Human life, at least in Tolstoy's telling, does not seem to conform so neatly to Cardozo's structure.[11] For Tolstoy, even a grievous wrong—the kind that can forever haunt two lives—may be a matter not of denying something to which the other was entitled but rather simply of causing losses that one shouldn't have. Perhaps that is not to "make life over" but to see life as it is.[12]

1.2 Two Ways of Relating

This book concerns the relationship between rights and wrongs—that is, wrongings.* Put another way, this book is about our claims on others—what others owe us and what we can demand from them. And it is about our complaints against others—what we can resent, rebuke, and call on others to repair. And, most of all, it is about the relationship between the two.

The two preceding stories highlight the fact that we relate to one another both before and after normatively laden moments and choices. Mrs. Palsgraf and the Long Island Railroad Company stand in one set of relations before anything happens and in another set of relations after the explosion. Natasha and Andrei stand in one set of relations during their

---

* As a terminological point, I use the word "wrong" in its noun form—e.g., "he committed a wrong"—to mean an instance of one person wronging another person. In this way, the use as a noun is associated with the use as a transitive verb—e.g., "he wronged her." Wrongs, in my usage, are committed against someone. This use should be contrasted with usages associated with the adjective "wrong"—the substantival use or the use referring simply to an instance of someone doing something that is wrong—which would not necessarily imply injustice directed against someone. In short, I distinguish "he did a wrong" from "he did wrong." Not all writers agree with my choice. David Owens, for example, specifically distinguishes between "wrongs" and "wrongings." He offers the following example: "If I concrete over the Grand Canyon, I have committed a wrong by disregarding its aesthetic value even if I have wronged nobody." David Owens, *Shaping the Normative Landscape* (Oxford: Oxford University Press, 2012), 45. Although Owens says that the assimilation of "wrongs" and "wrongings" is "a substantive normative claim," I think that we are in basic agreement despite our linguistic disagreement. I agree with Owens's substantive claim that there can be wrongful acts that do not involve wronging anyone. I simply resist calling such acts "wrongs" because, to my ear, "he committed a wrong" implies that there is someone who has been wronged. Owens's terminological choice means that, for him, "he did a wrong" and "he did wrong" mean the same thing, whereas I think that they mark a difference. Out of an overabundance of caution, I shall try to use the gerund "wronging" where there might be any possible confusion. Regardless, the reader should understand that I use the nouns "wrong" and "wronging" interchangeably.

courtship and in quite another after she casts him off. In each case, before-hand, we want to know what can be demanded and what counts as proper concern for the other. Afterward, there is hurt and loss, and the question is about the need for, or mode of, repair. The central question of this book—and the question on which Cardozo and Tolstoy appear to diverge—concerns the conceptual connections between these two perspectives. But there can be little doubt that interpersonal moral life is composed of relating ex ante and relating ex post.

Each perspective has its own distinctive characteristics. Before I act, your status may place constraints on the way that I may treat you. For example, I should not lie to you for my own gain. And I should not treat you as a convenient source of organs. These are not mere ordinary consider-ations; they seem to have a special force. They are sometimes described as "trumps,"[13] "side-constraints,"[14] or "exclusionary."[15] We have an inchoate understanding that these constraints spring from you and your moral status, although it is hard to say exactly what that means. It seems like I ought not do these things *because of* the sort of being that you are. We say that you are entitled to such treatment from me; it is owed to you. Relatedly, you typically have some control over the constraints on my action: you can permit my attempts at deception (as when we agree to play certain games), or you may decide to donate a kidney to me. That is, the way that a duty is owed to you may be manifested in your ability to claim, waive, control, or even transfer the duty in question.

We often characterize relations like these by saying that one person has *a right* that another act in a particular way. The right describes the way that its bearer constrains how others ought to act. But the language of "rights" can also be misleading, bringing with it additional baggage or le-galistic connotations. While my discussion will mostly proceed in the lan-guage of rights, the arguments might be just as well framed in terms of "claims." The crucial idea is that of an entitlement—legal or moral—that correlates with a duty owed by another. In such relations, the holder is a kind of authority with respect to the actions of others. We shape the ac-tions of others, and they too shape our conduct as we move through the world.

Moral relations, however, are not limited to forward-looking constraints on how we ought to treat one another. Moral agents also relate to one an-other in various ways after one party injures another—as one who has wronged and as one who has been wronged. These after-the-fact relations are found in our practices of complaint, accountability, resentment, compensation, apology, and forgiveness. For example, if I cause you harm by deceiving you, then you will have a complaint against me; even more so if I steal your kidney. It will not merely be the case that I acted wrongly, but also that I *wronged* you. Here again morality involves a particular sort of relationship between one agent and another. But this relationship exists ex post; it is not about shaping conduct going forward but rather about the repercussions of conduct afterward.

We can, in this way, identify two clusters of moral relations and associated moral practices—some that arise ex ante, shaping or constraining our actions, and others that arise ex post, making us accountable for our actions. The two lists in Table 1-1 offer some typical elements of these two clusters, though I don't take them to be precise or complete.

I take these clusters of relations to represent two different forms of relating to each other. I will typically describe these forms as ex ante and ex post, because I take them to be about a prospective, deliberative perspective and a retrospective, corrective perspective. But caution is required here. We are capable of asking, in advance, what matters will look like ex post; and we are capable of asking ex post what matters looked like at the time of deliberation. We can thus imaginatively adopt the alternative perspective, as when we ask beforehand, "Will I regret this?" or afterward, "Should I have known better?" Because of these imaginative capabilities, what I shall call the ex ante perspective is not truly limited temporally to the ex ante moment, and the ex post perspective is not limited temporally to the ex post. If one prefers, one might refer instead to the "perspective of deliberation" and the "perspective of grievance," or some such.[16] The important point is that relational phenomena seem to coalesce into two clusters.[17]

TABLE 1-1

Ex Ante		
rights	obligation	demanding
claims	duties to another	seeking/giving consent
entitlements	owing a duty	granting permission

Ex Post		
wrongs	holding accountable	apology
complaints	answerable to	forgiveness
grievances	owing a justification	compensation

The subject of this book—which I will often put in terms of the relation between rights and wrongs—is properly understood to be the relation between these two clusters. Are the ex ante and ex post relations merely different perspectives on the same underlying nexus between persons? Or are they manifestations of distinct ways that persons relate to each other—each not purely explicable in terms of the other?

1.3 A Supposed Unity

It is tempting to see all these relationships as essentially unified. Rights, the thought goes, place constraints on what we can do to each other *in that* we are liable to wrong others if we act in contrary ways. What it is to have a right is, at least in part, that one stands to be wronged if certain actions are not performed. On the flip side, one is wronged *just insofar as* one has had one's right violated—that is, just insofar as there is a violation of a duty one was owed. Having a right and being potentially wronged, then, are simply different perspectives on the same moral relation—much as the future and the past may simply be different perspectives on the same moment in time. On this view, the standing to demand an action is isomorphic with—indeed, the mirror image of—the standing to rebuke noncompliance. The relations are necessarily defined and understood in terms of each other—flip sides of the same coin. In short, to be wronged is to have had one's right violated, and to have a right is for it to be the case that some conduct would wrong you.

This unified picture is widely assumed across a range of contexts. In both ordinary and scholarly discourse, we often slide back and forth between talk of rights or claims and talk of wrongs or complaints. And theorists often take for granted that the concepts are mutually explicable. We have already seen one canonical statement of this view in Cardozo's axiom that "what the plaintiff must show is 'a wrong' to herself, i.e., a violation of her own right. . . . The commission of a wrong imports the violation of a right." Here is a smattering of other examples, across a variety of domains and normative commitments.

- Michael Thompson: "You have, as we sometimes say, a duty to Sylvia not to kill her. You 'owe' it to her not to kill her. Such language is perhaps a bit stiff, but we can put the same point more colloquially.

We can say, for example, that in killing Sylvia *you* wrong *her:* You would do wrong precisely 'to' her, or do wrong 'by' her."[18]

- Jeremy Bentham: "The distinction between rights and offences is therefore strictly verbal—there is no difference in the ideas. It is not possible to form the idea of a *right,* without forming the idea of an *offence.*"[19]

- Elizabeth Anscombe: "Justice as a personal virtue is that character in a man which means that he has a settled determination not to infringe anyone's rights. A wrong is an infringement of a right. What is wrong about an act that is wrong may be just this, that it is *a* wrong."[20]

- William Blackstone: "I am now therefore to proceed to the consideration of wrongs; which for the most part convey to us an idea merely negative, as being nothing else but a privation of right."[21]

- E. J. Bond: "It can only be true that I have a moral obligation toward you . . . if you have a moral right to demand something of me. . . . If I do have a moral obligation toward you . . . and I fail to honor that obligation . . . then you have been *wronged,* you have a justified complaint against me, a complaint justified *on moral grounds,* and you may be morally entitled to seek redress or reparation . . . ."[22] "Injustice (doing some person or persons a wrong) consists in the violation of rights; justice is respect for and protection of those same rights. . . . All these ideas are interconnected . . . If there is such a thing as injustice—and we know there is—then there are rights, for injustice consists in the violation of rights."[23]

- Judith Jarvis Thomson: "I will use 'Y wronged X' and 'Y did X a wrong' only where Y violated a claim of X's. So on my use of these locutions, they entail that Y acted wrongly; but they entail more than just Y acted wrongly—they entail that Y wrongly infringed a claim of X's."[24]

- The US Supreme Court (quoting the Connecticut Supreme Court): "An injury, legally speaking, consists of a wrong done to a person, or, in other words, a violation of his right. It is an ancient maxim, that a damage to one, without an injury in this sense, (*damnum absque injuria*), does not lay the foundation of an action; because, if the act complained of does not violate any of his legal rights, it is obvious, that he has no cause to complain."[25]

TWO WAYS OF RELATING

- David Owens: "What is it to do wrong in a way that wrongs someone? If X would wrong you by deceiving you then you have a right against X that he not deceive you; X *owes* it to you not to deceive you, he has an obligation *to you* [to] be truthful to you. And owing *you* the truth is different from merely being obliged to be truthful."[26]

- Arthur Ripstein: "I wrong you only by interfering with something to which you already have a right, or, as I shall put it, something you already have."[27]

- R. Jay Wallace: "The action that flouts [a directed] requirement will not merely be wrong; it will change the agent's normative relationship to another individual, wronging the person to whom compliance with the requirement was owed. This is, as it were, the ex post facto residue of the individual's claim against the agent to performance of the required action, in the case in which the claim has not been honored."[28]

In each of these passages, the writer takes the connection between our ex ante entitlements and our ex post complaints to be conceptually necessary, logically entailed, axiomatic, or just plain "obvious."

This common assumption plays two major roles: theoretical grounding and practical inference. Glimpses of each can be seen in the foregoing passages. First, the unity of these ideas is invoked by philosophers and legal theorists who are interested in the grounds for our directed duties. In virtue of what do we owe duties to others? In virtue of what do we have rights? The supposed unity can potentially help answer these questions. Bentham, who suggests that rights exist merely in virtue of the fact that some acts constitute offenses, provides a simple, thin example. For a deeper and more recent example, Stephen Darwall has influentially argued that morality involves "second-personal reasons"—reasons that stem from the authority of others to make claims on us. These reasons are, for Darwall, explained and constituted by others' ability to make complaints and hold us accountable. He writes, "If [someone stepping on your foot] accepts that you can demand that he move his foot, he must also accept that you will have grounds for complaint or some other form of accountability-seeking response if he doesn't. . . . A second-personal reason is one whose validity depends on presupposed . . . accountability relations between persons."[29] The idea is that our ability to make claims on each other presupposes our ability to address each other with complaints. Here, the supposed unity—what Darwall called "an interdefinable circle"[30]—is emphasized for theoretical purposes. It is thought to illuminate the nature and source of our obligations.[31]

The supposed unity is also invoked to draw more practical conclusions about particular concrete problems. It is taken to assist in determining whether a right exists or whether a wrong has transpired. Cardozo's reasoning in *Palsgraf* might be understood in just this way. There was a question whether Mrs. Palsgraf had been wronged. Cardozo takes himself to answer that question by pointing out that no right of hers was violated, which he couples with the assumption that one cannot be wronged without having had a right violated. The supposed unity comes in as the central axiom in Cardozo's decision. The opposite inference is also familiar: we might conclude that someone has rights precisely because it seems that they would have grounds for special complaint. These practical inferences—from the absence or presence of a right to the absence or presence of a wronging, and vice versa—reflect the pervasive practical impact of the assumed unity.

1.4 Wrongs and Rights Pushed Apart

Given its widespread endorsement and its significance in both theoretical and practical arguments, it is natural to ask whether these relations are as unified as often thought. Are rights and wrongs mutually defining? Does life conform to Cardozo's axiom?

This book describes a contrary view. Our ex ante normative relations, like rights and directed duties, do not map straightforwardly onto our ex post moral relations, like having a complaint or being wronged. There are two separable and independently functioning moral phenomena at work here. Our accountability relations ex post are not reducible to our entitlements ex ante—nor vice versa.

In the language of rights and wrongs, this book defends the view that rights and wrongs are distinct. I will argue that, although often intertwined, rights and wrongs do not always go hand in hand. Rather, they systematically diverge across a range of contexts. Neither presupposes the other, and it is a mistake to infer one from the other.

Appreciation of this practical divergence emerges alongside a recognition that rights and wrongs play substantively different roles in moral life.

Wrongs are not merely the outline left where rights have been taken away; rights are more than the glimmer of future liability. Taking these two relations to be reciprocals of each other fails to do justice to either one. It flattens our moral life, and it leads us into identifiable practical errors.

Rights-based theory is correct in seeing our lives as shaped by duties that we owe to others as a matter of respecting them as free and equal persons. The correlative to these duties is that each of us is entitled to certain treatment from others. Rights thus structure both how we ought to act and what we can demand of others. They carve out areas of life as ours, as a matter of our choice and not to be taken from us. It is of great significance to be the bearer of rights.

As Tolstoy seemed to appreciate, however, many of our most significant injuries at the hands of others arise out of matters over which we have no right.[32] They may stem from the violation of someone else's rights; or from the violation of general norms, not particularly owed to us individually; or from the denial of something—like love—to which we were never entitled in the first place. Our grievances cannot always be neatly traced to entitlements that we held beforehand. Nor, in turn, can rights be simply a matter of what gives rise to grievances. If we conceptualize rights as marking out wherever a person would have grievance, then rights will not structure our action as they should. We want, for example, to be able to say that Natasha was free—that Prince Andrei had no right—even as there was a potential to wrong. Moral relations need not come all in one set; moral life is more complicated.

In philosophy's constant two-way movement to theory and back to ordinary life, this book presses more toward a movement of return.[33] It aims to draw the reader back from certain theoretical commitments by attending to familiar features of human life and interaction that can be lost in the midst of theory.[34] But that characterization may make the project appear negative—merely dismantling a particular theoretical commitment. My aspiration is something more positive. If the task of philosophy is "the provision of rich and fertile conceptual schemes which help us to reflect upon and understand the nature of moral progress and moral failure,"[35] then this book aims to enrich our conceptual schemes. Nothing here is meant to reject the recent focus on relational normativity, from which both moral philosophy and the law have benefited significantly. To the contrary: I hope to show that, within relational normativity, there exists more richness to examine and to theorize.

1.5 A Methodological Caution

It is worth pausing, at this point, for an important methodological note. A reader might wonder whether this is all a semantic dispute. Is this just an argument about how we use the noun forms of "right" and "wrong"? Indeed, some of the passages already quoted seem to be asserting the unity as more or less definitional. Am I merely arguing over definitions?

No. I am not particularly interested in which words we use, though of course that can matter. One might stipulate that "wrong," when used as a verb or noun, refers only to rights violations. I would have no deep objection.[36]

My concern is with the underlying moral phenomena and practices. How do the cluster of relations that persons stand in ex ante bear on the cluster of relations that they stand in ex post? As I have tried to describe, we have robust practices associated with each perspective. We make claims on each other, and our existence imposes side constraints on each other's choices; on the other hand, we also engage in complaint, resentment, apology, forgiveness, and compensation. It is a substantive, not linguistic, question whether these relationships and practices align or come apart.

The argument for giving up the assumption that there is a necessary connection between having a right and being wronged is thus about correctly characterizing actual phenomena. It is driven both by concrete examples and by theoretical considerations about the different moral functions of these relations. These two aspects of the argument are deeply intertwined. I mean to argue that we cannot be true to the richness of our practices, across the range of cases that life presents, if we think that the ex ante and ex post are so tightly linked.

Keeping the focus on relationships and practices will help avert two merely linguistic responses that will persistently lurk as temptations. First, responses that take the form "that's just what we mean" are not truly addressing the underlying issue. For example, I will argue in Chapter 2 that some third parties, like Mrs. Palsgraf, are wronged. In response, one might simply insist that "wronged" refers to having had one's rights violated. Mrs. Palsgraf wasn't wronged because her rights weren't violated and, as a linguistic matter, that's just what it means to be wronged.[37] Such a response does not address the substantive claim that there exists another important moral relationship with a whole cluster of practices—call it what one may.

To deny this substantive claim, one must be prepared to say that the party in question does not have a special moral standing to complain, resent, apologize, compensate, be forgiven, and so on—that, morally, she is like any other bystander.

Second, responses that posit a moral relationship without any associated practical significance—mere placeholders—are equally problematic. For example, one might try to accommodate our sense that Natasha wrongs Prince Andrei by simply positing that he must have held some right of a different kind—for example, a right to her loyalty. The right is reflected in his special standing to assert a grievance. But, to engage my argument meaningfully, an assertion of a right should be associated with some practical difference that it makes *to the ex ante perspective*—some difference in deliberation, permissibility, enforceability, the standing to demand, the power to consent, or some such. If the "right" means nothing except that a person would be wronged by the conduct in question, then it is just a placeholder. Perhaps as a linguistic matter, we do sometimes use the words "right" and "wronging" in a placeholder fashion—"right" simply marking out who potentially has a grievance and "wronging" simply marking the fact that a right was violated. But my topic is whether our two clusters of actual practices and relationships—ex ante and ex post—line up, so I am not interested in linguistic usage that carries no practical significance. My focus is our moral practices, not how we label them.

In this spirit, I begin from the practices and phenomena that I associate with rights and wrongs. By Chapter 9, I will venture more in the way of philosophical analysis and definition. For now, the starting point will be our moral practices, with which I trust that the reader will have some intuitive facility.

1.6 Five Features of Rights

The idea of a right at issue in this book is, as I have said, bound up with a duty owed by another. These are what Wesley Newcomb Hohfeld called "claim-rights."[38] A person Y has a claim-right that another person X do φ if and only if X has a duty to Y to do φ. Notice that the duties in question are distinctly relational. I owe it *to you* not to step on your foot or take your organs; I owe it *to my promisee* to keep my promise; and I owe it *to my child* to provide for his well-being. These are not merely things that I ought to do in some general sense. The duty is, it is sometimes said, directed. I owe these duties *to a particular other person,* whom we can then describe as holding a right to the action in question.

It is notoriously difficult to pick out a single defining feature or set of features that characterize rights and directed duties, distinguishing them from mere interests, reasons, or nondirected duties.[39] I will not attempt it. Throughout this book, I will consider an array of features that regularly characterize rights and directed duties. Taken as a cluster, I believe that these features describe the distinctive normativity of rights and directed duties, even if no single feature or set of features is necessary or sufficient.

First, rights can often be waived by their holders, which is to say that the duties in question are under their control.[40] For example, if I make you a promise, then I am under a duty to perform and, importantly, you have the power to release me from that duty. That power reflects a way in which I am not merely under a duty, but under a duty *to you.* The will theory famously—and problematically—takes this control to be the essential feature of a right. One need not, however, think that such control is necessary for rightholding to agree that it is indicative. It reflects a directedness in the normativity.

A second common feature of directed normativity is that compliance can be claimed or demanded by a rightholder.[41] As my promisee, you have a special standing to call me to perform. Claiming performance consists not simply in mere descriptive assertion, simply pointing out that I am under a duty. Rather, it is an exercise of authority. Whereas others might note that I ought to keep my promise, you can demand it. This claimability, again, illuminates a way that my duty is uniquely connected to you.

Third, compliance can often be coercively enforced.[42] I have duties both to respect your bodily integrity and to be generous. But you—or someone else—may permissibly use force to make me comply with the former but probably not the latter. This enforceability suggests a way in which bodily integrity is a right and respect for it is owed to you. It is so yours that you can forcibly take it if necessary.

Fourth, rights seem to operate as trumps or side constraints, excluding certain facts from even entering into consideration.[43] To say that you have a right to your kidney is to say that society cannot take it from you, even where it might be beneficial on aggregate to do so. To say that a promisee has a right to performance is to say that whether to perform is, in at least some respects, settled, regardless of how advantageous nonperformance might now be. Rights and directed duties thus come with a kind of deontic structure.

Finally, and perhaps most elusively, rights and directed duties seem to have a special phenomenology, both for the duty-bearer and for the correlative rightholder. Confronted with a rightholder, one experiences one's choice as dictated by the status of the other party. The rightholder enters the agent's deliberations in an especially immediate way. To see another as a person, with rights, is to see certain actions as blocked off. Potential transgressions may be experienced—perhaps should be experienced—a bit like looking directly into the sun, as something that one practically cannot do. The rightholder is thus not merely a downstream beneficiary of our duties; she exerts a kind of direct pull on our choices themselves, lending them a distinctive phenomenology. Conversely, the rightholder experiences herself as exerting this pull on others. The experience of a rightholder is not merely a sense of security, but a sense of control or authority. In short, rights come with a particular feel.

Each of these features suggests, in some way or another, a relational kind of normativity. It is not merely that one has a reason (monadic), but that one is related to another (dyadic). Taken together, I think that these features are illuminating and cohesive. Even if none of them supply necessary and sufficient conditions, they point toward our concept of having a right. I will return to them throughout the book as the sort of features that would mark out a right or a directed duty. Rights will, paradigmatically, exhibit many—if not all—of these features. When we ask whether a person does or does not have a right, the question is about the applicability of these features.

1.7 Six Features of Wrongs

Wrongs also share a set of familiar features. First, there is a distinctive reactive attitude—what philosophers since P. F. Strawson have identified as "resentment"—that is fitting for one person to feel when another person wrongs them.[44] Resentment is thus distinguished from "sympathetic or vicarious or impersonal or disinterested or generalized analogues."[45] The distinction is clear enough: there is one emotional reaction to witnessing the cruelty of another, quite another to being the victim of cruelty oneself. Of course, both may occasion outrage, blame, negative judgment, contempt, and so forth. But there is something that is distinctively appropriate to the person offended or injured. I resent the person who cuts in line ahead of me, but I am merely censorious toward the person who cuts in line behind me. To parallel the earlier discussion of rights, one might say that being wronged has a particular phenomenology.

Second, and somewhat less routinely noted, wronging also has a distinctive phenomenology for the perpetrator. One who commits a wrong is apt to feel a directed, relational form of guilt. Any wrong action can occasion a general, undirected guilt—as when you forget to brush your teeth, or when you realize that your trash has blown away in the wind. But wrongings involve an identifiable other (or set of others) to whom one's guilt is oriented.

These internal, emotional features of wrongs are—unsurprisingly—connected with external practices. Thus, a third feature of wronging is the way that it makes appropriate a special form of interpersonal address: complaint. A person whom we have wronged can address us in a manner different from one who has merely observed our transgression. They have a special standing, which transforms "you shouldn't have done that" from detached criticism to personalized complaint. To make a complaint is more than mere assertion of a normative fact; it is an expression of grievance and a plea for repair.

Fourth and relatedly, where there is a wronging, apology is apt. Genuine apology involves a stance toward another as one who is wronged.[46] Saying whether there is a wronging thus often involves saying whether an apology would be appropriate.

Fifth, wronging often involves the aptness of (other) forms of remedial action—like compensation or repair.[47] If I am the one who has clumsily knocked your meal off the restaurant table, then my offer to buy you another is intelligible in a different way from if I am merely a bystander to your misfortune. What would be a gratuitous (and perhaps meddlesome) offer is instead responsive and not gratuitous (whether necessary or not). It is intelligible in this way precisely because there is understood to be something—a wrong—to which it aims to respond and make repair.

Lastly, forgiving is also associated with wronging. One who has been wronged typically can elect to forgive the wrongdoer. That is, they can give up their resentment or their complaint. This power to forgive is generally not available to others. You might forgive me for clumsily spilling your meal, but it would be out of place for the patron at the adjacent table to say that she forgives me—unless, of course, the food landed on her, which is precisely the point.

As in the foregoing discussion of rights, these features are not offered as definitional or as a set of necessary and sufficient conditions. Rather, these features can be used to recognize wrongings and to appreciate what is at stake in our discussions of them. They are interrelated. For example, directed guilt can feel just like imagining the resentment of another, or it can feel like the urge to apologize. Although I believe that these features form a cohesive package, I do not mean to claim that each feature is necessarily part of every instance of wronging. My point here is that, when we are talking about wronging, we are talking about the relation involving these features.

The reader might wonder at this juncture whether being wronged isn't simply a matter of having a special right or set of rights—a right to resent, a right to complain, a right to an apology, and so on. Some very good theorizing about wrongs has been done by scholars focusing on second-order rights, and I share some common ground with these scholars.[48] But I do not think that wrongs are best understood in terms of a set of second-order rights, at least where "right" means anything like the Hohfeldian claim-rights described in the previous section.[49] Wrongs, in my view, involve a kind of standing—the standing to resent, to complain, to forgive, and such. And I do not believe that standing can be reduced to rights; it is sui generis.[50] There is much more that could be said on this thought, but I trust that it will emerge in due course. And even if one disagrees about the distinction between rights and standing, it would not undermine the core thesis of the book. What is essential at present is simply that wrongs involve the aptness of these familiar emotions and practices.

1.8 Rights Theory

In prizing apart our ex ante rights and demands and our ex post complaints and grievances, I do not mean to deny that there are distinctively relational normative phenomena. Quite the contrary; I mean to contend that there are two realms of such relational phenomena, not just one. Ex ante, we view each other as the source of norms—as generating obligations that we owe to the other person. Ex post, we view each other as those to whom we are accountable—as able to address us with complaints to which we must respond. Our relations in both of these realms are, in Michael Thompson's words, "bipolar"—they bring together "a pair of distinct agents as joined and opposed in a formally distinctive type of practical nexus . . . opposing poles of an electrical apparatus . . . an arc of normative current . . . passing between the agent-poles."[51] We cannot fully capture these relations without a rich appreciation of what it is for there to be another person.[52]

Theorists drawn to such a relational conception of law or morality are often keen to focus on rights. Reasonably so. To have a right, in the Hohfeldian sense, is to be linked to another party who is under a corresponding duty. Rights thus characterize a kind of normative relation between parties. They draw attention to the way that parties have claims *on each other,* owe duties *to each other,* are accountable *to each other,* and commit wrongs *against each other.*

There is, however, significant controversy about how to fill in the content of this relation between persons. In particular, a debate has long persisted between so-called interest theories and will theories. Interest theories, beginning with Bentham and continuing through Joseph Raz, begin with the basic idea that rights serve to protect the interests of the rightholder. That is, the interests or reasons in favor of placing a duty on one party are what generate the rights of the other party. To have a right, then, is simply for there to be the proper connection between one's interests and the duties of another. Part of what is attractive in such an account is that it reduces the idea of a right to the seemingly more basic ideas of interests and the injuries that can be suffered to those interests. A right simply describes a protection against certain injurious conduct by others.[53]

According to a different view—the will theory—a right grants the rightholder normative control over the subject matter of the right. As Hart put it, a rightholder is "a small-scale sovereign."[54] Rights enact a kind of control over a certain choice or subject matter. To say that I have a right against your trespass is to say that, with respect to you, I have a certain kind of control over my house. For the will theory, the sense in which duties are owed to another agent is explained in terms of that agent's control. This focus of the will theory makes it attractive as a way to elucidate rights' relational character.

Both views suffer from persistent difficulties, which has led many scholars to find the debate between the theories intractable or stale.[55] A primary difficulty for interest theories is that not every impermissible setback to our interests counts as a violation of our rights. For example, if I hire someone

TWO WAYS OF RELATING

to give my mother a gift, my mother's interests will be set back if the person impermissibly fails to perform, but she doesn't seem to hold a right to performance.[56] Or if you wager on a baseball game, your interests might be set back if a streaker illegally runs onto the diamond and disrupts the pitcher, but his doing so hardly seems like a violation of your right. Examples like these illustrate that merely having an interest that is advanced by another's duty seems too weak to ground a right. The interest theory thus appears overinclusive. Modern permutations of the interest theory have developed more sophisticated ways of dealing with these problems,[57] but they persist.[58] A second difficulty for interest theories arises because some officeholders seem to have rights that are not about their own interests.[59] A journalist has the right to protect her sources; a parent has the right to educate his child. Such rights seem to be about giving the officeholder an entitlement to act in service of the interests of others.

The will theory faces its own problems. Most famously, it seems unable to explain the apparent existence of rights over which the holder cannot exercise control. As a result, the will theory faces challenges to explain unwaivable rights, like the right not to be enslaved or tortured, and rights held by those who cannot exercise the relevant control, like nonhuman animals, children, and the disabled.[60] Put generally, the will theory seems to fail to explain some of the most significant wrongs that we can commit.

I believe that decoupling rights and wrongings allows one to accommodate the central insights, and also to explain the central failings, of these competing theories. The interest theory seems to be correct in focusing on the moral significance of unjustified harms. The will theory, on the other hand, seems correct in drawing our attention to the distinctive ways that rightholders can shape our actions. But the interest theory generates too many rights claims, and the will theory acknowledges too few wrongs.

My suggestion is, roughly, that the interest theory provides the basic materials for an account of wronging and the will theory provides the basic elements for an account of rights. An individual is entitled to complain against another (thus, is wronged by another) if and only if she has a stake in the other person's action and the other person cannot offer a justification to her. This conception parallels the basic interest-theory elements of harm and justification. On the other hand, a person has a right against another if and only if that person has normative authority over some facet of the other person's conduct, typified by having a claim to certain action. This conception relies on the basic framework of the will theory. Viewed in this light, the seemingly intractable debate between interest and will theories reflects the existence of two different but equally real normative relations.

1.9 Autonomy and the Moral Community

Taking an even broader view, separating rights and wrongs potentially offers a way to capture two competing pulls in moral, legal, and political thought. My hope is to find an important place for rights and directed duties without letting them become the exclusive currency of relational morality. Rights are a critical feature of living autonomous lives. But the independence that they offer can threaten an understanding of ourselves as members of a moral community, as accountable to one another for what we do. This threat leads some to reject rights altogether—recoiling from the individualism of rights in favor of a moral collectivism. The perceived excesses of rights theory produce rights skepticism. Here too, the recurring debate may reflect the existence of two different relations, each capturing something different.

Rights theorists in the Kantian tradition are correct that rights are critical to—indeed, constitutive of—existing as free and equal persons. We each have spheres of freedom, structured by equality. Without such spheres, we would be unable to live our lives as we choose. To have rights is to have choices that are one's own, not subject to the control of others. Such freedom is not valuable only instrumentally. In some sense, it seems to capture what it means to be a moral actor entitled to the respect of other moral actors. In the words of Joel Feinberg, "Respect for persons . . . may simply be respect for their rights, so that there cannot be the one without the other; and what is called 'human dignity' may simply be the recognizable capacity to assert claims. To respect a person then, or to think of him as possessed of human dignity, simply is to think of him as a potential maker of claims."[61] Rights thus play a crucial part in our moral and political lives—they constitute us as separate, mutually respecting persons.

But rights can also come to monopolize our interpersonal discourse. It is a familiar criticism of rights-based thinking that it is overly atomistic and adversarial. To hold that we are all small-scale sovereigns of our own little domains is to carve up the entire moral landscape into mutually exclusive spheres of influence. Rights, on this territorial conception, begin to look like a zero-sum game. My normative power comes only at the expense of your freedom, and our interests become pitted against each other. We can

TWO WAYS OF RELATING   21

negotiate over where to draw the lines—what's in your sphere and what's in mine. But we are in a constant, normative turf war over what's in each of our spheres. As Karl Marx puts it, "The right of man to liberty is based not on the association of man with man, but on the separation of man from man. . . . It makes every man see in other men not the realization of his own freedom, but the *barrier* to it."[62] Rights, the worry goes, by their very nature set us against one another.

For some theorists, these concerns lead to thoroughgoing rights skepticism—a belief that rights are a counterproductive framework for human life. But that casts aside the crucial work that rights do.[63] Still, there is a legitimate concern in the criticism—the fear that rights can come to dominate our moral perspective. To be sure, we must recognize each other as separate and free individuals. But taking rights seriously can create an illusion that our accountability to each other is limited to avoiding trespasses on each other's spheres.[64] What happens outside our sphere, then, seems to be no concern of ours. We are separated—alienated—from one another. It is for this reason that Marx describes the rights as "of egoistic man, of man separated from other men and from the community . . . an isolated monad, withdrawn into himself."[65] This is no way to live. It ignores the essential fact that we live together and regularly have a stake in what is done to one another. Rights-focused theories underappreciate the social web in which we reside.

I want to reject the idea that delineating and respecting each other's spheres exhausts the way in which we are accountable to each other. I believe that, even acting within our spheres, we are accountable to others when we act badly in ways that matter to them. I'm connected to what you do not merely when you owe me a duty—not merely when I impose a constraint on your action. I'm also connected to what you do simply by virtue of being a member of the moral community. Whether you act rightly or wrongly, how you treat others, even whether you pursue truth and beauty are all matters in which I may potentially have a stake. By prizing rights and wrongs apart, this book aspires to make space both for the autonomy that rights safeguard and for the accountability that comes from living in a moral community.

In her poem "Renascence," Edna St. Vincent Millay confronts the precarious balance between bounded individual experience and moral feeling for the rest of the world. On the one hand, we inhabit our own small patch of ground—enclosed, perhaps, by "three long mountains and a wood."[66]

WRONGS AND RIGHTS COME APART

This circumscribed individual experience confines us, keeping us from the world at large. But were complete connection with others truly opened up to us, it would be destroying. Millay imagines it thus:

> For my omniscience paid I toll
> In infinite remorse of soul
>
> . . .
>
> Mine was the weight
> Of every brooded wrong
>
> . . .
>
> No hurt I did not feel, no death
> That was not mine; mine each last breath
>
> . . .
>
> East and West will pinch the heart
> That can not keep them pushed apart . . . [67]

We require both the boundaries of our own individual world and also emotional community outside ourselves. Rights are part and parcel of our boundaries; they define our individual territory of agency. But when all interpersonal life is understood only in this fashion, we become confined. It pinches our heart, denying our connection to others. Boundlessly opening ourselves to others is no alternative. It pinches our heart in another way, suffocating our autonomous self with the incursion of others' cares and aims. In both directions, one risks losing the balance between moral agent and moral community. Full moral experience—the full heart—requires more conceptual space. Against the theoretical pull, we must keep wrongs and rights pushed apart.

1.10 A Roadmap

The central part of this book is devoted to showing various ways in which the ex ante and ex post sets of relations come apart and serve divergent purposes in our lives. To this end, Chapters 2 through 8 develop various arguments that are loosely connected but also self-standing. Some chapters focus on the claim that rights and wrongs can exist without each other. Other chapters focus on the idea that rights and wrongs are qualitatively or functionally different such that we should see them as different relations even where they do co-travel.

These various arguments are independent in the sense that the reader might accept one without accepting others. I expect few readers to find every argument compelling. But the various arguments are intended to be mutually reinforcing. While perhaps any single set of phenomena or examples might be explained away or dismissed as idiosyncratic, the range and totality hopefully make such dismissal less plausible. So while the skeptical reader might pluck out the weakest pieces in an effort to divide and conquer, I hope that they will read on and remain open to the possibility that there is a pattern here, not simply an array of moral peculiarities.

Chapter 2 introduces the case for a divergence between rights and wrongs by focusing on cases in which third parties seem to be wronged even though no right of theirs has been violated. The chapter begins with situations in which the violation of one party's rights appears to wrong some other party. To take a simple case, if you kill me, then you will wrong my mother—though it will have been my rights that you violated, not hers. In cases such as this one, there is a violation of a right, but not the right of the person who now stands to assert a grievance. This is the scenario of *Palsgraf*. In the second part of Chapter 2, I consider cases in which arguably no rights violation occurs at all, only the violation of a more general duty. I suggest that we sometimes wrong one another by breaches of less individually directed norms, including public duties, norms of the market, duties to the self, and even aesthetic and prudential norms. As this suggests, the chapter gives wronging a quite extensive scope. This extensiveness may strike some as unpalatable, and the chapter closes by considering three possible objections in this vein.

Chapter 3 turns to rights and their function in our lives. Rights are normative—they shape how we ought to act going forward. I argue that potential wrongings are not suited to serve this action-shaping role. While avoiding the commission of a wrong will typically be functionally equivalent to respecting rights, this is not always true. Even where it is true, rights are directly reason-giving whereas potential wrongs are not. In short, one should aim to do what one owes to others and not aim to avoid wronging others. The gap between rights and wrongings can thus be seen in what shapes our deliberations.

Whereas rights hold primacy in the ex ante, deliberative perspective, they give way in the ex post, corrective perspective. Thus, in Chapter 4, I argue that the ex post questions about how to respond to wrongs—what we might think of as remedial questions—cannot be answered only with reference to rights. Even where there is an underlying right and it grounds a complaint, it does not always explain the character of the complaint that does arise. The magnitude and shape of a wrong aren't determined by the underlying right. Instead, various facts seen only in ex post perspective will matter. If I tread on your garden, what I owe you in repair may depend on whether I have ruined the flowers and which ones, whether I have profited by my trespass, and perhaps even how you experience your garden stroll the following day. The wrong—the thing for which I must make repair—thus has an internal nature quite apart from the right in question—your right to exclude me from your garden. In this way, even when a wrong is grounded in a rights violation, it is qualitatively distinct.

Chapters 3 and 4 thus form something of a pair. In each chapter, I will argue that, ultimately, one kind of relation holds primacy for a particular perspective. Rights and wrongs will often align, but when push comes to shove, potential wrongs do not determine how we ought to shape our conduct (Chapter 3), and the right violated does not determine how we ought to respond ex post (Chapter 4).

Chapters 5 and 6 also form a loose pairing, focusing on the moral activities of claiming and complaining. These activities involve asserting a right or a wrong, respectively. And these forms of interpersonal address may come apart.

Rights, we typically think, involve not merely being owed certain treatment but also being able to demand or claim that treatment. Chapter 5 focuses on cases in which we may stand to be wronged by conduct and yet we cannot claim anything as a matter of right. Four cases are considered: failures of beneficence, failures of gratitude, wrongful thoughts about others, and unjustified withdrawals of love. In each of these cases, a party may be wronged though she cannot claim a right to the contrary treatment.

Chapter 6 considers the opposite—cases in which one has a right to particular treatment and yet cannot complain upon violation of that right. Standing thus to complain does not appear necessary to rightholding. Three types of complaintless individuals are considered. First, norm transgressors—like criminals—can lose the standing to complain about violations of their own rights, even as they continue to retain the rights in question. Second, sometimes parties have no complaint because, as I shall put it, all ends well. The final part of the chapter considers nonhuman animals. I argue that nonhuman animals are rights-bearers and yet they cannot complain upon the violation of those rights—meaning that significant ex post relationships are unavailable. What all of the cases in the chapter illustrate is that having a right is not conceptually bound up with being able to complain or rebuke.

Chapters 7 and 8 offer a final pairing, each related to waiver. Chapter 7 considers what it means to waive a complaint. I argue that one can waive a complaint and give up one's standing to assert a grievance without surrendering the underlying right. I characterize this phenomenon as preemptive forgiving.

The opposite of preemptive forgiving are cases in which someone waives her right and consents to certain conduct of another and yet still finds herself with a complaint against that very conduct. In order to examine this possibility, Chapter 8 considers the phenomenon of exploitation. I argue that the familiar paradox of exploitation fades away if we see that rights and wrongs are separable. Exploitation, I will argue, involves treatment of another person that does not violate her rights and nevertheless wrongs her.

Perhaps none of these various arguments would, on its own, be enough to destabilize the assumption that rights and wrongs are necessary reflections of each other. But I believe that, taken together, they sketch a picture of two different moral relations, which play distinct roles in our moral experience. I hope that the reader will not, therefore, fixate on any questionable argument or unshared intuition in isolation, but will instead engage with the picture as a whole.

The final chapter of the book, Chapter 9, attempts to bring the ideas gleaned from the earlier chapters together in a positive account of rights and wrongs. The ultimate picture is one in which having a right involves being entitled to respect ex ante such that one has a claim on the conduct of the other person; wrongings, in contrast, depend on an ex post perspective, in which one finds oneself adversely affected by the conduct of another and yet that person cannot justify their conduct. Relational morality thus takes two different forms: one involving individual spheres of agency and entitlement, and another involving accountability to other members of the moral community.

These two forms of relating stand out on either side of our actions. There are, of course, connections and interactions between them. Such connections can lead us to bind them together. But that collapses our moral life. This book seeks an account of wrongs and rights that keeps them pushed apart.

2

Third Parties

In Charlotte Brontë's *Jane Eyre,* the eponymous heroine is summoned to the deathbed of the aunt who raised her. Mrs. Reed had been unloving, cruel, and vindictive toward the orphaned Jane, and they had parted with Jane declaring never to call her "aunt" again. But, at death, Mrs. Reed requests Jane's presence and confesses, "I have twice done you a wrong which I regret now."[1] The wrongs that Mrs. Reed goes on to enumerate are interesting. "One was in breaking the promise which I gave my husband to bring you up as my own child," she says. The second was lying to a wealthy foreign relation who was trying to locate Jane and support her. This lie, Mrs. Reed explains, was "because I disliked you too fixedly and thoroughly ever to lend a hand in lifting you to prosperity." In short, the wrongs she has done to Jane, as Mrs. Reed sees it, consist in breaking a promise given to someone else and in telling a falsehood to someone else.

This chapter concerns wrongs like these—wrongs done to one person by a promise broken to another, a lie told to another, or some other misconduct toward another. These are third-party wrongs; someone is wronged by the breach of a duty that was owed to someone else.

Recall that, in *Palsgraf,* Benjamin Cardozo denied the possibility of such wrongings. Because the railroad's duty to take care of the package was not owed to Mrs. Palsgraf, she was not wronged by the breach of that duty. She was a mere third party. The exclusion of third parties from those who may be wronged is a hallmark of the idea that wrongs are violations of rights. (More precisely, it is the restrictive half of the biconditional.)

Such third-party wrongs are, I believe, not merely possible but even unexceptional—everyday furniture in our moral lives. Our grievances often extend beyond our own rights, and our failures sometimes make us answerable not merely to rightholders but to others as well. Mrs. Reed's deathbed expressions of remorse—while they ought probably to have included a more direct apology for her cruelty toward Jane—were not at all incoherent. We do sometimes wrong each other by breaching promises to third parties and lying to third parties.

The third-party cases are a gateway. They are both an entry point to the structure that I will defend and a portal out to the real world from the confines of theory. In this spirit, I will, for the moment, rely somewhat on the reader's intuitive understandings and on the sketch of rights and of being wronged laid out in Chapter 1. I hope that the reader will have, on the one hand, an inchoate sense of the awkwardness of ascribing to Jane Eyre a right that Mrs. Reed keep her promise to her husband, or in ascribing to Mrs. Palsgraf a right over how another person's package should be handled. Such individuals are third parties. At the same time, I also hope that the reader will see that some third parties are not mere bystanders when things go badly. They have a complaint, which shows up in the way they relate to the wrongdoer and the wrongdoer relates to them. The third-party cases should thus suggest an opening where wrongs and rights may come apart. But for those inclined to be profligate and to ascribe rights to the injured third parties, or for those inclined to be stingy and to see no grievances in these parties, I will offer only partial replies here. The untenability of these positions fully emerges, I think, only as one considers the range of ways that rights and wrongs function in our lives. That will be the subject of the succeeding chapters.

2.1 Wrongs from the Violation of Others' Rights

2.1.1 CONTRACT BENEFICIARIES

Jane Eyre was the beneficiary of the promise Mrs. Reed made to her late husband. Such third-party beneficiaries—individuals outside a two-party promissory or contractual relationship who nonetheless stand to benefit from performance—are a natural example of the kind of parties with whom this chapter is concerned. They have caused no small difficulty for lawyers and philosophers alike.

In arguing for the will theory of rights—the idea that a rightholder is a "small-scale sovereign"[2]—H. L. A. Hart offered the now famous example

WRONGS AND RIGHTS COME APART

of a contractual third party to show that holding a right involves having control, rather than merely having an implicated interest.

> X promises Y in return for some favor that he will look after Y's aged mother in his absence. Rights arise out of this transaction, but it is surely Y to whom the promise has been made and not his mother who *has* or *possesses* these rights. Certainly Y's mother is a person concerning whom X has an obligation and a person who will benefit by its performance, but the person *to whom* he has an obligation to look after her is Y. This is something *due to* or *owed to* Y, so it is Y, not his mother, whose right X will disregard and to whom X will have done *wrong* if he fails to keep his promise, though the mother may be physically injured.[3]

Hart's claim is that the son (Y), and not the mother, is the rightholder. That is, the contractual duty is owed to the son. It was to him that the promise was made, and he who possesses the resulting rights. The mother is implicated and stands to benefit from performance, but the duty is owed not to her but to the son.

Hart's point here is about normative control over the performance. That the promise was made to the son, and not the mother, matters because it means that the son is the holder of something that the mother is not. As Hart goes on to explain, "it is [the son] who has a moral *claim* upon [the promisor], is *entitled* to have his mother looked after, and who can *waive* the claim and *release* [the promisor] from the obligation."[4] The mother, in contrast, does not have the same kind of control—she is not in a position to demand or to waive performance.[5] It is not her entitlement. The difference in normative control is what makes the son, and not the mother, the rightholder.[6] All of this is plausible.

But the last sentence of the block quote strikes me as, in part, false. Hart says that the duty is something owed to the son, and that *therefore* ("so") it is the son *and not the mother* who stands to be wronged. The inference here is straightforward, and it is not hard to find the unstated premise. Hart assumes, without stating it, that a person stands to be wronged by nonperformance if and only if performance is owed to that person. This is, of course, Cardozo's premise in *Palsgraf*. In Hart's hands, it underwrites a valid inference: the duty is owed to the son, not the mother; one stands to be wronged only based on those things that one is owed; *therefore*, the son, and not the mother, stands to be wronged.

I think, however, that we ordinarily would think that the mother stands to be wronged by the promisor. If the promise were broken, the mother and the promisor would seem to stand in the kind of relationship characteristic of one person having a grievance against the other. It would be perfectly appropriate for her to resent the promisor's nonperformance: her son arranged something for her, and as a result of the promisor's failure, she has not received it. Furthermore, one can imagine the promisor apologizing to the mother. One can imagine the mother forgiving the promisor.[7] It would be intelligible, perhaps even obligatory, for the promisor to try to compensate the mother for whatever ways she was left worse off. Indeed, in American law, an intended third-party beneficiary—like the mother here—has standing to sue for breach of contract.[8] In sum, the mother has a grievance, reflected in a standing to hold the promisor to account.

I believe these two descriptions of the case should be taken at face value. The mother *does not* have a right against the promisor—this is Hart's main point. But she *is* wronged by his breach. If this is correct, then the unstated premise that underwrites Hart's inference must be incorrect. It is not the case that one stands to be wronged only when one holds an entitlement.

Hart's premise was Cardozo's premise. One can find Cardozo himself reaching a similar result in a contract context.[9] In the 1920s, the City of Rensselaer hired the Rensselaer Water Company to supply water to the city. The company promised to furnish water for streets and sewers, for public buildings, and for fire hydrants. While this contract was in effect, there was a fire in the city, which spread to the warehouse of H. R. Moch Company, destroying the warehouse and all that was inside it. Moch sued the Rensselaer Water Company, alleging that the company had failed to provide water to the fire hydrants in accordance with its contract, and that the fire spread and destroyed the factory due to this failure.

Cardozo, writing for the New York Court of Appeals, viewed Moch just as Hart viewed the mother—a third party holding no rights over performance and therefore without standing to complain of breach. Acknowledging that "in a broad sense" the contract was "for the benefit of the public," Cardozo emphasized that "more than this . . . must be shown to give a right of action to a member of the public not formally a party."[10] To assert a complaint, there must be a duty owed to the complainant. The contract, according to Cardozo, involved "an assumption of duty to the city and not to its inhabitants."[11] Members of the public stood to benefit, but they were not rightholders and, as such, they could not be wronged by nonperformance.

Cardozo's opinion in *Moch* has fewer defenders than his opinion in *Palsgraf*,[12] and, without getting caught up in the legal details, one can understand why. As an intuitive matter, it's natural to think that Moch has a genuine complaint. Its warehouse burned to the ground because of the water company's breach of contract. That seems to be what matters. True, the contract was with the city, and the city thus held the rights to performance in a way that Moch did not. But why should that determine whether Moch has a grievance in the case of nonperformance?

One might, at this point, be tempted to offer a different account of these cases—one that locates some other, noncontractual right held by the mother and by Moch. Certain features of the examples may seem noteworthy. First, one might observe that both the mother and Moch may have acted in reliance on the word of the promisor. Second, one might think that the injuries to the mother and to Moch were foreseeable in a way that ought to have generated a duty to avoid them. Finally, it may appear significant that in both cases a special relationship existed between the third party and the promisee—that of mother-son and that of citizen-state. Perhaps one of these features might be the basis for a right to performance after all. These three topics—reliance, foreseeability, and special relationships— will be the subjects of the next three subsections.

Before turning to these topics, however, it is worth observing that there are contract beneficiaries who have neither a special relationship nor a reliance interest. Suppose that an eccentric billionaire decides that she wants to perform a random act of kindness by giving away a large sum to a stranger. She assembles a list of thousands of people who have contributed to the community—schoolteachers, nurses, veterans, and so on. At an event for these people, one person's name will be randomly drawn and a large cash prize will be awarded. There will be one of those oversize checks and confetti and whatnot. A professional has been hired to facilitate the lottery. When the name is finally drawn, it turns out to be you! But, in a Hollywood plot twist, the facilitator turns out to be a professional of a different sort—a skillful con man who has absconded with the money.

I contend that you would consider yourself wronged by the con man. I would. The feeling would not be merely the "Aw, shucks!" disappointment

THIRD PARTIES   31

that one might have upon discovering that your ticket was one digit away from winning the lottery. You would feel aggrieved. If you ever met the con man, you would have something to say to him. You might expect remorse, apology, and an effort at repair or restitution. He, in turn, might express repentance, seek to make repair, and attempt to earn your forgiveness. You would hardly be operating on a moral blank slate.

Contract law in most jurisdictions has evolved to recognize complaints of third parties.[13] Reliance is not typically required, nor is it the measure for recovery. While early cases often involved either family relations or creditor-debtor relations, it is now clear that the only important relationship that the third party must bear is that of being the intended beneficiary. So the law would likely recognize your complaint against the con man. Indeed, our fictional story departs only modestly from a more run-of-the-mill fact pattern: an attorney does not draft a will properly and the person who ought to have inherited sues the attorney.[14] In recognizing third-party suits in this circumstance and a wide range of others, the law seems to be responding to a felt need for justice between a party in breach and a party who has lost as a result.[15]

Even as the law recognizes a complaint here, it is not recognizing a right in the sense that Hart described. The third-party beneficiary does not control performance; absent special terms or circumstances, the power to waive or to modify the performance obligation resides in the promisee.[16] So while the law recognizes the third party's standing to bring a complaint for breach, that standing does not align with ex ante control.[17] One can readily appreciate why these ideas come apart. Although more than one person can be aggrieved by the same action, only one person can be "sovereign" at a time. Consider again the con man example. Although it may feel as though he has stolen money that was "as good as yours"—and that is roughly the basis for your complaint—you did not actually have a property right. When what is at issue is control, the difference between "yours" and "all but yours" is critical; we need determinate boundaries of control in order to live as free and equal agents.[18] But it's not clear that the scope of our grievances must map onto those boundaries of control.[19]

2.1.2 FALSEHOODS TOLD TO OTHERS

Turn to a different type of case: Suppose that, during a break at work, you wander out of your normal workspace and meander around in the far reaches of the warehouse. There you happen to overhear a coworker making small talk with a customer. Your coworker tells the customer that the expressway, which has been closed for repairs, is now open again. You don't think anything of it at the time. Later that day, however, you are suffering from an asthma attack and you need to rush to the hospital. You try to take the expressway only to find it closed, and you wind up mired in construction traffic and in a great deal of extra emotional distress and physical discomfort. The next day, you ask your coworker why he said the expressway was fixed. Your coworker says that he was lying because he found that customer obnoxious and deviously wanted to send him into a traffic jam.

Do you have a complaint against your coworker? I think so. The familiar package of practices and emotions would seem to apply. You might naturally feel some personal resentment, and you might even vocalize it ("What the hell? That really messed me up."). Your coworker may feel guilty. He might—indeed, perhaps should—inquire into the details of what you suffered in consequence of the lie ("How bad was it?" "How long were you delayed?"), not merely as a matter of politeness but with a sense that it makes a moral difference, that it shapes his appropriate response. An apology would seem to be in order. And the apology might be accompanied by context that serves as a partial excuse ("He and I have been frenemies since high school, and I was getting him back for a lie he told me"). Or it might come with an offer for some further repair ("I'll handle closing up tonight for you"). You might forgive the coworker—or not. In all of these ways, you would stand in the relation of one person with a grievance against another.

Can this relation be explained by your having a right to your coworker speaking truthfully or a right to rely on his statements? There is at least one reason to be doubtful: one might think that the relevant right belongs to the person addressed. Hugo Grotius explains the wrong of lying as "a violation of the existing and permanent rights of the person to whom a discourse, or particular signs, are directed."[20] These rights, for Grotius, derive from "a kind of tacit agreement" about what discourse participants "owe to each other in their mutual intercourse." From this understanding of the relevant rights, Grotius concludes that there cannot be a wrong to a third party:

> When a conversation is addressed to any one, who is not thereby deceived, although a third person, not immediately addressed, may

THIRD PARTIES

33

> misconceive the matter, there is no wilful falsehood in the case. . . .
> It cannot be said that an injury is done to the person, who acciden-
> tally and cursorily hears a matter, and misconceives it: for being no
> way concerned, there is no obligation due to him. As he miscon-
> ceives a thing addressed to another, and not to himself, he must take
> upon his own head all the consequences of the mistake. For, prop-
> erly speaking, the discourse, with respect to him, is no discourse,
> but an inexpressive sound that may signify one thing as well as
> another.[21]

Grotius is considering a case in which no wrong is committed against the
direct addressee, who is not deceived.[22] But the same argument would seem
to generalize to cases where the addressee is deceived. When you overhear
your coworker, the discourse is, with respect to you, "no discourse, but an
inexpressive sound that may signify one thing as well as another." Perhaps
the coworker and the customer were rehearsing a play, or rehashing some
incident from years before, or operating with some other shared understanding. You, as a nonparticipant, had no right that it not be so. The right
against falsehoods exists between those who have a tacit agreement about
a shared discourse; they have the control to shape what they are doing.
There's something correct here: the primary rights belong to conversational
participants as such.

From the idea that the right belongs to the addressee, one might infer,
as Grotius does, that there can be no wronging. For you to rely on a statement when not within the discourse, you "take upon [your] own head all
the consequences." That conclusion would seem to run contrary to our
practices of resentment, apology, repair, and forgiveness, as surveyed a moment ago. But one might be led to such a conclusion if one thinks that a
wronging must be undergirded by a right.

Yet again, we can find a version of the relevant inference in a Cardozo
opinion. In *Ultramares Corp. v. Touche, Niven & Co.*,[23] the question was
whether an investor could sue an accounting firm for false statements cer-
tifying a client's books. The defendant was hired by Fred Stern to prepare
and certify the company's balance sheet. This certification included statements that the firm had "examined the accounts of Fred Stern & Co." and
the balance sheet "is in accordance therewith," and that the balance sheet,
"in our opinion, presents a true and correct view of the financial condition
of Fred Stern & Co."[24] The accounting firm knew that Fred Stern would

likely show the certified balance sheet to investors and creditors in the ordinary course of business. Indeed, about a month later, Fred Stern requested loans from Ultramares Corporation. It agreed to loan money on the condition that it receive a certified balance sheet. Within the year, Fred Stern declared bankruptcy. The company had been teetering on insolvency all along. This had not been reflected in the balance sheet due primarily to a handwritten entry for $706,843.07 on the accounts receivable ledger. Had any attempt to verify this entry been made, it would have been found to be fictitious. Another suspicious entry in the accounts payable ledger and the discovery of inflated inventory numbers each could also have raised red flags. But the defendant did not uncover the problems, having apparently failed to audit the accounts with much care. Ultramares brought suit against the accounting firm for the losses it suffered on the basis of the false certification that the firm had issued.

The case thus raised the same three-party structure: Should the accounting firm be liable for its false statements to a party other than its client to whom the statements were given? The New York Court of Appeals, in an opinion by Cardozo, rejected the jury verdict in favor of Ultramares. The key to Cardozo's reasoning involved drawing a distinction between the duties of performing a careful audit and the duties of avoiding fraud. It was true, Cardozo reasoned, that the accounting firm had failed to exercise the care for which it had been employed. It had, in this way, violated the duties it owed to Fred Stern. But that failure would not itself amount to fraud, and the accountant's duty to the world of investors and creditors consisted in avoiding fraud.

Cardozo wanted to avoid the conflation of these different duties—one to the client and recipient of the speech and the other to the public at large—fearing that they might become "nearly, if not quite, coterminous" or "coincident."[25] Like Grotius, Cardozo thought that it is the party with whom the speaker directly interacts who shapes the speaker's primary duties to avoid falsehoods.[26] Less onerous duties (to avoid fraud) might be owed more generally, but the right to a careful accounting was owed to the company that hired the accountant. Then, on the premise that liability must track rights, the accountant's lack of due care in doing its job could not be the basis for liability to the world at large. If it could, that would "expose accountants to a liability in an indeterminate amount for an indeterminate time to an indeterminate class."[27] Cardozo thus refused to extend "the assault on the citadel of privity."[28]

THIRD PARTIES   35

I think that Grotius and Cardozo are correct that the right to truthful expression belongs to the addressee, not the third party. But I think that they are incorrect to infer that there is no wronging.[29] To return to the coworker example, it was the customer's rights that were violated by the lie; the wrong to you is collateral. Had your coworker not been lying and violating the customer's rights—had the two of them been operating with a mutual understanding (e.g., telling a fictional story)[30]—then you would not have the same grounds to complain.

One might argue, however, that you would still have a complaint: "You shouldn't say false things where someone else can hear them and might misunderstand." This framing suggests a possible right of yours—a right against the negligent spreading of falsehoods. One owes, according to this thought, a duty of care when there are foreseeable injuries that might result.[31] Your coworker's failure toward you is one of carelessness. You, the third party, hold a right, not to compliance with the conversational norms (what is owed the direct addressee), but to a kind of precaution. Had such precautions been taken and the statement been heard only due to surreptitious eavesdropping, then there would be no complaint.[32] According to this picture, there are basically three categories of listeners: (1) addressees, to whom there is a duty not to lie; (2) foreseeable third parties, to whom a lesser duty of care is owed; and (3) unforeseeable third parties (like eavesdroppers), to whom no duty is owed. Grotius and Cardozo were keen to distinguish (1) from (2); but perhaps (2) can still furnish an explanation for the wrong of the overheard lie.

There is much that is correct here. There are, of course, duties of care and wrongs of negligence (which will be discussed more fully in the next section). And I agree that they may be implicated here. So, as a description of a speaker's duties and the relevant rights of others, this tripartite picture strikes me as largely accurate. My contention, however, is that wrongs do not always align with this classification of duties. This is true in two respects.

First, appealing to negligence mischaracterizes the content of the wrong. Where the statement was a lie, the complaint does not sound in negligence. Consider your response to your coworker. Your press would be, "Why did you lie?" It would not be, "Why didn't you make sure that I couldn't hear you?" And consider how he might reply. Saying, "I could never have foreseen that you would overhear me," or, "I took precautions against being overheard," would seem close to laughable. They might be met simply with,

"Yes, but I did hear you." Whereas such considerations would be plausible responses if the coworker had not been acting wrongly toward the customer—had the two been rehearsing a play—they seem irrelevant where the statement was a lie. To say that one couldn't have foreseen the injury is responsive when the potential injury is what purports to make the action wrong; it is not a plausible reply when the action was wrong regardless.

Second, appealing to negligence unduly restricts the scope of complaints. Even a person whom a speaker could not foresee may, I believe, hold the speaker to account for a lie. As I initially described the coworker case, it's not clear how foreseeable the presence of another would be. To assess that, one would need to know more about the privacy of the far reaches of the warehouse. It could be quite a secluded spot, appropriate for sharing secrets or speaking without caution for being overheard. Surely there are such places. Even if it were such a place, I think that you have a complaint against your coworker. He lied and you were hurt by it. You were not a deliberate eavesdropper; you did nothing wrong. As such, though unforeseeable, your injury strikes me as grounds for complaint. It seems odd to insist that in all situations where one could not be faulted for, for example, telling a fictional story without precaution for an incidental listener's misunderstanding, one is therefore not answerable for lying.[33] Accountability for a lie outstrips the duty of care.

Both these points concern the significance of lying. My suggestion is that the liar opens himself to the complaints of affected nonaddressees—foreseeable and unforeseeable, irrespective of the precautions taken or forgone. This view, it might be noted, was also famously Immanuel Kant's: "Whoever tells a lie . . . must answer for the consequences resulting therefrom even before a civil tribunal and must pay the penalty for them, regardless of how unforeseen those consequences may be."[34] A key part of Kant's argument against lying to the murderer at the door was that one would be answerable for the consequences if, unforeseeably, the lie enabled the murder to happen. Now, I have no interest in defending Kant's claim that one should not lie to the murderer at the door. It seems to me that Kant was missing the fundamentally relational aspect—Grotius's insight that permissibility is shaped by the rights of the addressee (the would-be murderer having none). But I endorse Kant's thought about responsibility for wrongful lies.[35] Whenever someone tells a wrongful lie, that person cannot justify the harm that the lie causes to others.

THIRD PARTIES

37

That structure, I contend, characterizes your complaint against your coworker. Your grievance is not that you had a right to rely in the way that an addressee does, nor is it that you had a right to precautions being taken as a foreseeable victim. It is simply that the coworker's conduct was wrongful and that conduct turns out to have a bearing on you.

2.1.3 NEGLIGENCE

Persons to whom we have made promises or with whom we enter into conversation hold particular claims on us in virtue of those interactions. But we also owe duties to others absent any special interaction, just in virtue of their status as persons. You have a right to bodily integrity, which means that I ought not swing a baseball bat into your leg. It also means that I ought to take care in swinging a baseball bat in your vicinity lest it end up hitting you in your leg. You, in this way, shape how I ought to act. So there are at least two classes of people who determine what counts as permissible action—those with whom we have had some special interaction (e.g., promisees and conversation partners) and those whom we stand to injure if we act unjustifiably (e.g., people in the vicinity of my lie or my baseball bat). Third parties fit into neither of these classes.

The line between rightholder and third party is thus a matter of who shapes the duty-bearer's conduct. Promisees control the performance of a promise; conversational participants jointly determine the norms of speech among them; and a person's bodily integrity demands certain kinds of care. In each case, the essential idea is that another person matters, ex ante, to how we ought to act. Third parties—that is, nonrightholders—do not shape conduct in this way.

Mrs. Palsgraf was just such a third party according to Cardozo. The railroad employees ought to have taken more care in how they handled the rushing passenger and his package. But that was a matter of the risk to the passenger and his package. Their conduct was not wrong because it posed a foreseeable risk to Mrs. Palsgraf. As Cardozo put it, "The risk reasonably to be perceived defines the duty to be obeyed." [36] The risk reasonably to be perceived did not encompass Mrs. Palsgraf; she was, in this sense, a third party. That's not to say that the railroad owed her no duty; other failures (e.g., carelessly tossing the package into the crowd) would have foreseeably put Mrs. Palsgraf, standing on the platform, at risk of bodily injury. But this particular failure—not securing the package from falling

38   WRONGS AND RIGHTS COME APART

onto the tracks—did not. The kind of care that was lacking in this case was just between the railroad company and the passenger.

I think that Cardozo is correct about that. While there were many ways in which the railroad company ought to have taken the safety of people standing on the platform into account, this probably wasn't one of them. The conduct was defective simply because it risked damaging the package or hurting the passenger. It would be quite strained to say that, in ensuring that the package is not dropped, one should be concerned about nonowners who just happen to be in the vicinity (on the off chance that the package contains fireworks). Such a demand would indeed be for life "to be made over." Our actions are not shaped in this way, nor should they be.

Cardozo infers from this fact about the duty of care that Mrs. Palsgraf was not wronged by the failure. If the vigilance was not owed to her, then on what basis could she complain? This now familiar inference links the ex ante concern about action with the ex post standpoint of accountability. "Before negligence can be predicated of a given act, back of the act must be sought and found a duty to the individual complaining, the observance of which would have averted or avoided the injury."[37] This is a tempting argument.

But now consider matters from the standpoint of Mrs. Palsgraf. She was innocently standing on the railroad company's platform when she was struck by a large metal object, leaving her with injuries that would impair her significantly for the rest of her life. It was no mere natural accident, like an earthquake. Rather, these injuries were caused by human actions, and actions that ought not to have occurred. It seems to me that it would be an extraordinary person who would not feel the significance of the human error. The injuries would seem not merely tragic but unnecessary and avoidable. The actions and inactions leading up to the injuries would seem not events in which one had no concern—none of your business—but rather of deep personal significance. All of this would, I contend, naturally coalesce in resentment. Ordinary people would not see themselves as just unlucky, nobody's fault at all. No one thinks it surprising that Mrs. Palsgraf sued.

Or consider the standpoint of the railroad employee. Upon witnessing the effects of his sloppy conduct, the employee might feel immense guilt. He might apologize to Mrs. Palsgraf. That reaction would, I contend, extend beyond mere "agent regret," the remorse that one feels when, without fault, one's action results in bad consequences. Here, the employee knows that his actions were not without fault. Though this particular result was not to be foreseen, it was undeniably the result of his failure—not merely his actions, but his defective actions.[38] Only callousness would produce a reaction like, "What's it to her?" as though he were simply not meaningfully answerable to Mrs. Palsgraf.[39]

All of these facts point strongly, I think, to the idea that the ex post relations of answerability need not trace back to the ex ante rights and directed duties. They stand as evidence that a party may be wronged though it was not her rights that were violated.

The still-unconvinced reader may worry that my argument trades on difficult borderline examples. Cases like *Palsgraf,* the overheard lie, or the unintended listener are close and context sensitive, which (the argument goes) allows me to shift to suit my purposes between two possible interpretations. The third parties may or may not have had a right and may or may not be wronged. The appearance of any mismatch, it may be insisted, depends on emphasizing these different possibilities. But ultimately, either there's a wrong traceable to a right, or there's no wrong at all. Suitably specified, every case would turn out to be one or the other.

My argument is that we should not foreclose a third possibility. Imagining only two possibilities is too limiting. It forces us to say *either* that the third party ought to have shaped permissibility in advance *or* that the bystander was not wronged at all. This binary, I contend, offers inadequate texture. Sometimes we are not among those who shape the moment of choice, and yet we are among those whose lives are shaped by whether the choice was properly made.

To see vividly how ex ante concern and ex post injury can come apart, consider one of *Palsgraf*'s progeny. In *Flanders v. Cooper,*[40] a physical therapist allegedly used highly atypical methods, including hypnotism, for treatment of a joint disorder. This treatment was alleged to have implanted false memories of sexual abuse by the patient's father. The patient's father attempted to sue the physical therapist for negligence. He wanted to argue that he had been wronged by the physical therapist's improper treatment of his daughter.

The Maine Supreme Judicial Court—like most jurisdictions that have faced cases with this structure[41]—dismissed the complaint. When one considers the care owed ex ante, one can readily see why courts have reached this conclusion. A medical provider's duties with regard to medical treatment are exclusively owed to a patient.[42] Anything else would mean that medical providers should sometimes *not* do what they judge best for their patient. That would seem an intolerable outcome, and we have good reason to insist that medical providers are duty bound to provide what they judge best for their patients. In a choice about medical treatment, "the risk reasonably to be perceived" must be the risk to the patient.[43] As such, the father did not have a right with respect to his daughter's treatment. From the perspective of whose interests should have been shaping the treatment decision, the father was irrelevant.[44] Thus, if one believes—like Cardozo and the Maine Supreme Judicial Court—that whether a party was wronged depends on whether there was a duty owed to that party, the father's complaint must be rejected.[45]

But supposing the facts are as he described them, was the father wronged? As a matter of ordinary understanding, I think it would be almost bizarre to say that he wasn't. This incident quite possibly ruined his life. He was faced with as damaging an accusation as one can imagine. And it was all because his daughter's *physical* therapist mistreated her with hypnosis. To say that resentment and blame would be intelligible seems an understatement. Likewise, apology and forgiveness would be apt, with the only question being whether someone in the father's shoes could possibly forgive. In short, if the question is not whether the treatment decision ought to have taken the father into account ex ante, but rather whether the improper treatment decision resulted in accountability to the father ex post, then the answer looks entirely different. Indeed, I suggest that only someone in the grip of theory would think that these questions collapse into each other.[46]

2.1.4 THE LOVED ONE

The examples considered thus far illustrate ways that we can have a stake in what is done to another person without having a right over what happens. We may have this stake because we chance to be on the same railroad platform or in the same corner of a warehouse. But often it is because our lives are intertwined with others. A mother may have a stake in the promise given to her son, and a father may have a stake in the medical treatment given to his daughter. These familial cases may strike some readers as compelling but exceptional. I think that would be a mistake.

In William Shakespeare's *Much Ado about Nothing*, Claudio denounces his intended bride, Hero, at the wedding altar based on false evidence. Initially, Hero's father, Leonato, painfully fails to take his daughter's side.

THIRD PARTIES

But his character is redeemed as he comes to feel his child's injury as his own:

> LEONATO [TO CLAUDIO]: Marry, thou dost wrong me; thou
> dissembler, thou . . .
> Know, Claudio, to thy head,
> Thou hast so wronged mine innocent child and me
> That I am forced to lay my reverence by,
> And with gray hairs and bruise of many days
> Do challenge thee to trial of a man.[47]

Leonato considers not merely his daughter wronged by Claudio's accusations but himself also, enough to justify a duel. ("Wronged" is not common parlance these days, but it is delightfully rife in Shakespeare.) His resentment is natural and familiar—what parent wouldn't feel personally aggrieved by the grave mistreatment of their child? We have innumerable stories of parents seeking to exact justice for what has been done to their children or, occasionally, forgiving the wrongdoer.[48] In some cases, such parents may only be acting as agents of their child, but in many cases, they are responding to injuries of their own as well, though they be a third party.

One might observe, however, that Leonato's response dwells in an antiquated patriarchy where men held wives and daughters as a kind of property.[49] Is our sense that people may be wronged by what is done to their loved ones implicitly reliant on such ownership? Should we reject any belief in such wrongings as inconsistent with modern liberalism?

If we think that wrongs must consist in the violation of a right—that there can be no wrongs to third parties—then we face a dilemma: either we must say that parents and lovers have rights over the lives of others, or we must conclude that we are not in fact wronged by the mistreatment or killing of those we love.[50] I think that something has gone wrong to find ourselves in that dilemma. But accepting the phenomenon of third-party wronging allows us to escape this choice between being illiberal or unfeeling.

The dilemma is apparent in the common law's fumbling attempts to handle the status of loved ones. As a matter of traditional principle, one cannot seek damages for death or injury to another. That would be to violate the principle that one can sue only for the violation of one's own rights.

But, probably because such restrictiveness is simply intolerable, there have always emerged exceptions.

First, there were claims for "loss of consortium," which provided compensation for the destruction of an intimate relationship. As with Leonato, however, this idea traces to a patriarchal notion that a husband had a right to his wife's services.[51] In some jurisdictions, this unsavory origin led to the abolition of loss of consortium, often alongside the elimination of torts for adultery.[52] No longer, the thought goes, would anyone have a right to another's body; anachronistic conceptions of the household had given way to individual freedom.[53] Meanwhile, in other jurisdictions, loss of consortium has not been abolished but rather expanded—to wives, children, parents, and sometimes beyond.[54] The answer for these jurisdictions, it seems, was not to deny that husbands have cognizable interests in their wives. It was instead to recognize that any spouse, regardless of sex, has a cognizable interest in their partner. And, on similar grounds, children also have an important interest in their parents.

A second legal innovation provided a different way of redressing the harm a person suffers when their loved one's rights are breached. New tort actions opened the door to sue over the emotional distress occasioned by the death or injury of a loved one. But this too has been fraught. Initially keen to hew to the rule that one must have had a right of one's own violated, many jurisdictions muddled into the "zone of danger" rule, whereby you can recover emotional distress damages only if you were also in physical danger.[55] No recovery if you watch your child get run over from your porch, only if you were in the street.[56] Most (but not all) jurisdictions have now moved beyond this rule, allowing claims by close family who directly witness injuries to a loved one. But it's often unclear whether these claims are supposed to be grounded in a right that we have over the treatment of our loved ones, or simply an anomalous place where third-party wrongs will be acknowledged.[57]

Finally, the traditional prohibition on lawsuits for death has been displaced by wrongful death statutes. For some scholars, the fact that such actions are enabled only by statute reveals them to be the exception that proves the rule.[58] These suits aren't responding to true wrongs in the sense of rights violations. They are rather merely mechanisms "to empower certain nonvictims—persons who have suffered no rights violation."[59] Perhaps that is the internal logic of the law—that spouses and children and parents are not wronged by the killing of their loved ones—but then so much the

THIRD PARTIES

worse for the logic of the law. Interestingly, however, that was not Cardozo's understanding. "Death statutes have their roots in dissatisfaction with the archaisms of the law," he wrote, and through them "an independent cause of action is created in favor of the beneficiaries."[60] Here is how he explained them:

> The common law did not give a cause of action to surviving relatives. In the light of modern legislation, its rule is an anachronism. Nearly everywhere, the principle is now embodied in statute that the next of kin are wronged by the killing of their kinsman. The family becomes a legal unit, invested with rights of its own, invested with an interest in the continued life of its members, much as it was in primitive law. . . . The plaintiffs have a grievance above and beyond any that belongs to them as members of the body politic. They sue to redress an outrage peculiar to themselves.[61]

For Cardozo, family members are genuinely wronged by what is done to any one of them and it was a mistake ever to have thought otherwise. He explained this fact consistent with his belief that wrongs consist in rights violations by regarding the family as a unit, "as it was in primitive law." In a surprising reversal, purely individualized rights are not the answer to law's anachronism but rather the anachronism itself.

The dilemma is apparent: we must say that we hold rights over family members' lives or deny that we are wronged by what happens to our family members. Neither option is appealing. The dilemma can be escaped by decoupling rights and wrongs, simply by allowing that the family members suffer wrongs as third parties.

Some readers will appreciate the dilemma but will dismiss the problem as an anomaly. There is something peculiar about the family that may require special treatment, it will be acknowledged, but this says little about our normative concepts beyond that unique context. But this reaction is implausible—a kind of theory-driven refusal to engage with actual life. It ignores the fact that the family is not some small corner of how we live, but fundamental to people's interactions, values, and identities. It fails to grapple with the fact that humans are deeply social creatures and that the family is, to repurpose Cardozo's word, "primitive." It mistakenly regards our stake in what happens to our loved ones as categorically different from our stake in what happens to others in society.

44 WRONGS AND RIGHTS COME APART

There is a reason why Leonato's grievance still resonates today in spite of its patriarchal undertones. Having *a right* in another is an archaic idea best abandoned, but having *a stake* in another's life is certainly not. Our normative concepts of rights and wrongs are not so bound up with each other that we cannot recognize the significance of these stakes.

2.2 Wrongs from Wrong Actions

In the examples thus far, someone is wronged as a result of the violation of another person's rights. In such cases, there is still always some rights violation at play, and one might wonder whether wrongs are still tethered to rights in some way, even if vicariously. My aim now is to consider cases in which no particular rights violation has transpired. There is, I will argue, a continuity. Wrongs from the violation of someone else's rights bleed into wrongs simply from wrong action, a more general category.

2.2.1 COMPETITION WRONGS

I have emphasized the way that we often have a stake in how other people act, even when we are not a rightholder. Rights-oriented thinkers typically appreciate that we do have such interests, but they regard these interests as not fundamental to our interpersonal obligations. It may be true that your life will go better or worse depending on what I choose to do tomorrow, but that fact alone generally does not matter to how I ought to act. What matters is not whether you have a stake in my action, but rather whether you have a claim on me. We care not about harm per se, but about transgressions.

Competition is often the paradigmatic example. Here, for example, is how Ronald Dworkin describes the important contrast:

> We need to . . . distinguish[] between two kinds of harm you might suffer because other people, like you, are leading their own lives with their own responsibility for their own fates. The first is bare competition harm, and the second is deliberate harm. No one could even begin to lead a life if bare competition harm were forbidden. We live our lives mostly like swimmers in separate demarcated lanes. One swimmer gets the blue ribbon or the job or the lover or the house on the hill that another wants. . . . Each person may concentrate on swimming his own race without concern for the fact

THIRD PARTIES 45

that if he wins, another person must therefore lose. That inevitable kind of harm to others is, as the old Roman lawyers put it, *damnum sine injuria.* It is part of our personal responsibility—it is what makes our separate responsibilities personal—that we accept the inevitability and permissibility of competition harm.[62]

Dworkin's thought is that we are only answerable to others for violating their spheres of entitlement—crossing over into their lanes. People may be better or worse based on more than this—based on what happens in other lanes—but that's not something for which the swimmers in these other lanes are accountable. People's rights, not what they happen to have a stake in, are the touchstone of accountability. (I don't think that Dworkin can be credited with the recent emergence of "stay in your lane" as slang for "mind your own business," but the coincidence is remarkable.)

While I readily accept that some harming is permissible and not grounds for complaint, I do not think that we should conclude that we are wronged only when someone else crosses over into our lane. People can and do wrong us in ways that do not involve crossing into our lane. A closer examination of competition injuries reveals as much.[63]

Imagine that you run a mom-and-pop retail business with a few dozen employees. One day, a big-box store from a large national chain arrives in town. Its prices for comparable products are lower than yours. Initially you attribute this fact simply to economies of scale: of course they can charge lower prices because they're so much bigger. You focus on your comparative strength, advertising your store's personal service and commitment to the local community. But your business declines nonetheless. Month after month, you find yourself in the red, and you realize that you will not be able to stay in business. Knowing what you do about the industry, you find yourself increasingly perplexed at how the big-box store is able to offer such low prices and maintain a profit margin. You start to poke around and ask questions. You discover that your competitor engages in an array of problematic conduct toward its workers—systematic undercounting of hours worked, classification of many workers as "independent contractors" to avoid paying benefits, violations of workplace safety rules, and so on. Moreover, the competitor engages in various deceptive practices toward consumers—misleading advertisements, illusory rewards programs, bait-and-switch sales, and so on. You realize that it has been all these practices—things that you would never have done—that

46 WRONGS AND RIGHTS COME APART

have given your competitor the edge and driven your business to the brink of bankruptcy.

Have you been wronged? I think so. Any ordinary person is likely to feel resentment in that situation. Moreover, you might feel that you are owed repair—that your losses of these past months are illegitimate and should be made up to you. Supporting this view, the law, especially in the United States, may afford various avenues for you to sue the competitor and to recover damages.[64] We recognize that, in various pertinent ways, the competitor's conduct has created a normative imbalance between you.

The big-box store's actions are, however, most naturally construed as violations of the others' rights, not yours. It is the workers' rights and the consumers' rights that are being transgressed, at least most directly. The problem, to put it in Dworkin's metaphor, is not that your competitor has crossed over into *your* lane, but that the competitor has crossed into *others'* lanes.

In this light, the example looks like the three-party cases considered already. The big-box store has violated someone's rights (the workers' and the consumers') and you—basically a bystander like Mrs. Palsgraf—have wound up getting hurt. But the example also opens a gateway to an even broader conception of wronging—it is continuous with further cases.

To begin with, notice that other forms of advantageous misconduct could function similarly. Suppose that, instead of violating any rights of workers or employees, the big-box store acts badly in other ways. It cuts its costs by engaging in rapacious environmental practices, dodging taxes, siphoning government funds, and so forth. (For the clearest case, imagine these practices are illegal—environmental violations, tax fraud, etc. But that's probably not necessary. Even if the competitor is technically within the bounds of the law, it may be illegitimately profiting off loopholes and government largesse.) The case is no different. It's not essential that your competitor's advantage comes from violating someone's rights; it's essential that it comes from acting wrongly.

This observation prompts a natural thought: there is a rights violation here—a right that you hold against your competitor. In competition, including market competition, competitors have a right that other competitors not gain an advantage through violating the rules. That's cheating, and competitors have a right against cheating. So cases like these, the thought goes, are easily explained within a rights-based framework.

THIRD PARTIES

In some contexts, competitors undoubtedly do have such a right. If we are playing a board game and I am not following the rules, you are entitled to draw attention to this failure and demand that I correct it. I owe it to you to bring my play into compliance. One can see how such a right to compliance might be grounded by imagining a dialogue. You might point to the written rules and assert that, in agreeing to play the game together, we agreed with each other to abide by these rules. "Look, this is the rule of the game and you committed to playing this game with me." There are two elements here: established rules and mutual commitment among competitors to be bound by those rules. When both are present, then competitors generally have a right to each other's compliance.

That rights-based explanation works well for some wrongs in sports and games, but sports and games are artificial contexts.[65] It is a mistake to assume that all competition fits that model. The market, though socially constructed, is not some artificial system with artificial game-specific objectives and well-codified rules, mutually accepted by all competitors upon a demarcated entry. Rather, the market is built out of, and continuous with, ordinary life. While we may not always be in the market, neither is it something that we cleanly enter and exit like a poker game or a swim race.[66] Nor are we mere "players" with artificial ends; we are real people with true interests.[67] Indeed, the so-called rules of the market seem to incorporate most of morality and the law. So whereas the reason why a player ought not move a game piece in such and such way is typically explicable in terms of the rules and the fact that the player owes compliance to the competitors, the reason why a business ought not endanger its workers or deceive consumers seems to have virtually nothing to do with competitors—it has to do with the workers and consumers themselves. It may be hard even to say in advance who counts as a competitor, unless of course one simply means anyone adversely affected.[68] So it seems to me that many of the wrongs to market competitors are basically third-party wrongs. It is not that we have a right to everyone else's compliance by virtue of being in the market, but rather that we may have a stake in the conduct of others by virtue of the market.

This may be even more clear in real life beyond the market, where competition wrongs arise with even more organic nuance and complexity. Here too one may lose out on important goods because another transgresses—not against you but against another or against broader collective aims. One misses out on one's dream apartment because another applicant embellishes her application to the landlord; one is passed over for a promotion at work in favor of a coworker who will assist the manager in papering over, rather than addressing, the unit's lack of productivity; one's careful contribution to an intellectual discussion is overshadowed by another person's flashy obfuscation; one loses the love of one's life to a romantic rival who manipulates or deceives. Such injuries are ubiquitous. It would be perversely antagonistic, I think, to view ourselves as constantly having rights against one another as rival competitors. We should not respond to such cases by thinking that we simply need to be clearer about the lane lines in some metaphoric race.[69] And yet these injuries from others' transgressions are real, and they are personal. The stinging resentment that they can generate when suffered is not inapt; nor is the felt need to offer moral repair when we have been the illegitimate victor. In short, these are real wrongs—not because they are transgressions of rights but because we do not in fact "live our lives mostly like swimmers in separate demarcated lanes."

2.2.2 PUBLIC NUISANCE WRONGS

Even if one could make out a right of competitors that would ground competition wrongs, competition wrongs bleed into another type of wrong, not about competition at all. Dworkin, one will recall, introduced "competition harm" to point out that not all harm grounds constraints on our conduct. Granting the truth of that, my contention was that competition harm *caused by wrongful conduct* can seem to ground a wrong. If this were a unique feature of competition, then we should not see the same phenomena elsewhere, for other types of harm. But I think that we do.

Consider a sibling of Dworkin's argument about harm, this time from Arthur Ripstein:

> Suppose that you and I are neighbors. You have a dilapidated garage on your land where our properties meet. I grow porcini mushrooms in the shadow of your garage. If you take down your garage, thereby depriving me of shade, you harm me, but you do not wrong me in the sense that is of interest to us here. Although you perform an affirmative act that worsens my situation—exposure to light destroys my mushrooms—I do not have a right, as against you, that what I have remains in a particular condition.[70]

THIRD PARTIES

49

Ripstein's argument, like Dworkin's, is that bare harm does not ground any duty, nor therefore any complaint. And, again, I agree. As the example is described, the mushroom grower does not seem to be wronged.

But it does not follow that what the neighbor would need is a right.[71] Indeed, that seems doubtful. Modify the example to make the removal of the garage independently wrongful. Suppose that the garage was a historic landmark subject to state preservation laws. Though it may not look like much, the garage is the oldest structure in the area and was designed by a noted architect. To remove the garage legally would require the owner to go through a lengthy and prohibitively costly permitting process. So the owner has decided simply to flout the law, anticipating lax enforcement. The mushroom grower, who had believed her porcinis to be safe, finds them shriveling in the sun as a result of her neighbor's lawlessness.[72]

I think that, in this modified telling, the mushroom grower is wronged. She might naturally resent the loss of her porcinis. She might complain about the transgression, not merely as an ordinary community member. The garage owner, upon learning of the destroyed mushrooms, owes an apology (and not merely as an expression of regret). If the garage owner responded instead with "what's it to you?" (or perhaps "stay in your lane"), I think that we would regard him, not the mushroom grower, to be displaying a lack of moral vision.[73]

Notice how this example replicates the dialectic regarding competition wrongs. Ripstein, like Dworkin, points out that bare harm does not constitute a wronging. But adding general wrongfulness seems to change our judgment. In fact, this case would become a competition wrong if we added that the garage owner is a competing mushroom business. So if one thinks that competition wrongs depend on a unique right of cocompetitors, then one is in the odd position of believing that whether the impermissible removal of the garage wrongs the injured neighbor turns on whether the garage owner and the neighbor happen to share an occupation.[74]

All this suggests to me that, as a general matter, we may be wronged by wrongful conduct that affects us. It needn't be a violation of our rights; indeed, it needn't be a violation of anyone's rights. What's important is that it is a violation of shared or public norms. I call wrongs based on general wrongfulness "public nuisance wrongs" because they have the structure of public nuisance law. This old, cabined, and mostly disregarded legal action allows a private individual to sue for conduct that involves "interference with the interests of the community at large" but only if the plaintiff has suffered some personal harm, "harm of a kind different from that suffered by other members of the public."[75] I think that this tracks our moral concepts. When someone's wrongful conduct causes us personal harm—not merely the generalized injury of any member of the community—then we have an individual grievance. We are in a position to resent the conduct, not merely feel the indignation appropriate for any member of the community.

Through harm, transgressions of general norms seem to transform into particularized grievances. It is the difference between seeing a dog owner fail to pick up after her pet and stepping in it—mild indignation or detached judgment versus direct resentment and personal complaint. In explaining public nuisance, William Blackstone offers the example of a ditch dug across a roadway into which a man or his horse falls, causing injury.[76] Though the roadway is not the rider's any more than it is anyone else's—that is, though it is the right of all that is offended by the ditch—"for this particular damage, which is not common to others, the party shall have his action."[77]

Or consider an incident that happened a few miles away as I was writing: In a town that has an ordinance against fireworks, unauthorized Fourth of July celebrations caused a horse to panic and break through his metal fencing. The horse was found the next morning stuck in the nearby marsh where he had fled. Despite hours of effort by rescuers, he was ultimately too tired and hypothermic, and had to be euthanized, with his owner of the past thirty years alongside. Surely we do not want to say that this owner has no grounds for resentment, no personal complaint.[78] It does not matter that the ordinance was a general norm—not about private rights, and not about protecting horses. The public transgression fell on her and her horse, and that is enough.

One might, at this point, suggest that perhaps we all have a right to compliance with public norms. It's not just competitors who have a right to rule compliance—everyone does. Adherence to morality and to the law are owed to all of us, to the entire moral or legal community.[79] There is something to this thought. I will return to it in Chapter 9. But for now, notice that, if we are not careful, this suggestion threatens to obliterate directed duties as a distinctive category. If all duties are owed to everyone—if every wrongful act correlates with a right in every other person—then there would be nothing added in saying that you owe a duty *to me*. We want rights to designate the rightholder as having some distinctive status, and that risks

THIRD PARTIES

being lost if everyone is regarded as having a right all of the time. One might try to appeal to different kinds of rights, primary and secondary.[80] But that reply comes perilously close to conceding the argument. There would then be two different categories: primary rights, which demarcate control and risks to be perceived, and then the "right" of everyone not to be injured through noncompliance with general norms, which underwrites a standing to complain. That there are two such categories is, basically, my central thesis.[81]

There is, we might say, a difference between being owed something as rightholder and being part of the general community to whom right action is, in some more general sense, owed. Consider the following. In discussing the case of a doctor with too little of a drug to save everyone who needs it, Elizabeth Anscombe writes,

> Suppose I am the doctor, and I don't use the drug at all. Whom do I wrong? None of them can say: "you owed it to *me*." For there might be nine, and if *one* can say that, all can; but if I used it, I let one at least go without and he can't say I owed it to *him*. Yet all can reproach me if I gave it to none. It was there, ready to supply human need, and human need was not supplied. So any one of them can say: you ought to have used it to help us who needed it; and so all are wronged.[82]

Anscombe's assessment is that, in conditions of scarcity, no one has a right to the life-saving drug. No one can say that it is owed to them individually. And yet, if the doctor fails to give the drug to any of the needy patients, Anscombe thinks "all are wronged." Such a doctor is not merely a public nuisance but a public menace, forsaking human need when it could have been met. That wrongful conduct can be the basis for a wronging. In this sense, the doctor does owe something to the patients—not the drug itself, but rather accountability for her actions. That this latter category outstrips the former is my point. Where there is a general public norm—the demands of the law, morality, or simply "human need"—we are potentially accountable to the entire community who share in that norm when we breach it.[83] And where some member of that community has a special stake in the matter—whether it be a matter of where they grow their mushrooms or the drugs they need to live—our failure to abide by those norms constitutes a wronging.

2.2.3 IMPRUDENCE WRONGS

I will, speculatively, go a step further. In Charles Dickens's *Bleak House,* Richard Carstone, a likeable but irresponsible young man, becomes engaged but struggles to apply himself professionally. Because his guardian has allowed him to marry only when he establishes himself in a profession, his professional failures hamper his engagement. He remarks to a friend, "I love her most devotedly; and yet I do her wrong, in doing myself wrong, every day and hour."[84]

Because others have a stake in our lives and our actions, I believe that our imprudence and poor choices can wrong them. Undeniably, our own failures and struggles can be the cause of great pain for those around us. I believe that when these struggles are not simply misfortunes but rather are attributable to our imprudence or negligence, then we may find ourselves having to answer to those who are indirectly injured.

The biblical parable of the prodigal son is the classic illustration. After squandering his share of the family wealth, the son returns to his father and says, "Father, I have sinned against heaven *and against you.*"[85] The father famously forgives and welcomes the son back. The story is intelligible because we understand how the father might be wronged by the son's actions. If we could not, then the son's declaration that he has sinned against his father, his contrition directed toward his father, and his father forgiving him would all be incoherent.

The biblical telling might be taken to imply that the father had a right to his son's obedience and loyalty, echoes of Leonato's claims over Hero. The wrong would then correspond to a violated right after all. But the parable remains a resonant story because it does not require such patriarchal control. Consider a variation in a poem by Sarah Orne Jewett titled "A Farmer's Sorrow."[86] Jewett describes the sadness of a farmer who watches and reluctantly helps his child devote himself to schooling rather than taking over the farm:

> Dan's a professor, and they say he knows as much as most—
> But he don't know, and never will how much his learnin' cost.
> 'Twas him that should have had the place; 'twas father's 'fore
>   'twas mine.
> I'd like to kep' it in the name; but I ain't goin' to whine.

THIRD PARTIES

53

There is no claim to obedience; no purported right to the son's taking up the plow. Indeed, the farmer even assists the son in pursuing his education, accepting that it might be for the best. Still, there is sadness in any child turning away from family tradition. One might think that that sorrow is the subject of the poem. But the last verse adds another layer.

> Dan's kind of disappointed—he sees he ain't the first;
> There wan't the makings of the best, and yet he ain't the worst.
> They call him a good scholar; but there's much he's learned in
>   vain,
> If he don't think he'd farm it, if he could start again.

Why does it matter that the son regrets his choice? One answer is that it is merely another, separate sorrow; a further misfortune for the family to bear. But that strikes me as missing something important: it overlooks the way the son's mistake inflects the father's sorrow. Had the departure made the son happy and successful—had it been the right choice for him—then the farmer might have been left with merely a private lament at what was not to be, the loss of family heritage. That would have been just one of life's misfortunes, a tragic misalignment of desires. Instead, the loss comes from a mistaken choice; it was avoidable. Had the son seen things better from the start, then the farmer would not have had to face his sadness. And that difference alters the father's sorrow. An element of fault or responsibility enters the picture. Admittedly, we would probably still balk at saying that the son "wronged" his father, but notice how apology and forgiveness seem to become apt in a new way.

The parent-child context presents an especially stark form of one person having a stake in another's life choices, but it is not unique. A lover, like Richard Carstone, wrongs his partner by failing to apply himself. And the same can be true of others in our lives—the devoted teacher,[87] the invested coworker, the faithful friend. In a powerful scene in the film *Good Will Hunting,* Will, the naturally gifted genius (played by Matt Damon), casually remarks to his childhood friend Chuckie (played by Ben Affleck) that he intends to turn down his fancy job offers and remain in their working-class Boston neighborhood. When Chuckie objects, Will protests, "Why is it always this . . . I fuckin' owe it to myself to do this or that?" Chuckie cuts him off, responding, "No, no, no. No, fuck you. You don't owe it to yourself. You owe it to me. 'Cause tomorrow I'm gonna wake up and I'll be fifty. And I'll still be doing this shit. And that's all right, that's fine. I mean, you're sittin' on a winning lottery ticket and you're too much of a pussy to cash it in. And that's bullshit. 'Cause I'd do anything to fuckin' have what you got. So would any of these fuckin' guys. It'd be an insult to us if you're still here in twenty years." Moments later, Chuckie describes how every day he hopes to discover that Will has left for something better. Few people have the talents of Will Hunting, but most of us are fortunate enough to have others who have invested in us, who rely on us, or who care about us. We are answerable to them for our failures—not because they have rights over our lives but because they have a stake in them. And when the failure is bad enough, it may be a wrong to them—perhaps even "an insult."[88]

There is a way to see these wrongs as continuous with the third-party examples. In the third-party cases, someone is hurt as a result of the perpetrator's violation of a duty owed to someone else. In the present cases, someone is hurt by what might be regarded as the perpetrator's violation of a duty owed to himself.[89] Put this way, all of the cases involve having a stake in a duty owed to someone. For example, one might think that a parent is wronged by a child who thoughtlessly commits suicide in a similar way to how a parent is wronged by a drunk driver who hits and kills his child. In each instance, someone has wrongfully killed his child in violation of what the child was owed, with suicide merely adding the complexity that the "someone" was the child herself. I mention this framing not to defend it but to illuminate some continuity. If one considers self-regarding duties to be directed duties to the self, then the loving parent is straightforwardly in the role of a *third* party. If one rejects the coherence of a directed duty owed to oneself,[90] then the parent is a third party simply in the sense that he is not the holder of a correlative claim-right. Either way, the parent's grief takes on a special character when it is the result of a *wrongful* death.

Naturally, the clearest cases of self-regarding conduct wronging others will involve intimates; they are typically the ones who have a meaningful stake in our self-regarding conduct. And the clearest cases involve high-stakes failures—squandering one's life or one's talents—that have a morally laden quality to them. But I want to suggest (while appreciating that it may seem a step too far for some readers) that even these features are not necessary. Sometimes we are wronged even by the low-level imprudence of strangers, where our interests happen to be in coinciding jeopardy.

THIRD PARTIES

Imagine you are on a game show, and you accumulate significant winnings. But, in the final round, there is a twist. Another contestant has also been playing. And now, through a random draw, your fate has been attached to this other contestant: if he succeeds in the final round, then you will take home double your winnings; if he fails, you will take home nothing. The contestant knows nothing of this arrangement. (The point is to create drama for the viewing audience.) In the final round, the contestant deliberately chooses the more difficult challenge as an act of bravado, even though the payout would be the same. Then, as he is completing the challenge, he makes a silly blunder—say, fails to carry the tens in adding sums, or fails to listen carefully to instructions while focused on entertaining the audience with his antics. He loses—a result that might have been a satisfyingly deserved outcome after his sheer cockiness and stupidity but for the fact that you too have now lost.

I think that you have been wronged here. You might naturally resent the toll that this idiotic behavior has taken on you. One can imagine the contestant apologizing to you upon learning that his loss also meant your loss. And notice the structure of that apology. One form of contrition might be, "I'm sorry; I didn't know that I was playing for anyone else." But if you're like me, that would not be entirely satisfying. Your resentment didn't stem from his not foreseeing your interests (how could he?), but from the fact that he was being such an idiot. The more apt apology, I contend, would be, "I'm sorry; I really screwed that up." The wrong is grounded not in an other-directed duty but in the sheer boneheadedness.

Here's a real-world, legal example: In a dispute over water use in California, one downstream user questioned irrigation being done by farmers during the winter when their fields lay fallow. Legally, the farmers had priority as long as they were making reasonable beneficial use. Defending their winter irrigation, the farmers explained that it served to drown and kill gophers. The court rejected this use out of hand, holding that "whatever quantity of water was used by respondents solely for this purpose during the winter period was not devoted to a beneficial use." In the court's words, "This seems to us so self-evident that no further discussion of the point is necessary."[91] The legal regime around water rights is complex, but I think that the basic idea here is intuitive: If someone with priority is using water for their own beneficial use, then you have no complaint. And yet, when they are using it for something idiotic—like drowning gophers—then you do have a complaint. The complaint turns not on something owed to you but on the (literally) downstream effects of nonbeneficial conduct.

To some readers, this may all sound unduly censorious. To be clear, I do not mean to deny that we all have the right to be an idiot sometimes. My claim is about answerability when our idiocy should happen to affect the life of another. I do not think the right to idiocy entails impunity. We regularly and appropriately hold each other accountable for basic functioning as minimally competent agents in the world. Most of us can relate to the complaint that Bob Dylan expresses in the line, "He's sure got a lotta gall to be so useless and all / Muttering small talk at the wall while I'm in the hall."[92] We resent the sheer uselessness of others when it causes us injury—when we are in the hall waiting for them to shut up. To be sure, the prodigal son is a clearer wrong. But these cases reside on a spectrum. It seems to me to be a mistake to deny that spectrum—to think that there is some on-off switch for answering to one's imprudence.

More broadly, my contention is that rights—as important as they are—do not simply carve our actions into private self-regarding acts and other-regarding duties. There is some sense in which all our actions, even our selection and pursuit of our own idiosyncratic personal ends, connect with those around us. Consider Joseph Raz: "Rights are supposed by their proponents to be the foundations of morality in the narrow sense. . . . They set limits to an individual's pursuit of his own interests. . . . [But t]here is a fundamental objection to . . . the notion that . . . one can divide one's principles of action into those concerned with one's own personal goals and those concerned with others, in such a way that the principles are independent of each other."[93] Raz's point is that personal relations require that we see ourselves as, in some sense, acting in relation to others even in our personal pursuits—that there can be no cordoning off the personal from the moral.[94] The fact that even personal choices relate to others shows up, I am now suggesting, in our accountability for imprudence. Others do not have rights over our personal pursuits, but that does not mean that we are unconnected with, and unanswerable to, them.

2.3 Three Concerns about Expansiveness

The cases that I have described are meant to suggest that we can be wronged even when no right of ours was violated. Perhaps someone else's rights were violated; or perhaps there was simply a violation of public norms. My claim

THIRD PARTIES

is that, sometimes, such violations nevertheless give us personal grievances. Where the misconduct of another bears on us in a particularized way, we stand to be wronged by it, even if it is not a matter of our rights. If any of these cases are compelling, then it opens a conceptual space between rights and wrongs.

Many, however, will be concerned about the possibility of such a space. They will object that it would be an aperture to chaotic and unlimited accountability. Third-party wrongs may seem a Pandora's box, letting loose the possibility of all manner of dangerous and bewildering complaints. We may be subject to what Cardozo warned against: "a liability in an indeterminate amount for an indeterminate time to an indeterminate class."[95]

I suspect that most resistance to the preceding examples derives, consciously or unconsciously, from concerns in this vicinity. But there are different ways that this gut resistance might be fashioned into an actual objection. With the remainder of this chapter, I will address three different plausible objections related to overexpansiveness. None of them, I think, gives us reason to deny categorically the existence of third-party wrongs.

2.3.1 NORMATIVE INJURY

Intuitively, how we hold people accountable for any given wrong act should depend in some way or another on why that act is wrong in the first place. For example, more severe accountability seems appropriate the stronger (and more unrivaled) the reasons against an action. Unprovoked physical assault is a more serious wrong than a benevolent white lie, and that would seem to have much to do with the fact that the reasons against it are weightier. The person who commits the assault displays a greater indifference to others and the way that others matter. Accountability relations thus appear to be a response to the lack of respect for one's moral status.[96] If I assault you, then I implicitly say that I think you are someone who can be assaulted, who doesn't matter. Resentment and complaint may be regarded as responses to this implicit threat.[97]

From these very plausible thoughts, one might arrive at an objection to third-party wrongs. Third-party wrongs involve, basically by definition, parties whose moral status is not the grounds for the duty. When I assault you, I wrong you because I implicitly communicate that you don't matter, that your bodily integrity need not be respected. But my actions express no such thing about any others. Of course, there is something in my action that might cause anyone to be threatened—namely, the implicit message that I think some people can be assaulted. That might prompt blame and indignation from anyone. But, the thought goes, there is a specific injury—what might be called personal normative injury—that only you suffer. As Jay Wallace puts it, "The wrong that has been visited on one who suffers such an injury consists, at least in part, in the attitude of indifference to or contempt for one's specific claims."[98] Only you suffer this disrespect for a personal normative entitlement. As such, only you should feel resentment, which is a response to this particular injury. Third parties, though they may be harmed, suffer no injury to their normative authority, and that explains why they cannot be wronged. Put simply, the duty wasn't about them, and thus the breach isn't about them either.

There is, without a doubt, a special kind of injury involved in having *your* claim disregarded—a manifestation of a disrespect for you personally. A significant part of the sting in a rights violation can be the expressed disregard for the individual rightholder—the implication that the victim is worthy of less concern than others. And it is true that third parties do not suffer this kind of injury in the same way that a rightholder does.

All that I reject is that a wrong necessarily requires this specific kind of injury. A transgression can wrong someone without saying anything about them personally. Suppose that I assault you from behind one day. When you look up from the ground in bewildered pain, I say, "Oh, gosh, I didn't realize it was *you*. I thought that it was my nemesis. I would never do that to *you*." Undoubtedly this response on my part would mitigate certain fear and resentment on your part. It might make it easier for you to forgive me. But surely I have wronged you regardless. There is something for which I owe you an apology and for which you might forgive me. It would be comedic for you to dust yourself off and reply, "Alrighty then, nothing for you to apologize about."

There are two possible avenues of response at this point: to reinterpret the wrong here or to reinterpret normative injury. According to the first, one might cast the example as a wrong of carelessness. My having been mistaken actually does completely negate one potential wrong—willingly causing you bodily harm. But I have still wronged you by my disregard for you in not exercising more care. Your complaint, on this view, is that I should be more careful (when I commit my assaults).

This response strikes me as strained. For starters, it's too self-centered—the complaint ought not be, "You should do a better job looking out *for me*," but rather, "You shouldn't go around assaulting people." Furthermore, the

THIRD PARTIES

wrong cannot be merely about a lack of care because I may have been careful with respect to you. Your presence could have been completely unforeseeable—I might have taken every precaution to ensure that it was my nemesis I was attacking, or have had every reason to believe that it couldn't be you, only to be foiled by ill chance.[99]

A different line of response would say that normative injury should not be understood in such a personal way. The injury is not disregard for *your* normative authority as such, but rather just disregard for *some agent's* normative entitlement (which turns out to be yours). In committing the attack, I knew I was violating someone's rights and that's what matters. The normative injury consists in the rights violation itself. In support, it might be argued that there are reasons to abstract from particular individual identities and to focus on the agent qua agent.[100] Normative injury is properly regarded as about the agent in the abstract.

But now consider a variation on the assault case. Rather than mistaking you for my nemesis, I have correctly identified my nemesis and I fire an arrow from my crossbow straight at his heart. But at that very instant, he is startled by a bee, jumping out of my arrow's path. And behind him, you happen to drop down from a tree branch where you have been unforeseeably concealed, only to take the arrow unluckily in your stomach.

The abstract conception of normative injury will treat this case altogether differently from the mistaken identity example. In the mistaken identity case, there was a failure to respect *this* person, I simply didn't know that it was you. But in this second case, we cannot say even that. Without falling back on the negligence thought (rejected earlier), there is simply no way to say that I have failed to show proper respect for your normative status. My deliberation could not have involved anything about you, even qua anonymous agent.

This abstract conception of normative injury now faces two distinct problems: First, treating the misdirected arrow case as categorically different from the mistaken identity case is counterintuitive. In each, you receive a blow meant for another. Second, it seems implausible that my arrow lodged in your stomach doesn't wrong you. The law, for whatever it's worth, agrees. Under the doctrine of transferred intent, an intention to injure one person that results in injury to another person will be regarded as an intentional injury to that second person.[101] So my arrow fired to wound will ground a complaint for culpably causing your wounds. It does not matter whether your presence was foreseeable.[102] When my intention to

60 WRONGS AND RIGHTS COME APART

harm yields actual harm, I have committed a wrong to the harmed person. That the actual victim was not my intended victim (*de se* or *de re*) is simply no defense.

More generally, the abstracting response salvages the idea of normative injury only by emptying it of content. It is no longer about suffering some kind of personal disrespect; it is simply about the formal fact that one's right was or was not violated. There might be reasons why law or morality should reserve certain responses for rights violations. We could call this responding to normative injury (using the abstract sense), but it would be merely notional. The injury would not supply some independent grounds for rejecting third-party wrongs, in the way that the personal conception of normative injury might have; the injury would merely be defined to exclude such wrongs. My sense is that normative injury as an idea gets its intuitive credit from the personal version; the abstract version is not entitled to trade on that credit.

I fully accept that personal normative injury—the injury of someone not caring about *you* as a moral agent—is a serious phenomenon. And it is absent in third-party cases. What I deny is that such personal normative injury is essential to wronging. Each of us is not a disembodied normative authority. If wrongs turn on how a transgression matters to us personally, then there is no reason to focus only on normative injury. We also suffer real injuries when there is damage to our bodies or to the social and physical world in which we are enmeshed.

2.3.2 FREEDOM

A different argument for rejecting third-party wrongs, also sounding in concerns about expansiveness, focuses on freedom. According to this thought, accountability for an action is a kind of restriction on one's freedom. If you are answerable to me for some particular choice, then you are not free with respect to me—I have some control over your choice. If this thought is combined with the premise that the only justification for exercising control over another person is in support of one's own rights, then it would follow that one can only hold another to account for violations of one's own rights. Put another way, third-party wrongs might appear to be a violation of the liberal ideal of maximal freedom consistent with the freedom of others.[103]

This concern for freedom clearly animates some of the resistance to third-party wrongs, both in theory and in practice. In *Moch* (the fire

THIRD PARTIES   61

hydrant case) for example, Cardozo's primary concern with the plaintiff's position was the way that liability would impose an involuntary burden: "Every one making a promise having the quality of a contract will be under a duty to the promisee by virtue of the promise, but under another duty, apart from contract, to an indefinite number of potential beneficiaries when performance has begun. The assumption of one relation will mean the *involuntary* assumption of a series of new relations, inescapably hooked together."[104] Similarly, in *Ultramares* (the accounting case), Cardozo's concern about "indeterminate" liability is invoked "to enkindle doubt whether a flaw may not exist in the implication of a duty that exposes to these consequences."[105] In both cases, Cardozo's point is that liability to persons who were not rightholders would be an unjustifiable imposition, a limitation on our freedom. Third-party wrongs would give third parties a say over what we choose to do.[106]

As noted, this argument against third-party wrongs relies on two premises: first, that being answerable to someone else means an imposition on one's freedom; second, that the only permissible impositions on one's freedom are when one has a right oneself. I am skeptical of both premises, but especially the first.

I see little reason to think that, as a conceptual matter, answerability entails a lack of freedom. There is a difference between who gets to decide and whether they have to answer for it. Ex post accountability need not mean an assumption of ex ante control. When a student thinks that a teacher wrongs her by giving an unfair grade, the student need not be implicitly challenging the teacher's right to do the grading. Similarly, when I form the thought that you will wrong me if you trick my mother into leaving her inheritance to you, I am not implicitly asserting that I have any ex ante control—either that the disposition of the inheritance is a matter of my control or that how you treat my mother is something over which I might grant or deny permission. In both cases, to reply to the complaint with, "You're not in charge here," would involve a conceptual mistake. To assert a complaint is perfectly consistent with believing that one is not in charge. So too with resentment. And being subject to a complaint or to resentment is thus consistent with freedom, with being in charge.

But perhaps verbal complaints and reactive attitudes are cheap.[107] To be entitled to a coercively enforced remedy, one might say, is an altogether different matter. To be wronged in this stronger sense—the sense of interest to the law—means not merely the standing to grumble but the standing to do something about it.[108] And that, one might think, requires that one had a right ex ante. One is entitled to force someone to make repairs to the world only if that corner of the world was supposed to be under your control in the first place. Otherwise, it would be forcing someone to do the equivalent after the fact of something one could not have imposed beforehand.[109]

There are many reasons to be doubtful here. First, detaching wrongs from moral dialogue and personal reactive attitudes—from resentment, apology, forgiveness—risks losing any foundation in ordinary interpersonal life. Second, given that reactive attitudes can be a serious and primal sanction,[110] it strikes me as odd to treat the availability of legal remedies as encroaching on our freedom but not to regard reactive attitudes similarly. Third, it's not clear that remedies after the fact are best regarded as a continuation of ex ante control.[111]

For now, I shall make only one point. Would third-party wrongs, even with enforceable remedies, mean that we are less free? In an important sense, they would not. According to one attractive picture, freedom means having a robust sphere of personal sovereignty, a domain in which we are truly in charge, a set of choices where we get to dismiss the complaints of others simply by saying, "none of your business." Recognizing third-party wrongs need not shrink that sphere at all. As long as you stay within your sphere—as long as you act permissibly, within your rights—you are subject to *no additional constraints* on what you may do.[112] There's no reduction in your sovereign sphere. Your "freedom" is implicated only if you venture across the line. Should you trespass on another's sphere, then you may have to answer not merely to that person but to others as well. But why think that a loss of freedom?

Freedom, whatever it means, isn't about being able to act wrongly without facing others to answer for it. Consider an analogy: defense of others. Is it an imposition on our freedom if other people can intervene to defend one another? I don't see that it is, even though it does mean that we may be subject to the coercive force of someone other than the rightholder. Defense of others doesn't change our first-order obligations, even as it does expand the potential consequences for wrongful action. Likewise for third-party wrongs. In both instances, the sphere of permissible conduct is not contracted—all that changes is the repercussions for stepping outside that sphere.

THIRD PARTIES

63

Of course, that is a quite formal conception of freedom. In a more practical sense, expansive liability does place a burden on our freedom by chilling activity that carries any risk of violating the rights of another. This concern lurks in Cardozo's *Moch* and *Ultramares* opinions—who will take on potential liability to one person when that could carry with it liability to all? One frolics less freely in a space bordered by landmines than in one bordered only by fences. But in my view, that is simply what it means to live in a complex social world—that there are landmines afoot when we act wrongly. We get to choose how to act within our own sphere, and we get to shape and reshape the boundary lines with others. But we do not get to control the response that we face when we trespass.

2.3.3 CAUSATION

A final concern about expansiveness relates to causation. If our violation of one person's rights means that we may be accountable to others for the results, then where do we draw the line? Surely we cannot be accountable for everything, even events far down some distant causal pathway. *Palsgraf* is often (mistakenly) understood as a case about causation because, if the railroad could be held accountable for the unforeseeable chain of events that led to Mrs. Palsgraf's injuries, it may seem to open the door to liability for all manner of harms. If we allow for third-party wrongs, then a wrongful but relatively benign act that winds up causing a raft of injuries to wholly unforeseen third parties could open the door to a raft of unanticipated grievances. A single lie or misstep might mean that one has wronged some distant stranger. Our only refuge would be arbitrarily drawing some cutoff, as Judge William Andrews seems to concede in *Palsgraf*. A rights-based conception, in contrast, seems to offer a natural and principled limit: only those consequences within the scope of the right violated are attributable to the actor. Surely that is better than throwing the door wide open to the vast untamable winds of causation.

To my mind, it is actually a virtue of the view that it appreciates the unpredictability and expansiveness of potential wrongs and casts focus onto the hard questions about causation. The extent to which we are answerable for long and elaborate causal chains strikes me as a difficult but appropriately confronted question. Lawyers and analytic philosophers are professionally drawn to tidiness. But it seems to me that this is a place where life does not afford tidy answers, as literature sometimes shows us. When

64   WRONGS AND RIGHTS COME APART

we look carefully at interpersonal life, these questions seem to be among the most vexing. As George Eliot remarks, "The problem how far a man is to be held responsible for the unforeseen consequences of his own deed, is one that might well make us tremble to look at it."[113]

Consider an example from Robert Penn Warren's novel *All the King's Men*. One of the novel's subplots involves an upstanding character named Cass Mastern, whose one bad act consists of having an affair with his friend's wife, Annabelle Trice. Upon discovering the affair, Mr. Trice removes his wedding ring and shoots himself. A trusted family slave named Phebe finds the ring and gives it to Annabelle. Annabelle is unable to bear Phebe's knowledge of the circumstances behind her husband's death, and she sells Phebe into the appalling slave trade of the antebellum South. Mastern is deeply altered by learning what has happened. He writes,

> At that moment of perturbation, when the cold sweat broke on my brow, I did not frame any sentence distinctly to my mind. But I have looked back and wrestled to know the truth. . . . It was . . . the fact that all of these things—the death of my friend, the betrayal of Phebe, the suffering and rage and great change of the woman I had loved—all had come from my single act of sin and perfidy, as the boughs from the bole and the leaves from the bough. Or to figure the matter differently, it was as though the vibration set up in the whole fabric of the world by my act had spread infinitely and with ever-increasing power and no man could know the end. I did not put it into words in such fashion, but I stood there shaken by a tempest of feeling.[114]

This idea—that the moral significance of our failings ripples outward in unforeseeable ways—is an important theme in the novel. In fact, one might say that it is an important theme in all tragedy. Aristotle describes the tragic hero as "a person who is not superior in virtue and justice who passes into ill fortune, not because he is bad and vicious, but because he makes some error."[115] Tragedy relies on our understanding that one error or flaw can have grave ramifications for our fortunes, both material and moral. Although Cass Mastern could never have foreseen that his affair would have any bearing on the slave, he devotes himself to finding Phebe and saving her from the whorehouses. This quest, unsuccessful in the end, is intelligible as an attempted act of repair. Mastern sees himself as

THIRD PARTIES

owing something remedial to Phebe, to right the world that he has made wrong.

The point here is not the clichéd but true observation that all things are interrelated—the proverbial butterfly flapping its wings. Rather, the point is uniquely about *bad* acts—that badness seems to spread in a special kind of way. The butterfly that innocently flaps its wings isn't accountable for the hurricane, but Cass Mastern is accountable, in some morally significant sense, for the evils that result from his "single act of sin and perfidy." It is when we commit a bad act that we are morally accountable for whatever follows.

Theorists have appreciated the way that even unforeseen bad consequences can be imputed to our wrongful actions. This view was, as noted already, Kant's. At the beginning of *The Metaphysics of Morals*, he writes, "The good or bad results of an action that is owed . . . cannot be imputed to the subject. The bad results of a wrongful action . . . can be imputed to the subject."[116] If we lie, for example, then whatever unforeseen misfortunes follow can be imputed to us. In a different vein, Anscombe argues that you cannot "exculpate yourself from the *actual* consequences of the most disgraceful actions" by appealing to what was foreseeable; rather, "a man is responsible for the bad consequences of his bad actions."[117] And, in his dissent in the *Palsgraf* case, Judge Andrews argues that there can be liability for injuries to unforeseen plaintiffs. He writes, "It may be said this is unjust. Why? In fairness [the negligent person] should make good every injury flowing from his negligence."[118] The common thread is that, once one acts wrongly, one cannot escape responsibility for "the vibration set up in the whole fabric of the world," as Robert Penn Warren put it.

But, one might insist, there must be some limit.[119] Perhaps the Long Island Railroad Company wronged Mrs. Palsgraf, but the chain could go much further. Her resultant stutter causes an instruction to be misunderstood, causing a delivery to go to a wrong address, causing the intended recipient to be without medicine, causing his child to grow up without a parent. Surely the Long Island Railroad has not wronged this orphan. Where is the limit?

The answer is . . . causation. No doubt the question of what counts as a cause is immensely thorny. But it is the question that we should seek to answer. We want to know whether—or to what extent—the Long Island Railroad's negligence caused the child to grow up as an orphan. That one can often postulate some chain of but-fors should prompt us to think harder about causation, not to abandon the inquiry. Perhaps we must think more carefully about each counterfactual (e.g., how do we know the instruction wouldn't have been misunderstood anyway?). Perhaps if we are more properly Bayesian, it will prove epistemically untenable to believe causal claims involving long chains. Perhaps we are better served by moving away from all-or-nothing description and toward descriptions in terms of causal contribution, with wrongs fading in severity the further out one goes. I do not have a worked-out theory. But I don't think that law or morality gets to skip over a question that confronts everyone else, from historians and physicists to novelists and sportscasters.

Nor, importantly, would rejecting third-party wrongs eliminate questions of causation altogether. For example, had the explosion in *Palsgraf* caused the metal scale to fall not on Mrs. Palsgraf but on the owner of the original package, the causal question would be the same, though there would be no third-party involvement at all. So ruling out third parties is, at best, only a way to hide the problem from view a little.[120]

Recognizing third-party wrongs does involve accepting more expansive responsibility for the effects that our actions have in the world. That puts the question of how far to reach down the chains of causation on display. I think that is true to life and an important question, though indeed one "that might well make us tremble to look at it."

3

Shaping Action

Rights are action shaping. They define the contours both of what we are entitled to do and of what others are entitled to do to us. Our rights allow space where our agency can flourish, normatively shielded from interference. And conversely, the rights of others provide boundaries that are to be respected in our own actions. Looked at from either side, rights are fundamentally about describing the normative boundaries of our actions.

Recall the five typical features of rights described in Chapter 1: waiver, claiming or demanding, coercive enforcement, exclusionary reasons or side constraints, and a phenomenology of directedness. Notice what all of these features have in common. They each presuppose normativity. Rights are, it is understood, connected up with some subset of our duties; they are about what we ought to do. The philosophical debates over how to delineate rights and directed duties seek to characterize this subset. That is, they seek to illuminate the special features of those duties that are correlative to rights.[1] The common ground is that rights matter to what we should do or not do.[1] Shaping action seems to be the essential role of rights.

They accomplish this with a distinctive force. Rights and directed duties seem to involve a special kind of reason—perhaps especially pressing, or subject to certain conditions, or exclusionary, or just phenomenologically unique. Rights are of such great importance because they tell us—often decisively—how we should act. Though there may be debates over how exactly to distinguish it, in thinking and talking about rights, we are concerned with this distinctive normativity.[2]

In describing relational normativity, it can be tempting to appeal to a connection with wronging. We can find the normativity of rights, the

68 WRONGS AND RIGHTS COME APART

thought goes, in the potential wrongings that their violations would produce. Rights are action shaping *in that* wronging another is something to be avoided. One might, in this way, think that Cardozo's axiom—that a wrong consists in the violation of a person's rights—illuminates the normativity of rights and directed duties.

There are two slightly different forms that this thought can take. First, one might think that the fact that a person stands to be wronged is itself a *source* of normativity. On this view, the potential wronging gives one reasons to avoid a course of conduct. For example, Elizabeth Anscombe writes, "What is wrong about an act that is wrong may be just this, that it is *a* wrong."[3] Anscombe seems to be suggesting that the fact that an action would wrong another is an important aspect or description of *why* one ought not perform that action. The potential wronging is explanatorily prior; it grounds the reasons for refraining.[4]

A different idea is captured by Arthur Schopenhauer when he writes, "The concept of wrong is the original and positive, and the concept of right, which is opposed to it, is the derivative and negative."[5] Schopenhauer's idea was that our experience of wronging is an experience of interpersonal morality. He believed that we encounter morality by encountering what it is to wrong another person, extending our will so far that it interferes with another's. This is a point about apprehension, not about grounding. Accordingly, one might think that the fact that an action would wrong another person doesn't *generate* or *ground* a reason not to do it, but rather it is merely part and parcel with there being a reason not to do it. To recognize that an action would wrong someone is to recognize a certain kind of reason, but it doesn't ground them. Along these lines, Stephen Darwall argues that, when we appreciate how an action would open us to the moral complaint of another person, we appreciate the moral reasons against that action.[6] For Darwall, accountability relations and second-personal reasons "comprise an interdefinable circle," such that neither has priority in grounding the other.[7]

I will not dwell on the differences here. What is important for either of these views is that wrongings are—just like rights—inexorably tied to the same distinctive normativity. The action-shaping quality of a right inheres in the action-condemning quality of a wronging. Rights and wrongs are thus different windows onto the same normative relation, the same special set of directed reasons and duties.

SHAPING ACTION

In this chapter, I will argue that wrongings are not action shaping in the way that rights are action shaping.[8] That is, I will argue that the fact that an action would wrong someone does not figure into what one ought to do in the way that rights do. To be precise, my thesis in this chapter will be the following: the fact that X's φ-ing would wrong Y does not constitute a reason for X not to φ—at least, not in the way that the fact that Y has a right that X not φ constitutes a reason for X not to φ. Strictly speaking, that is what my overall argument requires. I will, however, frequently say simply that potential wrongings do not provide any reasons—leaving out the further qualifier "in the way that rights provide reasons." This locution is simpler, and it is what I believe. But a full defense of this unqualified claim would require engaging with thorny questions about the nature of reasons. It is in vogue to say that "reasons are cheap" and to be skeptical of generalizations that anything is not a reason.[9] With respect to wrongings, I am not convinced, but I don't wish to get hung up on this. If one is drawn to profligacy about reasons, then my claims that potential wrongs do not provide reasons for action should be read as saying that potential wrongs do not provide reasons for action *in the way that rights do*. That is the important thesis: wrongs are not normative in the way of rights.

This thesis, when combined with the premise that rights are action shaping, yields a broader argument: if it is essential to rights that they are action shaping, and if wrongs are not action shaping as rights are, then rights and wrongings cannot be mirror images of each other. Rights describe something normatively potent, whereas potential wrongings are comparatively inert. We see rights and wrongs come apart in thinking about how each matters to action.

The remainder of the chapter is structured as three separate but related arguments for the claim that potential wrongings are not action shaping. First, I argue that there are certain promissory wrongs that do not correlate with duties. The second argument scrutinizes the role of potential wrongs in the context of conflicted choices, arguing that they do not play the action-shaping role that rights do. Finally, I step back from the particular cases and argue that wrongings are not action shaping because they represent a fundamentally ex post perspective, drawing analogies to regret and legal liability. What hopefully emerges is a unified picture of the way in which wrongs, by their nature, are detached from action in a way that rights, by their nature, are not.

3.1 Promissory Wrongs without Action

If our directed duties and the potential wrongs we might commit are just mirror images of one another, then they will not come apart. That is, there will not be cases in which a potential wrong exists without an accompanying reason for action. But I believe that wrongs and reasons do come apart in precisely this way. In this section and the next, I present cases in which a potential wronging does not correlate with the kind of normative significance that one would expect to characterize rights and directed duties. Here, I will be concerned with certain promissory wrongs, which can arise when we commit ourselves not to an action but to a state of affairs.

3.1.1 COMMERCIAL WARRANTIES

To begin, consider the express commercial warranty. A seller of goods might say, "I promise you that the powertrain on this car will last for 60,000 miles," or, "We guarantee that this product is safe and reliable." Similarly, a service provider might say, "I promise that this work will last at least three years," or, "We guarantee that your house will no longer sink into the ground."[10] Warranties like these are commonplace and a critical feature of commercial life. Notably, they may be offered after the good has been fully manufactured or after the service has been completed.[11] There is, at that point, nothing left to be done.[12]

If the powertrain fails or the house sinks into the ground, then the seller will be answerable to the recipient. In this way, a warranty seems at first blush to be the exercise of a normative power akin to, or perhaps a subspecies of, promising. Just by uttering certain words, the seller makes it the case that a buyer will have a complaint against her where he otherwise might not. Warranting is the power to create a kind of liability. Of course, warranties carry a kind of legal connotation. But I think we should see it as a moral phenomenon as well. Consider the host who says, "I promise that there are not nuts in the carrot cake," or the teenager who says, "I guarantee that the party will be over by ten o'clock."[13]

Warranties exemplify the fact that we sometimes use the language of promises to refer to guarantees that a fact will obtain. Are such warranties actually promises? Can we promise that the world will be a certain way? Oliver Wendell Holmes Jr. found no problem in thinking so: "An assurance that it shall rain tomorrow, or that a third person shall paint a picture,

SHAPING ACTION 71

may as well be a promise as one that the promisee shall receive from some source one hundred bales of cotton, or that the promisor will pay the promisee one hundred dollars. What is the difference in the cases? It is only in the degree of power possessed by the promisor over the event."[14] Holmes's argument, which is a powerful one, is that we can and do make promises over which we do not have *complete* control, so why shouldn't we be able to make promises over which we lack *any* control?

Granting this continuity, there is also a difference here. We might distinguish between *promising to* (do something) and *promising that* (some fact will obtain). Philosophers typically assume that one promises an action within one's control, and then one is bound by a duty to perform that action.[15] The promise is action shaping; it gives one a special kind of reason to perform the promised action. *Promising-that* does not seem to fit that model.[16] With a warranty, if the product does not turn out as warranted, then the buyer has a complaint against the seller. But though it can be the basis for a wrong, the warranty may not generate any action-shaping duties. It's not about action. It's about a fact obtaining in the world. Sometimes it's a fact over which the guarantor has complete control; sometimes it's a fact over which the guarantor has very little control; and sometimes it's a fact over which the guarantor may have no possible control.

One might resist this characterization of warranties as a kind of *promising-that*. On the one hand, one might contend that the warranty is not actually a *promise that* some fact will obtain but rather a *promise to* repair, replace, or indemnify the purchaser if the product fails.[17] Some warranties are, by their terms, precisely that.[18]

But for many warranties, such an interpretation seems unsatisfactory. Suppose that I'm your roofer. I've done various repairs for you, and now you've hired me to replace your roof. At the end of the job, I promise you that the roof will last for at least twenty years. It fails miserably the next winter. On these facts, I do owe it to you to replace the roof and indemnify you for your losses. But that would not be *performance*; it would be a remedy for a failure. One can see that it is remedial in various ways. First, notice that there would be a moral residue: even if I replace the roof, I still owe you an apology for the failure.[19] If all that I promised was to replace it if it failed, then this apology should seem peculiar. Second, one can see that the guarantee was not merely a promise to repair in the ways we would talk about it. Suppose that someone asked you, "Should I trust Nico's promises? Has he ever given you a bad one?" I think that you would and should say, "Yes, his roof didn't last like he said it would." You might follow up by noting that I had repaired things. But I don't think you would regard the events as instantiating my keeping my word. Finally, one can see that the promise is not merely to indemnify by noting that it would be bad faith for me to operate all along anticipating a strong likelihood that I will issue a replacement.[20] If my saying, "I promise that the roof will last twenty years," meant simply, "I promise that, if the roof doesn't last twenty years, I will fix it," then it would be fine for me to say that knowing—even planning—that it won't last. But generally that would not be acceptable precisely because the guarantee means something different from a conditional promise to repair. For all these reasons, many warranties are not merely conditional promises to repair or to indemnify. They are, as they sound, guarantees that the world will be a certain way, such that the recipient has been wronged if it is not.

Rather than contending that warranties are merely promises to indemnify, one might take the opposite tack and argue that *promising-that*—including the making of warranties—is not truly promising at all. *Promising-that*, one might contend, is just a special form of assertion. Whatever liability it generates is not promissory but rather liability for misrepresentation.

Undoubtedly, we do sometimes use the language of promising and guaranteeing as a form of assertion, but I don't think that's the way to understand the commercial warranty. If we must draw a firm dichotomy between promises and representations, then I think that the liability for warranties is typically promissory. At least sometimes, saying, "I guarantee that this roof will last twenty years," is not merely an emphatic way of asserting that the roof will last twenty years.

For what it's worth, the law has had to contend with whether to treat warranties as promissory liability or a kind of misrepresentation—which would require that the statement be heard, believed, and acted on. In the United States, it is now widely accepted that liability for breach of express warranty does not require reliance; it's treated as promissory in that the defendant is on the hook simply for having given her word.[21] And this makes sense when one recognizes the continuity between express warranties and simply specifying a promise. One might, as part of a manufacturing contract, say, "I promise to deliver widgets that will last for ten years." There would be little doubt that the guarantee would be part of the promise,

SHAPING ACTION

73

operating merely as a specification of what is to be delivered. So it would be odd to think that saying, "I promise that these widgets will last ten years," is something altogether different—no longer part of the promised performance. This was basically Holmes's point: once we recognize that one can promise someone that he will receive one hundred bales of cotton of a particular quality, it is a short step to thinking that one can promise that a fact will obtain. So if we must categorize warranties as either promises or representations, then they seem to be the former.

The better lesson may be that drawing a hard-and-fast separation between promissory liability and liability for misrepresentation is a mistake. It obscures the fact that, in most promises, two elements are typically present. If I promise to take you to the airport, I thereby give myself reasons of a special kind to take you to the airport (action shaping) *and* I guarantee a fact (namely, that you will be taken to the airport by me). When we say "I promise," we typically effect both of these changes in the normative landscape at once. We create a duty and we make it the case that we will be accountable for a nonoccurrence.[22] These effects are interwoven. So rather than seeing a categorical divide between promises and representations, I think that it is better "to distinguish the guaranteeing force from the obliging force of a promise."[23]

Though they typically arrive together, these different forces can and do come apart. We can cancel the standard implicatures, teasing apart the guaranteeing force and the obliging force. For example, we say things like, "I promise to make every effort to take you to the airport."[24] This locution doesn't generate different reasons or action guidance for the promisor; the obliging force is exactly the same. I should deliberate similarly, and the same actions will count as impermissible. What the locution does (if successful) is cancel the normally implied guaranteeing force—it acknowledges the possibility that you will not be taken to the airport by me. It indicates that there are possible sources of failure beyond my control for which I am not taking responsibility. Such disclaimers can be valuable, facilitating negotiation over how to bear risks.[25] But they involve giving a promise with less than the standard force.[26]

Just as there can be an action-shaping effect without a guarantee, there can, I contend, also be a guarantee without shaping action. In such cases, the promisor issues an utterance that does not oblige her to do anything, and yet it does make it the case that the promisee will have a grievance

74 WRONGS AND RIGHTS COME APART

against her if the promised state of affairs does not come about, at least when offered after the work is fully completed—the commercial warranty operates in this way. The seller's words are meant to guarantee that a fact will obtain, but they are not meant to create any action-shaping duty. The commercial warranty, in this context, is a promise whose action-shaping significance has been shrunk to zero. It is the basis of a promissory wrong, but it generates no promissory duty.

The promise does not have the standard force—both guaranteeing and obliging—because it is basically impossible for the seller to do anything. If one promises to provide a car with a powertrain that will last 60,000 miles, then one presumably takes on an action-shaping duty to manufacture or procure up to that standard. But when the warranty is offered only as the car is being driven off the lot, there's no action left to be guided. So all that the promise does is create a guarantee.

I say "basically impossible" because there are, of course, still things that the seller *could* do to make the powertrain last. She might of her own accord show up to check and replace the engine oil. Or she might take it upon herself to repair area potholes and clean the roads of dust and other potential engine contaminants. But that would be absurd. We recognize that the seller is not obliging herself to do such things, even if we think that they would be ways to ensure that the powertrain does, in fact, last 60,000 miles. Instead, she has offered a bare guarantee, which is, I am suggesting, a promise with part of its normal force atypically absent.

3.1.2 PROMISES TO FEEL AND TO BELIEVE

I want to suggest that a similar structure can explain a range of other atypical promises—promises where an action-shaping duty to perform is somehow blocked or inoperative. In the commercial warranty, this happens because there's no action to be taken. Something similar may explain other promises that are not straightforwardly promises to act.

To begin, consider the promise to feel or not to feel a particular occurrent emotion. Such promises are not unfamiliar: "I promise not to feel angry," "Promise me that you won't feel sorry for me," "I won't feel even the slightest pang of jealousy, I promise."[27] Promises like these can be important for negotiating emotional interactions and building trust. Here, for example, is part of an 1801 letter by Eliza Southgate—a remarkable eighteen-year-old girl from Maine who would go on to marry the future governor of New York City before dying at age twenty-five from childbirth complications:

> I had flattered myself, when I commenced this correspondence, to reap both instruction and amusement from an undisguised communication of sentiments. I had likewise hoped that you would not think it too great a condescension to speak to me with that opennes[s] you would to a female friend. However, I shall begin to think it is contrary to the nature of things that a gentleman should speak his real sentiments to a lady. Yet, in our correspondence I wished and expected to step aside from the world and speak to each other in the plain language of sincerity. . . . Do not imagine from what I have said that the most disagreeable truths will offend me. *[I] promise not to feel hurt at anything you write, if 'tis your real sentiments.* But, cousin, don't trifle with me; do not make me think so contemptibly of myself as you will by not allowing me your confidence.[28]

One can, I think, immediately appreciate the significant value of Ms. Southgate's promise. How else does an eighteen-year-old girl in 1801 elicit candid intercourse rather than protective paternalism? We should not dismiss such expressions as simply ineffectual. Her correspondent would, I believe, have a grievance if his subsequent sincerity prompted Ms. Southgate to be hurt.

And yet one does not, in general, choose to feel hurt. Ms. Southgate's promise may give her reasons to adopt various strategies to control her reactions, but it does not directly give her reasons not to feel hurt. That's not because feeling hurt is not reason responsive. It is; one can have better or worse reasons for feeling hurt. But feeling hurt is not, generally, within our guiding control. The promise can't be action shaping in that way. For this reason, it seems to me to be a bit strained to describe Ms. Southgate as taking on a *duty* not to feel hurt.

I suggest that Ms. Southgate's promise—like the commercial warranty— is devoid of obliging force and yet retains its guaranteeing force. The fact that what is promised is, in this circumstance, beyond her control makes the promise partly ineffectual, but not entirely. It's not directly normative; it doesn't create a duty not to feel hurt or give her correspondent a right that she not be hurt. But nonetheless, Ms. Southgate's promise makes it the case that she will wrong her correspondent if she is hurt by his sincerity. It puts her at risk of a wronging.[29]

Related to the promise to feel is a promise to believe. Here, again, promises can be an important tool for negotiating emotionally fraught situations. Imagine a child who has been victimized by an adult and is reluctant to tell his story for fear that it will fall on deaf ears. One can imagine a parent saying, "You can tell me. I promise I'll believe you." Or consider the dynamic between someone saddled with excessive self-doubt and a friend or lover trying to offer reassurances. In her anthem on what she needs in a man, Sheryl Crow sings, "Lie to me/I promise I'll believe."[30] Her point seems to be that, sometimes, we just need to hear that everything is going to be okay or that we are better than how we see ourselves. But such needed words may not be forthcoming if they will only be disbelieved and dismissed. As in the child case, a promise to believe can be an important commitment in exchange for the other person's testimony.

I think that the promisee in these cases is wronged if the promisor does not ultimately lend credence to the testimony. If the adult does not believe the child, or if the doubter ignores the lover's assurances, they commit a wrong. And this is not merely a point about outward behavior or effort; there would still be a wrong if the person outwardly manifested belief while internally giving the testimony little to no credence.

Still, promises to believe are problematic. They cannot straightforwardly generate an action-shaping duty because belief is not straightforwardly responsive to any consideration one might have. Belief is responsive to evidence. A promise to believe against one's known evidence will be dubious. Consider an example from the end of Henry James's *Wings of the Dove*. Densher has long deceived Milly, who has become aware of the deception and now lies dying. Densher is confronted by Milly's companion, who requests that Densher deny that there has been any deception, to put Milly at peace. Densher asks the companion, "Do *you* believe it?" Despite having very good evidence of Densher's deception, she responds, "What I believe will inevitably depend more or less on your action. . . . I promise to believe you down to the ground if, to save her life, you consent to a denial."[31] Here, it is hard to credit the promise as truly a promise to believe. She knows that Densher has lied. Her words are, at best, a promise to act as if she believed him.

So why not say the same about the promises to the child and to the reassuring lover? If our beliefs are only responsive to evidence, then aren't

SHAPING ACTION

all promises to believe merely promises to act as if? I think not. A promise to believe can be a guarantee that, when presented with evidence, one will give it credence. That is, one can promise *that* one will believe; what one cannot do is promise *to* believe. What Milly's companion's promise lacks is any introduction of new evidence that she might or might not credit. There's no future epistemic response for her to guarantee. In contrast, where there will be new evidence, promises to believe can have guaranteeing force. They can make it the case that we will wrong someone if we do not believe her, even though they cannot directly give us reason to believe her.

3.1.3 WICKED PROMISES

In the preceding examples, the promises lacked obliging force because there was no action to be taken. The same effect can, I think, arise when statements intended as full-fledged promises—intended to have both obliging and guaranteeing force—partly misfire, having no obliging force, leaving only their guaranteeing force.[32] The problematic promise fails to generate a duty but nonetheless generates a wrong from breach.

If this is correct, then the question, "Is the promise binding or not?" turns out to be too simple a dichotomy. We can say that the promise has misfired in one respect while it has succeeded in changing the normative landscape in another respect.

Consider the promise to do something immoral or illegal—the wicked promise. Philosophers have repeatedly debated whether such promises are binding.[33] Each side has its appeal. On the one hand, it's hard to see how one could place oneself under a duty to do that which one ought not do. On the other hand, it seems that there can be genuine grievances for broken promises even when wicked—so-called honor among thieves.

The standard philosopher's example is a promise to rob a bank, but here's a more fanciful example. In *Frankenstein*, Victor promises the Creature that he will create for it a companion. But he reconsiders, thinking, "Had I a right, for my own benefit, to inflict this curse upon everlasting generations? . . . Now, for the first time, the wickedness of my promise burst upon me."[34] The language here is striking: Victor breaks his promise when he comes to believe that he has no right to do the thing that he had promised. And perhaps he is correct in that assessment. If he had no right to do the thing to begin with, then plausibly he could be bound by no duty from having promised.[35]

And yet it hardly need follow that the Creature is not wronged by Victor's breach. We understand that he is, and that the revenge he takes on Victor is grounded in that wrong. Thus the philosophical puzzle: the wicked promise seems simultaneously *void ab initio* and also the basis for legitimate resentment.

One might, at this point, try to explain the apparent wrong to the Creature in some other way. Perhaps it is not the breach of promissory duty that wrongs the Creature—since, after all, there could be no such duty—but rather the act of making the wrongful promise in the first place, purporting to have the authority to do so. As we already saw in the warranty context, one might try to interpret the purported promise as a kind of misrepresentation.[36] But this approach is problematic.[37] Because it claims that the wrong consists in making the promise, it would mean that Victor wrongs the Creature even if the Creature releases him from the duty or even if Victor goes ahead and creates a companion for the Creature. Once the wicked promise is made, the wrong is a fait accompli. But that seems incorrect. By promising, Victor makes himself liable to commit a wrong—perhaps destined to commit a wrong one way or another—but that is a matter of his future conduct.

So we are back to the puzzle of saying either that there is a duty to do what one ought not or that there is no wronging. The persistent intractability of this question arises, I suggest, because there are simply two different senses in which the wicked promise might be binding.[38] The wicked promise cannot generate true deontic reasons for an action that ought not be performed. It cannot give a right that was not the promisor's to give. And yet the wicked promise may still operate as a guarantee.[39] One might still be answerable when the world does not go according to one's word. In this way, wicked promises seem to me to create wrongs that are not correlated with action-shaping duties.[40]

3.1.4 SEXUAL PROMISES

As a final example, consider yet another problematic promise: a promise to have sex. Hallie Liberto offers the following schematic example: "Take John and Jane, young adults in college. Enthusiastic about John's upcoming football game, Jane promises John that she will have sex with him after the football game if his team wins, as an incentive for him to train harder and perform his best in the game. . . . John's team wins."[41] Liberto argues that John should not accept the promise from Jane and that, if it has already been accepted, John should release Jane from her obligation. But that assessment assumes (as Liberto affirms) that the promise is obligation generating. I want to focus on that question. If not released, does Jane owe a duty to John to have sex with him? Is Jane's promise action shaping?

Liberto provocatively argues that "positive sexual promises generate promissory obligation."[42] Her argument for this conclusion runs explicitly through the existence of a potential wronging. Here is how she summarizes: "When Jane promises John to have sex with him, she incurs an obligation to have sex with him. This obligation might be outweighed by competing moral considerations, as with any promissory obligation. However, if John chooses to hold Jane to her word, Jane wrongs John by refraining from sexual activity with him."[43] To her credit, Liberto explicitly acknowledges the premise in this argument: "I assume that promissory obligation is a directed duty to a promisee such that the promisor *wrongs* the promisee by breaking the promise."[44] For Liberto, wronging is the hallmark of directed duty. Because she thinks that Jane would wrong John by breaking her promise, she concludes *on that basis* that the promise does generate an obligation, albeit one that should be released. In other words, Liberto assumes that there are two alternatives: either Jane's attempted promise is invalid and makes no change in the normative landscape, or else Jane does successfully promise and that generates promissory obligation. Liberto's belief that Jane would wrong John convinces her of the second alternative.

I'm cautiously willing to accept, at least *arguendo,* that, under some properly described conditions, Jane might wrong John by promising to have sex with him and then not doing so.[45] John might end up foreseeably and innocently disappointed, and he might have an intelligible grievance that she brought about this disappointment. John might feel hurt or even resentful; Jane might apologize or aim to make it up to him in some other way; he might forgive her. These retrospective practices are coherent only insofar as we think that the promise was efficacious in creating a wronging relation.

But I believe that Liberto is incorrect in inferring on the basis of this potential wrong that the promise generates a directed duty. Consider Jane's deliberative standpoint. How should her promise factor into her choices after the football game? Suppose that she finds that she is not sure that she wants to have sex with John. Should her promise enter as a significant consideration, perhaps tipping the balance? My view is that it should not. Jane's decision whether to have sex should be, I think, entirely responsive to whether she wants to have sex. The fact that she would break her promise—that John would have a complaint and that she would owe him an apology—seems to me to be irrelevant to her choice whether to have sex. There might be a potential grievance, but it is not action shaping.

Even if one thinks that the promise should enter into Jane's deliberation somehow,[46] my argument requires only a more modest claim: any deliberative significance is not that of a directed duty. It does not have that deontic force. If I promise to take you to the airport, that promise doesn't merely provide me with any old reason. It's decisive against ordinary personal preference. In fact, that seems to be the essential action-shaping feature of promissory obligations and other-directed duties—they exclude from deliberation certain ordinary or personal considerations, like not feeling like it. But it seems highly implausible that Jane's promise should shape her deliberations *like that*. Proper deliberation for her surely doesn't require ignoring whether she would like to have sex—thinking only that she owes it to him. Insofar as directed duties are supposed to be about a special kind of normativity, then Jane is not under a directed duty to have sex with John.[47]

One might, at this point, try to say that Jane's wrong would be that of misrepresenting her feelings: "You shouldn't have misrepresented how you felt." But this replicates the same problem that we saw in trying to explain the wicked promise as a misrepresentation; it treats the wrong as a fait accompli upon utterance. That just doesn't fit.

Rather, I would suggest that, after she has promised, Jane is in a kind of limbo. She has not *already* committed a wrong of falsely raising expectations. What she does will determine whether she has committed a wrong. If she fails to follow through on her promise, then she will have wronged John by raising and disappointing his expectations. Still, as already argued, that fact does not mean that she owes John a duty to perform, assuming we understand by that something that would shape her deliberations. I believe that description best captures our intuitions about the case. But this option is only available if we abandon the assumption that wrongings are the mirror image of directed duties.

There is a continuity, the reader is probably noticing, across all of the cases that I've considered—the commercial warranty, the promise to feel, the promise to believe, the wicked promise, and the promise to have sex. It is natural to think their capacity to generate duties must stand or fall together. Critiquing marriage vows, Percy Bysshe Shelley remarked, "To promise for ever to love the same woman, is not less absurd than to promise to believe the same creed."[48] If viewed as creating action-shaping duties

SHAPING ACTION

that directly shape our deliberations, then there would be something absurd in many of the promises that we make in life.

But even where promises may not bind our choices directly, we should not say that they are not directly binding. These promises bind in one sense—they generate potential wrongs—but they do not bind in another, transferring rights or generating action-shaping duties. They put the promisor in what I characterize as a kind of limbo. The guarantor has done something that may or may not turn out to be a wrong. There is a potential wronging, and yet that does not shape forward-looking deliberation. This understanding is possible only if one is willing to accept that the existence of a potential wronging is not the same as the existence of a right or a directed duty.

3.2 Wrongs and Tiebreakers

The previous section focused on certain promissory wrongs—showing that they do not connect with action in the way that rights do. In this section, my goal is to offer a second range of cases—not focused on promising—in which there is a potential wronging and yet that potential wronging provides no reasons for action, at least none like rights do. For this, I'll consider cases in which an actor's choice seems pulled equally in two different directions. Can the presence of a potential wrong tip the balance or break a tie, as some additional right might? I think not. Potential wrongs seem not to shape action in these cases, suggesting the bare wrong is not itself a reason for action in the way that a right is.

3.2.1 THIRD-PARTY WRONGS AS TIEBREAKERS

Suppose that as a hobby you engage in recreational pyrotechnics. You enjoy spending your Saturday afternoons setting off various elaborate explosives and fireworks. There is a secluded plot of land where you and other local enthusiasts often practice. This is legally permitted, and there are signs notifying people to beware. There is, however, an obligation to broadcast a loud warning message before detonating any device. One day, you go out to the park and set up an elaborate explosive display. The display is on a timer to allow you time to get safely away from it. For some reason, today it slips your mind to broadcast the warning signal. After you have walked away and are looking back, you see that two familiar local children have approached the device. One is a girl who has no family and no one who cares for her. The other is a boy with extremely loving parents who would be absolutely heartbroken if he is injured or killed. You have enough time to get one child away from the device, but not both.

Both children have a claim to be saved. And whichever child you do not save will certainly have been wronged by your negligence. In Chapter 2, I argued that third parties, like family members, may be wronged by actions done to others. Here, I think that you would wrong the parents if their son died at your hands. It would, for example, be quite coherent for the parents to resent you, demand an apology, forgive you, and so forth.

It might be tempting to explain the wrong to the parents as correlative to a right that the parents have that their child not be killed. Is there such a right? Insofar as rights are about action shaping, we might reframe that question: Does the potential wrong to the parents correlate with an action-shaping duty bearing on your deliberation?

I think not. I believe that the fact that the little boy's parents stand to be wronged does not play any role in what you should do—and it certainly does not play the action-shaping role that we would like rights to play.

Consider, first, whether the potential wrong to the parents should be treated as a reason to save the little boy. There are strong, balanced reasons for saving each child. The fact that failing to save the boy would also wrong some related parties does not seem to provide any further reason. It is no reason at all. It would be erroneous—perhaps downright pernicious— to think that the existence of the parents can decide between the otherwise evenly balanced claims of the two children. It is not something that you should think about. Whatever status the parents have, it does not inform your choice.

Now, admittedly, this is a complex case. The fact that one should not, on account of the parents, choose the boy over the orphan girl does not conclusively show that the potential wrong to the parents provides no reason. It would be a mistake to assume that reasons can always be added. There are many ethical contexts in which an additional reason will not settle or even bear on a decision. Many things that would generally provide a reason—say, the opportunity to save a friend's crystal vase—could not be used to settle the choice between saving the girl and the boy. So perhaps the potential wrong to the parents similarly provides a reason, but one that is outweighed or silenced or otherwise inoperative in this scenario.[49]

SHAPING ACTION

Though this response may sound plausible, I think there are strong grounds for doubting that explanation here. First, the potential wrong to the parents is no comparatively small matter like a vase; killing someone's child may be about as grievous an injury as one can inflict. If it were a reason, one would think that it would be a significant one. Second, it is not clear that there is any sense or context in which the wrong to the parents would matter to deliberation. While a reason need not function as a tiebreaker, it must be capable of functioning in some way or in some context.[50]

Perhaps, one might suggest, we should view the parents as providing a reason contrastively: the potential wrong to the parents does not provide a reason to save the boy over the girl, but it does provide a reason to save the boy rather than do nothing. But does it? It seems to me that the boy and his rights provide all the reason to save.

Alternatively, one might suggest that the parents provide a reason counterfactually. The crystal vase provides a reason in this sense: if it were not for the children, then the vase would be a relevant consideration. One might suggest something similar about the parents: if the boy's rights were not present, then the wrong to the parents would matter. But it's hard to make sense of that claim. Were it not for the boy's rights, there would not be a wrong to the parents at all. It's only because the boy's rights are being violated that the parents are wronged. Parents are not, absent special circumstances, wronged by rights-respecting treatment of their children. The potential wrong depends on the conduct already being wrongful for some other reason. It cannot, then, count as yet another reason in this determination. Put this way, it is not that the third parties are morally irrelevant but that, from the deliberative perspective, the wrongs they might suffer are epiphenomenal.

Even if I am wrong about this and the potential wrong to the parents is a reason in some capacious sense, my argument only requires the weaker claim: the potential wrong to the parents is not a reason *of the special kind that rights generate*. The potential wrong to the parents is not associated with any ex ante claim on your conduct. The parents could not (properly) demand that you save their child over the familyless girl. Of course, they would hope for such a choice, but it would be wholly inappropriate to assert that you owe it to them to make such a choice. Nor should you consider yourself to owe it. It would be to treat as demanding a consideration

84 WRONGS AND RIGHTS COME APART

that is not entitled to that status, elevating the parents from stakeholders to claimholders. To do so misapprehends the significance of the parents. They do not have an ex ante entitlement that guides your choice of conduct. The relationship with the parents exists only downstream. They are not significant in the way that having a right implies.[51]

3.2.2 DIRECT WRONGS AS TIEBREAKERS

The pyrotechnics example has a number of peculiar features. One might think that it turns on something special about third parties. Perhaps third-party wrongs are oddly not action shaping but "regular" wrongs are.

I don't think that the case turns on the third-party aspect; the same dynamic can arise without it. Consider a modified version of the pyrotechnics example. Again, you negligently fail to activate the warning signal. When you look back, you see that a little girl is in the dangerous area. You have just enough time to rush back and save her. But unfortunately, at that very moment, another child is blown by an unforeseeable tornado gust into the area. This second child—a little boy—is now equally at risk, though he is there through no fault of yours.

I contend that it is permissible to save either child. You are not under a duty to save the little girl. Nonetheless, if the little girl is injured, you are accountable in a different way from the way that you would be for the injuries to the little boy. We might say that the little girl stands to be wronged, whereas the little boy stands to be tragically injured.[52]

One might object that, actually, you would wrong whichever child you don't save. It is only because of your negligence that the little girl is in jeopardy. Were she not there, then you could save the little boy without any choice. Thus, if you don't save the little boy, that failure too is because of your negligence. According to this thought, your negligence wrongs the little boy by creating a dilemma where there otherwise wouldn't be one. (If you are tempted by this thought, notice that it already suggests a belief in third-party wrongings. You were negligent with regard to the little girl. If this negligence grounds a wrong to the little boy, it would seem to be as a third party.)

As the case is described thus far, perhaps this response is correct. But the already baroque example can be embellished to remove this possibility. Imagine that, in addition to broadcasting a loud warning signal, the safety protocol sets in motion various mechanical gates that lower to block access to the danger area once everyone has cleared. As before, you forget to activate the safety protocol. When you look back, you see the little girl in the danger zone, but fortunately, you have enough time to run back and save her. But this wouldn't have been possible if you had activated the gates—they would have blocked your path. So, fortuitously, the very negligence that put the little girl at risk is what makes the rescue possible. Now, as before, the tornado gust blows the little boy into the danger zone (and the gates, had they been down, could not have prevented this). In this modified story, it is no longer true that you would have been able to save the little boy if you had not been negligent. Still, I contend that it is permissible to save either child. The fact that the little girl, but not the little boy, stands to be wronged does not mean that you are under a duty to save the little girl.

One might argue that, in fact, one has a duty to save the little girl, which is a compensatory continuation of one's original duty of due care.[53] In this sense, one owes it to the little girl to save her, just as you owe it to someone you injure in a car accident to pay his medical bills. Rescuing might thus be considered a form of remedial action, owed to a rightholder as such.

There are good reasons to resist this thought. If rescue—let alone preferential rescue—were a form of compensation, then it should generally reduce the amount of other compensation owed. But it doesn't. If a doctor imperils a patient through malpractice but is able to recover, save the patient's life, and limit the damage, the doctor does not owe the patient less in compensation than she would if a different doctor had been the one to do the saving. Acting to save the person whom one has imperiled doesn't count as a remedy; it merely mitigates the scope of one's wrong. It is about containing one's moral liability, not about discharging it. I see even less reason to think that *preferential* rescue can be a compensatory duty. The negligent doctor doesn't owe any less in compensation if she left other patients on the operating table in order to save the one she negligently imperiled.

3.2.3 BETWEEN TEMPORAL PERSPECTIVES

Let's take a step back and try to diagnose what is going on in these cases. In all of the pyrotechnics examples, there is a temporal aspect—one is situated in a moment where one can preempt one's own wrongdoing. One might think that the wrong inheres in the negligence itself. The moment that you forget to sound the warning, you have wronged the imperiled child. I think that's not quite right, but there is something in it. It's true that one's wrongful conduct inheres in the negligence. But I think it would be a mistake to think that *the wrong* is already consummated at the moment of negligence—that what happens next doesn't affect the wrong committed.

I suggest that the rights violation inheres in the act of negligence, but the wrong involves within it the subsequent consequences and harms. The little girl's right—what she was entitled to from you—was to have the safety protocol followed. You owed this care to her. And, in this respect, you failed—already. This explains why you do not have a duty to save little girl. What she was owed has passed. She was entitled to the warning.

But though the duty violation is complete, the wrong that you have done her depends on what happens afterward.[54] The wrong from your failure has yet to materialize fully. In this way, the stories are set in a moment of limbo. Duties have been breached, but the resultant wrongs have yet to unfold. It is this limbo that generates the peculiar disconnect between reasons and wrongings in these cases.

In this vein, consider an observation from Frances Kamm: "May I kill one person now to stop a threat I started yesterday that will soon kill five people? I think not."[55] Kamm's point is that the demands of rights cannot be captured by a requirement to minimize one's rights violations. In a way, this is the point I have been making. Rights are about shaping action. One ought not place a threat that will kill five people; one owes it to those people not to do it. But once one has, one has breached that duty—even though the wrong has yet to be realized. One is left in a limbo where the duty has been breached and yet the wronging has yet to occur. And in this limbo, the breached rights do not figure in one's deliberation in the same way; their normative authority has elapsed. What Kamm's example shows, I would say, is that, even if five rights might typically have more force than one, you cannot violate one person's rights in order to avoid wronging five others. The different temporal perspectives make all the difference.

In this chapter thus far, I've offered arguments trying to pump intuitions from somewhat unusual cases. But the surveyed cases are, to my mind, only vivid manifestations of a general truth about wronging and action. If these cases have seemed idiosyncratic, it's because they are. They share this odd temporal setting, which I have described as a kind of limbo. The actor has done something that may, depending on how events turn out, ripen into a wronging. In the commercial warranty, issuing the promise might ripen into a wrong to the consumer. In the pyrotechnics case, your negligence might

SHAPING ACTION   87

ripen into a serious wrong to the parents. In neither case is the wrong already established from the outset, and yet its potential does not shape our action. The die has already been cast.

This idiosyncratic temporal situation serves to illuminate an essential difference: wrongings involve an ex post perspective whereas shaping action is necessarily forward looking. The cases illustrate the tension between perspectives by situating the actor in a moment that is neither fully ex ante nor fully ex post—a kind of limbo. When we are fully in the ex ante perspective, thinking about whether to commit a wrong can look akin to considering a person's rights. When we are fully in the ex post perspective, thinking about what rights a person had can meld into asking whether there was a wrong committed. Their essential difference gets masked by the fact that there's only one perspective before us. We are like someone who has only seen each of a pair of twins separately and does not appreciate that there are two different people. It is only when both are seen together that the difference is apparent. In the limbo between ex ante and ex post, where there is the possibility that a wrong might do action-shaping work apart from rights, the difference between them is revealed.

3.3 Action and the Ex Post Perspective

The same fundamental difference exists always, if less obviously, between truly action-shaping considerations and ex post considerations. Wrongs require a perspective that involves a completed action and is thus unconcerned with action shaping. Thus, even where a potential wrong does coincide with reasons against the action, the potential wrong is not itself action shaping. I think that one can see this by reflecting on the phenomenology of deliberation. There is something off about going through the world attempting to avoid wronging others. That would be misdirected; it would be to have one's eye off target. To think about what wrongs one might commit would be to attend to something epiphenomenal—something from a downstream perspective. Such misdirected attention may be innocuous or even salutary, but it is nonetheless directed at something other than the right-making features of one's action.

The best way that I have found to illustrate this thought is by way of analogy. Aiming to avoid wrongs is, I will argue, a bit like a lawyer determining the right thing to do on the basis of what will avoid liability. Or, similarly, it is a bit like the person who goes through life trying to avoid having regrets. Such modes of deliberation are misdirected. They involve focusing on something other than the right-making features. That's not to say that one ought not deliberate in these ways. Doing so may result in just as good choices, or it might even help a person to make improved choices. The point is not to say how any real person ought psychologically to deliberate. Rather, by thinking about modes of deliberation, I hope to illuminate what count as right-making features of action—justifying reasons. My claim is that wrongs are not directly bound up with them in the way that rights are.

3.3.1 LEGAL LIABILITY

In a major, well-known study, a collection of law and economics scholars examined how jurors arrive at punitive damage awards.[56] What they found was that jurors behaved in a number of highly "puzzling" or "problematic" ways (a result that surely did not disappoint the funder, ExxonMobil). One of the results that the economists found puzzling was that jurors seemed to penalize businesses that engaged in cost-benefit analysis.[57] Jurors awarded higher punitive damages when a business weighed the costs of potential injuries or deaths in deciding to pursue a particular course of action than if the business engaged in no such analysis. Even more striking, the higher the cost that a business assigned to potential injuries or deaths, the higher the punitive damages jurors awarded. To the economists, this was bizarre: the more safety conscious a business's cost-benefit analysis, the more the business got punished.[58]

I may be with the jurors here. If I were on a jury and a corporation had anticipated legal liability of $10 million and gone ahead anyway, then the first thing that I would want to do is hit that corporation with more than $10 million in damages. Why? Presumably part of this reaction stems simply from an aversion to cost-benefit analysis. But I think that there is a further source of antipathy.[59]

There is something deeply misguided about viewing one's reason for complying with the law as equivalent to one's personal reason for avoiding legal liability. The liability-anticipating corporation treats its reasons against wrongful conduct as fully captured by the cost of legal liability. In this way, the corporation operates just like Holmes's iconic "bad man," treating the law as "a prophecy that if [it] does certain things [it] will be subjected to . . . compulsory payment of money."[60] The economists may view this as natural. For them, the point of legal liability is to generate a reason to avoid socially

SHAPING ACTION 89

detrimental conduct without deterring socially advantageous behavior. So deliberating about potential liability should be functionally equivalent to deliberating about one's moral reasons to avoid the conduct.

The noneconomists among us, however, find something deeply misguided here. We know that Holmes's bad man is—for lack of a better word—bad.[61] We appreciate that there is a difference between aiming to fulfill one's legal duties and aiming to avoid legal liability. The point is not merely that legal liability may be inaccurate, as not every transgression will be detected and penalized. Rather, it is about the mode of deliberation. Even a well-intentioned corporation that wanted to avoid any legal transgressions per se would, I think, be making a mistake if it viewed its reasons for care as based on avoiding doing anything legally wrong. The corporation should seek to minimize injuries because it cares (or its members care) about what it owes to the users of its products—not because it doesn't want to be liable.

In 1981, former Securities and Exchange Commission chief accountant John C. Burton stated that he thought the accounting profession "has spent so much time avoiding liability or trying to avoid liability over the last decade that it has begun to lose sight of what its social purpose is in some degree."[62] We can make perfectly good sense of this thought. Ideally, one's deliberative eye should be trained on one's duties and ends. Avoiding liability seems, in a way, epiphenomenal. Of course, potential liability may indeed motivate actors, but it is not a justifying reason. To appreciate someone else's legal rights is not merely to appreciate that one would be subject to legal liability. The right is an action-shaping feature of the deliberative perspective; the potential liability is not.

3.3.2 REGRET

Having just picked on economists and praised ordinary human preferences, let me flip things around. Economist Richard Thaler studied people's responses to the following example: "Mr. A is waiting in line at a movie theater. When he gets to the ticket window he is told that as the 100,000th customer of the theater he has just won $100. Mr. B is waiting in line at a different theater. The man in front of him wins $1,000 for being the 1,000,000th customer of the theater. Mr. B wins $150. Would you rather be Mr. A or Mr. B?"[63] What Thaler finds, surprisingly, is that many people would prefer to be Mr. A. The reason, apparently, is that some people think that the additional $50 is not enough to offset the regret of just missing out on \$1,000. Thaler found this irrational, and I must admit that I agree.

Why does this seem irrational? One might think that, because one has no control over where one stood in line, it's irrational to regret it. But it isn't actually true that one lacked control; one could have gotten in line one spot earlier if one had only avoided dilly-dallying. Lack of control might be meant in a different way, though. One couldn't control whether one stood in the winning spot in line given that one had no idea which spot that would be or even that there would be such a spot, so regretting one's chosen place seems irrational. But that seems wrong too; it's perfectly common to regret an action as a result of unforeseen (and even unforeseeable) consequences. "I really regret not listening to my normal radio station yesterday—I heard that they picked my name out of the phonebook and were prepared to give me a prize if I had been listening and called in." "Man, I wish that I'd gone last night—I never would have guessed that David Beckham would crash a random neighborhood party." So I don't think that the irrationality is thinking that Mr. B would feel regret at missing out on the big prize.

What, then, might be odd in saying that one would rather be Mr. A? I think the answer is that there seems to be something amiss about *making a choice merely to avoid regret*.[64] That is, what is odd is not thinking that Mr. B would feel regret, or even thinking that Mr. A is likely the happier of the two. What is odd is thinking that this fact counts as choiceworthy— that one would elect to be Mr. A and forgo hard cash.[65] Although the self-help industry urges us to "live a life without regrets," there is something misdirected in aiming to avoid regret. Avoiding regrets is a proxy—an indirect way to capture one's present reasons. It is not itself choiceworthy. From the first-person deliberative perspective, it seems odd to treat regret as a reason, rather than as a proxy for one's other reasons.[66]

Consider an example. There is considerable evidence that, among Olympic medal winners, bronze-medal recipients tend to be happier than silver-medal recipients.[67] This result is attributed to the fact that silver medalists have to contend with having just missed out on the gold. But now imagine that you know this fact and you find yourself at the end of the Olympic marathon battling another runner for second place, the leader having a commanding lead. Does the fact that the silver medal will come with more regret count as a reason to settle for the bronze? Surely not. The future regret does not count in *that* way. Had your coach told you, "Don't

SHAPING ACTION 91

let yourself have any regrets about this race," she would have meant that you give every bit of effort possible—the very opposite of settling.

The point here is about the proper focus of ideal deliberation, about what actually counts as a justifying reason. It's not about results. Two people, one of whom aims to live a fulfilling life and the other of whom aims to live a life without regrets, may end up living similarly. My point is that the latter person's deliberation is nonetheless aimed at something that is not truly a justifying reason. He has surrendered the immediate deliberative question of what he ought to do for the epiphenomenal question of how his actions will appear when evaluated in retrospect.[68] His deliberation proceeds by way of an imagined rearview mirror. And this redirected view, though perhaps a helpful proxy, can actually be in subtle tension with the true stance of agency.[69] These aren't the fundamental normative facts—the justifying reasons.

3.3.3 POTENTIAL WRONGS

My claim is that the potential complaint of, or wrong to, another person is similar to legal liability or regret. Even if seeking not to wrong others results in the same behavior as seeking to fulfill one's duties, it is not tracking one's justifying reasons directly. It attends to a derivative consequence rather than the fundamental normative facts.

You should act as you owe it to others to act. If you have wronged someone, then you have generally done something along the way that you ought not to have done. But the thing that matters is what one ought to do, not the potential wronging. It is the duty that bears the normative significance. In this sense, the fact that X's φ-ing would wrong Y does not constitute a reason for X not to φ.

Perhaps this should come as no surprise. Subjunctive conditionals do not typically capture fundamental facts.[70] The fact that a cup *would* shatter *if* it were dropped does not explain its fragility; instead, something about its molecular structure does. Similarly, I have suggested, the fact that an action *would* be regretted *if* performed does not explain why it should not be performed. And, similarly still, I suggest, the fact that an action *would* wrong someone *if* performed does not explain why one shouldn't perform that action. In each case, the conditional analysis doesn't track the fundamental explanation.[71]

One might have thought that the relation between wrongs and duties was different—that wrongs were more intimately bound up with directed duties. To see a potential wrong, one might have thought, just is to see a reason for action. Jay Wallace, for example, writes, "Interpersonal recognition is achieved when we act in a way that deprives others of a warrant to resent our treatment of them."[72] This is not so much false as confusing matters. It is like saying that a meaningful life is achieved when we act in a way that deprives our future self of a warrant for regret. Interpersonal recognition is not fundamentally about avoiding the warranted resentment of others. It is about taking into account what one owes to others. Metaphysically speaking, directed duties are different from wrongs. The difference can be appreciated by seeing that one is action shaping and bound up with justifying reasons—and the other is not. For the purpose of right action, one is directly significant and the other is epiphenomenal.

Why, then, have so many philosophers thought that the potential wrong that we might commit against another constitutes an important reason not to pursue an action, even the essential moral consideration? The answer is that focusing on the wrong that one might commit is a way of drawing our attention to the other person, something all too often missing. In a famous passage in *Middlemarch,* George Eliot describes young Fred Vincy, who has recklessly borrowed money that he is unable to repay: "Curiously enough, his pain in the affair beforehand had consisted almost entirely in the sense that he must seem dishonorable and sink in the opinion of the Garths: he had not occupied himself with the inconvenience and possible injury that his breach might occasion them, for this exercise of the imagination on other people's needs is not common with hopeful young gentlemen. Indeed we are most of us brought up in the notion that the highest motive for not doing a wrong is something irrespective of the beings who would suffer the wrong."[73] What focusing on potential wrongs does, to its credit, is ensure that the reasons for obeying morality are not "something irrespective of the beings who would suffer."[74] By focusing on wronging, one draws attention to the fact that moral obligations are often not just free-floating, but rather they are owed to other persons. Emphasizing the wrong that one would do to another is a way of shaking someone from a merely monadic conception of duty. It is a way of exhorting someone to recognize the relational character of moral duties. It can be powerfully motivating.

But sometimes a statement that is evocative along one axis will sacrifice accuracy along another. Something can be a powerful motivating reason, even as it is not properly a justifying reason. Notice that legal liability and regret can also serve exhortative functions. Someone might say, "Don't get us into any legal trouble," without meaning that breaking the law is acceptable so long as it isn't detected. The potential legal consequences are referenced just to evoke the significance of legal obligations. Similarly, the slogan "Live a life without regrets" resonates because it evokes the significance of every choice to a meaningful life as a whole.

It is a feature of poetic description that sometimes the best way to make a person feel the force of something is not to describe the thing itself but to describe some other connected thing. My suggestion is that thinking of one's potential wronging has this sort of poetic truth to it. It draws our attention to both the stakes and the source of our moral obligation; it reminds us both that our moral compliance matters to the life of someone else and further that this someone is the source of our moral obligation— that morality is relational. When I consider the wrong that I might commit, I am forced to consider the person whom I would wrong.

But we should not infer justifying reasons from what is psychologically motivating. It's tempting to think that the potential wrong to a parent is a reason not to harm their child because one might say, "Think of her innocent family." But there are innumerably other evocative things that one might say: "Think of the innocent gap between her teeth when she smiles," "Think of all the birthdays that she will never get to enjoy," and so forth.[75] Though perhaps motivating, these are not truly justifying reasons. They are ways of getting someone to see the reasons that he or she already had— or, put another way, to see the other person as a person, as a source of reasons, as a rightholder.

This poetic truth shouldn't be mistaken for metaphysical truth. Although thinking about the wrong that we may do can serve to draw our attention to the duty that we owe another, it is the duty and not the potential wrong that is normatively significant.[76]

This point helps to clarify what it is to have a right. It is to be a source of reasons—or, more strongly, the source of a duty—for someone to act in a particular way. To be a rightholder is to deserve a place in someone else's action. That place in another's action is neither because of nor mutually constituting with accountability relations. Those descriptions fail to grasp the conceptual independence. One's rights are a source of the reasons; accountability only comes later, depending in part on whether someone conformed to the reasons that she had. To understand the action-shaping character of rights, we must appreciate the way that they are not mirror images of wrongings.

4

Repair

Whereas rights call for action, wrongs call for reaction. When one person has wronged another, the two stand in a relation that makes certain practices and emotions potentially appropriate in response. These may include resentment, revenge, apology, atonement, compensation, reparation, forgiveness, and so on. In the law, we talk of "remedies"—the legal relief afforded to the victim of a wrong. In morality, we are more likely to talk of "repair"—the process of restoring an interpersonal relationship marred by a wrong. The ideas are different variations on the same theme. In both law and morality, we understand that a wronging involves an imbalance and that, although we cannot truly turn back the clock and erase the wrong, we can take steps to undo the imbalance and to rebuild the relations between the parties.

If one understands a wrong to be a matter of the violation of a right of the victim, that understanding will shape the contours of appropriate response to the wrong. Thus, in his great treatise, William Blackstone wrote that, "as all wrong may be considered as merely a privation of right, the one natural remedy for every species of wrong is being put in possession of that right."[1] It is a simple and appealing syllogism.

In this chapter, I intend to reverse Blackstone's reasoning, to deploy it as *modus tollens* rather than *modus ponens*. Insofar as every wrong does not have the one natural remedy of being put in possession of the violated right—and I shall argue they do not—wrongs cannot be considered merely the privation of a right. Our remedial practices reveal that wrongs have a character of their own, quite apart from the rights whose violation may have given rise to them. Wrongs—as seen through what they demand in

REPAIR 95

remedy or repair—cannot be understood merely in terms of a right that has been violated.

4.1 Three Features of Making Amends

Our practices of moral repair are rich, wide ranging, and remarkably context sensitive. Even our array of terms and concepts is striking. We talk of "making amends," "making good," "atonement," "repair" and "reparations," "remedying," "restitution," "rectification," "redress," "recompense" and "compensation," and so on. While each of these terms carries its own nuances, they share an idea that, in the aftermath of a transgression, a person can take actions that will respond to wrongdoing in a way that at least partly makes things better, bringing back together—however imperfectly—what has been torn asunder by the wrong. (Many even share that idea etymologically: mending, re-putting, and at-one-ment.) In this sense, these are actions that partake of what Aristotle called "corrective" justice.

I do not aspire in this chapter to offer anything like a full theory of moral repair.[2] On the contrary, I wish to be as ecumenical as possible. My argument requires only some minimal assumptions about the structure of reparative actions (or at least an important subset thereof). What is important is that the reparative actions with which I am concerned are relational, have what I will call a size and shape, and are responsive to wrongs.

4.1.1 RELATIONALITY

First, the forms of repair with which I am concerned are fundamentally relational. They link the wrongdoer and the victim. One makes amends *to* another, offers restitution *to* another, apologizes *to* another, pays compensation *to* another, and such. To be sure, there are acts that a wrongdoer might undertake that are private, perhaps even internal, or that are not offered to the victim. We thus sometimes talk of "atoning" or "making amends" in forms that apparently have nothing to do with the victim, instead involving unrelated offsetting good works. Even in these contexts, there may be a relational structure with the transgression being regarded as against God, or the community, or the world at large; the wrongdoer is then correspondingly making amends to God, or to the community, or to the world at large. But regardless, whether one thinks that

96 WRONGS AND RIGHTS COME APART

all amends-making is relational or not, my focus is on those reparative actions that are.

Aristotle famously characterized the operation of corrective justice in mathematical terms. Whereas distributive justice concerns a kind of equality in ratios—that each person's holdings be in equal ratio to their desert—corrective justice concerns arithmetical equality.[3] The injustice is conceptualized as a loss to the victim and a reciprocal gain to the wrongdoer. As illustration, Aristotle imagines a line with the point of division shifted from its midpoint, the reduction in one portion of the line identical to the increase in the other. Equality then requires correction of loss and gain by way of a transfer *from* the wrongdoer *to* the victim. Merely alleviating the victim's loss, or merely disgorging the wrongdoer's gain, would not on its own restore the equality between the two. In the imaginary line, equality cannot be restored only by adding to one side of the line what was lost or by subtracting that amount from the other; what is required is adding back what was taken *from* one side *to* the other side. The mathematical imagery thus emphasizes the relational character of corrective justice—what the wrongdoer owes and what the victim deserves are not separate but tied together in a formal way.

4.1.2 SIZE AND SHAPE

Aristotle's mathematical imagery also draws attention to the way that reparative actions come in different magnitudes. This is especially obvious when money is involved. Compensation or reparation payments might be larger or smaller. Similarly, providing an alternative, substitute, or otherwise offsetting good might require more or less. So too is there a magnitude in apology and expressive acts of repair. Apologies come in different sizes, and we readily distinguish between a big apology and a small one. These differences may even be marked out in various cultural norms, including how lengthy or repeated the apology should be, whether it should be accompanied by symbolic gifts, and whether it should be accompanied by physical gestures like bowing or prostration.

In saying that repair has a magnitude, I do not mean to assume that it can be assimilated onto a single metric; indeed, it seems to me that it cannot. Reparative actions vary in form as well as magnitude. In this sense, vectors might be a better mathematical image. Repair can point in different directions, and it can have greater or lesser magnitude in whatever direction it points. But what is essential for my purposes is merely that reparative responses are not all the same: some are bigger, some are smaller, some are structured one way, some another. Put simply, reparative actions have different shapes and sizes.[4]

A slight aside: One might object to my inclusion of apology in the catalog of reparative acts. Aristotelian corrective justice, it might be said, is about justice in holdings; it is about material justice and the rightful condition. Apology, in contrast, is not material and not a matter of rights; it is a matter of the agent's virtue. Thus, the objection would go, apologies have no role in corrective justice.

This thought should be resisted.[5] It is true that there might be some corrective justice (as performed by a court of law) without any apology from the wrongdoer.[6] And it is true that bare apology may often look too paltry to be called corrective justice. But apology and material remediation are complementary responses to the moral imbalance created by a wrong. Their tight connection can be appreciated by seeing that, in many contexts, each may fail without the other. An apology unaccompanied by readily available material repair may be problematic, false, or even disingenuous. We look askance at the CEO who apologizes for corporate conduct but refuses to dip into the company's profits to pay compensation; so too the state that apologizes for historical injustices or dispossessions without any accompanying effort at material repair.[7] Conversely, the mere rebalancing of material holdings does not effectuate corrective justice, but it can when accompanied by apology. The thief who unapologetically returns the stolen goods as a "gift" has not made amends or realized corrective justice; but the apologetic thief who makes the same material transfer does. Apology thus seems to form an important part of the package of remedial action. And regardless, the important thing is that apologies share the features of reparative actions on which my argument turns: they are relational, they come in different shapes and sizes, and they are responsive to wrongs.

4.1.3 RESPONSIVENESS

Finally, I take as a premise that reparative action is responsive. One doesn't just make amends, apologize, or offer compensation out of the blue. One makes amends *for something,* one apologizes *for something.* The reparative action is responsive not merely in that it comes after and is prompted by a wrong, but in the deeper sense that appropriate reparative action depends on the nature of the wrong.[8] That is, *how* one makes amends depends on *for what* one is making amends. Or put yet another way, the nature of the wrong affects the shape of the remedy.

It is important to be precise here, and it may be useful to distinguish two different versions of responsiveness. The language of "repair," "remedy," and "correction" lends itself to a strong conception. When one repairs a broken machine, one makes it work again—ideally, "as good as new." To provide a remedy for sickness is to restore the patient to health. To correct a mistake is to eliminate it, leaving behind what is right. These images suggest a strong kind of responsiveness: reparative actions aim toward the elimination of what is wrong and the restoration of what was before or what ought to be.

On this strong view, reparative responses have a particular ideal shape, dictated by that to which they respond. If my car's engine leaks oil, I might respond by periodically adding more, but that would not count as *repairing* the engine. Repair would mean finding and eliminating the leak. Similarly, if I have a torn ligament in my knee, I might take pain killers to allow me to go about my day, but that would not count as a remedy; surgery, on the other hand, would. Reparative action, on this understanding, is not merely responsive but actually corrective. It corresponds directly with the nature of the problem that it aims to address.

Recall Blackstone's syllogism: "As all wrong may be considered as merely a privation of right, the one natural remedy for every species of wrong is being put in possession of that right." It is not hard to supply the unstated minor premise: a natural remedy restores what has been deprived. This is the strong idea of responsiveness. And it is Aristotle's idea of corrective justice: justice requires restoring the equality by transferring back all and only what was wrongfully taken from the victim by the wrongdoer. It requires making the victim whole. Reparative action doesn't merely respond to the wrong—its shape is *determined* by the wrong because it responds by undoing.

This strong conception of responsiveness has appealed to theorists at least since Aristotle. I believe in some version of it myself. But just as it has always had natural appeal, there have always been problems. It may seem to take the imagery of repair and remedy too literally.[9] Some wrongs simply cannot be undone. There may be permanent physical injuries or emotional scarring or even death. Moreover, even where the harm itself is not completely irreversible, efforts at repair may be better understood as redress

REPAIR 99

rather than as single-mindedly focused on what came before. Just as torn jeans might be repaired by a patch that hardly aspires to return them to the way they used to be, so too our practices of moral repair might seem like they are better regarded as seeking workable responses in the aftermath of wrongs, not their undoing.

Still, even skeptics of the strong conception of responsiveness will maintain that reparative actions are shaped by the wrong in some way. This might be put in terms of being "proportional" or "fair and reasonable" or some such. Everyone accepts that sending a Hallmark card is not a proper response for murdering someone's grandma and buying a Rolex is not a proper response to being a few minutes late for a lunch date.

We might, therefore, describe a weaker conception of responsiveness. On this weaker conception, more severe wrongs will, generally speaking, require more significant reparative responses. Similarly, different classes of wrongs (e.g., economic vs. emotional) may require different forms of reparative response. The wrong may not fully determine the size and shape that the reparative response should take, but there will be something like covariance between them.

For the purposes of the argument in this chapter, I will assume only a very weak conception of responsiveness. The argument relies on the following premise:

> If φ is a more appropriate reparative response to x than ρ would be (including if φ is appropriate and ρ is not), and if ρ is a more appropriate reparative response to y than φ would be, then x and y are different.

This formulation is meant to be ecumenical. It is significantly weaker than the minor premise in Blackstone's syllogism. It assumes neither that there is a single appropriate response to any given wrong nor that all appropriate responses seek to undo the wrong. It assumes only that there is some range of appropriate responses to any particular wrong, and that there is variation in those ranges across different wrongs. This premise will be true on any plausible conception of responsiveness. And it is all the argument this chapter requires.[10]

One final note here: In describing appropriate reparative responses, I am appealing to an idea of "fittingness."[11] In this sense, some action might be an appropriate reparative response and yet not what an agent ought to do,

WRONGS AND RIGHTS COME APART

all things considered. If apologizing to you for stepping on your foot will let the serial killer know where we are hiding, then I shouldn't do it, although it would be an appropriate response in the sense at issue here.

4.2 Moral Repair and Ex Post Considerations

Insofar as moral repair comes in different shapes and those shapes are at least weakly responsive to the nature of the wrong committed, we can potentially learn about the nature of wrongs by examining our practices of moral repair. Our remedies can be a window onto the wrongs themselves. In adopting this approach, we are not unlike the physician who might use knowledge about what tincture cures a set of symptoms to help pin down the nature of the malady, or the mechanic who might use knowledge that a tap of the hammer in such and such spot will get the machine running again to figure out the nature of the underlying mechanical problem. In each case, by looking at a reparative response, we can learn about what it is that is being addressed.

The remainder of this chapter is devoted to using this strategy to think about wrongs—in particular, the connection between wrongs and rights. Is the nature of a wrong—as viewed through what it would take to respond to it appropriately—determined by the right that was violated?

I believe that the answer is no. I will argue that an appropriate reparative response depends not only on the nature of the right that was violated but also on entirely ex post considerations. Two different instances of the same rights violation might require radically different remedial responses. This is true, I will suggest, in at least three respects.

4.2.1 SOME EXAMPLES

Start with some schematic descriptions of a few relatively straightforward interpersonal wrongs:

> *Broken Marriage:* Anna is married to Alexei. She falls in love with someone else, and she abandons her marriage to Alexei.

> *Genetic Material:* George is Henrietta's doctor. In the course of cancer treatment, George biopsies one of Henrietta's tumors. Without Henrietta's consent, George keeps and regenerates the biopsied cells and uses them for scientific research.

Workplace Equality: Natalie and Gordon are professional friends and partners in the same firm. They take on various projects together, working alongside each other. But as time passes, it becomes clear that Natalie is doing more of the work, and Gordon is receiving more of the credit.

Classroom Insensitivity: Christopher teaches a small undergraduate writing class in which Chantel is enrolled. A few weeks into the semester, he confuses Chantel for the only other Black student in the class.

These examples are each inspired by much more complex stories,[12] but I have deliberately described the cases in only skeletal terms. It is important to the argument that, in each case, there are a variety of ways that the story might be filled in. Indeed, I intend for each case to call out for further specification.

In each of these examples, one party wrongs the other, at least absent further details that might alter that *ceteris paribus* assessment. Moreover, in each case, one can plausibly describe the duty owed to the other person that has been breached. Anna vowed her love and fidelity to Alexei, and she has broken those vows. George owed a duty not to perform medical procedures on Henrietta without her consent. Gordon owed it to Natalie to contribute as a partner and not to take credit for her work. Christopher owed it to Chantel to get her name right.

In pointing to these transgressions, there need be no implication that the conduct is egregious or that the people involved are monsters. Even good people can fall out of love, fail to disclose something that might not have seemed material at the time, not carry their weight in a joint project, or misspeak in public. But *ceteris paribus,* they are wrongs. Each victim might complain against or reasonably resent the treatment. And they thus present the problem of moral repair: What could or should each wrongdoer do in terms of making amends? What would the shape of appropriate reparative action be?

My contention is that we cannot answer these questions by knowing only the nature of the right that has been violated. We need to know more—and not just more about the context leading up to the incident, which might give the duty particular features. We need to know details about what happened following the violation. Filling in those details one

WRONGS AND RIGHTS COME APART

way might make appropriate one kind of repair that would be inappropriate if the details were filled in another way. The contours of moral repair are only fully visible from the ex post standpoint. This is true, I will argue, in at least three ways.

4.2.2 RESULTANT HARM

First, the appropriate reparative actions depend on the extent of the harm caused by the action. What is owed by way of apology and compensatory action will depend significantly on how much harm is caused.

In *Broken Marriage*, how Anna ought to orient herself toward Alexei depends significantly on the extent to which she has hurt him. If Alexei is left truly scarred and heartbroken by her departure, it will be quite different from if he is hurt less severely or even finds himself relieved. If Alexei finds a new partner whom he comes to regard as the true love of his life, Anna's orientation toward him can be quite different from if he never recovers. This is not to deny that, regardless of any of these details, Anna has wronged him and owes it to him to adopt a stance of apology and contrition. But the shape and extent could be radically different. If we imagine a conversation between the two decades later, we can imagine a story that would make Anna renewing her apology for what she did to him appropriate and perhaps even obligatory. But we can also imagine a story in which Anna's apology decades on would seem unnecessary, self-aggrandizing, and perhaps even insulting to Alexei.

In *Genetic Material*, we can perhaps even more clearly imagine a full range of possibilities. Perhaps George's research on the cells comes to nothing, they are destroyed, and Henrietta suffers nothing apart from the fact of the violation. On the other hand, perhaps the research becomes significant and public, Henrietta's genetic code is published, embarrassing family secrets are revealed, and her life is turned upside down. (In the real-life case of Henrietta Lacks, the key feature of the story that distinguishes the case from innumerable others in that era is the outcome of the research.) George owes an apology either way, and perhaps even compensation. But the scale of the apology and the compensation would vary immensely. What might seem like massive overkill in the first case—say, erecting a statue to commemorate what happened to her—could seem meager and insensitive in the second.

With respect to *Workplace Equality*, it may be important to know both the extent—material and emotional—to which Natalie is made worse off

REPAIR   103

by having to do more than her share of work and the extent to which she loses out on certain goods. Once again, it is easy to imagine quite divergent possibilities. In one, Natalie's personal life unravels under the burdens of work that she shouldn't have had to do, and Gordon basks in professional acclaim and opportunities in which she hardly gets to share. In a different story, Natalie handles the extra work with little difficulty, and when the projects fail, Gordon's outsize apparent responsibility actually ends up shielding Natalie. In either case, Gordon has treated her unfairly and owes her something by way of recognition and apology. But in the first story, his moral debt is much greater, and his actions should reflect that.

Finally, consider *Classroom Insensitivity*. It is a notable—sometimes even cruel—feature of insensitive conduct that its impact can be wildly divergent and context dependent. Chantel might barely notice or genuinely laugh it off, and a passing apology might be all that's necessary or appropriate. Indeed, going further in attempted repair might prove to be a worse offense than the original. (In the real incident from which I have borrowed names, the professor was fired after issuing an overdramatic nine-page apology to the entire class.) On the other hand, one can imagine a scenario in which the harm inflicted is significant. Perhaps Chantel—already strained to the breaking point by feelings of alienation—is brought to tears in front of laughing classmates, or she is nudged over the line to withdraw from school. If these are the consequences, a more grave, heartfelt apology accompanied by further offers of support and assistance would seem not only appropriate but correct.

In each case, a set of reparative actions and orientations that would seem appropriate if the story were to unfold one way would seem inappropriate if the story were to unfold a different way—and vice versa for a different set. The shape that repair must take seems only to come into focus ex post. This is not a novel observation. Philosophers have long puzzled over "moral luck," in particular what Thomas Nagel referred to as "outcome luck."[13] In the law, what is sometimes called the "eggshell skull rule" holds the defendant responsible for whatever damage results to the particular victim. Moral repair takes on divergent shapes depending on outcomes.

If this is correct and if moral repair is responsive to the wrong (in the sense specified earlier), then this should mean that, in each of these cases, there may be different wrongs that result from the very same violation. We don't really know the wrong that Anna or George or Gordon or Christopher commits until we know what resulted from their actions. The wrong isn't simply given—like a mirror image—by the right violated. Wrongs are their own distinctive thing; and it is they that we seek to repair.

Admittedly, this is a simple argument, and rights-based thinkers are not oblivious to the fact that resultant harm matters. They can insist that the violation of the same right constitutes the same wrong, but that the same wrong can come in different magnitudes—the way that the same shirt might come in different sizes. Or they can say that their important claim is that the right violated dictates the *nature* of the wrong, conceding that the wrong itself will have a magnitude in a way the right does not. While such moves are available, they put strain on the theory, and this strain is rarely acknowledged or confronted.[14] Our everyday practices of moral repair seem to presuppose that wrongs are quite different things from rights violations.

4.2.3 THE FORM OF REPAIR

The previous section argued that, from the same rights violation, different reparative actions might be appropriate depending on what harm results. If repair is responsive to the wrong, then this difference implies that different wrongs can stem from the same rights violation. Viewed in this way, wrongs are not purely constituted by rights violations.

Still, as just acknowledged, this argument is compatible with the reply that the right in question determines the appropriate *form* of the moral repair, if not its magnitude. This somewhat obscure suggestion gets some traction when one appreciates that injury is itself a comparative idea—it requires measuring the injured state against some uninjured state. Rights and duties, it might be thought, provide the comparison point. To know how George has hurt Henrietta, for example, we want to compare her situation with what her situation would have been if he had respected her rights. Moral repair, it might be thought, responds to precisely that difference.

The idea can be illustrated with the Aristotelian imagery of a segmented line. Rights, it might be said, describe the axis and the equilibrium point. When there is a rights violation, the departure from the equilibrium point will be of greater or lesser magnitude. That departure is a contingent matter, but rights will tell us all we need to get back: move in such and such direction until you are again at the point of equality. Rights, it may thus be said, do determine the structure of moral repair, even if not its particular magnitude.

I want to suggest that even that is not true—even the form that the reparative action takes depends on factors other than the right that has been violated, factors that require the ex post vantage point.

Consider the story of George and Henrietta: How should George understand the wrong that he has done to Henrietta and the reparative actions that might properly address it? My contention is that we cannot answer that question until we know what has ensued. Imagine, as before, that George's research leads to publicity about Henrietta's genetic material. Not only do details of her own sickness become public, but so too do her children's genetic predispositions and previously concealed paternity within her family tree. What George initially regarded as innocuous scientific work on cells that Henrietta would never know she missed instead comes to reshape Henrietta's life. In such a world, it would be appropriate for George to take actions that would try to address and mitigate these injuries. He might, for example, destroy the cells and his research. He might voluntarily offer her a nondisclosure agreement. If he were to offer financial settlement at all, it should be expressed as compensation for the harms that she has suffered. He probably should not offer to pay retrospectively the standard remuneration given to voluntary donors. His apologetic stance should be that of saying, "I wish that I had never done this to you." This might look straightforward: the reparative actions are shaped by comparison with a counterfactual world in which the right was respected.

But now imagine a different story. George's research takes off and advances medical science; George earns professional acclaim, and he develops a patent that proves wildly profitable. Henrietta, meanwhile, is not made worse in any appreciable way; she remains anonymous but empty-handed. In this world, quite different reparative actions would seem appropriate. Destroying the research would appear misguided and perhaps wrongful. Attempting to conceal Henrietta's role might look positively perverse. And offering financial remuneration—perhaps a share of the patent—would seem reasonable. His apologetic stance should be that of saying, "I wish that I had gotten your consent," or perhaps, "I wish that I had not profited at your expense."

In these two different stories, the repair is shaped by comparing the world against some counterfactual world. But it is not the same world. In the first story, the salient counterfactual is that in which Henrietta's cells were never taken; in the second, the salient counterfactual is that in which George didn't unilaterally profit from her cells. Insofar as the reparative actions and orientations are a reflection of the wrong, then the wrongs in these two stories seem to be different.

Notice, however, that these two orientations are mutually incompatible. One cannot wish that George never used the cells and simultaneously wish that he paid a fair price to use them. One or the other of these things could be true, but not both. That incompatibility forecloses what might be a tempting reply on the part of the rights theorist—that the two wrongs are explained by two different rights, the right to bodily integrity and a right not to have someone profit off one's body. Ordinarily, when two different obligations are violated, then there is nothing amiss about attempting to make repair for both. If I'm late for our lunch and spill your coffee as I arrive, then I owe you two apologies, as well as a new coffee and an extra consideration for your time in the future. But in George's case, one reparative orientation or the other is appropriate—but not both. Indeed, attempting to adopt both orientations simultaneously would be impossible. George has committed a single wrong. But depending on how events unfold, not just the magnitude but the very orientation of his reparative act will be different.

A similar point can be made about the other cases. Consider Anna and Alexei: How should Anna understand the wrong that she has done to Alexei? Suppose that Alexei remains heartbroken and alone, never giving up the wish that Anna would have stayed. Anna might then appropriately see herself as having deprived Alexei of the happiness, meaning, security, and other goods that he could have had in a continued married life together with her. Her apologetic stance should be that of, "I'm sorry that I destroyed the future that we might have had." As a matter of repair, it would make sense for her to try to offer him what little substitute she could—continued friendship, perhaps even some companionship in the travails of old age, and a continued appreciation for the good memories they share. It would be insensitive for her to throw out their photo albums and mementos, constantly emphasize the dysfunctional features of the marriage, and shy away from the worthwhile.

On the other hand, imagine that Alexei promptly finds a new wife, his old high school sweetheart. He is happy in this new marriage, his only two sources of sadness being that it is now too late in life to have children with his new partner and that he considers his divorce to have been a sin. He does not regret that Anna left but rather that he was ever taken in by her charms in the first place. He sees her as having wasted the best years of his life in a charade. In this unfolding, it would seem quite misguided for Anna to try to play a continuing role in Alexei's life. Her best reparative actions might be to make herself scarce. She should throw away the photo album, or at least keep it to herself. Her apologetic stance should be not that she didn't give him what she promised but that she ever made him those promises. This is a distinct and incompatible reparative orientation from the first. It focuses on a different counterfactual. It views Anna's wrong differently, not just as a matter of magnitude but in its very form.[15]

The dueling counterfactuals are even easier to appreciate in the case of Natalie and Gordon. The wrong arises because Natalie is doing a larger share of the work and not receiving commensurate credit. This might be rectified by Gordon doing more of the work and compensating Natalie for the ways that she has covered his part in the past. Or it might be rectified by ensuring that Natalie receives the credit and remuneration that reflect her share of the work. These are orthogonal reparative orientations. I don't think that we can say ex ante which would be appropriate. If, by the time Gordon gets around to making repair, the project is going well and looks to be a smashing success, it might be inappropriate for him to swoop in and only then try to do his share. He may, at that point, owe it to Natalie to give her the primary credit. On the other hand, if the project turns out to be a failure, Gordon can hardly make repair by clarifying to the world that it was really mostly Natalie's work, not his own. Without knowing how matters stand ex post, we cannot say what the proper reparative orientation should be for Gordon, let alone its magnitude.

Finally, consider Christopher and Chantel. Undoubtedly, Christopher owes Chantel an apology, but what kind? This is not merely a question about magnitude or intensity, but also about form. Should Christopher's apology be public? Should it explicitly reference the racial dimensions or not? These are not easy questions, and they are context sensitive. My claim is that their answers may be affected by how things unfold after the transgression. Imagine that Chantel and the other Black student immediately roll their eyes, and one of them mutters "typical" under her breath. A few white students start snickering. Another white student, oblivious to the error, speaks up to comment on what Chantel had said and repeats the name error. It may, at this point, be appropriate for Christopher to pause a moment and offer a robust apology that is not merely a quick aside only to Chantel. Contrast that with a case in which Chantel immediately blushes and shrinks in her seat, visibly mortified by the name slip. Here it may be much more appropriate for Christopher to offer his apology as a quick aside, move on rapidly, and then perhaps follow up later with a private, second apology. These are different sets of reparative actions, each more appropriate based not on the nature of the duty but on what has unfolded.

One might argue that the difference here is not about fittingness—that the same apology would be fitting either way—and that the difference instead only reflects the influence of practical considerations. I don't think that's correct. The difference arises because there are two quite different possible injuries that might flow from the same error. On the one hand, the injury might consist in making Chantel feel alienated, drawing attention to ways that she is different and unrecognized within the social group. Insofar as that is the nature of the injury, explicit and public apology may only compound the injury—drawing yet further attention to her and her difference. On the other hand, the primary injury might consist not in creating an awareness of differential treatment (that may be no surprise to Chantel at all) but rather in its manifestation in such a casual and unacknowledged form. To find oneself disrespected in everyday places and to believe that the pattern goes unnoticed by others can be awful; it is as though one is subjected to collective gaslighting. If that's the nature of the injury, then the passing private apology might only compound it. In other words, the different apologies are fitted to address very different injuries, even as either could be the result of the same error on Christopher's part.

4.2.4 THE EXPERIENCE OF THE VICTIM

I've tried to illustrate that, for the very same violation, the appropriate reparative orientation of the wrongdoer may vary significantly—in magnitude but also in form. Even knowing the rights and duties in question, we don't know ex ante what the shape of reparative action should be ex post. Some of this ex ante indeterminacy comes from uncertainty about how concrete events will unfold—Will George's research be a success? Will Gordon and Natalie's projects? Will Alexei's high school sweetheart come along? Will the white students snicker? But as the foregoing discussion has already intimated, much of the indeterminacy arises from the different possible ways that the victim may experience or interpret the injury themselves.

In recent years, there has been a call to take seriously and center the lived experiences of victims. I think that one way to understand the importance of this call is by appreciating the way in which the same transgression will often come with different possible reparative orientations. Selecting the proper orientation will then be a matter of attending to the experience of the victim. To know what duty you have violated—what you ought to have done differently—does not fully tell you what you have actually *done* to someone. To know that, you will need to attend to them, listen to them.

This makes clear a third respect in which the appropriate reparative actions cannot be determined ex ante. Not only is there more than one shape, but one cannot specify even a complex conditional mapping from the right violated to the appropriate repair. It might be tempting to say, for example, that Natalie ought to get such and such if the project is a success and such and so if it is not. But even that's not true. We need to see how Natalie experiences her injury. Gordon's appropriate reparative orientation does not depend only on extrinsic material facts about the result of the enterprise, but also on how Natalie reacts.

Moreover, the victim's experience may shift, and the appropriate reparative response may shift with it. In the real-life case of Henrietta Lacks, the family's initial demands were for privacy protections; but later they sought recognition and financial settlement. They went from seeking anonymity to dedicating a public statue. We can easily imagine Alexei going back and forth between wishing that Anna had stayed and wishing she'd never entered his life. As these shifts occur, the appropriate reparative orientation shifts with them. It is a familiar feature of suffering a violation that one's understanding of it changes over time; and, correspondingly, it is an important feature of moral repair that it is not static.

This may look like it gives a lot of power to the victim. In fact, I think that the problems arise precisely when one sees it as a *power*. One way that corrective justice theorists try to explain the election of legal remedies is as a continuation of the rights of the plaintiff. For example, the original owner of stolen goods can seek to recover the market value or the proceeds of the thief and, according to these theorists, that option reflects the fact that the owner's rights include a power to sell. As Ernest Weinrib puts it, "Consistently with corrective justice, the option replicates at the remedial stage the content of the plaintiff's substantive right."[16] The role of the victim in determining the appropriate reparative action is regarded as a kind of normative control, a manifestation of their rights.

This understanding opens the door to opportunism and abuse. That the experience of the victim dictates the appropriate reparative orientation does not mean that the victim simply gets to choose and control at will. They are accountable to the truth, their truth. We can imagine Alexei making complaints of both forms—that Anna is depriving him of their life going forward and also that she has taken the best years of his life from him—and alternating back and forth between them in a manner calculated to make Anna feel the most guilt and give him the most by way of repair. If centering the victim meant that Chantel simply gets to choose what reparative actions she wants to demand of Christopher, we could readily understand the anxiety that some people express about such centering. And if centering the victim meant giving the victim a power to be wielded as they choose, we could see why victims might perversely become attached to their wounds.[17]

But centering the victim should not be understood as giving a power. The victim's experience significantly (though not definitively) shapes the wrong, and, as such, the victim ought to receive a kind of epistemic deference. There is a truth about what wrong has been committed, a truth that turns on the victim's experience and thus about which we must largely trust their testimony. But receiving a kind of deference is not the same as receiving discretion. It is not a power to choose, but rather an immunity from being questioned. In this spirit, the law typically frames these issues in terms of estoppel—that there are some things that the wrongdoer cannot be heard to question—rather than as a matter of the victim simply having a right to choose. That strikes me as the correct understanding.[18] There is a fact of the matter about the injury that a wrongdoer inflicts. And it is to this injury that reparative actions should respond. But this is a fact that can only be known ex post and with attention to the victim.

4.3 Wrongs as What We Repair

4.3.1 PUTTING THE PIECES TOGETHER

Let me put the pieces of the argument together now. According to the responsiveness idea, if one reparative response is more appropriate to the wrong than another would be in one situation, and vice versa for another situation, then those are two different wrongs. According to the previous section, for the same rights violation, one reparative response may be more appropriate if matters unfold one way, and vice versa if things unfold another way. Thus, the very same rights violation can give rise to different wrongs, depending on how matters look ex post. And if that's correct, then wrongs—the things that we seek to apologize for, make amends for, repair,

REPAIR 111

and so on—are not constituted by rights violations. This is Blackstone's syllogism in reverse.

We naturally think that repair means giving back to a wronged party whatever was taken from them. We speak of making someone whole. In this picture, the wrong is a kind of tearing asunder and repair is a putting back together. A piece of Aristotle's line has been separated off and just needs to be put back into its place. What we need to put back is the same thing that was there before it was removed.

But matters are not that simple. Things look different at one time from how they do at another; time and events change things. Repairing a puzzle is not straightforward when the pieces can merge and morph. One is not just trying to return whatever was there before. Instead, repair must involve something new—something that will require seeing what was there before *and* how things look now.

Wrongs have this character of a morphing void. They may arise from the fact that a right has been taken from us, but their shape is not determined only by the shape of the right that was taken. It also depends on the course of the world. That is, the nature of a wrong depends on certain facts that only come into existence once the wrong is committed. In this way, a wrong is its own thing, sculpted by the unfolding of events.

One piece of evidence for this—the piece of evidence leveraged in this chapter—comes from wrongs being the things that we attempt to repair. Such repair is often unsuccessful or incomplete. But when we seek to make amends, there is some feature of the moral universe that we aspire to repairing. Reflection on that aspiration reveals that wrongs are not the mirror image of rights. They are distinctively ex post.

4.3.2 LEGAL REMEDIES AND THEORIES OF PRIVATE LAW

This chapter has mostly avoided discussing legal remedies. The basic claim is about our foundational interpersonal concepts. It applies even where the only tribunals are those of conscience and social judgment. But, of course, the law has always confronted questions of remedies—often in sharper and more pressing forms than moral philosophy—and the dynamics that I have drawn out are familiar in the law of remedies. The story of Anna and Alexei captures the alternating pulls of what a contract lawyer might call the expectation measure and the reliance measure of damages. The story of Henrietta and George suggests the divergent appeal of compensatory damages and disgorgement. I believe that there is much to be learned from how law has evolved to address remedial questions. But in framing this chapter outside the law, I have tried to make manifest that these are not distinctly legal issues—that the same problems arise when we address non-legal questions, like how to apologize.

Still, it may be worth saying a few words to situate my understanding in relation to current theories of private law. Speaking broadly, a persistent divide has existed between corrective justice theorists and theorists who regard private law as creating social rules. Corrective justice theorists, taking inspiration from Aristotle, see private law as instantiating a form of interpersonal justice, with legal remedies serving to correct rights violations. In modern formulations of corrective justice, a core idea is the "continuity thesis": when a wrong occurs, the *normative* relation that existed between plaintiff and defendant continues to remain the same, despite the *material* injury. If I steal your car, your right to the car continues to exist—it's still your car.[19] Or, put slightly differently, my duty and associated reasons not to interfere with your car continue to exist.[20] For corrective justice theorists, this normative continuity is crucial to legal remedies. The proper remedy is a matter of giving legal effect to the normative relation that was there all along. Remedies are the flip side of rights.

In contrast, other theorists regard private law as creating a set of social rules. Such theorists range across legal realism, law and economics, critical legal studies, and distributive justice. What unites this motley group is a belief that private law is not wholly explicable in terms of interpersonal rights. Questions of legal remedies are antecedent to, or at least partly independent of, considerations about rights. For the legal realist, the legal right to your car amounts to nothing more than the remedies available to you if I take it. For others, what remedies the law should give you are (at least partly) a matter of social values—how strongly do we want to deter theft, how valuable is security in ownership, how will this contribute to wealth and inequality, and so forth. Rights are the flip side of the legal protections we offer.

Often the divide is characterized in terms of rights-based theory versus instrumentalism or, secondarily, in terms of relational versus social justice. But it should be clear that the divide is perhaps just as much about the relationship between the ex ante and the ex post, between backward-looking and forward-looking orientations.[21] Corrective justice theory regards the ex post as continuous with the prior ex ante, and remedial questions are, in a way, backward looking. The question is, What right did the plaintiff have? For the opposing views, remedial questions are partly forward looking: What protections should society give to people? For these views, the ex post remedial question is continuous with the *future* ex ante.

I reject the continuity idea, backward looking or forward looking. What wrongs exist ex post is a different matter from what rights there were or will be. That's not to deny that there will be connections between them, but they are not the same. I share corrective justice theory's focus on relational justice—that the concern of private law is a justice between this plaintiff and this defendant. But I do not believe that the wrong suffered by a plaintiff is simply a matter of the right violated. That the wrong is not so determined is shown by the different remedies that may be appropriate for the very same violation.

For those familiar with private law theory, this argument may resonate with civil recourse theory, recently advocated by John Goldberg and Benjamin Zipursky.[22] Civil recourse theory shares much with corrective justice theory, but it diverges around remedies. Like corrective justice theory, it conceives of private law as distinctively responding to rights violations and thereby realizing a valuable form of interpersonal relation. But civil recourse theory rejects the continuity thesis and the idea that the law repairs or corrects. There is no single remedy picked out by the underlying right. Instead, private law empowers individuals with a structured way to react against those who have violated their rights. It provides a legal recourse—a legally sanctioned channel for responding to violations—which must be fair and reasonable. But precisely what recourse the law should authorize will depend on various considerations, perhaps including institutional and even instrumental ones.[23] The view is meant to be pragmatic.

There is much in this chapter that should be amenable to civil recourse theory. We both reject the continuity thesis, seeing a gap between rights and remedies. But we locate the gap in different places. Whereas civil recourse theory sees the gap as existing between wrongs and what we offer as remedies, I see the gap as existing between wrongs and rights. The comparison might be represented as in Table 4-1.

TABLE 4-1

CORRECTIVE JUSTICE:	remedies	*correct*	wrongs	*reflect*	rights
CIVIL RECOURSE:	remedies	*do not correct*	wrongs	*reflect*	rights
MY VIEW:	remedies	*correct*	wrongs	*do not reflect*	rights

TABLE 4-2

	Remedies are directly tied to ex ante rights	*Remedies are based on other factors ex post*
Remedies are determined by the wrong committed	Corrective Justice	My View
Remedies involve considerations beyond the wrong	Social Rules Views	Civil Recourse Theory

This comparison draws out the fact that civil recourse theory and my own view both reject the continuity thesis, but in different ways. We find different places to locate the lack of continuity. The comparison also draws out the way that we both hold on to different aspects of corrective justice theory. Civil recourse theory retains the conceptual claim that wrongs necessarily reflect rights violations. In contrast, I retain corrective justice theory's claim that the appropriate remedy is determined by the wrong.

The view defended here can thus be regarded as sharing (and rejecting) elements of both corrective justice and civil recourse theory. The connections might be represented in the two-by-two matrix in Table 4-2.

Like corrective justice theory, I believe that remedies are a matter of the wrong done. Like civil recourse theory, I believe that remedies depend on factors beyond the nature of the underlying right. These independently plausible ideas can be maintained simultaneously by thinking that the nature of a wrong depends on more than the nature of the right violated.

Here is a way to put the thought in the spirit of this chapter: What are wrongs? They are what we remedy. With a richer conception of wrongs, we can maintain that remedies are about correcting wrongs, while rejecting the inclination to link everything all the way back to rights and duties.

5

The Unclaimable

In Leo Tolstoy's telling of Natasha and Prince Andrei's story, Natasha wrongs Andrei by casting him aside in a fit of caprice. Their story throughout the remainder of *War and Peace* is shaped by the existence of a wrong between them. But as noted in Chapter 1, it is hard to understand that wrong in terms of a violation of Andrei's rights. One reason is that Andrei had explicitly disavowed any commitment on Natasha's part. But even apart from that, it might seem incorrect to describe the wrong to Andrei in terms of rights because love is not something to which a person generally has a claim or a right. And yet, the withdrawal of love—or the redirection of it to another—can be among the most painful wrongs.

This chapter concerns certain relational goods—like love—that, for whatever reason, cannot be claimed even by those who plausibly deserve them. These unclaimables provide some of the most natural examples of wrongs that are not correlative with rights. Reflecting on them—the way that their denial can give rise to wrongs and the way that they cannot be claimed as a matter of right—can offer intuitive access to the separability of wrongs and rights.

What may be less clear is what lessons to draw from these phenomena. Perhaps what they illustrate is not the fracturing of ex ante and ex post normative relations but rather a gap between duties and rights. (It is for this reason that I take these unclaimable goods to be supporting, rather than leading, evidence, only introducing them now in Chapter 5.) In the second half of the chapter, I consider two different objections in this vein.

5.1 Four Unclaimables and the Wrongs That Flow from Them

In the following sections, I discuss four relational goods that seemingly cannot be claimed. Each of these is a philosophically rich topic, and I do not pretend to do them—let alone the literatures surrounding them—anything like justice. What I hope to suggest, in each case, is the mere plausibility that (a) the good in question cannot be claimed as a matter of right and (b) nevertheless there are wrongs that consist in the denial of these goods.[1]

5.1.1 BENEFICENCE

Beneficence is the classic philosophical example of good action that cannot be claimed. Immanuel Kant famously categorized beneficence as an "imperfect" and "wide" duty, a duty of virtue rather than a duty of right.[2] John Stuart Mill described as "the specific difference between justice and generosity or beneficence" that justice requires "something . . . which some individual person can claim from us as a matter of moral right."[3] And here is how Adam Smith put it:

> Beneficence is always free, it cannot be extorted by force, the mere want of it exposes to no punishment; because the mere want of beneficence tends to do no real positive evil. It may disappoint of the good which might reasonably have been expected, and upon that account it may justly excite dislike and disapprobation: it cannot, however, provoke any resentment which mankind will go along with. . . . The mere want of the beneficent virtues, though it may disappoint us of the good which might reasonably be expected, neither does, nor attempts to do, any mischief from which we can have occasion to defend ourselves.[4]

The basic thought is that beneficence—though it would produce more good in the world—is not something to which a would-be recipient is positively entitled. And as such, resentment is not appropriate for failures of beneficence.

(This conception of beneficence raises important concerns that are mostly orthogonal to the topic here. Many theorists, particularly consequentialists, have made compelling arguments that there can be strict duties to aid.[5]

THE UNCLAIMABLE 117

In emergencies and in contexts of background injustice—that is, in the real world—providing aid probably is strictly obligatory at least some of the time. We might even say that, in such contexts, the needy have a right to the assistance. There are thus hard questions about the scope and demandingness of our duties of aid, and, in answering these questions, it may turn out that some aid does not fit the foregoing characterizations of beneficence at all. But I wish to leave these hard questions to the side—my concern is beneficence to which the would-be recipient is not entitled as a matter of right, wherever one draws that boundary.)

Is Smith correct that, because beneficence is not something to which one is entitled, one cannot be wronged by a mere failure of beneficence? I think not. To begin, recall Elizabeth Anscombe's example of a doctor with a finite amount of drug, insufficient to save all her patients.[6] As Anscombe observes, none of the patients can say that the doctor owes the scarce drug to him; nobody has a right to the drug. And yet—Anscombe observes—if the drug is not used at all, "all are wronged."[7] This strikes me as a correct description. A patient who suffers while the drug is left needlessly unused can properly respond with resentment, not merely general "dislike and disapprobation." The wrongfulness of letting the drug go to waste seems to generate a personal complaint in those who might have benefited.

Professional medical responsibilities and the public dimensions of health care resources admittedly make this a complicated case. One might try to explain the apparent wronging on the basis of some other right—perhaps each patient has a right that the drug be used, or perhaps they have a procedural right to a fair chance at the drug, or perhaps there is a collective right of all the patients to the drug. I do not think that any such explanation will prove satisfactory—for each patient, the wrong consists in not getting the drug given that it was left to waste. But it is not necessary to get bogged down in that here.

It will suffice to see that the phenomenon Anscombe observes is a general one. Imagine that, on your way to work, someone on the street outside your office asks you for the apple that you are visibly carrying, telling you he is hungry. Perhaps you ought to give it to him, but he is not entitled to it. He does not have a right to it. Even he seems to acknowledge that— this is why he makes a request, rather than a demand.[8] The apple is yours, and you may have need of it. For all he knows, it's all you have for lunch today, it's your safeguard against collapsing from hypoglycemia, or it's already promised to a colleague.

But now suppose that he watches through the window as you deposit the apple on your desk, as you often do with fruit, where it languishes for several days until the desiccated remains are thrown in the trash. Can he now resent your declining to give it to him? I think so. His complaint is the same as that of Anscombe's patients: "It was there, ready to supply human need, and human need was not supplied."[9]

Perhaps resentment is still premature. Although the man has some good evidence of what likely happened—namely, that you didn't need the apple and just carelessly left it to waste—he cannot rule out other explanations. Perhaps you really did have a good reason to decline at the time. So rather than resentment, perhaps all that he has is the standing to raise the question, "Hey, why did you say I couldn't have your apple, and then just leave it to rot?" If you have no good justification, then I think that you owe an apology. It is no answer to say, "What's it to you? It was my apple."

It is one thing to say that some choice is within your discretion, and another thing to say that you are immune to accountability for how you exercise that discretion. Beneficence is "always free" in the sense that it is a matter of discretion; acts of beneficence are not strictly required. But when one exercises discretion in a manner that reflects not a reasonable judgment but rather neglect or indifference or perversity, then that action may wrong others.

On this characterization, the wrongs from lack of beneficence can be regarded as continuous with certain wrongs of malevolence. I have in mind here a class of cases that has given the common law fits—what sometimes is called "abuse of rights." A few examples will give the flavor. In *Hollywood Silver Fox Farm v. Emmett,* the defendant instructed his son to fire a gun near the property boundary in order to disturb the skittish foxes that the plaintiff farmed on the adjacent land, hoping to drive the plaintiff away.[10] In *Burke v. Smith,* the defendant built a fence for the purpose of depriving a neighbor of light and air—a classic "spite fence."[11] In *Fortune v. National Cash Register Co.,* an employer dismissed a sales representative, who was explicitly an at-will employee, the day after the employee had procured a $5 million order on which he would receive a commission.[12] One could go on.

The puzzle arises because, in each of these cases, the defendant's conduct appears to be within their rights. One generally has a liberty to shoot a gun or build a fence on one's property; and employers are granted the legal right to terminate an at-will employee at their discretion. So the plaintiffs

THE UNCLAIMABLE

do not seem to have a claim-right against such conduct. The very description under which these cases are sometimes grouped—"abuse of rights"—gets called an "oxymoron,"[13] "either self-contradictory or vacuous."[14] But there is no contradiction at all if one distinguishes between what is within one's ex ante sphere of control and what one can complain against ex post. That seems to be the structure of these cases: one has discretion to use one's property or fire employees—but if that discretion is used in perverse or malicious ways, one can be held to account for it by those injured as a result.

My suggestion is that exercise of beneficence has a similar structure. None of Anscombe's patients has a claim to the drug; its use is up to the doctor. But if she fails to use it on anyone, then all are wronged. The man on the street does not have a claim to your apple; it's yours and you have the prerogative to use it as you see fit. But if you simply leave it to rot, then he is wronged.

In 2007, real estate mogul Leona Helmsley created a national stir by leaving $12 million in a trust fund for her dog, Trouble, while disinheriting two of her four grandchildren.[15] The media and the public expressed outrage, both generally and on behalf of the grandchildren in particular.[16] Of course, in one sense, Helmsley's action was merely a failure of beneficence. Testators have discretion over their estate; grandkids don't have a right to inherit. But some exercises of testamentary discretion strike us as unjustifiable, and the conspicuously exorbitant bequest to the dog at the expense of the grandchildren was viewed by many as wronging them.

5.1.2 GRATITUDE

Alongside the comments on beneficence quoted earlier, Smith makes a related remark about gratitude: "The man who does not recompense his benefactor when he has it in his power, and when his benefactor needs his assistance, is, no doubt, guilty of the blackest ingratitude. . . . He is the proper object of the highest disapprobation. . . . He is the object of hatred . . . not of resentment. . . . To oblige him by force to perform what in gratitude he ought to perform . . . would, if possible, be still more improper than his neglecting to perform it."[17] Gratitude—the proper response to beneficence—seems to share with beneficence the quality of being a duty, but not claimable. Right, but not a right. As Claudia Card puts it, "The benefactor does not have a *right* to one's acting in accord with [responsibilities of gratitude] but only *deserves* it (or doesn't)."[18] Although we speak of "debts" of gratitude, they are, in Barbara Herman's words, "curious debts . . . since they are owed to benefactors, but cannot be claimed or waived by them."[19]

If gratitude is not claimable, then one might question whether its denial can wrong anyone. Perhaps Smith is correct that ingratitude is a basis for "the highest disapprobation" but "not . . . resentment"—an offense against civil society generally but not truly an offense against the benefactor.

This undirected conception of gratitude simply does not seem to capture our interpersonal experience. Ingratitude strikes us not merely as a general failure of virtue—a display of bad character—but as a personal offense against the one deserving of gratitude. In *King Lear,* we understand Goneril and Regan to be not merely acting badly but wronging their father by their ingratitude, even as the King's narcissistic demands for recognition are his own failing.[20] Indeed, within families, perceived failures of gratitude often ground long-lasting, simmering resentment. Of course, many times that resentment is excessive or altogether unwarranted, but we do not appear in doubt about the aptness of resentment if the charge of ingratitude is valid. Resentment makes sense because ingratitude is not merely a failure to acknowledge a good but a failure to acknowledge the person behind the good.[21] Ingratitude is something for which we can apologize, and something for which we can be forgiven. Even the notion of "debts" of gratitude carries with it the idea that there is something relational—something owed to the giver.

In addition to not capturing our interpersonal practices, there is a second reason to reject a nonrelational understanding, related to the way that duties of gratitude can be a tool for enforcing oppressive social hierarchies. Relations of beneficence involve a kind of inequality, and gratitude seems to be a mechanism for navigating that inequality—both guarding against disrespect or advantage-taking while allowing the reassertion of the recipient's agency. Gratitude says, "I see you, and I see that you see me." A bit like a promise, well-functioning gratitude can be a way to mutually navigate vulnerability. But if failures of gratitude are understood as offenses against all civil society, then gratitude risks becoming precisely the opposite—a tool for enforcing social hierarchy, for making people bend a knee.[22] So a secondary reason to see ingratitude as a wrong *to the benefactor* is to insist that ingratitude is *only about the benefactor*.[23]

This creates the philosophical puzzle: If gratitude is owed to benefactors who stand to be wronged by its refusal, then why is there not a right

THE UNCLAIMABLE 121

to it? Why can it not be claimed? A promising answer is that claiming or demanding gratitude would be self-defeating. There are different ways to develop this thought. For one, it might seem that any benefactor who attempted to claim gratitude would thereby undermine their acting out of benevolence, which is the grounds for gratitude in the first place.[24] Demanding it would thus make it no longer warranted. A second, slightly different thought would be that gratitude should be a spontaneous expression of the recipient's emotion, and that gratitude given in response to a demand would simply fail to be that. Demanded gratitude would be like requested laughter—not real. A third variation is suggested by Herman's account of gratitude: if gratitude is a way for the beneficiary to reassert their agency, then it is crucial to gratitude that the benefactor not be in control.[25] All of these explanations are plausible, and there's no need to try to adjudicate among them. What is important is that the unclaimability of gratitude seems to be deeply built into it.

5.1.3 THOUGHTS (AND BELIEFS)

"But what if I think you killed Cock Robin, when as things turn out you did not? I think we might in the ordinary way say I wronged you and did you a wrong, though it can hardly be thought that my merely harboring that thought was my violating a claim of yours."[26] Judith Thomson makes this observation in *The Realm of Rights,* but she then sets such usage aside as not her focus. Nowadays, nobody says, "you wronged me," and barely anyone would choose the construction, "you did me a wrong." But back when such locutions were in usage, they seem to have been applied as much as anything to beliefs, opinions, distrust, and other forms of thought. I think there is intuitive force to such applications, even though we do not think that anyone has rights or claims over our thoughts—even though thoughts are unclaimable.

For a very long time, philosophers have been interested in the ethics of belief and, with the recent philosophical focus on "wronging," some have defended the idea that our beliefs can wrong others. Consider the following example from David Owens:

> Undeserved attitudes can also wrong. Suppose I come to believe, without any great evidence, that my brother drove my father to an early grave. When my brother learns of this belief, he will feel traduced. Perhaps I never express the belief to anyone and he discovers

122 WRONGS AND RIGHTS COME APART

> it quite inadvertently by reading my diary. Outrage, indignation, etc. are in order here quite apart from fear of further harm or damage: my brother may feel this way even if we are already estranged. Nor does he think that his being wronged depends on his having found out what I think of him (i.e. on the distress that discovery causes). Rather he simply values being regarded as a decent person and the fact that my belief is both ungrounded and against his interest ensures that it wrongs him.[27]

On ordinary understandings, the brother is wronged.[28] Indeed, instances of failing to believe or to trust have always been paradigmatic wrongings.[29] Not only that, Owens's diagnosis seems like the natural one: the brother is wronged because the belief is ungrounded and negative. An appeal to rights—saying that the brother has a right against such belief—is likely to seem incorrect.

In Owens's case, the wronging arises out of the content of the belief. But wrongings can also arise from the process of belief formation. Focusing on the effect of social structures, Miranda Fricker frames as "testimonial injustice" "a distinctively epistemic injustice, as a kind of injustice in which someone is *wronged specifically in her capacity as a knower.*"[30] Fricker's core examples—for instance, the woman who is given less credibility because she is assumed to be emotionally blinded—resonate intuitively. Such injustices are all too familiar, and a victim of such injustice is right to resent it. But though Fricker opens her book lamenting "the inattention to the rights and wrongs of our epistemic lives,"[31] she never talks about "rights" again. That is perfectly understandable. Although epistemic wrongings are intuitive and familiar, the idea of a right to credibility (or to a fair share of credibility) feels far less natural. And making a claim or demand for credibility has a paradoxical quality about it.

All this suggests that beliefs are another example of something that can wrong but that is unclaimable. But discussions of this topic can veer into thorny questions about doxastic control and pragmatic encroachment. Rather than entering these thickets, I want to focus on nondoxastic mental activity—wondering, fantasizing, coveting, imagining, hoping, daydreaming, loathing, and so on. The same combination of wronging and unclaimability appears here as well, with fewer lurking questions about control.

(Still, it is worth noting that this is all a spectrum. Belief is significantly a matter of attention, and directing attention is a mental *activity*.[32] Iris Murdoch's famous example of M and D—in which M "observes . . . or at least reflects deliberately" about D and discovers a more favorable view of her—makes the point excellently.[33] Murdoch emphasizes that M is active in changing her beliefs about D. Belief almost always has some active component. In Owens's example earlier, we might say that the wrong consists in "harboring" the belief, especially given the elements in the family history that would not support the belief were one's focus turned to them.)

It is striking that, whereas modern Western philosophical ethics is almost exclusively focused on action, religious ethical teachings heavily govern thought. To take an obvious example, the Ten Commandments ends by proclaiming, "You shall not covet your neighbor's house. You shall not covet your neighbor's wife, or his male or female servant, his ox or donkey, or anything that belongs to your neighbor."[34] Read naturally, these are prohibitions on thoughts and attitudes, rather than action. But some of the great thinkers in this tradition, evidently concerned with how even God's law could apply to anything but action, have interpreted "coveting" as a kind of action. Maimonides distinguished "coveting" from "desiring" and maintained that "coveting must involve a deed."[35] Thomas Aquinas reconciled matters by distinguishing "interior" and "exterior" acts, concluding that sin, "insofar as it is voluntary, must needs always include some act, at least the interior act of the will."[36]

The Christian image of internal sin is certainly alive in modern culture. In a famous *Playboy* interview, then–presidential candidate Jimmy Carter said the following: "I try not to commit a deliberate sin. I recognize that I'm going to do it anyhow, because I'm human and I'm tempted. And Christ set some almost impossible standards for us. Christ said, 'I tell you that anyone who looks on a woman with lust has in his heart already committed adultery.' I've looked on a lot of women with lust. I've committed adultery in my heart many times."[37] While the statement generated a lot of satire, it perhaps helped Carter because Americans were sympathetic with his honesty and with the sentiment that he expressed.[38] We seem to regard some thoughts as wrong, even as we sometimes indulge them; we recognize them as a kind of "deliberate sin."[39]

But "sinful" is not the same as wronging someone. Your bad thoughts are, one might contend, just between you and God. They may be failures of virtue and symptoms of bad character, but that does not show that thoughts alone, unaccompanied by external action, can wrong. Why think that mere thoughts can be wrongings?[40]

First, just consider the natural reactive attitudes. How would you feel to learn that someone actively daydreams about your embarrassment or failure? Or occasionally conjures violent or sexual fantasies about you? Or engages in unwelcome religious prayer concerning you or your loved ones?[41] I posit that your reaction would not be detached disapproval; it would be personal resentment. Second, note how natural it is to apologize for thoughts that one harbored—and also to forgive the thoughts of others. Third, one can promise thoughts. Imagine, for example, the husband who promises his dying wife that he will remember her every day for the rest of his life. If, as his life evolves, he finds himself going days without her memory occurring to him at all, could he not deem himself to be breaching his promise and thereby wronging her? Fourth, notice how thoughts have a different character if the person in them is real or fictitious. As a boy growing up, I had something of crush on Maid Marion. (Sadly, becoming Robin Hood is no longer a career goal.) If I engaged in some fantasizing and daydreaming about Maid Marion, that seems fairly innocent. Only the most puritanical would call that "sinning in the heart." But the same fantasies, if they are about the girl who lives down the street and has no idea, take on a different character. In that case, there is someone real who is implicated, who might object—whom I might be wronging. Finally, notice that our assessment of thoughts about someone may be shaped by the person's own conduct. If you scrutinize Dwayne Johnson's body as a benchmark against which you compare others, I don't think you're wronging him; he can have no complaint. But a similar treatment of your coworker almost certainly would wrong them. All of these features suggest that some bad thoughts are not merely unvirtuous in a detached sense—but that they can involve a transgression that is relational, that they are something that we do to another.

One might now swing to the opposite pole: Perhaps there are wrongings, but doesn't that show that there are rights? From what has just been said, it looks like we can be owed certain thoughts and that the contours are in some sense under our control—a matter of promising, waiver, and so on. There may, of course, be problems with *legal* rights over thoughts, but why not say that there are *moral* rights over thoughts?

If by that we mean only "stands to be wronged," then there is no problem. But for many people, there is an intuitive discomfort with saying there are rights to others' thoughts. I think that discomfort stems from the connection between rights and claiming, demanding, and control. To say

THE UNCLAIMABLE 125

that someone has a right is, we understand, to say that the person has a kind of authority. And as much as we may accept that our thoughts can and do wrong others, our minds seem like they should be a matter of nobody else's authority. In this respect, some aspect of the original idea—that mere thoughts are between you and God—has enduring appeal.[42] Your mind is supposed to be your own free domain.[43] The unclaimability—as in the case of beneficence—seems tied to a kind of discretionary sphere.

There might also be parallels to be drawn with gratitude. Gratitude, by its nature, seems like it must be given, not demanded. Perhaps something similar is true of mental activity. Proper respect—or the lack thereof—seems to be at the heart of wronging thoughts, and it is a cliché that "respect cannot be demanded, it must be earned." So in a way, the unclaimability of thoughts may arise from a self-defeating quality. Consider the caricatured demand of the frustrated parent or stodgy school principal in a comedy: "You listen to me, young man!" Part of the humor in the line comes from the obvious paradox in it: you can't get someone to truly listen by demanding it. This quasi-paradoxical quality to demanding thoughts may just be part and parcel with having private authority over our own minds.

The way that these two points may work in tandem can be seen by thinking about instances where people attempt to impose themselves on other people's minds. The Leona Helmsley will, in addition to giving millions to the dog, also conditioned the bequests to the two inheriting grandchildren on their visiting their father's grave annually. Presumably this was to ensure their remembrance of him. Such a demand seems simultaneously exceedingly controlling and also absurdly self-defeating; fond remembrance does not work that way.

5.1.4 LOVE (AND SEX)

Return, lastly, to love. Andrei and Natasha's story is relatable. The wrongs of broken love, even without broken promises, are ubiquitous. For many of us, the most searing wrongs that we will ever commit or suffer occur in the context of romantic or familial relationships. Admittedly, many such wrongs involve, at least as a component, some straightforward rights violations—at least morally speaking. Everyone has a right not to be lied to, belittled, gaslighted, abused, and so on. Morally, we have a claim to that much. But those violations hardly seem to exhaust the romantic wrongs that we commit and suffer. Often, the wrong consists simply in the thoughtless or

126 WRONGS AND RIGHTS COME APART

ill-conceived withdrawal of love itself. And yet, one does not have a right to the love of another. It is these less straightforward cases that present a puzzle about unclaimables.

Consider, for example, the following passage from Anthony Trollope's novel *The Eustace Diamonds* describing the situation of a character named Lucy Morris:

> Frank Greystock was not her lover. Ah,—there was the worst of it all! She had given her heart and had got nothing in return. . . . Then she remembered certain scenes at the deanery, words that had been spoken, looks that had been turned upon her, a pressure of the hand late at night, a little whisper, a ribbon that had been begged, a flower that had been given;—and once, once—; then there came a burning blush upon her cheek that there should have been so much, and yet so little that was of avail. She had no right to say to any one that the man was her lover. She had no right to assure herself that he was her lover. But she knew that some wrong was done her in that he was not her lover.[44]

Lucy does not view herself as having a claim on Frank's love—they are decidedly not engaged or in any other way committed to each other. And yet Lucy feels that there has been so much between them that he should be committed to her. That he is not her lover feels like a betrayal of what they have had and thus a betrayal of her.

Lucy's perceived wrong is not just the antiquated result of Victorian honor and morals. One finds similar assertions of romantic grievance—and associated public sympathy and indignation—throughout popular culture, from reality TV contestants to rom-com characters stuck in the "friend zone" to ballads of heartbreak. Taylor Swift, to take a prime example, has dominated the charts with songs of the betrayal, injury, and resentment from withdrawn love. Here is a passage from one of her most iconic songs:

> 'Cause there we are again in the middle of the night
> We're dancin' 'round the kitchen in the refrigerator light
> Down the stairs, I was there
> I remember it all too well
> And there we are again when nobody had to know
> You kept me like a secret, but I kept you like an oath

THE UNCLAIMABLE 127

Sacred prayer and we'd swear
To remember it all too well, yeah.
Well, maybe we got lost in translation, maybe I asked for too
    much
But maybe this thing was a masterpiece 'til you tore it all up
Runnin' scared, I was there
I remember it all too well
And you call me up again just to break me like a promise
So casually cruel in the name of bein' honest
I'm a crumpled-up piece of paper lyin' here
'Cause I remember it all, all, all.[45]

Swift's story is not unlike Lucy Morris's. Notice how, for both, the grievance[46] flows from remembering the tender moments—"scenes at the deanery" and "dancin' 'round the kitchen in the refrigerator light." The remembrances give rise to a complaint: How could you cast me aside after what we had? The complaint isn't self-focused—"you owed it to me"—but outwardly focused: "How could you tear that up?"

One might disagree with Lucy's and Swift's assessments that they were wronged (though I do not). The important question is only whether their orientation is conceptually coherent. Is it even intelligible to assert a wrong without pointing to something to which one had a claim? My hope is that the examples speak for themselves here. These are stories that have emotionally resonated with millions of readers and listeners; they must be tracking something recognizable.

Of course, one could try to find claims that would fit these grievances into a more rights-like framework. The natural candidate would be that all-purpose tool of contract law: the implied promise. Lucy Morris, the thought would go, was led on by Frank Greystock. In the "pressure of the hand late at night" was an implied promise to her. And it is breach of that implied promise that constitutes the wrong. Lucy's mistake is not thinking herself wronged but thinking that she had no claim in the absence of an express promise. So too with Swift—the wrong consists in the breach of a promise, of what they "swore" to each other.[47]

An appeal to implied promises obscures more than it illuminates. We can say that there are implied promises. We might even insist that there are implied promises when they have been explicitly disavowed, as in Andrei and Natasha's case. But what do these implied promises amount to?

128   WRONGS AND RIGHTS COME APART

And is it their breach or the conduct itself that is the true grounds for the wrong?

In Chapter 3, I argued that some promises create only potential wrongings, not action-shaping claims. Promises to love would seem to be like that. One cannot acquire an obligation to love because love is not something done out of obligation. This is not because there are no reasons for love; one can have reasons to love or not to love a person. But a promise cannot supply such a reason. It's the wrong kind of reason. So if we appeal to implied promises in these cases, it is not because unspoken promises are the source of reasons and obligations, the breach of which gives rise to the wrong. Rather, such framing merely reflects—rather than explains—the potential wronging.

This point is further confirmed by considering the actual grievance. An aggrieved lover might point to a broken promise, but in most cases, I venture that the breach of promise is epiphenomenal at best. The broken promise is not the substance of the complaint at all. This is nicely brought out by the story of Andrei and Natasha, where promises have been disclaimed. It's also, incidentally, brought out by Taylor Swift: her complaint isn't that her lover broke a promise, but that he broke *her* like a promise.

Trying to conceptualize the wrongs of denied love in a claim-based way is not only unilluminating, but it can be positively misleading and distorting. Insisting on the existence of a right or claim as a prerequisite to asserting a grievance can both foster misguided rights talk and subvert real complaints. Amia Srinivasan's widely read essay "The Right to Sex" clearly elucidates the problem (albeit discussing sex rather than love). Srinivasan is commenting on the liberal feminist response to Elliot Rodger, the twenty-two-year-old man who murdered five people, including two women, during a shooting at a sorority at the University of California, Santa Barbara. Rodger became representative of so-called incels, who are, as Srinivasan puts it, "a certain kind of sexless man: the kind who is convinced he is owed sex, and is enraged by the women who deprive him of it."[48] What Srinivasan notes is that liberal responses focused on critiquing male sexual entitlement, not on the social dynamics of sexual desire. Liberal feminists responded to Rodger by saying that nobody has a right to sex—that how other people conduct their sex lives is a matter of their freedom. But as Srinivasan astutely draws out, that orientation risks insulating sexual desire from any interrogation and complaint. If we say that Rodger simply could not have any complaint against the sorority women who wouldn't sleep with him

THE UNCLAIMABLE 129

because there is no right to sex, must we also say that a Black woman has no complaint against the man who declares that he is only interested in white women? What about when a person is told they cannot be desired because they are too fat? As Srinivasan puts it, "A feminism that totally abjures the political critique of desire is a feminism with little to say about the injustices of exclusion and misrecognition suffered by the women who arguably need feminism the most."[49]

Srinivasan challenges her reader "to dwell in the ambivalent place where we acknowledge that no one has a right to be desired, but also that who is desired and who isn't is a political question, a question often answered by more general patterns of domination and exclusion."[50] What would dwelling in such a place look like? Here is a suggestion: nobody has a right to be desired, but one can be wronged by the denial of desire. The incels' primary conceptual mistake (as opposed to their many factual mistakes) is not that they believe a person could have a grievance against those participating in an exclusionary sexual hierarchy but that they infer from a grievance to an entitlement. And the liberal feminist response, in a way, replicates this mistake by saying that nobody has a right to sex and inferring from that to the conclusion that there can be no injustice in being rejected. Both see the rights and injustices as necessarily conjoined—and that's a mistake. When one tethers entitlements and grievances in this way, one is liable to believe in entitlements that are not real (the incels) or rule out complaints that should be taken seriously (the liberal response).

Tolstoy saw these distortions. In *Anna Karenina,* Levin says to himself, "Yes, she was bound to choose him. So it had to be, and I have nothing and no one to complain about. I am myself to blame. What right did I have to think she would want to join her life with mine?"[51] In saying this, Levin infers from the fact that he had no right to Kitty's affection to the conclusion that he can have no complaint when she rejects him. Tolstoy's reader, however, knows that Levin is conceding too much: of course Kitty's love is not a matter of right, but that does not mean Levin has nothing and no one to complain about.

5.2 Two Counterarguments

Cases like these show us something about the contours of rights and grievances. But one might question whether they support the claims made throughout the rest of the book. Do these cases really display any divergence between the ex ante deliberative perspective and the ex post perspective of accountability? Are they not instead merely illustrations of the limits of rights, the limits of making claims on others?

There are actually two different counterarguments available here. First, one might say that the foregoing examples merely reflect the division Kant drew between the doctrine of right and the doctrine of virtue. All of these cases arguably involve duties of virtue—which by no accident were headlined, for Kant, by beneficence and gratitude. Duties of virtue concern what an agent ought to do, and their breach is a moral failure. But what we are *owed,* this reply would continue, is a matter of external freedom. The cases all revolve around internal moral or interpersonal failures. What the cases reflect is thus not a divergence between the perspectives of deliberation and accountability, since duties of virtue do matter to the deliberating agent, but rather a divergence between internal and external freedom—what it is to be virtuous and what it is that we owe to others in the world.

Here is a second, different counterargument: These examples concern directed duties that are, for special reasons, not claimable. The unclaimability may be a matter of preserving a kind of freedom or a function of some relational goods losing their value if they are not freely given. Regardless, what they reflect are directed duties with the claimable quality that we normally associate with rights subtracted away. But there's still duty owed to someone else to guide the agent's choice. The examples thus do not reveal any divergence between the ex ante perspective of deliberation and the ex post perspective of accountability—rather, they reveal a divergence between directed duties and claimability. They show that not everything that is owed can be claimed.

I suspect that readers will be somewhat attracted to both of these replies. Indeed, I am myself. The first thing to observe, however, is that they are in direct contradiction with each other. The crux of the first reply is that, insofar as we have departed from the domain of rights, these are not things that we are owed. The crux of the second is that these are things that we are owed in spite of not having any claimable right. If you are attracted to both replies, then it must be because of an ambiguity or equivocation around what it means to *owe* something to another person.

I suggest that our different senses of "owe" reflect the difference between rights and wrongings. On one sense of "owe," we owe something only when there is a correlative right or claim. On another sense of "owe," owing a duty is just a matter of someone standing to be wronged.

THE UNCLAIMABLE   131

Philosophers have taken, in recent years, to using the phrase "directed duties," and it seems often to capture this second sense of "owing."[52] But this term of art may obscure more than it illuminates if it leads us to think that there's some feature of the deliberative standpoint—some particular kind of duty—that then explains the accountability relations. "You owed it to him, and that's why he was wronged." The second reply—if it is to be an objection and not merely a reformulation of my thesis—depends on having such an independent notion of directed duty.

Consider gratitude. There is admittedly some intuitive pull toward the thought that the gratitude is owed to the benefactor and that the benefactor is wronged precisely because the duty was owed to him. But how are we to characterize this owing?

Consider two recent efforts. Tony Manela describes gratitude as something to which one has "an imperfect right"—the imperfectness of the right being that it is not "sturdy enough to support a speech-act as forceful as a demand."[53] This characterization makes it sound like other rights, but of a weakened form. But what is the imperfect right? "An imperfect right, as I define it, is a special standing characterized by license to unrebukably resent and to remonstrate in the face of noncompliance."[54] Fair enough, but that is just a description in terms of the ex post relations of accountability after all.[55]

Adrienne Martin offers a characterization that, unlike Manela's, aims to be explanatory in terms of some ex ante power. According to Martin, "rights entail the standing or permission to direct specific actions," but there is something different—what she calls "personal expectations"—that correlate with mere directed duties. Personal expectations "entail only the standing or permission to direct the adoption of broad ends, leaving latitude regarding the means to be taken."[56] The benefactor, the thought goes, does not get to demand any particular form of gratitude, but they do get to demand that the beneficiary be grateful in some generalized sense.[57]

But, as Martin appreciates, it's not like benefactors may immediately demand of beneficiaries, "You should be grateful." So what does standing to direct the end but not the means look like? Here is Martin's example:

> Suppose time passes: the beneficiary has recovered from their misfortune, and multiple apt moments for a simple "thank you" have passed unmentioned. Nor has the beneficiary expressed gratitude or appreciation in any other way. It would surely be legitimate for

132　WRONGS AND RIGHTS COME APART

> the benefactor, at this point, to begin to feel hurt. Then, one day, the beneficiary begins to regale the benefactor with a self-congratulatory narrative about their recovery from that original misfortune, giving no credit to the benefactor. At this point, the hurt feelings bloom into resentment, and a little direction would not be amiss: "You know, you've never even said 'thank you' for the help I gave you then?" This direction is legitimate not because the beneficiary suddenly has a claim on a performance of this particular social convention, but because enough evidence has accumulated that the beneficiary has no notion that they ought to be grateful.[58]

I find it telling how much this sounds like an ex post complaint. As far as I can see, it *is* an ex post complaint. Martin's use of the word "direction" is jarring, as the utterance ("you've never") is not really directive but plaintive. Imagine the beneficiary responded with, "Oh, I appreciate that bit of direction. Now that you mention it, thank you for the help you gave me." If I were the beneficiary, I would consider that response obtuse or patronizing—I wasn't giving a direction but protesting a failure. Apology, not simply compliance, is the appropriate response.

In making these points, I do not mean to be objecting to using "owe" or "imperfect right" or "personal expectation" to mark out places in moral life where someone stands to be wronged. But we should not confuse that with "owing" or "rights" of the form that plays a distinctive role in shaping our conduct ex ante.

If that's correct, then these unclaimable relational goods do illustrate the divergence seen in other chapters, and they do so precisely because there is something correct behind both counterarguments: These cases involve wrongful (unvirtuous) actions within agents' sphere of autonomy, not rights violations. And yet there is also a sense in which these are things that we owe to others—they are not merely free-floating duties; they can generate wrongs.

6

The Complaintless

Not all victims of rights violations can complain. In Chapter 4, I observed that the nature of a wrong may depend on how the injured party frames the complaint. But some parties can't frame a complaint at all. Consider the following remarks from Jeffrie Murphy about psychopaths: "[The psychopath] is socially dissimilar from the majority of his fellows in his lack of moral feeling, by his failure to be motivated by a recognition of the rights of others and the obligations he has to them. Thus, he is in no position to claim rights for himself. He violates a condition for the possibility of reciprocity which is . . . in turn a presupposition for intelligibility of the whole obligation-rights language game." Murphy concludes, "If this is so, of course, then the psychopath cannot be wronged, can be done no moral injury."[1] Supposing it is true that the psychopath cannot be wronged, does that mean that psychopaths have no rights?

This chapter argues that one gap between the ex ante realm of rights and the ex post realm of complaints exists because, even where a right is violated, having a complaint also requires that one be able to relate to the violator in the manner distinctive of holding to account. Where this is absent—as in the psychopath—the violation of a right may leave no wronging in its wake. One can have rights without complaints.

I will consider three different ways that one might be unable to complain against a rights violation and yet still be a rightholder. First, one might lack standing where one's own conduct prevents an appeal to the relevant norms. Thus the psychopath imagined by Murphy—as well as the more ordinary moral transgressor—may lack the standing to complain when the norm that he has himself flouted is not followed. Second, one might lack the standing to complain because one has nothing to complain about. Here,

134 WRONGS AND RIGHTS COME APART

I focus on cases in which, as I will describe it, "all's well that ends well." Some rights violations not only are harmless but also unfold in such a favorable way that they do not wrong. Finally, a creature might have no complaints because it simply cannot complain—because accountability relations of the relevant sort are not intelligible to them. Nonhuman animals (or at least many of them) fall into this category. I argue that they do have rights, even if they lack the capacity for issuing complaints or holding us to account.

Each of these three types of cases presents a challenge for the view that directed duties—and especially rights—are necessarily linked with the standing to hold us to account. Before turning to these three cases, however, the chapter begins with some remarks on the idea of moral standing.

6.1 Standing, Authority, and Relationality

There is a common idea that, in order to be a rightholder, one must have a kind of standing. The nature of this standing is a much more disputed question. Standing to claim, to demand, to hold to account, and so forth—all have their appeal and defenders.

Moreover (and less frequently appreciated), there seem to be two different ways that standing might relate to being a rightholder. Having a right might consist in a kind of standing, like, say, the standing to demand. But sometimes standing is understood as a kind of precondition to rightholding. Consider the following description: "To violate a right is to wrong the holder of the right. It is to fail to do what is owed to the right holder. That indicates that someone or something can hold rights only if it is the sort of thing to which duties can be owed and which is capable of being wronged. In other words, moral standing is a precondition of right-holding."[2] Moral standing—understood here as a capacity to be wronged—is taken to be a "precondition" for being the bearer of rights. "Standing" here refers to a kind of moral status—the status of belonging in the moral community. Conceptually at least, one might have this kind of standing without having any particular standing to make a claim or complaint.[3] It can be useful to appreciate the difference between these two senses of "standing": particular standing—the standing to make particular claims or complaints—and the general standing constitutive of belonging to a moral community. In the law, for example, we might ask if taxpayers have standing to challenge expendi-

THE COMPLAINTLESS   135

tures on vouchers to religious schools. But we might also ask whether trees
have standing. The first asks about a particular form of normative power
or authority; the second asks about having the proper kind of status to
have any cognizable form of normative power or authority. Standing can
thus capture a particular potential, or it can capture a kind of general
status that is a precondition for any instance of the particular.

One picture of the connection between these ideas can be found in the
work of Stephen Darwall. According to Darwall, morality is importantly
"second-personal." By this, Darwall means that our moral obligations are
owed to others—unlike general directives—in that they are based on reasons with which we address one another.[4] For Darwall, it is only insofar
as reasons are second-personal that we can direct each other practically, by
making demands directly on each other's wills, rather than epistemically,
by pointing out relevant normative facts. This suggests that second-personal
reasons have, built into them, some conception of authority.[5] This authority
is a kind of standing. As Darwall puts it in a now-familiar example, "When
you demand that someone move his foot from on top of yours, you presuppose an irreducibly second-personal standing to address this second-
personal reason."[6]

In a reply to Darwall, Jay Wallace questions how the authority of second-
personal address, which seems to depend on an act of the addressor, can
be the basis for moral norms, which do not seem to be similarly contingent. He begins by noting a peculiar feature of the gouty toe example:

> As Darwall initially develops the example, the victim's protest is
> lodged after the point at which pressure is applied by your foot to
> the gouty toe. This has puzzling consequences, if we take seriously
> the idea that it is the addressing of a claim or demand that is the
> source of distinctively second-personal reasons. The claim or de-
> mand that is at issue in this case is the victim's protest, which we
> should understand as creating a reason for you to desist, in virtue of
> the victim's authority to make demands of precisely this nature. This
> suggests that you did not have a second-personal reason to refrain
> from stepping on the victim's toe until the protest was issued. This
> cannot be right, however. Surely we want to say that you have an
> agent-relative reason not to step on someone's gouty toe that is (to
> some degree) prior to and independent of any complaint that might
> be issued after the toe has actually been stepped on.[7]

Notice the temporal element here. Wallace's point is that Darwall seems to be moving from ex post accountability to ex ante reasons. But if holding accountable is exercising authority, then this order of operations looks puzzling; most authority doesn't work like that. A soldier does not have a reason to march until the order is given—the authoritative address (the order) creates the reason. Moral reasons look different. The reason not to step on the gouty toe is not created by the protest; it was there all along.[8] If the reason exists antecedent to second-personal address, then it doesn't seem like the second-personal reasons come from the authority of the individual person—for example, the person whose toe it is.

It is from here, as I understand it, that Wallace and Darwall part ways.[9] Wallace rejects the appeal to *exercising authority*.[10] Wallace shifts to seeing relational normativity as, in some sense, the primitive. As he puts it, "What makes a reason second personal is . . . that it is implicated in a structure of relational or 'bipolar' normativity."[11] The fundamental idea, for Wallace, is that individuals have claims on one another. We don't create the special reasons by making claims—the reasons are there as part of our having claims.

Darwall, in contrast, rejects (or perhaps disavows) the idea that second-personal reasons arise from an *individual's* authority. The reasons of morality are second-personal in the sense that they can be addressed to us by any member of the moral community—including ourselves. We see this in the impersonal reactive attitudes (indignation) and in self-regarding emotions (guilt). Relational morality of claims and complaints is thus only one form of second-personal reasons.[12] Second-personal reasons more broadly presuppose the authority of the moral community.

This debate is not easy to follow. But I think that it may be illuminating of the conceptual space around standing. My conjecture is that Darwall and Wallace are each after a different notion of standing. Roughly speaking, Wallace is seeking the individual standing involved in making claims. And Darwall is seeking the standing involved in being part of the moral community.

And I think (to lay my cards on the table without any argument yet) each of them gets something correct. Wallace is correct in saying that the normativity of claims doesn't come from some authority that is bound up with lodging protests or having reactive attitudes—rather, it is built into the structure of relational normativity. Darwall is correct in saying that the reasons of morality are, in some sense, addressable by all persons in the moral community—that a crucial feature of morality is that it is a matter that all of us can raise with each other. But in my view, both of them are a bit too enamored with the Strawsonian idea that normativity is tied to holding to account. Whatever connection exists is a looser one. We are better off saying (with Wallace) that relational normativity is simply composed of claims and directed duties, and (with Darwall) that the moral community can address to us the reasons involved in such claims (and others besides) in the form of holding accountable.[13]

I hope that this hazy suggestion may become clearer over the remainder of the chapter. In examining the cases of complaintless individuals, I hope to show that, despite lacking individual grievances, the complaintless nonetheless have claims or rights. Put another way, they remain members of the moral community, and they are still a recognizable source of reasons for us. They have standing where that means the moral status of belonging to the community of rightholders. But that general standing is not a matter of their having the particular authority bound up with holding us to account—for they do not have that standing.

6.2 Transgressors and Provocateurs

Not everyone has the standing to complain, to resent, or to hold the actor responsible. In the simple case, someone lacks standing to complain when the action in question is not her business—such as if she has no particular interest at stake in the matter and she is not owed any particular duty with regard to the action. But there is another way that someone may lack the standing to complain, which does not involve being a disinterested party. This arises when someone has rejected a particular norm, usually through action but possibly only through speech.[14] As John Rawls puts it, "A person's right to complain is limited to violations of principles he acknowledges himself. A complaint is a protest addressed to another in good faith. It claims a violation of a principle that both parties accept."[15] What counts as acknowledging a principle is a tricky question, but when one entirely flouts a moral norm, it may become the case that one cannot legitimately appeal to that norm as the basis for a complaint against another. G. A. Cohen labels this *tu quoque*.[16]

Consider an example:[17] You are in a pub discussing sports with some locals. Sick of their baseless praise for their preferred soccer team, you casually respond, "Arsenal is a bunch of whiners and cheats." The man at the stool next to you, apparently a hothead, immediately lands a right hook to your chin, then, laughing, he starts to walk out the door. You feel no continued threat, only a wounded ego. Let's suppose that the correct thing to do is to turn the other cheek.[18] But you give in to your temptation, pull him back by the shoulder, and retaliate with a swing of your own. Ex hypothesi, you have acted *wrongly*. Your pastor at the other end of the bar has every reason to be appalled by your behavior.

But I do not think that the guy who hit you first can legitimately complain that he has been wronged. After striking you, he is in no position to complain about an analogous action done to him in response.[19] Consider how ridiculous it would sound for him to say, "You have wronged me—I demand your apology for this act of unnecessary violence." This is not, of course, to say that he has lost all standing to complain about anything. If you had escalated the conflict by throwing a grenade instead of a punch, he would be in a position to complain about that. And he might yet be in a position to complain about your insults to his favorite team. But he cannot, I think, complain about receiving a punch in response to his own punch.[20]

There are interesting and complicated questions about the scope of standing that is lost when one violates a norm: How similar must the violations be to each other? How proximate in time? When does one regain one's standing after a violation? Does one only lose standing to complain with regard to one's victims or with regard to the entire moral community? There are not simple, cut-and-dried answers to these questions. But the fact that we recognize them as good questions already suggests that we see the phenomenon. (One doesn't scrutinize the contours of an object that one cannot see at all.) The loss of standing has hazy boundaries and a lot of context sensitivity, but I take the bar fight case to be a relatively clear one. The second transgression is temporally close; it is the victim of the first transgression to whom the complaint would have to be made; and the character of the transgressions is almost identical.[21] The guy who throws an unprovoked punch has no real complaint when he receives a punch in return. He has already disregarded the very norm that he would seek to invoke. His complaint is vulnerable to the *tu quoque* response.

While like misconduct opens one to the *tu quoque* response, I don't think that is the only way that a party can lose standing to complain. The same thing occurs where the party's own misconduct leads to the other party's subsequent conduct. As Cohen puts it, "In this second type of silencing

THE COMPLAINTLESS

response you are disabled from condemning me not because you are responsible for something similar or worse yourself but because you bear at least some responsibility for the very thing that you seek to criticize."[22] In other words, where a party's wrongful action leads to, provokes, or otherwise causes the subsequent bad act of another, that fact may undermine the party's standing to complain.[23] Distinguishing these ideas, one can see that the bar fight example involves an overdetermined lack of position to complain: the would-be complainant both did the same thing (*tu quoque*) and provoked the complained-of conduct.

The law contains various doctrines—particularly from equity—that instantiate these ideas. Unclean hands, estoppel, *in pari delicto,* good faith, waiver,[24] unconscionability, and duress can all arguably function in this way. Such doctrines are understood to be "a shield, not a sword"—they do not establish rights in one party, but they undermine a complaint of the other party. They are often framed in terms of what the plaintiff "cannot be heard to say."

Focus on the doctrine of unclean hands, which is captured by the maxim, "Those who seek equity must come with clean hands." In operation, this means that one who has acted wrongly may have their complaint dismissed, regardless of their rights.[25] The standing to complain comes apart from the underlying rights.[26] To get the flavor, consider a high-profile modern attempt to invoke the doctrine. In 2008, the artist Shepard Fairey created the iconic "Hope" poster of then–presidential candidate Barack Obama using an image he found online. As it turned out, this was an Associated Press (AP) photograph. Although the poster had originally been created primarily to help the Obama campaign, Fairey began earning significant royalties. When the AP learned that Fairey had used its image to create the poster, the AP sued, alleging that Fairey's use of the photograph without obtaining a license violated its copyright. Among the replies in Fairey's countersuit, Fairey argued unclean hands. Fairey cited dozens of examples of the AP copyrighting and profiting from photographs of artists' work, including his own, without obtaining licenses.[27] In making this argument, Fairey was not alleging his own compliance with copyright law (although he did separately maintain that also). The point of the argument is that, even if the AP had rights to the Obama photograph that were violated by the poster, the AP had no standing to complain. The argument was not aimed at absolving Fairey's conduct, but at showing that the AP had no legitimate grievance.[28]

140   WRONGS AND RIGHTS COME APART

If one believes that the normativity of rights is bound up with the possibility of complaint, then cases like these will look perplexing. Saul Smilansky argues that such cases present a deep moral paradox—what he calls "the paradox of moral complaint." Smilansky argues that the paradox arises because there are two basic but conflicting ideas about moral complaints. The first is what has just been discussed: "Morally, a person cannot complain when others treat him or her in ways similar to those in which the complainer freely treats others."[29] But according to Smilansky, this idea conflicts with what he calls the "unconditional nature of some moral standards," the idea that moral standards apply unconditionally such that anyone can be held to them and anyone can complain when they are violated.[30] Smilansky argues that both ideas seem to have a basis in a "legislative" (i.e., Kantian) conception of morality, according to which when one acts, one thereby legislates a principle about the permissibility of one's action.

There is one obvious way out of this paradox: disconnect moral complaint from moral constraint. The moral standards can apply unconditionally to the agent in her deliberation, and yet these moral standards would not necessarily correspond with any ex post complaint. Smilansky notes this possibility but immediately dismisses it because "what this would imply, seems merely to change the paradoxicality rather than to solve it."[31] But what is so paradoxical in this? Smilansky only says (with an exclamation point no less) that this would mean that "it may be impermissible to treat [someone] in a certain way, but if this is done he nevertheless cannot complain!"[32] But that's just to restate the idea, not to offer an argument against it.

The true reason, I take it, that Smilansky balks at a disconnect between moral constraint and moral complaint is that he views such a disconnect to be in tension with the "legislative" conception of morality. Normativity, on this view, involves recognition of something lawlike, so that, when one acts for a reason, one is ratifying a principle for others as well. And thus the reasons that we have for action are the same reasons that others can use to address us. We can't separate moral constraint and moral complaint because the authority of the criminal saying "you cannot do that to me" is the same as the authority of our conscience saying "you cannot do that to him." The individual's standing to complain is equivalent to the authority of morality and the moral community. They rise and fall together.

THE COMPLAINTLESS   141

I think this position conflates individual standing to hold to account and moral standing in the sense of being part of the moral community. Moral reasons plausibly are, by their nature, applied equally to all members of the moral community. One has a kind of standing, then, just in virtue of being a member of the moral community—and even flagrant transgressors are still persons, still rightholders.[33] We do not get permission to torture torturers, and the state is justified in prosecuting both participants in the bar fight, not just the one who throws the first punch. But there is a separate question of what kind of standing—if any—a particular individual has to hold another to account for violations. And it is that individual kind of standing that the norm transgressor loses.[34] Our practices of holding one another to account—both personally and impersonally—may presuppose authoritative moral reasons. But the reasons do not stand and fall with the relevant individual holding one to account. And we can see that by recognizing cases in which the moral reasons are still present even in the absence of the standing to complain.

One might concede some version of this picture and yet argue that the case of the complaintless transgressor does not illustrate any divergence between what we owe to individuals as a matter of our deliberation (ex ante) and what we are accountable to them for (ex post). By appealing to the moral community—the thought would go—one is no longer talking about duties owed to the individual. The duty not to punch the guy at the bar or not to torture the torturer is owed not to the individuals but to the community at large. Our duties aren't about rights any longer, but about avoiding lawlessness.[35]

This response does not seem to me to do justice to the obligations that are at play in these cases. The obligation not to punch the guy in the bar is entirely continuous with other moral obligations. The guy, like everyone else, has a right against unnecessary physical violence. He is a person, and you owe it to him not to treat him that way. He may not be able to complain if the right is violated, but that should not be understood to mean that the right has been altogether forfeited, and some other, different principle is needed to explain the wrongness of violence. You have the same kind of reason not to punch him, regardless of whether he can complain.[36] Similarly, even if the AP had unclean hands, it would still have been perfectly coherent for Fairey to seek and obtain their license; they did still have the copyright. So I don't think one can escape by suggesting that the impermissibility in these cases stems from other reasons, not those of rights.

6.3 When All's Well That Ends Well

Moral transgression does not strike me as the only instance in which someone's rights are violated and yet the person has no complaint. A person may also have no complaint because they have nothing to complain about. This can happen when, with the benefit of hindsight, we can see that all has ended well. In that fortuitous circumstance, one doesn't have a complaint—one isn't wronged.

Caution is necessary here because the idea cannot be simply that no harm means no wrong. There can be—as Arthur Ripstein has emphasized—harmless trespasses, situations in which someone is wronged by some interference, even though that interference causes no manifest harm.[37] Ripstein makes out the idea of harmless trespass with examples that are vivid, compelling, and fun. Here is one:

> Suppose that, as you are reading this in your office or in the library, I let myself into your home, using burglary tools that do no damage to your locks, and take a nap in your bed. I make sure everything is clean. I bring hypoallergenic and lint-free pajamas and a hairnet. I put my own sheets and pillowcase down over yours. I do not weigh very much, so the wear and tear on your mattress is nonexistent. By any ordinary understanding of harm, I do you no harm. If I had the same effects on your home in some other way, no one would suppose you had a grievance against me, let alone that you should be able to call the law to your aid. Your objection is to my deed, my trespass against your home, not to its effects. . . . The harm principle cannot provide an adequate account of either the wrong I commit against you or the grounds for criminalizing it.[38]

Ripstein is quite enamored with this type of example.[39] For him, examples like this reveal an important insight into the nature of rights and wrongings. Because the wrong cannot be explained by reference to any harm, it must instead be explained in terms of the unauthorized nature of the action. And this generalizes: wrongs are, at their core, about unauthorized interference.

THE COMPLAINTLESS   143

It is noteworthy how artificial the examples all are—one must introduce hypoallergenic and lint-free pajamas, not to mention (presumably) a lack of discovery.[40] Still, there is little doubt that the examples constitute genuine wrongs. They conjure a clear reaction that the victim has been violated. If the victim discovers the trespass, he could certainly complain against it. And the transgressor—in his hypoallergenic pajamas—could not escape accountability by saying "no harm, no foul."

One might insist that Ripstein's examples are not truly harmless by introducing a more capacious conception of harm.[41] Though plausible, I will not pursue that here. Absent a more complicated understanding of harm, we should grant Ripstein that there are harmless wrongs. And thus we cannot say that someone has no complaint simply because they have not been harmed.

But it does not follow that all trespasses—that is, all violations of rights—constitute wrongings, irrespective of the harm done. Consider a different kind case. Suppose that you are alone in your house when you suffer a terrible fall and are in an extremely painful but not life-threatening position. I hear your cries for help from the road and come to the door. But I find it locked. Moved by your audible pain, I set myself to breaking down the door. Hearing what I am doing, you call out to me, instructing me not to break down the door but instead to go around to the back door. But, wrapped up in being the hero, I do not listen to you, kicking down the door in a glorious burst of splintered wood and broken glass. I am then able to get you to medical professionals, who tell you that your situation really was bad and you could have suffered significant injury.

Have I wronged you in destroying your front door, against your explicit demand? Plausibly yes. This supposed wrong probably pales in comparison to my having saved you. And you might seem ungrateful if you complained about it. But nevertheless, it was your door and your body, and it should have been up to you; I should have listened and complied. In that sense, I have violated your rights in kicking down the door. So maybe I have wronged you, albeit a wrong that should probably be overlooked. The law, for what it's worth, does impose liability for harm carelessly caused in the course of a rescue.[42]

But now add one more fact: when you get home from the hospital, you discover that—unbeknownst to you at the time—the back door had been deadbolted all along. I could never have gotten in that way. Had I desisted and tried the back door, it would only have wasted time. You

144 WRONGS AND RIGHTS COME APART

would have suffered more and then eventually acquiesced to my breaking down the door.

It seems to me that the thing to say, at this point, is that you have no complaint. You simply have not been wronged. It is still true that I violated your rights by kicking down the door. It was, as we have said, your door, your body, and I ought to have proceeded only with your authorization. But as it turns out, you have nothing to complain about. All's well that ends well.[43]

The operative feature of this case is not that the violation turned out to be harmless. It wasn't harmless, and moreover Ripstein's examples show that harmlessness is not sufficient to render a violation not a wrong. The essential feature is also not that you were ultimately benefited; one can wrong a person even while benefiting them if one does so through wrongful means.[44]

Nor, I think, is the essential feature that you lose your standing to complain because of your debt of gratitude.[45] For one thing, that explanation would seem to apply even without the back door being locked. But in my view, the back door having been locked clinches a firmer lack of complaint—there being nothing to complain of. Second, notice that similar cases could arise in which the rights violation does not end up benefiting the recipient (and thereby creating a debt of gratitude) but rather advances some other valuable goal that the rightholder endorses. For example, imagine that I was trying to get into your house not to save you but rather for the urgent need of some stranger, and you were just advising me remotely over the phone. In such a case, it would seem unnatural to explain your eventual lack of complaint in terms of a debt of gratitude. The key thing in either case, it seems to me, is that my action achieved an end that you endorsed (getting into the house) and that, with the benefit of hindsight, you would have endorsed my action as the means to achieve that end. This is the sense in which you have nothing to complain about: in the ex post perspective, you don't wish that I had acted otherwise. So what do you have to complain about?

One might point to so-called normative injury. Isn't there still a wrong that consists in the violation of your authority per se? As a categorical claim, that strikes me as something that only someone driven by theoretical commitments would say. Sometimes the violation of one's authority is an offense in its own right, even if all ends well. A child typically cannot avoid accountability to their parent for, say, taking the car without permission by saying, "But look, Dad, nothing bad happened." (Although query whether the parent is wronged in such cases.) And where there is reason to be on guard about proper respect—such as past interpersonal history or background social inequalities—then the rights violation might per se ground a complaint, even if all ends well. But these seem like special cases—the exceptions that prove the rule.

In the example as I have described it, there's no reason to take offense at the failure to respect your rights as such. And it seems to me that you have nothing to complain about. It's not just that it would be petty for you to complain that I, the good soul who came from the street to answer your calls for help, did not properly respect you; it would be downright wrong-headed to complain. In order to have a complaint, one must have something that answers the question, "What's it to you?" We care about our rights for many good reasons. They can protect us from harm, and they also allow us to govern our lives as we choose. We may just not want strangers sleeping in our bed, no matter how harmlessly. But caring about one's rights per se—even when there is no harm, no frustration of one's ends, no evidence of disrespect, nothing else that answers the question, "What's it to you?"—is a kind of fetishization.[46] There was a right that was violated, but it doesn't generate any ex post relation of accountability.

6.4 Nonhuman Animals

6.4.1 ANIMALS AND COMPLAINTS

Throughout the Middle Ages and as late as the sixteenth century, nonhuman animals were routinely brought to trial. E. P. Evans collects many such cases with fascinating and absurd details. For example, he describes an occasion in which rats were charged with "having feloniously eaten up and wantonly destroyed the barley-crop."[47] Lawyers debated what sort of summons would properly provide notice to the rats and whether they could safely appear in court. Other oddities range from a counselor being appointed to represent slugs that were threatened with excommunication to extensive disputes over whether accused animals should be tried as clergy or laypersons.

To us, these practices seem absurdly misguided. Evans himself described them in quite censorious terms.[48] These prosecutions seem to involve treating animals as persons in a way that is wholly inappropriate—as though they are accountable to us just as our fellow humans are. We humans have the remarkable ability to give and demand justification of each other's actions. We are accountable to each other, and we hold each other to account. And we have legal institutions built on these relations. But for the most part, we cannot relate to nonhuman animals in this way. They cannot give us justification for their actions or recognize our contention that they have acted without justification. We should not expect them to do so. So it seems ludicrous to haul a pack of rats into court.

Just as animals cannot answer the complaints that we make, animals generally cannot address us with complaints in the full normative sense. Of course, as anyone who has spent any time around animals knows, they can express dissatisfaction: they can whine, growl, whimper, struggle, and so on. But they mostly cannot complain in the special way that persons can complain. They cannot engage in a dialogue about how we ought to have acted. In this sense, rats are no more fit to be plaintiffs than defendants.[49]

By saying that nonhuman animals generally lack the capacity to complain, I mean that they cannot form the thought. That should be distinguished from the actual ability to articulate a protest. If I am bound and gagged such that I am prevented from any expressive action, this does not mean that I lack the capacity to complain in the normative sense. I am capable of thinking the complaint, even if my circumstances prevent its expression. So when I say that nonhuman animals lack the capacity to complain, I do not simply mean that they lack the language abilities to address complaints. Of course, their lack of our language doesn't help, but I mean that they cannot complain in the sense that they do not share our conceptual framework.[50]

In *Fellow Creatures,* Christine Korsgaard describes "two . . . different possible forms of cognition."[51] In one form, creatures have aims—they regard certain things as good or bad for them—and they act in order to achieve these aims. Such cognition includes valuing, and it can also include a great deal of intelligence and awareness. But we can distinguish this form of cognition from what Korsgaard calls "rationality" or "normative self-government." This second form of cognition involves not just there being reasons for one's action but the conscious reflection on, and choice of, those reasons.[52] Normative self-government enables the evaluation of reasons—deciding what does or does not count as a good reason, what does or does not justify an action. As Korsgaard puts it, "We human beings, unlike the other animals, think of ourselves and our lives in normative terms."[53]

Of course, this is a general categorization, and there will be some intermediate cases and variation. But I share Korsgaard's belief that there is, generally speaking, an important distinction to be drawn here, and that it roughly captures a division between human cognition and that of most other animals.[54] (Though some animals—most pointedly the great apes but perhaps many others as well—may fall closer to our side of the spectrum.)[55]

This rough distinction between merely acting in pursuit of ends and normative self-government illuminates the sense in which nonhuman animals generally lack the capacity to complain. Even if nonhuman animals could express all their thinking to us, they would probably not express something of the form "you *ought* not do that to me" (where the "ought" here is meant in a normative and not predictive sense). They cannot complain, then, insofar as they cannot question our *justification* for our actions. Making a complaint or holding accountable requires the ability to understand and think about action in normative terms—that is, as based on reasons. Nonhuman animals might think our actions bad in the sense of disagreeable, but they cannot evaluate or engage with our reasons.[56] And as such, animals cannot complain in the sense of judging our actions to be unjustified—the sort of understanding that undergirds a reactive attitude like resentment. They cannot address us with that kind of complaint.

Of course, as I have already noted, animals are capable of addressing us—even addressing us with what might be casually described as a complaint. If I am eating a particularly good-smelling bit of cheese and my dog is in a feisty mood, she might whine or bark, which seems an awful lot like a complaint that she isn't getting a share. If I stop rubbing her belly, she will invariably paw at me to continue. These sorts of behaviors are a testament to the way that nonhuman animals, especially domesticated ones, are capable of expressing themselves to us. And among the things that they can express are ideas like, "I don't like that," or imperatives like, "Don't stop!"

But if what I have said is correct, there is still something that a dog mostly cannot do—question or appreciate whether our actions are justified or unjustified.[57] It seems to me that we are quite aware of this inability. It is what produces the distinct sort of regret we feel for causing even justified discomfort to animals. We know that our animals cannot understand that there is a good reason for spaying them, or giving them vaccination shots, or caging them for their own safety. We cannot explain to them why we have built a road through their home or trapped and relocated them, even on the occasions when such actions are justifiable. Even relatively young children can be offered reasons (or the assurance that reasons exist) for the unpleasant things that we put them through, but nonhuman animals cannot.

There is thus an important relation that we—tragically in a way—generally cannot have with nonhuman animals. We cannot act toward them in ways that are justifiable or unjustifiable *to them;* we cannot stand in relationships of justification with them. When we harm them, there is a sense in which there is nothing that we can do. We can, of course, utter words of apology or perform acts of penitence, but we cannot truly engage with them in the relationship of apology and forgiveness. With animals, though we can rebuild trust, we can never truly be forgiven. Something like this, I think, explains why nonhuman animals are experienced as "innocent" and why their suffering can cause a distinctive sort of distress.[58] They are complaintless.

But do we not wrong animals? Given the immense cruelty and unfeeling indifference with which we treat the other animals, when the question is posed in that way, it would be misguided to say that we do not wrong them. There is a sense of "wrong" that marks out violations or captures any kind of wrongful treatment, and goodness knows we treat the animals wrongfully. So if the choice is between saying that we do or do not wrong them, we must say that we do; we cannot absolve our conduct toward them. But at the same time, it seems to me more accurate to say that the question is poorly formed—that it is asking about a predicate that does not precisely apply here. The relationship of wronging—that of having a valid complaint against—seems inapt for our relationships with animals.[59] For the most part, we can stand to them in the relationship of one who has harmed and one who has been harmed, but not exactly in the relationship of one who has wronged and one who has been wronged.[60] They just lack the capacity to relate in that way. Consider how natural it is to explain certain human matters by way of a fact about wronging—for example, "She behaves in that way because she has been wronged." With an animal, we are unlikely to offer such an explanation—we say, instead, that "she has been mistreated" or "she has been abused." The concept of wronging is, we appreciate, unfitting. Though animals *suffer* like we do—often, just like we do, and at our hands—they do not exactly suffer *wrongs* like we do. The concept just does not fully and perspicuously apply.

6.4.2 ANIMALS AND RIGHTS

Although nonhuman animals cannot complain against our actions, we can and do owe duties to nonhuman animals (and do not merely have duties regarding them). Put another way, nonhuman animals have rights, even though they are unable to hold us accountable. Insofar as this is true, it presents a problem for the view that directed duties are bound up with the capacity to hold accountable.

But why think that nonhuman animals can be owed duties, can be the bearers of rights? After all, there is a plausible conception of what it is to be owed an obligation that says that it involves a party who stands to be wronged. If animals cannot complain in that way, it might look like our duties concerning persons are relational in a way that our duties concerning animals are not. As T. M. Scanlon puts it, "If we have reason to care about the justifiability of our actions to other rational creatures, but not to nonrational ones, then our actions toward them are governed by a further class of reasons."[61] This view need not be callous. Such a view can acknowledge that we have reasons and duties—perhaps very strong reasons and duties— not to treat nonhuman animals badly.[62] But these reasons would not be the stuff of rights, of relational normativity, of what we owe them.

Note, at the outset, something peculiar about the idea that animals cannot be owed duties because they cannot enter into relationships of justification and accountability. The argument purports to say something about how we ought to act toward other creatures based on how those creatures are capable of responding to or viewing those actions once they have been performed. What we owe, going forward, is taken to depend on how it would be viewed in retrospect. But why think that what is owed prospectively depends on the capacity to view matters in a particular way retrospectively?[63] Suppose, albeit quite fancifully, that there were a human with the complete inability to remember—or even form thoughts about— anything that has happened in the past, even the immediate past.[64] Such a person, by virtue of this cognitive disability, would not be capable of making complaints or holding us accountable. But we should not infer that there cannot be obligations owed to such a person. Undoubtedly, such a person would be incapable of having important relationships with us. But it does not seem to follow that this person could not be the recipient of directed duties, the holder of rights. The sense of "owing" that is bound up with rights seems to concern a prospective orientation—what treatment is required and the character of that requirement, not how or whether we will be held accountable.

I am confident that, though they are complaintless, animals are owed duties and have rights. And not in some lesser fashion than you or I. In what follows, I will point to four features of our relations with animals that suggest that they have rights in a full sense—that our duties with respect to nonhuman animals have features characteristic of rights.[65]

First, the moral phenomenology of our relations with nonhuman animals is that of owing duties *to them,* not merely about them. Unlike beautiful art or untamed wilderness—objects that might have intrinsic value sufficient to generate reasons to treat them in various ways—we see in nonhuman animals that they are other creatures. They have a stake in how we treat them, but beyond that (for that is true of plants as well), we see them as other beings. We can look into an animal's eyes and know that it is looking back at us.[66] There is a consciousness—a perspective on the world, a "thou"—to whom what we do will matter.

A story from biologist Marc Bekoff suggests this moral pull penetrates even the most sanitized empirical settings:

> A doctoral research project I was once involved in required us to kill the cats we were studying. However, when I got "Speedo," a very intelligent cat that I'd secretly named—secretly, because we weren't supposed to name "subjects"—for the final exit from his cage, his fearlessness disappeared as if he knew that this was his last journey. As I picked him up, he looked at me and asked, "Why me?" Tears came to my eyes. He wouldn't break his piercing stare. Though I followed through with what I was supposed to do and killed him, it broke my heart to do so. To this day I remember his unwavering eyes—they told the whole story of the interminable pain and indignity he had endured.[67]

What one sees in the eyes of an animal—"the fierce green fire," as Aldo Leopold famously described it[68]—is not inanimate or passive or impersonal. I may recognize beauty in a work of art that I am about to destroy and suddenly conclude that it is inappropriate to destroy it. To arrive at this conclusion is to see a value in the world that gives me a reason for action. But to see the emotion in an animal's eyes is more than this. It is to see another being engaged in the struggle of living.

In this way, animals are not merely the impersonal loci of value (pleasure) and disvalue (pain). As Bekoff put it, it is not merely pain but also "indignity" that the animal's eyes make a claim against. We recognize in animals a moral status demanding respect that is not simply the acknowledgment of empirical qualities like sentience.[69] Raimond Gaita describes an incident in which he considered "putting down" a badly wounded cat by hitting it over the head with a shovel:

> My awareness of the brutishness of what I had intended to do to Tosca had nothing to do with my estimate of whether it would have been painful for her. I assumed that if I had hit her with sufficient force I would not have caused her pain. Our attention, when we think about these matters, is too easily drawn to what the animal will feel and we think too little of what our actions mean. We think about the pain we will cause but not the dishonor we will inflict. To see the difference one need only reflect on how desperate the circumstances would have to be before one would consider killing a human being by crashing a shovel onto her head, and how terrible it would be to do it no matter what the circumstances and no matter whether one thought (rightly or wrongly) that they justified it. . . . Was I wrong to intend to kill Tosca that way? I think I was. . . . [70]

Gaita sees that our duties to nonhuman animals are, at least in part, duties to treat them with respect. As he remarks shortly after the Tosca story, "One day—and it may not be too far away—we may . . . become deeply ashamed of how impoverished our sense was of animal dignity. We may become incredulous that we could ever have left animal corpses on the road to be run over again and again."[71] But the respect Gaita gestures towards is not merely abstract reverence, but rather a sense of recognition. What he owed Tosca was to see her as a fellow mortal. Our duties are inflected by recognizing them as beings with their own perspectives on the world, navigating their lives alongside ours. That gives our duties a phenomenology of directedness.

Second, that nonhuman animals are other creatures also means that they can engage in a kind of proto-claiming and proto-waiver.[72] They cannot, of course, assert or waive their rights as such. But they can display preferences about how they are treated, preferences that may resonate with what we appreciate as our duties. We experience animals as consenting to our touch or demanding the delicious cheese. Admittedly, these are not consent and demands in the conscious, normatively robust sense. But the fact that we experience them as consent or as a demand implies that we see our duties as having the same directed quality—and the animal as potentially rights-bearing. The animal doesn't merely have interests but exerts a kind of authority over how we may permissibly treat them.

A third reason for thinking that nonhuman animals have rights is given by the deontic character of our duties. Our duties with respect to nonhuman animals, like our duties to each other, seem to be subject to distinctive constraints against aggregation and trading off.[73] Such constraints reflect the directedness of duties. That I cannot take your organs and distribute them in order to prevent the death of five other people reflects the fact that I owe something to you particularly, and not merely to the world generally.

Our relations with animals seem to have this deontic character. It would be wrong, I think, to kill one healthy dog in order to distribute its organs to five other dogs. Most would agree that the wrongness of dogfighting does not depend on the amount of human entertainment that it provides. Suppose that one could run a dogfighting operation the profits from which would be sufficient for one to save many more dogs from abandonment, disease, starvation, or euthanasia in shelters. A small number of dogs would face suffering and death in the dogfighting ring, but far more dogs would be saved. I believe that such actions would still be impermissible.[74] These intuitions strongly suggest that we have duties that are owed to the particular dogs that would suffer—by being made the innocent canine organ donor or the innocent charity pit dog. The considerations of aggregate welfare are excluded, trumped, subject to a side constraint. That is, the animal has a right against such use.

Fourth and finally, at least some of the time, we view it as permissible to enforce coercively the duties that are owed to nonhuman animals. When we enforce these duties, we view ourselves as acting on behalf of the animals in a sense that goes beyond merely acting for their benefit—we see ourselves as defending their rights.

In general, it is not our place to intervene against others just because they act wrongly. Someone may squander their talents or resources such that they are clearly acting in ways in which they ought not, and yet their doing so will not warrant coercive intervention. For example, if an artist chooses to destroy his work even though its artistic value means that he ought to share it with the world, I am not permitted to take the art away and stop him. Coercion requires something more.

Our obligations to animals, however, seem to include this additional something. If the artist were torturing his cat, then it would be permissible for us to intervene and remove the cat from his possession. In fact, although our legal regime is otherwise quite stingy in its recognition of nonhuman animals, anticruelty statutes have long afforded nonhuman animals a set of rights (albeit quite narrow and substantially underenforced). Not only public authorities but even private persons may plausibly use force to protect animals sometimes—like stopping the cat from getting tortured. That's not being a busybody; it is instead acting in defense of another.[75] Reflecting this public sentiment, a wide range of jurisdictions have recently adopted so-called hot car laws, which provide civil immunity to private citizens for certain interventions on behalf of animals in distress (e.g., breaking into a car to save an animal at risk of overheating).[76] The permissibility of intervention—especially private intervention—in these cases only makes sense if we think the animal has a right at risk of being violated. We don't let people go around trespassing and destroying other people's property in the name of enforcing undirected duties. But here the intervention is warranted insofar as it is protecting rights—not merely ensuring another's general rule compliance. It thus seems like we all—even conservative state legislatures across America—have some inchoate sense that animals have rights of their own.

6.4.3 TRUSTEES FOR THE COMPLAINTLESS

I have been arguing that nonhuman animals have rights, even though they are complaintless. They show how we can owe a duty to another party even where the party would not have a complaint if the duty were violated. If this is correct, then it presents a problem for theories that tie rights or relational normativity to complaint or demands for justification.

The point at the end of the previous section—that we can act on behalf of the rights of nonhuman animals—suggests a possible response. Although nonhuman animals cannot complain or demand justification, perhaps our owing them directed duties can be captured by the fact that we could complain or demand justification on their behalf. Scanlon suggests, without full endorsement, this possible response for contractualism: "A contractualist view can accommodate this intuition [that obligations are owed to animals] if it holds that in deciding which principles could not reasonably be rejected we must take into account objections that could be raised by trustees representing creatures in this group who themselves lack the capacity to assess reasons."[77] Darwall makes a similarly noncommittal suggestion of this approach: "Although I am bound to insist that moral obligation, like the concept of a right, cannot be understood independently of authoritative demands, the thought that moral obligations can be owed to beings who lack second-personal competence might be able to be elaborated in terms of trustees' (for example, the moral community's) authority to demand certain treatment on their behalf (perhaps also to claim certain rights, compensation, and so on, for them). Thus, Dr. Seuss's character the Lorax (a free and rational being) declares, 'I speak for the trees.'"[78] Having trustees to make the legal complaints on behalf of animals is also suggested as a way forward for the awkward legal status that nonhuman animals are currently afforded.[79]

There is something appealing in this trustee model. One might try to put it this way: Nonhuman animals—unlike norm transgressors or those for whom all ends well—do have a complaint; they just don't know anything about it. Theirs is not a problem of standing but a problem of capacity. So, the thought goes, someone else can exercise their standing for them.

But what does it mean to say that animals have the standing to complain or demand justification but they merely lack the capacity? It cannot mean that animals could make complaints against us if they were capable of making complaints. That looks like a tautology: they could if they could. If maple trees were capable of complaining, then couldn't they have a complaint against being tapped? Heck, if my car could address me, might it not object when I miss an oil change?

The better, nontautological way to understand the idea requires seeing two different meanings of "could"—one of standing and one of capacity. When we say that the cat "could" complain against being tortured if it had the capacity, we mean to be saying that we owe it to the cat not to torture it. The cat has rights. In contrast, we don't owe anything to cars—though we may have duties concerning cars. What we are saying, then, in saying that a cat could complain if it had the capacity is merely that the cat has a certain status in our moral community.

There is nothing incoherent in that. Indeed, it makes good sense for contractualism, which is concerned with finding a set of rules to govern our moral community. The "reasonable rejection" in contractualism is all

THE COMPLAINTLESS   155

basically hypothetical anyway. To the extent that nonhuman animals have an individual perspective on the world, then their hypothetical voice might matter in contractualist reasoning.[80] Their imagined complaints would be used as a schematic to capture a kind of moral status—to think about how we should treat them, what we owe them.

But that is quite different from saying that rights are bound up with standing to complain or to demand justification in any individual, actual sense. What we see in nonhuman animals, I think, are creatures to whom we owe duties, where that is wholly disconnected from their being able to hold us accountable. If you were to look into the eyes of a dog gasping for breath in a rapidly overheating car, the felt duty would have nothing to do with a sense that the dog would hold you to blame. It's true that you might hold yourself to blame, but that's just because the dog has moral status—is a fellow mortal—and you owe it to her to try to save her. It's about standing in the moral community.[81]

6.5 Offensive Associations

There's something potentially offensive in the grouping of this chapter, and I want to close with a few remarks about that. At the beginning of the chapter, I quoted Jeffrie Murphy arguing that the psychopath cannot be wronged. Murphy goes on to argue that the psychopath is "more profitably pictured—from the moral point of view—as an *animal*."[82] As he puts it, "The psychopath, by his failure to care about his own moral responsibilities, his failure to accept them even if he recognizes them, becomes morally dead—an animal rather than a person." This is a philosophical endorsement of a standard bit of rhetoric: it is frequently said of those criminals viewed as particularly bad that they are "animals."

This comparison is unfair and offensive—in both directions. The suggestion that criminals should not be treated as fellow humans is offensive. And it can become an excuse to indulge some of our own worst instincts—tribalism, prejudice, and revenge. One can equally say that using "animal" as a pejorative to mean subhuman is offensive and unfair to animals. Despite their innocence, animals are made exemplars of moral debasement and exclusion from the moral community.

This chapter might seem to endorse the comparison by grouping the cases together. To make matters worse, I've also included people who are not hurt at all, materially or normatively. This might seem to bolster yet another set of unfair ideas: namely that criminals are better off being punished, and that nonhuman animals don't suffer.

Of course, I believe none of these things. But if what I have argued is correct, then we can see one truth in the comparisons without endorsing any of the callousness. Moral transgressors, the fortunately unharmed, and nonhuman animals are all, in different ways, without the ability to call us to account for our actions—to expect or demand that we stand in relations of mutual justifiability with them. Transgressors lack the moral authority to complain; when all ends well, there's no basis for complaint; and animals, by their very nature, are incapable of complaining. These are very different kinds of disabilities. But they are similar insofar as they are all beyond mere physical inability. In each case, there is no possibility of a complaint. And in this sense, the victims do not suffer wrongs when they suffer mistreatment.

But it need not follow that we do not owe duties to transgressors, to the fortunately unharmed, or to animals. Indeed, I have argued that they all do have rights, not merely that there are duties concerning them. So the psychopath and the nonhuman animal are similar, but not, as Murphy would have it, because both are utterly without rights. They both have rights. What they lack is the possibility of complaint.

7

Preemptive Forgiving

This chapter defends the possibility of preemptively forgiving. That is, I defend the claim that one can forgive an action before the action has taken place. Forgiving need not be retrospective. I suspect that some—perhaps many—readers will initially balk at this idea. There is a rich philosophical literature on the nature of forgiveness, and it has almost always assumed that forgiving occurs exclusively in response to past actions of others. But I will argue that forgiving need not be retrospective, that this is a coherent, a perhaps even familiar, moral possibility.

Of course, it is hardly controversial that, in some circumstances, people can prospectively alter the normative status of another person's action, relieving that person of being blamed for the action. Granting permission or consent can, in the right circumstances, make another person's action permissible where it otherwise would have been impermissible. So there is nothing foreign about a person releasing another prospectively.

My claim, however, is that, before an action is performed, it may be possible to forgive the action in question without thereby granting permission or consent. In other words, I will argue that, in at least some circumstances, one can do something before another person acts that releases that person from one's censure without, at the same time, releasing her from the duty that she owes. The possibility of preemptively forgiving illuminates the gap between ex ante directed duties and ex post accountability. Preemptive forgiving suggests that one can waive one's complaint—one's standing to hold another accountable—without necessarily waiving the relevant duties that one is owed.

The chapter proceeds in three sections. Section 7.1 examines what I take to be the two basic arguments against the possibility of preemptively forgiving. One argument focuses on the connection between forgiving and granting permission, the other on the connection between forgiving and emotion. I begin with in-depth explication of these arguments because, if preemptive forgiving is possible, then much can be learned from turning these arguments on their heads. As in Chapter 4, *modus ponens* becomes *modus tollens*. Section 7.2 consists of my argument that preemptive forgiving is possible. I offer a series of examples and arguments to suggest that preemptive forgiving can occur without collapsing into a grant of permission. I then reject the reply that these apparent instances of preemptive forgiving are actually instances of promising to forgive in the future. Section 7.3 completes the argument, drawing the implications that preemptive forgiving holds for distinguishing complaints from claims, wrongings from rights.

7.1 The Arguments against Preemptive Forgiving

Forgiving typically happens ex post. Philosophical accounts of forgiveness often assume that this is a necessary feature of forgiving—that forgiving can only occur after the act that is forgiven. The following statement from H. J. N. Horsburgh is representative: "There can be no question of forgiveness unless an injury has been inflicted on somebody by a moral agent. There must be something to forgive."[1] But this explanation is insufficient unless it is coupled with some reason for thinking that future actions cannot be part of our metaphysics. Certainly there must be something to forgive, but why can't the something be something that hasn't happened yet?

Ultimately, I mean to argue that we can forgive an action that is yet to be performed. The main argument for this claim, however, does not come until the next section of the chapter. I forgive (now) the impatient reader who wishes (in the future) to skip ahead to that part of the chapter. Before turning to examples of preemptive forgiving, however, I want to discuss the arguments for the idea that forgiving is necessarily retrospective.

7.1.1 FORGIVING AND PERMISSION

There is an argument—what I will call the *First Argument against Preemptive Forgiving*—that, if pressed, I believe many philosophers would be inclined to endorse. David Londey offers a particularly nice articulation of the basic idea:

PREEMPTIVE FORGIVING

> Forgiving someone for something is quite a complex act, as can be seen from the fact that the utterance "I forgive you for doing A" only has its full intended illocutionary force if a number of conditions are satisfied. In the first place, it must be the case that you have already done A—I cannot forgive you for what you have not done (although I can either predict that I shall forgive you if you do A, or give you permission to do it, thus removing any question of having to forgive you for it in the future).[2]

The thought here is that forgiving must occur ex post because anything beforehand would be something other than forgiveness—perhaps permission or prediction.

The argument purports to stem from the nature of our moral concepts. The claim is not merely that, as a contingent and empirical matter, acts of forgiving come after the wrongful acts that they reference. Rather, it is the conceptual claim that an act cannot be an act of forgiving if it precedes the wrongful act that it references.

Why think that forgiving is necessarily retrospective? The thought—exemplified by Londey—is that forgiving would cease to be forgiving if it occurred beforehand. Prospective forgiving is impossible because that conceptual space is already occupied by other forms of interpersonal address. In particular, prospective address with normative (rather than predictive) content would collapse into granting permission. The thought is that forgiving operates as a form of release, but releasing someone beforehand would constitute granting permission, not forgiveness. Preemptive forgiving is supplanted by granting permission.[3]

The connection between granting permission and forgiving is natural. Both, it seems, can be performatives.[4] Both involve changing one's relationship with another by virtue of some expression. When I say, "I grant you my permission to ϕ," under the proper conditions, that utterance changes what is permissible for you to do. That is, saying it makes the world different; it is not merely reportive. Similarly, when I say, "I forgive you for ϕ-ing," under the proper conditions, that utterance makes things different between us. It alters our moral relationship.

Not only are forgiving and granting permission both performatives; they both appear to effect somewhat similar alterations in the moral landscape. Both, for example, can sometimes be accomplished by saying, "It's okay."

160   WRONGS AND RIGHTS COME APART

They share an element of moral release. From the recipient's perspective, permission operates to release one from a duty. From the speaker's perspective, permission operates to waive one's right or claim. For example, if I grant you permission to draw water from my well, then I have waived my right to exclude you from the well and you have been released from your duty not to take water from the well.

Forgiving can also be viewed as a release. Again, this can be seen from the perspective of either the recipient or the speaker. From the recipient's perspective, forgiveness operates as a release from a moral debt. One is released from being any longer held to account morally for a wrong. Symmetrically, from the speaker's perspective, forgiving involves giving up some form of holding the other person accountable. Famously, forgiving can be characterized as, in some fashion, relinquishing one's resentment.[5] As Pamela Hieronymi has pointed out, resentment here should not be understood as simply a bare negative emotion from which we try to rid ourselves.[6] Rather, resentment is a judgment-sensitive response to a wrong; it is a complaint or a protest against one's treatment.[7] To forgive, then, is to give up or forsake this protest. For example, if you have injured me by cutting down my apple tree but I forgive you, then I have given up resenting you and you are released from bearing such censure.

So forgiving, like permission, dissolves some moral connective tissue.[8] But even granting this similarity, why think that forgiving would *collapse into* permission if it occurred beforehand? Why suppose that preemptive forgiving would offer *the same thing* as permission?

The answer is the common assumption that is the subject of this book: the assumption that claims and complaints are flip sides of the same coin. From what has been said so far, forgiving and permission involve different moral releases: granting permission waives a claim-right and releases someone from a duty, whereas forgiving waives a complaint and releases someone from a moral debt. But one might think that rights and directed duties are bound up with complaints and reactive attitudes—different aspects of the same moral connection between persons.

If that's correct, then forgiving and permission do start to look like conceptual siblings. Permission waives a claim and forgiving waives a complaint, but each ultimately dissolves the same underlying connection between agents. The only difference seems to be the temporal context.[9] This idea— that permitting constitutes the prospective analogue of forgiving—is sometimes explicit. For example, Piers Benn argues that one can only forgive on one's own behalf, "much as I can offer someone my own services, but not the services of another without first gaining their permission."[10] Or, to take a less high-brow example, this parallel seems to be presupposed by the slogan, "It is easier to ask for forgiveness than permission."[11] Either way, the idea is that permission and forgiveness are different manifestations of what is ultimately the same normative shift. A similar assumption is often found in legal argument too. For example, in patent cases, courts regularly assert that a nonexclusive license (i.e., granting permission) is equivalent to releasing liability (i.e., waiving a complaint).[12]

These reflections might give the impression that, far from being impossible, preemptive forgiving is possible and familiar—we just call it "granting permission." The final step in the argument involves showing that granting permission cannot count as a form of forgiving. The reason is that forgiving does not make an action permissible. To forgive an action is not to say that what was done was not wrong or not blameworthy.[13] Unlike condoning, which implies that whatever putative wrong has been committed was not objectionable, or excusing, which implies that the actor was not blameworthy for the wrongful act committed, forgiving must retain the view that the action in question was impermissible and blameworthy. "It's okay," in the context of forgiving, does not mean, "It was okay." As Seana Shiffrin puts it, "In response to another's wrong, we have the elective power to forgive, but forgiveness involves, among other things, recognition of a past wrong, not a power to make it the case that a wrong was never a wrong."[14] So granting permission cannot be forgiving's preemptive form.

This is the First Argument in a nutshell: if it were possible, preemptive forgiving would essentially amount to granting permission, but then it would no longer be a form of forgiving at all. For precision, here is a more formal articulation:

(1) *If preemptive forgiving were possible, then it would involve X forgiving Y for ϕing in the future.*
(2) *A person forgives another iff she gives up her standing to complain against the person.*
(3) *Thus, if preemptive forgiving were possible, then it would involve X giving up the standing to complain against Y for ϕing in the future. [From 1 and 2]*

162 WRONGS AND RIGHTS COME APART

(4) *X has a claim/right against Y not to φ only if X would have the standing to complain against Y if Y φs.*

(5) *Thus, if preemptive forgiving were possible, then it would involve X giving up the claim/right that Y not φ. [From 3 and 4]*

(6) *A person grants permission to another to φ iff she gives up her claim/right that that person not φ.*

(7) *Thus, if preemptive forgiving were possible, it would involve X granting permission to Y to φ. [From 5 and 6]*

(8) *Granting permission makes an instance of φing permissible.*

(9) *Forgiving someone for φing does not make an instance of φing permissible.*

(10) *Therefore, preemptive forgiving is not possible. [From 7, 8, and 9]*

The argument turns on important assumptions about the nature of forgiving (2, 9) and the connection between moral concepts (4). If, as I shall argue, this argument is incorrect, then that may shed new light on these assumptions.

7.1.2 FORGIVING AND EMOTION

Before turning to the argument for preemptive forgiving, there is another argument worth discussing. It starts from a different perspective on forgiveness. The First Argument relies on the idea that forgiving, like granting permission, can be a performative. But not everyone accepts that idea. For many, true forgiving consists not in words but in a change of heart.[15] The thought is that "forgiveness is primarily a matter of changing how one feels with respect to a person who has done one injury."[16] Forgiving, then, is not a speech act at all but rather an attitudinal shift. Consider Trudy Govier and Wilhelm Verwoerd:

> "I forgive you" is not a performative in the way that "I promise you" is. If a woman says "I forgive you" to her husband, who has confessed an affair, but then continues to remind him of it, appeal to his unfaithfulness to score points in their domestic battles, and nag him about his comings and goings, all this goes to show that regardless of what she said, she has not forgiven him. The emotional and attitudinal shifts involved in forgiveness occur over time and, in a case of serious wrongdoing, will typically involve considerable reflection and struggle.[17]

There is a shift in attitudes that this woman has not yet adopted. And we might naturally describe this by saying that she has not "truly" forgiven her husband. One might conclude, as Govier and Verwoerd have, that forgiving cannot be accomplished by utterance.

The idea that forgiving requires an attitudinal shift is the basis for the *Second Argument against Preemptive Forgiving*. It runs as follows: forgiving requires relinquishing negative reactive attitudes; one only acquires negative reactive attitudes after an action is performed; therefore, forgiving can only occur after an action is performed. In other words, preemptive forgiving is impossible because one has not yet experienced the wrongdoing and acquired the resentment that forgiving relinquishes. Recall Horsburgh's remark that there "must be something to forgive." The Second Argument gives this thought content by explaining that, if nothing has happened yet, then there is no emotional response to overcome.

There are two important and contestable premises supporting the Second Argument. First, it assumes that forgiving exclusively or principally involves attitudinal changes. That is a strong claim. Acknowledging that forgiving often refers to an attitudinal shift need not mean that there is not also a performative aspect. Some elements or forms of forgiving—some release—might occur without the paradigmatic attitudinal shift. For example, in Govier and Verwoerd's example, the wife's utterance "I forgive you" does effect an important change.[18] After the wife utters this, her continued expressions of resentment become less appropriate.[19] By speaking as she did, the wife surrendered at least some standing to complain or to demand further apologies.[20] Her utterance altered the discursive norms going forward; it changed what it was appropriate for her to do and say.[21] One way to understand this is as something like a promise not to hold the other party to account—"a promise not to use the past against the future."[22] In this way, the expression of forgiveness can function to change what one may and may not do, much like a promise does. Forgiving thus seems to have an outward dimension, irrespective of attitudes, that shapes how we relate to one another.

One might still insist that this is only derivative, the attitudinal shift ultimately being fundamental. For example, immediately after acknowledging that forgiving has both performative and attitudinal aspects, Margaret Holmgren writes, "Viewing forgiveness as a performative puts the cart before the horse. We must first determine whether an *attitude* of forgiveness is an appropriate response to wrongdoing. . . . If we believe that

164 WRONGS AND RIGHTS COME APART

an attitude of forgiveness is morally appropriate in a given situation, but we have not yet managed to overcome our resentment, we will have to decide whether it is better to be honest with the offender or to offer him the peace of mind that he might gain from hearing us say 'I forgive you.'"[23] Holmgren makes it sound like, whatever the illocutionary force of forgiving might be, the attitude of forgiving is conceptually prior. To utter "I forgive you" without the attitudinal shift is not "honest."

This assumption that the attitudinal shift, and not the utterance, constitutes "true" forgiving—an essential premise of the Second Argument—strikes me as severe. It precludes the more neutral position that "either can be considered manifestations of forgiveness and, depending on the circumstances, exercising one of these is not inferior to exercising both."[24] In a range of circumstances, forgiving apart from an attitudinal shift serves important purposes. Sometimes, the speech act will precede changing our attitudes and serve as a first step along the way. We may want our child to say, "I forgive you," then later remind him that he forgave the person whom he is now treating resentfully. On other occasions, the speech act may have important effects in terms of welcoming a person back into a group or community. For example, it may be important to declare that one forgives one's coworker so that others in the office can move on, even if one has not gotten over it oneself. It seems unnatural to claim that instances like these are not real cases of forgiving or are somehow infelicitous forgiving.

The Second Argument also turns on another rather strong premise, namely that reactive attitudes only arise after a wrong act is performed. Of course, that is the paradigmatic case. But it may also be that one sees in advance that a wrong is going to be committed and begins to acquire the negative attitudes beforehand. For a vivid example, consider the following passage from a Kazuo Ishiguro novel, explaining the bloodlust of soon-to-be genocide victims:

> I speak of people at the end of a brutal road. . . . Now comes an invading army of overwhelming size. The fort may hold several days, perhaps even a week or two. But they know in the end they will face their own slaughter. They know the infants they circle in their arms will before long be bloodied toys kicked about like cobbles. . . . They know this is to come, and so must cherish the earlier days of the siege, when the enemy first pay the price for what they will later do. In other words . . . it's vengeance to be relished *in advance* by those not able to take it in its proper place.[25]

PREEMPTIVE FORGIVING · 165

Anticipatory reactive attitudes can be seen in more mundane examples as well. Consider the emotion felt when you see that a driver whom you have watched weaving in and out of traffic is about to cut you off. Sometimes our emotional reactions never arrive first, knowing what's coming. Such anticipatory resentment can make sense, in part, because we resent the fact that the person *would* commit the wrong, which is revealed to us in our anticipation. If a spouse believes that a partner is going to cheat, resentment may be intelligible partly as a response to the lack of trust that has been created, as evidenced in the belief. But that's rarely the whole story. Anticipatory resentment is partly resentment of the future act itself.

As I will argue, I believe that preemptive forgiving is possible and that the Second Argument is false. But this is not to deny its force. One virtue of the Second Argument is that it explains why preemptive forgiving is not paradigmatic forgiving. Even if it is possible, preemptive forgiving will always be, in a way, an imperfect form of forgiving because of how it is situated relative to our emotional responses. Paradigmatic forgiving involves both performative elements and shifts in attitudes—attitudes that paradigmatically arise ex post. Preemptive forgiving does not look like this, and that is philosophically significant.

7.2 Preemptively Giving Up One's Complaint

7.2.1 SOME INITIAL EXAMPLES

Superficially, at least, it looks like we can engage in forgiving one another preemptively. We can say things like, "I forgive you if you do such and such." For example, in Stendahl's *The Red and the Black,* Madame Rênal, fearing that her lover is ending their affair, dramatically writes to him, "I shall never survive our final separation by a single day.... Go! I forgive you if you love me no more.... It is a small thing in my eyes to pay for the happy days that I have just passed in your arms with the price of my life."[26] Madame Rênal appears, at least, to be forgiving her lover for the departure that he has not yet made. Somewhat differently, in a legal context, a contract might state, "I hereby waive my complaints should such and such happen." Ostensibly, locutions like these forsake some entitlement to hold another accountable before the action in question occurs.

But ordinary language is hardly decisive, and one might insist that utterances like these aren't truly examples of forgiving or waiving a complaint. In fact, locutions like these might appear to be ways of granting permission, lending credence to the First Argument. "You won't hear me complain"

166   WRONGS AND RIGHTS COME APART

can be a colloquial way to say, "You have my permission." Reading significance into the difference would be pointless parsing of words. I mean to resist this view.

The case for preemptive forgiving requires not mere linguistic evidence but evidence from the functioning of our ethical practices. Consider an example. Two soldiers are in a foxhole in an advanced position when an explosive device wounds one of them. Although the camp is only a few miles away, the wounded soldier is unable to get up the steep hillside, even with the other soldier's help. They are able to call for assistance, but they are informed that it will be several hours before aid can be dispatched to their location. The unharmed soldier promises that he will stay by the wounded soldier's side until help comes. But after an hour of sitting in the cold rain, the unharmed soldier is visibly shivering and the gunfire is approaching. The wounded soldier says, "I forgive you if you leave me." The soldier leaves.

One might say that the soldier has acted wrongly by leaving. He has broken his promise and abandoned his comrade. Insofar as he has acted wrongly, it is because he has violated the obligations that he owed to his fellow soldier. But how can we make sense of this evaluation in light of the wounded soldier's statement? There cannot be a violation of the soldier's obligations if those obligations were waived. One possible response is to say that the wounded soldier didn't really mean what he said. Although it looked like waiving or forgiving, the statement was merely a ritualistic expression of appreciation or sympathy. This is not implausible and might, in some situations, be the correct interpretation. But it has the disadvantage of refusing to take the wounded soldier's statement at face value. Although he said that he wouldn't hold it against his comrade, it turns out that he can hold it against him.

I want to suggest that there is another possibility: the wounded soldier has waived his future complaints and yet has not released the other soldier from the obligation he owes him. He does not relieve his comrade of his obligation, but he has disclaimed holding him to blame for its violation in the future.[27] This possibility takes the wounded soldier's statement at face value—he forgives the other soldier. But it does not treat that as equivalent to waiving the duty that was owed to him. If one assumes the strong conceptual tie between obligations and complaints, then there are only two possibilities—either the statement had no real moral significance or it was a waiver of the obligations owed to the wounded soldier. My suggestion is

PREEMPTIVE FORGIVING 167

that there is an intermediate option: waiving the complaint but not the obligation.

Lest one get too caught up in one example, consider a second from one of the most oft-told stories in the Western tradition:

> Jesus was troubled in spirit and testified, "Very truly I tell you, one of you is going to betray me." His disciples stared at one another, at a loss to know which of them he meant. One of them, the disciple whom Jesus loved, was reclining next to him. Simon Peter motioned to this disciple and said, "Ask him which one he means." Leaning back against Jesus, he asked him, "Lord, who is it?" Jesus answered, "It is the one to whom I will give this piece of bread when I have dipped it in the dish." Then, dipping the piece of bread, he gave it to Judas, the son of Simon Iscariot. As soon as Judas took the bread, Satan entered into him. So Jesus told him, "What you are about to do, do quickly." But no one at the meal understood why Jesus said this to him.[28]

Although its meaning is the subject of some controversy, Jesus's conduct toward Judas is often read to express something like the statement, "I forgive you for what you are about to do." But Judas's action was still wrong and a sin. Interpreting Jesus as forgiving Judas's betrayal in advance is not taken to imply that he granted permission or that it was any less a betrayal.

Whether or not forgiveness is the correct biblical interpretation is unimportant. Insofar as this interpretation is intelligible, it illustrates a moral possibility. It's conceptually coherent to think that Jesus forgave without granting permission. The story thus provides an example of preemptively waiving one's prerogative to hold another accountable without, at the same time, waiving one's entitlement to be treated justly.

One way to see that the waiver of complaint in these examples does not operate as a waiver of the duty is to consider the evaluation of some other member of the moral community. While the wounded soldier in the first example and Jesus in the second example may both have given up any complaint about the wrongfulness of the act done to them, this would not stop the rest of us from blaming the wrongdoers.[29] Not only could we say that the acts are blameworthy, but, more importantly, we could say that the acts were a violation of duties owed to the other person. Although the wounded

168   WRONGS AND RIGHTS COME APART

soldier may be barred from saying it, the rest of us can say that, in leaving him, the unharmed soldier violates the duty he owed to his wounded companion. And regardless of whether Jesus preemptively forgave him, the rest of us can say that Judas betrayed Jesus—violated his duties to him. If this is correct, then waiving the complaint does not mean the elimination of the directed duty. The right—understood as the Hohfeldian correlate of that directed duty—survives the waiver of the potential complaint.

One thing that the two foregoing examples have in common is that both involve situations in which it would be hard to imagine the mere words making the action permissible. In the foxhole case, it's possible that nothing the wounded soldier might say could truly release the other soldier. The soldier knew the situation when he made the promise, the promise is reinforced by background norms of soldiering, and the wounded soldier is now vulnerable. Similarly, in the Judas story, it seems hard to imagine that anyone can grant permission for—can truly make permissible—a betrayal.

It is probably not a coincidence that preemptive forgiving appears in examples like these. The sense that the rights in these examples are largely unwaivable operates to cancel the conversational implicature between waiving one's complaint and waiving one's right. While normally preemptively waiving a complaint might be understood to imply permission, that implication is blocked in these cases.[30]

Still, I don't believe that unwaivable duties are necessary for preemptive forgiving. The implication can be blocked in other ways—for example, by explicit statement. Suppose a woman promises her down-on-her-luck friend that she will take her on a camping trip. As the weekend approaches, however, the woman receives an invitation to a professional event that might be a prime career opportunity. She explains the situation to her friend, essentially requesting to be released from her promise to go camping that weekend. Imagine the friend responds by saying something like this: "If you want me to let you off the hook, the answer is no. You promised me, and you owe me this. But I can't make you go. If you decide to bail on me, I understand and I forgive you. I know this is a tempting opportunity for you, and we've all been there. So I won't complain or hold it against you." I believe that there is nothing contradictory or incoherent in this. The friend refuses to release the promise, but she nonetheless forgives the prospective breaking of that promise—that is, forsakes the future complaint she would otherwise have. Both these things must be explicitly stated because, other-

PREEMPTIVE FORGIVING

wise, the one might imply the negation of the other. But this implication can be blocked by explicit disavowal.

7.2.2 PREEMPTIVE FORGIVING'S FUNCTIONS

Even if these examples suggest that preemptive forgiving might, theoretically, be possible, one might wonder what purpose it could serve. Resistance to the phenomenon might be partly based on the sense that it can have little function and is therefore at best anomalous. In this section, I want to explore the possible motivations for preemptively forgiving. I hope to suggest that there are actually a wide variety of contexts in which preemptive forgiving may serve a valuable function.

First, preemptive forgiving may arise where granting permission is impossible. As already noted, one way that this can happen is if the right in question cannot be waived. Consider the following passage from Herbert Morris:

> It is only each person himself that can have his choices respected. It is no more possible to transfer this right than it is to transfer one's right to life. . . . If without our permission, without our choosing it, someone used us as a shield, we may, I should suppose, forgive the person for treating us as an object. But we do not thereby waive our right to be treated as a person, for that is a right that has been infringed and what we have at most done is put ourselves in a position where it is inappropriate any longer to exercise the right to complain.[31]

Morris's claim here is that there is an inalienable right to have one's choices respected. The inalienability is demonstrated by the fact that the most one can do is forgive or, as he puts it, put ourselves in a position where we can no longer complain. Another way that granting permission may be impossible is if permission is not one's to give. In some cases, third parties have standing to forgive—like the parent after their child is harmed.[32] In such cases, a party will not be in a position to grant permission and preemptive forgiving will be all that is available. For example, imagine that a divorced parent recognizes that the other parent is on the verge of ducking out of their children's lives. That parent could not give permission insofar as the duty is owed to the children. But the parent might, I think, say something like, "I forgive you if you abandon them" (assuming that abandonment is not simply unforgivable). Here, again, the possibility of preemptive forgiving makes sense because granting permission does not seem possible.

Second, preemptive forgiving may make sense when one anticipates that forgiving ex post will not be possible. The vivid case arises when one anticipates death. When, for example, the wrong countenanced is one's own killing, then preemptive forgiving is the only option.[33] But one might anticipate being unable to forgive afterward for less dramatic reasons. One might know that one will be beyond communication, or one may worry that one will forget the transgression so completely that one would forget to forgive. Particularly interesting cases, I think, arise when one anticipates being unwilling to forgive ex post. Suppose that you see your beloved child poised to do you a severe wrong. Knowing yourself prone to holding grudges excessively, you fear that, once the wrong is committed, you will be unable to bring yourself to forgive. But at present—before the sting of the injury has been felt—you want to express your present stance toward the wrongdoing as, though wrong, not destroying your relationship. Like the person who anticipates death, you want now to forgive out of a fear that you will be unable to do so later.

Third, preemptive forgiving may be a useful mechanism for avoiding conflict.[34] One may have a coworker or neighbor who one sees is set on committing a wrong. The resulting tension might be undesirable—because it is awkward or because it would require a waste of energy. Forswearing resentment in advance may be a means to defuse the tension before it arises. This function may be particularly important where there are conflicting understandings of the relevant norms. I forgive you if you parody my god, not because I think it permissible but because I recognize that your beliefs are quite different from mine.

A related fourth possibility is that preemptive forgiving may serve as a token of goodwill. A poetic example can be found in one telling of the Scottish story "The Lovers of Gudrun." One man says to the old friend with whom he is now in conflict, "Let us never forget . . . the joyous days of old and the love that knit us together. Let us forgive whatever ill the one may have done to the other—yea, let us forgive beforehand whatsoever of wrong may yet fall out between us—so that our love may be remembered of men and not the strife into which we are surely drifting."[35] Here, preemptive forgiving is viewed as a way to express goodwill for the purpose of mending a friendship. But the gesture might be equally used to build, not just rebuild, a relationship.

PREEMPTIVE FORGIVING

Fifth, preemptive forgiving may function compassionately to relieve the burdens on a wrongdoer in anticipation of a wrong. We may, in certain circumstances, want to relieve the transgressor from some of the burdens—like guilt or punishment—that he or she will feel in facing a difficult choice. For example, imagine that you have been helping a friend battle addiction. You see that she is in danger of using again, but that she is deeply pained by the guilt of letting you down. The guilt associated with her backsliding may be, one can imagine, as destructive as the substance abuse itself. Wishing to mitigate the damage, you may want to express the fact that you forgive her for what she is going to do, even though you do not condone it. Something similar, I think, motivated the Obama administration's decision to announce that they would no longer prosecute families that negotiate with kidnappers. This announcement did not make negotiating permissible—the legal prohibition was retained—but it did acknowledge that the government would no longer hold people accountable for violations. Preemptive forgiving, in these cases, serves as compassionate relief to avoid compounding the harm of an inevitable transgression.[36]

Relatedly, a sixth purpose for preemptive forgiving arises when someone is excessively concerned with avoiding committing a wrong. Although inadequate attention is more common, occasionally people are overly concerned about avoiding wrongs. When this is the case, preemptive forgiving may help someone to apply the appropriate level of care. For example, imagine that an experienced actor and a novice are rehearsing a love scene involving various forms of physical contact. The novice is extremely tentative, afraid of clumsily touching the other actor inappropriately. Seeing that this fear is undermining the scene, the experienced actor might tell the struggling novice that the actor forgives any inappropriate touching that might inadvertently occur.[37] This is not permission to grope; it does not make inappropriate touching appropriate. But it may help to alleviate the excessive caution that is undermining the scene. Only by relieving future blame can they engage in the shared activity successfully. Liability waivers, as I'll discuss momentarily, can also serve something like this function.

Of course, liability waivers are not always a mechanism for enabling joint activity unhindered by fear of liability. Sometimes they are a negotiated concession, and this suggests a seventh purpose that preemptive forgiving may serve. I may agree to forgive you for the bad thing that you are contemplating only in exchange for something from you or from someone else. Negotiated forgiveness is familiar in political contexts, but something

172   WRONGS AND RIGHTS COME APART

similar happens even in interpersonal cases. One can agree to forgive because one is getting something in return.

Eighth, preemptive forgiving may be a way to avoid hypocrisy. In the camping trip example, the self-deprecating statement, "We've all been there," helps makes sense of the friend's preemptive forgiving. It helps the listener understand how the speaker can, on the one hand, insist on the existence of the duty and yet, on the other hand, forgive its transgression before it has even occurred—or, put another way, how she can retain her claim even while forsaking any future complaint. Perhaps some self-deprecation—a recognition of one's own sins or a recognition of one's own luck in not sinning—is at the root of all acts of forgiving.[38] Even if it is not, preemptively waiving one's complaint may be an acknowledgment that one would not have standing to complain against some particular wrong.

Finally, preemptive forgiving may serve an important function where a conflict exists between *pro tanto* obligations. By preemptively forgiving, I may acknowledge that another person has an all-things-considered duty to do something that the person has a *pro tanto* obligation to me not to do. For example, suppose that you have mistakenly made two conflicting promises about what you will do on Saturday. Recognizing that your promise to take your mother to the doctor is more important than your promise to meet me for lunch, I might tell you that I forgive you if you have to cancel. That need not be a present release of your promissory duty. As described, you still have a duty to me to try, if possible, to make it to lunch (e.g., if the doctor cancels). Forgiving here functions as an acknowledgment that you now face other competing obligations, may breach, and are forgiven if you do.

As many of these examples suggest, preemptive forgiving may offer only an imperfect response to nonideal circumstances. But this should not lead us to say that these are not truly instances of forgiving. Something meaningful occurs. Preemptive forgiving—even where the forgiving is not paradigmatic and comprehensive—serves important functions in our interpersonal lives, nonideal as they often are.

7.2.3 PREEMPTIVE FORGIVING VERSUS PROMISING TO FORGIVE

There is an important reply to consider at this point. In the face of the foregoing examples, a skeptic might attempt to recharacterize them as promises to forgive in the future. That is, one might insist that presently waiving one's future complaint or resentment is impossible, seeing instead only promises not to complain or resent. This response avoids detaching rights from the standing to complain. The person doesn't lose his or her standing to complain. When the violation occurs, the person still *has* the complaint, but she has promised not to avail herself of it. One might bolster this response by noting that, in the law, people frequently make promises to hold others harmless—that is, covenants not to sue—and that such promises seem to be our way of waiving an unformed future complaint. I wish to make several points about this response.

First and most importantly, this response strikes me as simply unable to explain our moral experience adequately. The response implies that forgiving requires that something be done in the future, even if that is just refraining from holding the other person accountable; what I have been calling preemptive forgiving is merely a prologue to the actual forgiving. But this interpretation seems implausible when one imagines that the future action is, or becomes, unavailable. Suppose that the wounded soldier says, "I forgive you if you leave me," and then loses consciousness. Minutes later, as gunfire approaches, the unharmed soldier leaves. Through binoculars from a safe distance away, the soldier sees his wounded comrade struck by an explosion and killed, having never regained consciousness. According to my view, the wounded soldier already forgave the act of leaving. But the promise-to-forgive response would say that he only promised to forgive it, and now he is dead. We can imagine this difference mattering if the surviving soldier is plagued by the question of whether his friend forgave him.[39] I see no reason to say that the forgiveness was inadequate or incomplete.[40] So even if there are some cases that should be interpreted as promises to forgive, I do not believe that all can be.

Second, this response is somewhat unstable. When one tries to spell out the idea of a promise to forgive, it seems to collapse into either preemptive forgiving or a promise that one cannot give. Consider first how it might collapse into preemptive forgiving. Recall that, according to certain views, performative forgiving is basically like promising. Forgiving can be understood, more or less, as a promise not to hold a past wrong against the wrongdoer. If that's right, then a promise to forgive would be a promise to make a promise in the future. Now, that's a weird structure. In certain instances—for example, land purchases and wedding engagements—we do promise, contingent on certain conditions, to make a promise. But if I say, without any conditions, "I promise you that tomorrow I will promise

174   WRONGS AND RIGHTS COME APART

you that I will take you to the airport," then it is tempting to say that I have already effectively promised to take you to the airport. Similarly, unless it is conditional, the promise to forgive may start to look like present forgiving.[41]

Now, one might respond by saying that the promise to forgive *is* conditional—it depends on the wrong being committed. But this gets tricky. Is the promise to forgive conditional, or is the not holding accountable conditional?[42] The reason for thinking that the promise must be conditional is, presumably, that the conditions for forgiving are not yet in place until after the wrong is committed. Forgiving, one might insist, requires an emotional transition, not merely a rational choice. One cannot give up holding another accountable until one experiences the resentment. But this point can lead to instability in the opposite direction. If that is the worry, then why think that one can make a promise to experience the emotions in this way? Once forgiving is viewed as a matter of having and releasing certain emotions, it no longer looks like something we are in a position to promise. Thus, interpreting all apparent instances of preemptive forgiving as promises to forgive starts to feel precarious.

Third, even if the promise-to-forgive account were able to overcome these problems, it would risk losing the connection between having a complaint and having the standing to complain. What I have been describing are cases in which one seems to retain a right and yet one seems to have given up the standing to complain upon the right's violation. On my view, having a complaint is understood in terms of certain words, practices, and emotions being fitting. The promise-to-forgive response explains the significance of preemptive forgiving in terms of reasons to act, not reasons of fittingness. It posits a sense of "having a complaint" that is detached from what one can, morally speaking, do. "Having a complaint" in this sense means simply that one had a right violated. It becomes a placeholder.

The artificiality of insisting that the preemptive forgiver still "has a complaint" is plain when one considers its implications. Is every waiver of a complaint like this? Is it impossible to forsake one's moral complaint and only possible to promise not to use it? Note that the same points might apply to waiving a right. Why not say that one never waives a right but only promises not to exercise it? These questions highlight the fact that a waiver is importantly different from a promise. Once one sees the difference, then the only sense of "having a complaint" that will be left is as a placeholder.

7.2.4 LIABILITY WAIVERS AS PREEMPTIVE FORGIVING

The distinction between preemptive forgiving and a promise to forgive—which can feel abstract and elusive—can be concretely illuminated by thinking about run-of-the-mill liability waivers. I believe that we cannot properly understand liability waivers unless we appreciate the possibility of presently surrendering a yet-unrealized future complaint.

When I go to a ski resort and I sign a liability waiver releasing the resort from liability if I break my leg, I am not thereby giving them permission to break my leg. One natural way to interpret this is to say that I have given up any complaint that I may have should they violate my rights. I have given up my complaint without giving up my rights. That is, I preemptively forgive the ski resort if they break my leg.

This is not, however, the way that liability waivers are always conceptualized. An attorney might say that liability waivers are promises not to sue. Superficial appearances seem to confirm this. Liability waivers are often couched as "an agreement to hold harmless" and "a covenant not to sue." This is contract language. So it looks like liability waivers are not present waivers of a legal complaint but rather contractual promises not to exercise whatever legal complaint might arise.

But that's not the right way to conceptualize them. Liability waivers are not promises of future conduct but present waivers of future unrealized complaints, and one can see that in the practical legal effects. The law's typical response to breach of a contractual promise is to require the breaching party to pay damages. If you breach your contract to buy my goods, then I can sue you and make you pay me for the profits I've lost. But liability waivers don't typically work like that. If I sue the ski resort for breaking my leg, my lawsuit will get dismissed. The ski resort doesn't sue me to recover their losses as a result of my lawsuit. So if the liability waiver is actually a contractual promise not to bring suit, then why does it operate to bar a lawsuit? Why doesn't enforcement of a liability waiver take the form of an action for expectation damages?

A first answer might be that the covenant not to sue operates as a bar to a suit because, if it did not, pointless circularity would result. The defendant could turn around and sue the plaintiff for whatever damages were recovered, so it is simply more efficient to bar the action to begin with. Here is how one legal treatise explains it: "A covenant not to sue . . . is a bar to the original cause of action. This is to avoid circuity of action; for if the

176   WRONGS AND RIGHTS COME APART

plaintiff in the original action were to recover, the defendant could recover precisely the same damages back for breach of the covenant to forbear or not to sue."[43] The circularity makes it pointless to have a separate action for damages, so it's simpler to bar the original action.

But it will not always be pointless. Suppose, for example, the plaintiff values the expressive function of obtaining a judgment,[44] even if she will have to forfeit any damages right back to the defendant. I may want the court to declare that the ski resort wronged me, even if I have to break my promise not to sue them and I will have to turn over any damages that I receive. Another significant difference will arise where the damages for breach might exceed the damages obtained in the underlying case. For example, if I sue the ski resort, the resort may wish to counterclaim for breach of contract and recover *additional* damages, such as its attorney fees. Can it do this? A minority of jurisdictions do conclude that a party in breach of a covenant not to sue can be held liable for attorney fees.[45] The thought is that a covenant not to sue is a promise and subject to the normal remedies for breach.[46]

There is, however, a second option. The covenant not to sue can be viewed not as an additional promise but rather as a present waiver. Here is how an early opinion from the Supreme Court of Michigan puts it: "An agreement never to sue . . . operates as a release. Not as it has so often been said, upon the principle of avoiding circuity of action, but because in substance and effect it is a release. . . . We think it is clear that an agreement not to sue . . . is never a distinct and independent undertaking, upon which an action is maintainable, but a mere modification or extinguishment . . . and as such may be availed of in defense."[47] What the court is keen to express here is that the covenant not to sue should not be conceived as its own separate promise. To allow a separate action for damages would be, as another early court put it, "marking out a crooked path for litigants to travel, and one that was in nowise contemplated by their contract."[48] The waiver is only a release.

The leading case on this issue is a Second Circuit opinion by Judge Henry Friendly. The crucial passage declares,

> Certainly it is not beyond the powers of a lawyer to draw a covenant not to sue in such terms as to make clear that any breach will entail liability for damages, including the most certain of all— defendant's litigation expense. Yet to distill all this out of the usual formal covenant would be going too far; its primary function is to

serve as a shield rather than as a sword. . . . In the absence of contrary evidence, sufficient effect is given the usual covenant not to sue if, in addition to its service as a defense, it is read as imposing liability only for suits brought in obvious breach or otherwise in bad faith.[49]

Judge Friendly's point is that, while one could make a full-blown contract not to sue, the ordinary liability waiver should be read as something that merely releases the other party—something that can be used as a shield but not as a sword. A majority of American jurisdictions follow this approach.[50]

I think that Judge Friendly gets this precisely right. Ordinarily, when one agrees not to sue, what one intends to do is give up whatever future complaint one might have. It is not meant as undertaking a contractual obligation, but rather as a present release. It is waiving one's complaint, not promising not to complain. The jurisdictions that take the opposite view have, I think, been handcuffed by not recognizing this as a conceptual possibility. They have not appreciated the gap that exists between having a right and having a complaint—the gap that preemptive forgiving opens up.

7.3 The Significance of Preemptive Forgiving

If the arguments against preemptive forgiving are wrong, then one or another of their central assumptions must be mistaken. These arguments must have mischaracterized the nature of forgiving or the nature of our normative concepts or both. We can thus draw lessons from the possibility of preemptive forgiving.

A first lesson concerns the nature of forgiving—performative or attitudinal. The Second Argument against Preemptive Forgiving relied on two important premises: that forgiving necessarily requires an emotional shift and that the necessary reactive attitudes cannot be present until after wrongdoing takes place. Insofar as preemptive forgiving is possible, one or both must be false. I am skeptical of both, but the more interesting lessons concern the first.

Examples of preemptive forgiving are generally examples of forgiving operating more as a performative. Preemptive forgiving might thus generate an argument against—or at least a challenge for—accounts of forgiving that characterize forgiving as essentially attitudinal. One temptation in reacting to the debate between attitudinal and performative accounts of forgiving is to conclude that there are simply two different phenomena, both labeled as "forgiving," and examples of preemptive forgiving might look to support that. In one sense, the wounded soldier forgave his comrade, and in another sense, he never had the chance. There is performative forgiving and attitudinal forgiving, and that's all there is to it. This solution, however, is rather unsatisfactory. There must be some deep connection.

Based on what I have said about preemptive forgiving, I will briefly venture a hypothesis: All forgiving is giving up one's complaint, but this can happen in two ways. A complaint involves both a standing and an invocation. One can give up one's complaint—that is, forgive—by giving up either the standing or the invocation (or both). I have been characterizing performative forgiving as surrendering one's standing. It is a declaration that alters the appropriateness of making a complaint. Attitudinal forgiving can also be viewed as giving up one's complaint. Earlier, I mentioned Hieronymi's thought that the attitude of resentment is a form of protest. If this is right, then giving up one's resentment is giving up one's protest—or, we might say, one's complaint. The attitude shift in forgiving occurs when one relinquishes the attitude of complaint or protest.[51] The two forms of forgiving, then, are unified as forms of giving up one's complaint. This hypothesis is made palpable through preemptive forgiving's illustration of surrendering standing in a nonreactive way.

In the context of this book, perhaps the more significant lesson is to be drawn from reexamining the First Argument. In this light, preemptive forgiving can offer another window into the connection—or the disconnect—between our interpersonal concepts. Recall that the First Argument relies on a premise about the relationship between having a right or claim and having the standing to complain or resent. We can now run this argument backward. Preemptive forgiving shows the possibility of relinquishing one's standing to complain without thereby releasing someone from his or her duty. If so, then having a right or claim is not necessarily tied to having the standing to complain.

At the risk of being pedantic, this reverse argument might be laid out as follows:

(1′) *If preemptive forgiving were possible, then it would involve X forgiving Y for ϕing in the future.*

(2′) *Forgiving someone for ϕing does not make an instance of ϕing permissible.*

PREEMPTIVE FORGIVING

(3') *Granting permission makes an instance of ϕing permissible.*

(4') *Thus, if preemptive forgiving were possible, then it would involve X forgiving Y for ϕing in the future without thereby granting permission. [From 1', 2', and 3']*

(5') *A person forgives another iff she gives up her standing to complain against the person.*

(6') *Thus, if preemptive forgiving were possible, then it would involve X giving up the standing to complain against Y for ϕing in the future without thereby granting permission. [From 1' and 5']*

(7') *A person grants permission to another to ϕ iff she gives up her claim/right that that person not ϕ.*

(8') *Thus, if preemptive forgiving were possible, it would involve X giving up her standing to complain against Y for ϕing in the future without X giving up her claim/right that Y not ϕ. [From 6' and 7']*

(9') *Preemptive forgiving is possible.*

(10') *Therefore, it is possible for X to give up X's standing to complain against Y for ϕing in the future without X giving up her claim/right that Y not ϕ. [From 8' and 9']*

(11') *Therefore, it is not the case that X has a claim/right against Y not to ϕ only if X would have the standing to complain against Y if Y ϕs. [From 10']*

The premises—save for the claim that preemptive forgiving is possible—are copied directly from the First Argument.

The conclusion of this revised argument is the rejection of that now-familiar axiom—that having a right and having the privileged standing to complain of a wronged party are necessarily and conceptually bound up with each other. These things can, and often do, go together. That's why preemptive forgiving is atypical, nonparadigmatic. But it's quite possible and conceptually coherent. Preemptive forgiving, in which a party gives up her standing to complain while continuing to be owed the duty, seems to provide yet another example of these normative concepts coming apart.

Of course, no one thinks that it is always appropriate to hold another accountable whenever one's rights have been violated. A wrongdoer may have an excuse that would relieve accountability. Or some other consideration, like the potential for harm or the passage of time, may render it inappropriate for a victim to bring forth her complaint. Everyone would acknowledge that one's complaint upon being wronged will be defeasible in these sorts of ways.

But preemptive forgiving offers a bigger challenge. In cases of excuse, the victim still has the standing to complain—this is why the excuse is given to her—but the wrongdoer has an answer to that complaint. In cases where there is some reason not to complain, the victim again retains the standing to complain, but she ought not exercise that standing. In preemptive forgiving, however, having a right threatens to come apart, not merely from successful and appropriate complaint, but from the standing to complain whatsoever. The sense in which a preemptive forgiver cannot complain is not merely that any complaint would be defeated or wrong; complaint is made inapt. If that is correct, then preemptive forgiving offers a glimpse into a gap between two concepts of relational normativity—rightholding and the standing to hold accountable. Standing to hold accountable is not just the ex post reflection of rightholding, but something detachable from it. That is why it can be waived without waiving the right.

One might wonder how this picture fits with my contention that rights are ex ante and complaints and wrongs are ex post. After all, isn't the lesson of preemptive forgiving that we can sometimes do things with our complaints ex ante? But my view is not that we can only think about rights in the ex ante moment and wrongs in the ex post moment. Quite the contrary. In fact, it is those who view rights and wrongs as flip sides of the same coin who are closer to thinking that, for they see only one relation, just considered at different times. I see two relations. Each is shaped by its distinctive perspective, ex ante and ex post. But they are both, in a sense, always separately there for us. One of the remarkable things that we can do as conscious, self-governing, temporally extended agents is think about one normative perspective while we inhabit another. That is how we can give up a complaint that we don't yet have; that's why it's possible to preemptively forgive.

8

Exploitation

In Chapter 7, I argued that a person can waive a complaint against a particular action without granting consent or permission—what I referred to as preemptive forgiving. In this chapter, I explore the converse question: Can a person consent to an action and yet still have a complaint against such action? Put even more starkly, can a person be wronged by conduct even though she has waived her right against it?

From an exclusively rights-based perspective, the answer would appear to be no. If one waives one's right, then there would seem to be nothing to ground a complaint. One cannot, it might be thought, grant permission and then complain when the recipient makes use of that very permission.[1] Following that line of thinking, Joel Feinberg writes, "One class of harms . . . must certainly be excluded from those that are properly called wrongs, namely those to which the victim has consented."[2] This conclusion may seem to follow directly from a relational conception of morality. While perhaps an action could be wrong in a generalized sense despite consent, it could not be *a wrong to that person* if she has genuinely given her consent. After all, consent seems to be all about changing the moral status of an action—transforming something that would be a wronging into something that would not.

There is, however, a moral phenomenon that has caused fits for this simple picture: exploitation. It has been occasionally observed, often with puzzlement, that exploitation can appear morally problematic without harm or a lack of consent. This has befuddled theorists. How could an action wrong someone if that person consents to it and is not harmed by it? Predictably, various theorists have attempted to deny one or another of these apparent features. Perhaps such actions are not in fact wrongings;

perhaps there is not in fact full consent; or perhaps they are not truly mutually beneficial.

In this chapter, I mean to defend the straightforward appearance: exploitation can involve a wrong despite the victim's consent and benefit. In particular, I will focus on the idea that exploitation can involve a wronging even though the victim has consented. If that's accurate, then exploitation reveals the possibility of waiving a right and yet still standing to be wronged—the inverse of preemptive forgiving. That possibility looks to be foreclosed by exclusively rights-based approaches, which is why exploitation has bedeviled such views. But separating wrongs from rights provides the resources to take our intuitions about exploitation at face value.

This is no accident. Part of my aim in separating wrongs from rights is to appreciate that, as important as rights are, they do not exhaust our interpersonal moral relations. It is true that each of us is, in an important sense, our own sovereign. That gives consent decisive significance over many matters. But if the argument in this book is correct, then our moral relations with one another are not exhausted by respecting that sovereignty. We are often answerable to another for acting badly, even where the person calling us to answer had no sovereign power that was violated. Exploitation is yet another place where this is evident.

8.1 Exploitation's Puzzle

"Exploitation" can refer to a wide variety of interactions. In a broad sense, it describes any interaction in which one party takes advantage of another. One party gains by virtue of an unfair transaction with another. In the classic Marxist example, the capitalist exploits the worker by acquiring the surplus value of the laborer's work—taking what is not his—simply by virtue of owning the means of production.[3] Broadly speaking, then, fraud, deceit, physical coercion, and appropriation of others' entitlements might all be characterized as instances of exploitation. Such exploitation can be harmful and rights violating.

I will focus, however, on a narrower category of exploitation—what may be described as consensual, mutually advantageous exploitation.[4] In such cases, a person willingly consents to an exchange with another person and that exchange is, in fact, mutually beneficial. Nonetheless, we might still say that one party is "exploiting" or "taking advantage of" the other person. There are many familiar examples that might, under proper circum-

EXPLOITATION

stances, be regarded as consensual, mutually beneficial exploitation—sweatshop labor, sex work, organ selling, surrogacy agreements, and so forth. In such cases, a party may knowingly consent to the exchange, and they may do so out of a reasonable belief that they will be better off by doing so, and yet we might nonetheless condemn the resulting transaction as exploitative.

Cases of consensual, mutually beneficial exploitation are puzzling for rights-based theories. They appear to present instances of morally problematic interactions—indeed, of wrongs—in spite of the parties' consent and benefit. For example, a sweatshop laborer arguably consents to work in oppressive conditions and her circumstances are genuinely improved by doing so, and yet she seems to have a complaint against working in such conditions.[5] A surrogate mother arguably waives her parental rights with regard to her child and yet she may be wronged by having her newborn child taken from her. In short, the exploited party seems to waive their rights, and nevertheless, we typically think that the exploited party is wronged.

Importantly, the victim of exploitation is wronged *by their exploiter.* An impoverished individual may be done an injustice by the social system that put them in that position, but exploitation seems to imply a wrongdoer—an exploiter. In this way, the very idea of exploitation can seem to imply a wronging. As one writer puts it, "To exploit people is to wrong them, however much or little they may lose or you may gain from the act."[6] For many rights theorists, this creates a puzzle: How can someone consent and yet still be wronged?

A typical response is to deny one side of the paradox or the other.

On the one hand, one might contend that—contrary to appearances—when people face such a lack of alternatives, their choices cannot amount to consent in a morally transformative sense. Their choices are compelled by "the coercion of economic necessity."[7] The apparent consent in such cases is illusory and ineffectual. It's like having an economic gun to one's head. As Lord Chancellor Northington penned in 1762, "Necessitous men are not, truly speaking, free men, but, to answer a present exigency, will submit to any terms that the crafty may impose upon them."[8] This conceptualization allows us to account for the apparent wrong of exploitation. It is—like theft—the wrong of taking from another without his or her consent. One reaches this conclusion by, at least in part, denying the agency of the victims of exploitation.

184   WRONGS AND RIGHTS COME APART

On the other hand, one might contend that—contrary to appearances—consensual exploitation does not wrong the exploited party. There are two possible routes here. First, one might think that the combination of consent and benefit means that the supposed exploitation is, in fact, permissible. On such a view, we should not be taken in by our initial discomfort.[9] Our sense that exploitation is morally bad is perverse "fastidiousness" or "self-righteousness."[10]

Perhaps more palatably, it is possible to maintain that exploitation is in some sense morally bad and yet not *a wrong* to the exploited party. Feinberg, for example, writes, "In these cases there is no wrongful loss for the exploitee, who can himself have no grievance."[11] Nonetheless, he regards exploitation as what he labels a "free-floating evil." By this, Feinberg means to say that exploitation is "an occurrence or state of affairs that is rather seriously to be regretted" and yet "clearly not the ground of plausible grievance."[12] This position, at least, leaves space for the idea that exploitation is morally problematic. But it still insists that there can be no wronging where there is consent. Where exploitation involves abuse or coercion, it will rise to that level; but other exploitation—mere low wages, for example—will not implicate rights in that way.[13] And thus it will not wrong.

8.2 A Wrong Despite Consent

None of these options strikes me as a plausible strategy for explaining every apparent instance of exploitation. Some instances involve a lack of meaningful consent. Others may ultimately constitute free exchanges such that we should not see them as wronging anyone. But it seems to me that there are cases that will fall between these categories. There will be some individuals who will think something like, "I know that I signed up to be treated this way, and I know that I could quit if I wanted, but I still feel aggrieved and resentful at being treated this way."

In what follows, I mean to make out the coherence of such a thought. I will offer some first-person testimony from individuals in two classic spheres of exploitation: sweatshop labor and prostitution. The picture that I hope to paint is that some victims of exploitation see themselves as freely consenting and yet also see their exploiters as wronging them in the transaction. I believe that our moral theory shouldn't demand that we say that this combination of thoughts is inherently mistaken—that we should not have to respond to such people by telling them either that they are

EXPLOITATION

incorrect in seeing themselves as freely choosing or else that they have no grievance against their exploiters. Our moral categories should allow us to say that someone has genuinely waived certain rights and yet still has a legitimate complaint.

One cautionary note: Many—perhaps most—instances of exploitation in the real world involve such a lack of meaningful choice that they should not be regarded as consensual at all. Many—perhaps most—are also cruel and deeply harmful. I want to be clear that I am in no way denying these realities. My claim is that these are not the only problems, that these categories do not fully capture the wrongs that exploitation inflicts. The focus on consensual exploitation is to show that a rights-based framework will not suffice to explicate fully the wrong of exploitation. But it is not to deny that the world is rife with rights violations—coercion, oppression, and violence.

8.2.1 SWEATSHOP LABOR

In the 2015 documentary *The True Cost*,[14] filmmakers follow Shima, a twenty-three-year-old worker in a garment factory in Dhaka, Bangladesh. Shima came to Dhaka at an early age for the economic opportunities. During the course of the film, she makes the difficult decision to return to the village where her parents live and leave her daughter there to be raised by them. The choice to work in the factory away from her daughter is heartrending. But Shima seems to view it as a sacrifice that she chooses to make for her child, reflecting,

> I feel heartbroken. I don't want my daughter to have to work in a garment factory like me. I feel bad [about leaving her], but I think I will be happy one day when she has a good future. She will be a good human being and people will say that, even though Shima worked in a garment factory and stayed in Dhaka, away from her child, she gave a good education to her child and raised her as a good human being. If she gets a good government job, or gets married to a good man, then people will say that and I would be very proud of that. That yes, I struggled, but I tried my best not to let her go through this. That I raised her well.

Shima views herself as choosing to sacrifice for her child. There can be little doubt that her choices are shaped by her poor economic circumstances. But it also seems that her choices are her own and that she is, in a way, proud of them. Shima takes ownership in other ways too—organizing a union among the factory workers.

But even as she takes ownership of her work, Shima nonetheless seems to find it deeply exploitative. In an emotional scene, she explains, battling through tears,

> There is no limit to the struggle of Bangladeshi workers. Every day we wake up early in the morning, we go to the factory, and work really hard all day. And with all the hard labor we make the clothing. And that's what people wear. People have no idea how difficult it is for us to make the clothing. They only buy and wear it. I believe these clothes are produced with our blood. A lot of garment workers die in different accidents. . . . It's very painful for us. I don't want anyone wearing anything, which is produced with our blood.

Shima's sense of injustice here is palpable. She sees herself and those around her as victims of the factory owners and the global consumers. Even as she is proud to sacrifice, she sees a wrong being committed against her and her fellow workers. Shima's sense of injustice is hardly unique. Many sweatshop workers surely feel the sting of exploitation. In 2012, an Indian worker named Sakamma commented to a human rights tribunal, "It hurts us to be paid so little. I have to do this and they sell one piece of clothing for more than I get paid in a month."[15]

Must we say that Shima and those like her either are coerced against their will by poverty or else have no complaint? I think that we should be reluctant to do so. We should be inclined to take the appearances seriously—namely, that Shima is making a responsible choice for her daughter's future and yet is being wronged all the same. She has consented and yet still has a legitimate grievance.

8.2.2 PROSTITUTION

In 2007, the *Guardian* interviewed Karen, a prostitute in a London suburb.[16] She was not the victim of human trafficking or drug addiction but a fifty-something former administrator. Karen explains her initial entry into prostitution by saying, "I started going on blind dates and it slowly started to evolve into having sex with strangers. . . . I had a bad month, financially, as I invariably would, and it started as a trickle. I had always been curious about doing it—I think I was trying to prove to myself that actually prostitution was OK." She notes that chronic fatigue had made conventional work difficult: "Just driving to work and back every day would exhaust me. . . . I have to factor in a lot of rest in my life." Prostitution offered an alternative way to earn a living. As she explains, "To keep myself going and pay my bills and save for my pension, I probably need to see five a week. . . . I can almost control my workload." Karen faced real pressures and financial and psychological issues—including the trauma of a sexual assault in her twenties—but it is hard to read her words and regard her as simply unable to consent to her interactions.

Nevertheless, Karen sees her trade as deeply exploitative. Her words could hardly be stronger: "I believe there is a conspiracy to turn women into readily accessible semen receptacles. Men are twisting this now to make women think it's a level playing field and it's equal and liberating. No, it suits men, it's convenient for men. That's what is so insidious." Describing her work itself, she says, "Some people say that prostitution is actually a man paying to rape a woman. I think that is true in a lot of cases. Although it is a business arrangement, he is getting off on the fact that the woman doesn't want it. Basically you've consented to being raped for money." She later notes, "I will never trust a man again." The resentment here is vivid. It's clear that Karen views herself as wronged by the very transactions that she sees as paying her bills. That orientation seems perfectly coherent.

This account is not representative, but neither is it completely exceptional. In a 2018 interview, a sex worker, Lottie, is asked if she is "comfortable" with the work. She responds, "I have no choice. Without sex work I would be poor."[17] But when asked whether she sees the work as consensual, she says, "We can turn down the money, but it's really hard. . . . No one is forcing me, but I would be pretty broke without the work. I certainly wouldn't have Chanel bags and ready to wear without sex work." There is ambivalence here, but ultimately Lottie seems to view her choices as her own.

Like Karen, Lottie nonetheless regards her clients as wronging her. She explains, "I was already wary of men when I entered this industry, but now I truly despise them. . . . Their behaviour is just so damn ugly and insulting towards me." When asked if her clients look down on her, Lottie responds, "Oh god yeah . . . I'm treated as subhuman, they literally think I should work for free/inhuman prices, you're basically a slave in their eyes that they shouldn't have to pay for. That's how they see us. As slaves." Her resentment, like Karen's, is visceral.

I believe that we should accept the way that Karen and Lottie view their circumstances. We should not think that there is anything incoherent in their simultaneously believing that they have consented to their work and yet that their clients wrong them. If our moral categories force us to say either that there was some failure of consent or else that there could be no wrong here, then those moral categories are impoverished.

I do not mean to suggest, of course, that most prostitution should be regarded as consensual. There are good reasons for fearing that it is not.[18] Women in the sex trade are often underage, trafficked, and driven by desperation.[19] We should unequivocally recognize the pervasive coercion that occurs in these realms. But we must also be wary of the paternalism of always framing the wrongs of prostitution as a failure of consent.[20] It is perhaps better to be frustrated at what is offered by the binary of consent and nonconsent.[21]

Rights—and associated concepts like consent—can have a frustrating imperialism. I think we should resist. That sex workers—like Karen and Lottie—are often exploited and wronged by the men who purchase their services should not lead us necessarily to reject the meaningfulness of their choices. If it does, we need a richer set of concepts. The alternative is to accept both that there is consent and that there is a wronging. One may have consented to sex for money and yet be wronged by the man who takes up that arrangement.

8.3 Is There a Right Not to Be Exploited?

I am suggesting that we take the phenomenon of exploitation at face value. We should accept that it involves a wrong—sometimes a grievous wrong—to the exploited party even though that party has in fact consented to the exploitative arrangement. We can accept this position if we accept that wrongs can arise without an underlying right violation. In short, separating wrongs from rights offers the resources to account for the phenomenon of exploitation on its own terms.

There is, however, an obvious and important possible reply. One might contend that, in fact, exploitation does violate a right of the victim—namely, *a right not to be exploited*. Such a right would be separate from the rights that are the subject of the transaction.[22] For example, we might think that a worker has various rights over her labor and also, separately, a right not to be exploited. In accepting an employment agreement, the worker consents to sell her labor in exchange for payment. She thereby transfers certain rights over her labor or the fruits thereof. But, the thought goes, she does not thereby waive her right not to be exploited. That right remains, and it grounds the wrong if the employment is exploitative. The sweatshop laborer, for example, consents to the work, but she doesn't consent to being exploited. The prostitute consents to sex for money but not to being degraded. The wrong consists in a violation apart from the thing for which consent was given.

Is there such a right not to be exploited? We should immediately set aside one piece of evidence for a such a right—namely, our sense that exploitation wrongs the victim. That exploitation seems to wrong—and not merely to be wrongful in the abstract—is powerful evidence for finding a right *if one thinks that wrongs must be underwritten by a right*. But that is precisely what I deny. So some other argument is needed to settle the question. Otherwise, the rights-based reply is rather empty. If the only reason for saying that there is a right not to be exploited is in order to accommodate our sense that exploitation involves a wronging, then such a right is what I have called a mere placeholder. For the rights-based account to be meaningful, there must be some other work that the supposed right not to be exploited can do.

One might respond that such a right does play an important role. It correlates, one might say, with the directed duty not to exploit another person. And insofar as this duty shapes our action in the relevant ways, the right not to be exploited is not some mere placeholder. I mean to argue against this view. That is, I mean to argue that the supposed right not to be exploited does not play any of the roles that rights typically play in shaping action (which, to be clear, is not to deny that the wrongs of exploitation are serious wrongs).

In order to make this argument, I will again consider the paradigmatic features of rights that were introduced in Chapter 1. As I have made clear, I do not mean to claim that rights must have any of these particular characteristics. But when all of them are absent, it is hard to see what meaningful role a right is meant to be playing. My contention is that the supposed right not to be exploited does not function in any of these ways.

8.3.1 CONTROL OR WAIVER

First, notice that the right not to be exploited would almost certainly have to be inalienable. Practically speaking, if a party could consent to being exploited, then the right would provide little protection. A would-be exploiter could simply elicit consent to the exploitation and inoculate the transaction. Even without explicit consent, it would be hard not to infer an implied waiver unless the right were inalienable. It would be quite odd to think that a sweatshop worker consents to long, grueling work for low pay but does not implicitly consent to being exploited—unless, of course, we thought that the latter consent were simply impossible.[23] Inalienability would thus seem to make the right practically coherent.

That the supposed right would be inalienable is not itself a problem; it might even be an advantage. Conceiving of the right as inalienable would also make it fit with other dignitary rights that a person cannot surrender. One can no more consent to be exploited than one can consent to be a slave, the thought might go. One can waive one's particular rights, but one cannot waive one's status as a person rather than a tool. Or, to draw a different comparison, one can no more consent to be exploited than one can consent to be discriminated against. Certain kinds of respect and equal treatment are things that we are always owed.[24]

I do not want to suggest that there cannot be inalienable rights, or that this could not be such a right. But it does mean that one role that a right might play—delineating a matter over which one can exercise choice or control—is not available. There are, however, other, more plausible roles for the supposed right not to be exploited.

8.3.2 DEONTIC CONSTRAINT

A second role that rights—especially inalienable rights—can play is demarcating deontic constraints. Rights, in this sense, reflect the fact that one cannot override the relevant duty for the sake of some other good or some other person. Part of what it is to say that I have a right to my life is to say that you cannot kill me even if you might save others by doing so. If there is a right not to be exploited, one would imagine that it too would provide a kind of deontic constraint. Those who are attracted by a rights-based account will, most likely, have something like this feature in mind. And it is tempting because exploitation can appear to be categorically impermissible.

EXPLOITATION

I mean to argue that the norms of nonexploitation do not operate as a deontic constraint in this way. Consider an example. You are a young ornithologist attempting to do fieldwork in a remote part of the rainforest. In order to do such work, you need a field guide with knowledge of the local geography, flora, fauna, conditions, and survival practices. You apply for and receive a grant to pay for a guide, which is good because you are a poor adjunct and have no other available funds. The grant earmarks $5,000, which is a fair market rate for a guide in your region. Unfortunately, the guide whom you initially hire backs out at the last minute, and there are no others available. You are informed, however, that you will do just as well going to the region and hiring a guide on the spot from the local indigenous population, who know the area extremely well. When you arrive at the local village, you find that there are indeed many villagers with the requisite skills and eager to take on the task. The villagers are largely poor, subsistence farmers, and this represents a massive opportunity for them. Most families could spare at least one member while still maintaining their farm operations. You make a plan to interview all the interested applicants and select the one you deem best.

But the night before the interviews, the villagers come to you and suggest that, for $5,000, they would prefer to support your expedition collectively. Rather than a single individual receiving the full payment, which they regard as a massive windfall, they offer to provide you with a team of people who will serve as porters, cooks, guides, and so on—splitting the fee among them. If you accept the offer, you will have a team of people servicing your every need—cooking your food, carrying your gear, washing your clothes, constructing makeshift latrines, disposing of insects and reptiles that infiltrate your supplies, and so on. You had not planned to hire out this work and escape handling these burdens yourself. Many of their tasks will be dirty, strenuous, or mildly risky. And the villagers would be working for months on end at what will amount to a couple of dollars per day. Having the team will, however, significantly improve your expedition's prospects by giving you many more hands and by freeing you to devote your own time more completely to the ornithology work.

You initially balk at the suggestion. You suggest that the villagers agree among themselves that the person selected share the wages with the others. But they explain that they would not trust the chosen guide to follow through, nor would they accept being put in what they would regard as a debt to that person. You wonder whether you might pay the guide less and

192   WRONGS AND RIGHTS COME APART

simply gift the extra money to the village, but that would violate the terms of the grant and it would offend the villagers, who want employment, not charity. So you are left with the choice of selecting one guide or paying the same amount for the full team of extensive labor.

I want to suggest that accepting the team of villagers will involve exploitation in a way that hiring a single guide would not, and yet I also want to suggest that it is permissible to accept the proposal.[25] That conjunction should not be true if each of the villagers has an inalienable right not to be exploited correlative to a deontic constraint on how you must treat them.

Consider first the claim that it will constitute exploitation. It seems to me that the relations of inequality—both material and expressive—created by this arrangement make it rather paradigmatic exploitation.[26] For your own intellectual project, you will be paying very low wages for hard physical labor in a manner that will reinforce the differences wrought by global injustice. Were it an option, you might reasonably prefer simply to gift the money to villagers. Instead, the nature of the expedition will leave you with a moral debt to the villagers, even as they appreciatively take on the work. You may feel at every turn that you owe it to the villagers to express sympathy and appreciation—perhaps even apology—in a manner not typical of ordinary contracting parties. Should the research project yield fame and fortune, you might reasonably take yourself to owe it to the village to pass on some of the material gains to them—not as charity but as a kind of restitution or deferred compensation. In short, the arrangement would create a moral imbalance between you—an imbalance for which remedial steps would be appropriate if they could be respectfully taken.

If it is exploitative, then perhaps it is impermissible to hire the team of villagers. Perhaps you should insist on selecting a single guide, refusing to exploit. But that strikes me as incorrect. The villagers have expressed their preference for the team arrangement, and it is an intelligible preference. The arrangement may preserve a kind of distributive justice among the villagers—preventing one from receiving a massive windfall and the others nothing. And your research will benefit as well. It seems to me that, in the face of these benefits to all involved, it is permissible to accept the villagers' proposal.

But notice that these aggregate benefits are not normally the sort of considerations that would justify infringing a right, especially an inalienable right to respectful treatment. The exploitative character of the arrangement does not seem to operate as a side constraint in the way that we might expect from a right. If there were truly a right not to be exploited—in a nonplaceholder sense—one would expect it to operate as a stronger prohibition.

It is easy to think that nonexploitation is a deontic constraint. That's because it will be rare that a transaction will require exploitation. After all, typically the surplus from an exploitative transaction can be redistributed more fairly, meaning that there will typically be some nonexploitative alternative. That is, one can usually just share more of the benefit with one's transacting party. But not always, as the villager case illustrates.

Consider another example where a right against exploitation seems too strong. Price gouging during disasters is often taken to be a paradigmatic case of exploitation. But suppose that, during a hurricane, a local hardware store can price-gouge on the expensive generators suddenly in high demand among affluent mansion owners and use the increased revenue to subsidize batteries for low-income families. It's not clear to me that this would be impermissible, though stealing property from the affluent for the same purpose ordinarily would be. If there were a right not to be exploited, it's hard to see why it would be different from theft. But exploitation does not seem to offer such a strict prohibition. Exploitation, I contend, seems to mark out a kind of wronging more than it seems to impose a deontic constraint.

8.3.3 ENFORCEABILITY

Third, a common hallmark of a right is that it can be enforced, either by the rightholder or by others. If I try to take your kidney without your consent, you—or some third party—might use force against me to prevent that. Not all rights have this character, but it's another way that a right not to be exploited might be more than a mere placeholder. So can individuals coercively enforce the duty of others not to exploit them?

It doesn't seem like it. One who finds that her negotiating party is seeking to exploit her cannot then engage in fraud to obtain a fair contract. The fact that an employer is exploiting an employee will be no defense if the employee embezzles the wages he would have received in a fair transaction. The law, at least, does not afford potentially exploited parties the kinds of self-help options that it typically affords to rightholders in order to protect their rights.[27]

One might point to the unconscionability doctrine in contract law as a counterargument here. It makes exploitative contracts "voidable," which

194 WRONGS AND RIGHTS COME APART

is to say that it empowers exploited parties to make unfair terms or agreements legally unenforceable. But the unconscionability doctrine is "a shield, not a sword."[28] It is a way to answer the complaint of another, preventing an exploiting party from going to court and asserting the wrong of breach.[29] One cannot sue another party for unconscionability; nor, typically, can one use unconscionability to unwind a completed transaction.[30] Unconscionability doctrine thus seems to be less about creating a right against exploitation and more about denying legal recourse to those engaged in exploitation.

Though individuals do not seem to be able to enforce privately a supposed right against exploitation, public law does contain various coercive prohibitions that seem to be, at least in significant part, prohibitions on exploitation. Minimum wage laws, consumer protection laws, elements of housing law, and anti-price-gouging statutes all seem aimed at preventing exploitation. Laws like these are important and reflect a commitment to the idea that exploitation is wrongful. One should not conclude, however, that these laws recognize a right not to be exploited. They may target exploitation as a matter of public welfare and public morality, not as a rights violation.

In fact, there is some powerful evidence that public regulatory law does not regard exploitation as a rights violation. We frequently forgo regulatory responses that could target exploitation out of a concern that such laws would only end up harming those whom the laws are designed to help.[31] We fear that prohibiting sweatshops will not improve working conditions but instead cost people their jobs; we fear that overly forceful banking regulation will not provide access to fairer interest rates but rather prevent the poor from accessing credit at all; and so on. If we thought that people had a right—an inalienable right—against being exploited, then these arguments would look somewhat odd. We wouldn't typically tolerate rights violations merely because allowing them makes the victims better off.

8.3.4 DEMANDING

Rights typically afford their bearer a power to claim or to demand. They confer a kind of standing. Whereas a bystander can point out that an action violates a duty (mere assertion), a rightholder can demand that the actor comply with his duty. Having a right enables a special kind of speech act. One might contend that, even if victims do not have an enforceable right against being exploited—enough to ground defensive actions or a legal

EXPLOITATION 195

cause of action—they do have a special standing to demand better treatment. Workers, for example, might picket to demand better wages. Might not the plausibility of making a demand, and not merely a request, reflect there being some right?

It is undoubtedly true that victims or potential victims of exploitation have a special standing of some kind. I grant that they stand to be wronged. Moreover, in typical cases where exploitation is impermissible, the victims or potential victims can point to this impermissibility. This means that, in ordinary cases, the victims have a powerful moral position: you are acting impermissibly and we stand to be wronged. The picketing workers may be correctly saying just that. One might think that that is precisely what demanding amounts to.

But now consider the villagers. Can they demand that the ornithologist not exploit them? It's hard to see what this would mean. Whereas the picketing workers are suggesting that the employer ought to act differently (e.g., pay them more) where that is an available option to the employer, the villagers are not in a position to say that the ornithologist acts wrongly. They cannot demand that the ornithologist act differently. Indeed, they want the ornithologist to act precisely this way. And yet, I am suggesting, they may still reasonably resent the treatment, even as they recognize its preferability. Theirs is a complaint untethered from particular impermissibility. It is a complaint about the ornithologist's interaction with them, but it's not impugning the ornithologist's individual choices so much as the world at large. The wrong stems from being an instrument and instantiation of broader injustice.

So there does not seem to be a standing to demand if that means something action shaping, something tied to permissibility. As noted, however, there does seem to be a standing to demand in some sense. But I think that is merely a recognition of a potential wronging. It is the ex ante anticipation of an ex post relation. If that anticipated wronging matters prospectively, I think that it is not because it determines permissibility but rather because it adds a directedness.

8.3.5 THE PHENOMENOLOGY OF DIRECTEDNESS

It is that directedness to which I turn last. The phenomenology of a duty—the fact that we experience ourselves as owing certain conduct to another—suggests that the other has rights and is not merely the object of a general duty. While hard to explicate rigorously, we experience certain duties as owed to a particular other. In Chapter 6, I argued that our duties toward nonhuman animals can have this directed quality, bolstering the idea that talk of rights is apt. One might deploy a similar argument here: We experience the duty not to exploit as directed. When confronted with a potentially exploitative transaction, seeing the person on the other side of the transaction should provoke the sense of duty not to exploit. That is, one might argue that the phenomenology of exploitation is *as something that I owe it to this person before me* not to do to them. I consider this feature to be the most compelling potential argument that there is a (non-placeholder) right not to be exploited.

Still, I am not convinced. As an initial point, in the case of nonhuman animals, the phenomenology goes alongside the other features discussed earlier—in particular, deontic constraints and enforceability. The directedness there makes sense as an internal reflection of certain objective dimensions that the duties have. Here, if my preceding arguments are correct, directedness would be standing on its own.

More significantly, I want to question the phenomenological claim on its merits. Imagine that you are faced with a potentially exploitative transaction. Consider, yet again, the ornithologist who is offering backbreaking porter services for pitiful wages. You would probably feel some moral pressure to avoid the transaction. You might feel uncomfortable, guilty perhaps at the injustice of the inequality between you. You might consider whether there could be alternative transactions that would better preserve dignity and equality. You might even form the thought that no person should relate to another person like this. Such moral sentiments might lead you to avoid even a mutually advantageous transaction.

But it's not clear that any of this is a matter of experiencing a duty *to the other person*. After all, the other person is there before you asking that you engage with him. In this light, your moral concern seems aimed not *at him* but at something more abstract.

So I would contend that the phenomenology of exploitation is more conflicted. You feel simultaneously that you owe it to the person before you to take his choices seriously, and yet also that it is wrong to participate in an arrangement that treats any person in this way. I suspect that affluent Westerners who have traveled in poorer parts of the world are familiar with this paradoxical moral experience.[32] Global injustice can create a dilemma—engage and risk exploitation, or refuse for the aloof purpose of keeping one's hands clean. Insofar as noninteraction most cleanly avoids exploitation, avoiding exploitation may appear to be more about the agent's moral integrity than about the other person.

The same point can be made by noting the significance of gain. Exploitation requires that the actor benefits from the transaction. To know whether I am exploiting you, I cannot look merely at what I am doing to you, but must also look at what I am getting. An action would generally not constitute exploitation if there were nothing being gained.[33] But whether the actor benefits has little to do with the other party; it has everything to do with the actor. If there is a norm against exploitation, it can be obeyed simply by never profiting, regardless of what one does to others. Put this way, it hardly looks like a norm about what is owed to others. So, in this way too, the phenomenology of exploitation does not seem straightforwardly directed; rather, it seems to significantly concern the exploiter's own moral position.

Still, there is a sense in which one's experience is directed—namely that the exploitation would create a wrongful relation between you and this other person. There is a potential wronging. But that is not exactly the same as owing it to this person not to engage with him in this way. Thus, exploitation has a conflicted phenomenology: avoiding exploitation does not seem to be for the other person, and yet exploitation would wrong that person. This seemingly paradoxical phenomenology arises, I suggest, precisely because we have an inchoate understanding that what we owe someone and what might wrong that person can come apart.

8.4 Exploitation, Action, and Material Effects

The foregoing argumentation largely turns on finding a mismatch between what counts as exploitation and what an agent's first-order duties prohibit. Nonexploitation, I am contending, is not exactly an other-based constraint on our action. Rather, exploitation describes a way that interaction can create moral imbalance or the need for moral repair. It describes a kind of wrong—a respect in which conduct can be susceptible to the complaint of another. Exploitation is not about rights or duties but about a kind of problematic receipt of benefits and about a resulting alienation from each other.

Some readers will be resistant. Modern liberal theories of exploitation generally want to pinpoint where the exploiter goes amiss.[34] That puts the focus on the exploiter's action from the deliberative perspective. Exploitation, on these views, is a kind of voluntary advantage taking. Seeking a particular wrongful choice of the exploiter, these theories typically suggest that the exploiter artificially or unfairly restricts the options of the exploited party. The exploitative transaction is wrongful, even if voluntary, because the exploiter has kept an option off the table.[35] The sweatshop offers the choice between no wages and sweatshop wages but offers no choice for a living wage. The price gouger offers a choice between forgoing a necessity and paying an exorbitant price, taking off the table the option of paying a fair price. Exploited parties consent to an option among those offered, but they don't consent to the restriction on their set of options. Theories of this sort face persistent and deep problems,[36] but they have the apparent benefit of pointing to what the exploiter *does* that is wrong.

From such theories, it follows that exploitation will not occur—could not occur—when options are restricted due to something other than the choice of the putatively exploiting party. Exploitation, on these views, describes a way that a party impermissibly structures a transaction. It cannot arise if the party doesn't structure the transaction. On these grounds, some readers may balk at my descriptions of the ornithologist example. My contention is that exploitation inheres in the receipt of inequitable benefit from the villagers. But, it will be replied, if she could not offer any other option than she did, how could it be exploitation?

I think that this reply is misguided. Exploitation names a kind of wrong that may—or may not—be a matter of the exploiter withholding an option or structuring the transaction. My primary interest, of course, is not the label "exploitation"—it is to show that there is a non-rights-based kind of interpersonal grievance that can arise even in voluntary transactions. Still, in this final section, I want to offer some reasons for thinking that the kind of wrong that I am describing is properly regarded as the essence of exploitation. It is truer both to the animating Marxist tradition and to the way that we would like to use the concept in modern criticism.

Return now to the challenge: How could something constitute exploitation if the actor could not offer some other, better option? The ornithologist could do nothing else, so it couldn't be exploitation. It's a tempting thought, especially for a liberal.

But now consider a different story. An idealistic young barista has been selling her hand-sewn dresses online in small numbers, and what had started as a hobby has become a source of income to supplement her wages from

EXPLOITATION

the coffeeshop. She would like to take the next step and turn her dress business into a company, maybe even a career. The apparel industry is highly competitive, but she has some well-received designs, positive customer reviews, and appealing branding, all of which make her optimistic. The challenge is that she must radically scale up her production. Having no personal wealth, she needs outside financing to make that happen. She speaks to banks and venture capital firms. All of them, recognizing that it is a competitive market, expect certain sales margins and sales volume. The better the financing options, the more formidable the expectations. She comes to see that, unless she contracts with sweatshops in Southeast Asia for her manufacturing, as all the competing apparel companies do, she will not be able to achieve those benchmarks and her funding will dry up. She doesn't like it, but it's the only pathway she sees to create a viable company.

As I have described the example, the barista cannot offer a better deal to the sweatshop laborers. She offers this deal or else her company never gets off the ground and she cannot offer them any deal at all. This is merely a thought experiment; the empirical question whether the story accurately depicts the situation of most modern entrepreneurs doesn't particularly matter. (I do think that it at least partly reflects the situation of many.) What is important is that, if exploitation requires the possibility of offering the victims a better deal, then the hypothetical barista does not engage in exploitation by commissioning the sweatshop labor. That's true even if she's paying laborers one dollar to make garments that ultimately sell for one hundred dollars. It's what she had to do to be in the market and offer anything, so—one might say—she has not engaged in exploitation.

I think that this liberal position would be a betrayal of the core critical aspect of exploitation. It would relegate the concept to apply only to greedy actors—those who press an advantage to extract *extra* value inequitably. Rather, I think, the concept applies usefully to anyone who extracts inequitable value. It's about a kind of morally problematic benefiting.[37] It may be performed greedily, but it may also be performed almost helplessly.

Without diving into the contentious world of Karl Marx interpretation, I note that this picture seems to be roughly aligned with Marx's view. As one writer summarizes, "For Marx, this [is] a structural fact about capitalism: we are all locked into structures where all we can do to survive is to exploit others, and to degrade our own natures in the process."[38]

Exploitation, on this view, is not so much about individual fault. The structural context makes it the case that, perhaps unavoidably, we interact in ways that create impaired human relations.[39]

This makes sense when one sees exploitation as less about a particular choice of the exploiter and more about material transaction. For Marx, exploitation was at least partly a quasi-scientific concept, referring to a particular material phenomenon in which one party obtains value from the labor of another.[40] Exploitation simply describes this process of one benefiting from another. Within the literature on Marx and exploitation, there is extensive debate over whether Marx even had any moralized concept of exploitation.[41] I don't want to wade into that interpretive question. But it is noteworthy that the Marxist idea begins—and perhaps even ends—with the material fact of value extraction. That's not such a counterintuitive idea. In the barista example, if she is paying laborers one dollar to make garments that ultimately sell for one hundred dollars, it's natural to say that there is ipso facto exploitation happening.

The material transaction has relational consequences. For Marx, it had descriptive implications concerning the breakdown of human relationships. It created alienation, destroyed solidarity. It also has moral implications, at least if one adds some further moral premises.[42] If the material benefit is undeserved or unjustifiable, that creates a kind of morally impaired relation. That is, the sheer material facts raise a relational problem and a moral problem.

This understanding connects exploitation with an aspect of the ex post perspective that has been a theme elsewhere. The ex post is tied to the way that the world has gone. In relating ex post, we are trying to account for not only the particular choices that we made but also the material facts about what has happened between us. Thus, when wrongful conduct toward one party has an impact on a third party, there may be a wronging (Chapter 2); when seeking appropriate moral repair, facts about the material repercussions matter (Chapter 4); and when the world turns out sufficiently favorably, there might even be nothing to account for (Chapter 6). Rights-based theorists often emphasize that sheer material harm is not morally significant on its own. I agree with that. But I believe that material harm can give rise to a question of justification: "Why did you do that thing that hurt me?" And that question, I contend, introduces normative considerations of all sorts. The unjustifiability need not be about the victim; it suffices that the harm derived from something wrong.

Here I'm suggesting an analogous structure. Material benefit to the exploiter paired with general unjustifiability is enough to create a wronging relationship. Material benefit extraction lacks normative significance per se, but it opens a question of justification: "Why are you getting so much from me?" And this puts on the table a full array of moral considerations. It is not essential that the unjustifiability be grounded in the exploiter's individual conduct. It may be more general features of society that are unjustifiable. Still, that unjustifiability gives the material benefit an interpersonal moral valence. The wrongness need not be about the exploiter's choices; it suffices that the benefit derived from something wrong.

In sum, the puzzle of exploitation melts away, I think, when one appreciates the differences between ex ante and ex post interpersonal relations. With that difference in mind, it is not surprising that one might consent to something and yet still be wronged by it. Consent removes a prohibition; it licenses conduct. But that is hardly a guarantee that, in actual effect, the conduct will not create a moral imbalance, impaired relations, and a need for moral repair.

In fact, exploitation is not the only place where a relation of wronging springs up in spite of consent. Recall Leo Tolstoy's story: Prince Andrei explicitly waived any right to Natasha's hand. He consented to her remaining free. And yet she wronged him in exercising that freedom so injudiciously. Consent hardly immunized Natasha's actions from creating an injury and a need for repair. While it was true that there was nothing to which Andrei was entitled—nothing that he could demand ex ante—that did not mean that he could not be wronged by what transpired. Exploitation is similar. Consent does not immunize a transaction from wronging a participant. Though it means that a person does not have a right to something different, they may still be wronged by what materially transpires.

9

Relational Dualism

Those who have traveled this far now deserve affirmative accounts of rights and wrongings, respectively. The preceding chapters have all—at various junctures—presupposed, implied, gestured at, or sometimes even explicitly described features that I take to define these relations. But I have, as yet, mostly avoided providing any full-fledged theory.

In this final chapter, I will aim to pull together ideas and to impose some structure. But I do so with some hesitation. For one thing, the theoretical claims here are largely tentative, as much hypotheses as conclusions. Moreover, I worry that readers will fixate on anything that looks like a determinative theory at the expense of what has led there. The heart of this book and whatever account it has to offer exists in the pages that have come before this. I believe there is more to learn about our moral relationships— or at least more I am capable of illuminating—by careful examination of how we relate to one another than by theory building.

So my request of the reader is this: Do not give what I say here outsize importance. If you find that I do not succeed in offering a satisfying account, that is not a reason to shrug off the preceding chapters, but rather a reason to engage with them all the more. If you find that I do offer something even partly satisfying, it is only so because it emerges from what came before. Either way, what I offer here is as much detachable addendum as it is culminating account.

9.1 Three Dualities

Discussions of rights, wrongings, and directedness are characterized by a number of divisions. Three different dualities, which crop up over and over in these discussions, stand out. Two have already been observed; I will note them again and then add a third.

First and most familiar, theoretical discussions of rights and directed duties have divided between interest theories and will theories. Each offers something appealing, and yet each faces seemingly insurmountable objections. Interest theories understand directedness in terms of harm and the role that avoiding harm plays in undergirding our duties. But interest theories struggle with expansiveness, seeming to award rights to third parties. They also struggle to capture the sense that having a right involves not merely passively benefiting from a protection but also a kind of agential authority.

Will theories offer the inverse virtues and vices. They focus on the authority that rights seem to involve. But they can appear too restrictive, not satisfyingly capturing some of the most grievous violations that rights should guard against. Perhaps more damningly, their singular focus on individual freedom and agency seems to ignore the material ways in which sheer harm matters and in which our lives are interconnected.

Here is a second duality: discussions of rights and directed duties seem to envision both forward-looking and backward-looking functions for the concepts. For some writers, the essential feature of rights is that they describe special (perhaps exclusionary) reasons or constraints. Their essential role is in shaping action. For other writers, the key feature of directedness is a kind of accountability. That a duty is owed to another matters not to its normative force but to the way in which one will be answerable after a violation.

Recent discussions of morality's relational character have been heavily influenced by an appreciation for the essential role played by emotions and attitudes in our experience of agency and in turn of morality. But no less essential to our experience of agency—perhaps even a prerequisite for reactive attitudes—is our conscious experience of a temporal perspective.[1] We see a future that might unfold in untold many ways (whether or not it is truly metaphysically undetermined). Deliberation seems to require as much. As agents, we live in a world of possibilities. And then when we look back at our choices, we see another manifold: the ways that things might have gone. These alternative histories affect us and our relationships with each other.

> Footfalls echo in the memory
> Down the passage which we did not take
> Towards the door we never opened.[2]

204 WRONGS AND RIGHTS COME APART

These perspectives of ex ante and ex post—encasing a moment of action—are ineliminable features of human experience.

Inevitably, they shape our moral emotions, relationships, and practices, all of which are inflected by the way that we imagine different possible futures and different counterfactual histories. It is our blessing and curse, as moral agents, to regard our interactions both before and afterward. Unlike the skylark, "we look before and after,/And pine for what is not."[3] Given that our temporal perspectives—ex ante and ex post—are so essential to agency and morality, it strikes me as unsurprising that our moral concepts and practices should differ between them. If our very perception of action is different before and after, why should we be surprised if our moral concepts also operate differently before and after?

Let me add a third duality that one finds in discussions of rights, wronging, and directedness. Moral philosophers often appeal to two different concepts in describing our moral relationships: respect and justification. For some, interpersonal obligations are ultimately about respecting persons' moral significance; for others, they are about ensuring that our actions are justifiable to one another. Of course, philosophers generally don't reject either idea, but they tend to privilege one or the other. For some, respect is the crucial idea, with acting justifiably being simply a component or by-product of treating others with respect. For others, interpersonal justification is what gives content to the otherwise indeterminate catchword of respect.

Consider first respect. There is natural appeal in the thought that the directedness of rights and duties has to do with the way they constitute respect for the other person. The fact that I owe various obligations to you seems to reflect a recognition of you as morally significant. I must attend to your moral status; I must see you as having a sort of authority with regard to me. To have rights seems, in this way, to involve being an object of proper respect from others.

This connection between rights and respect has a heritage in the Kantian idea that "a person . . . possesses dignity (an absolute inner worth) by which he exacts respect for himself from all other rational beings in the world. . . . Humanity in his person is the object of the respect which he can demand from every other human being."[4] Modern theorists have fruitfully developed this thought as an explication of what it means to have rights. Warren Quinn, for example, argues that rights are entailed by proper respect for persons: "A person is constituted by his body and his mind.

They are parts or aspects of him. For that very reason, it is fitting that he have primary say over what may be done to them—not because such an arrangement best promotes overall human welfare, but because any arrangement that denied him that say would be a grave indignity. In giving him this authority, morality recognizes his existence as an individual with ends of his own—an independent being. Since that is what he is, he deserves this recognition."[5] The basic idea is that rights are bound up with respecting persons as the morally significant beings that they are—"a response to a characteristic of persons that makes persons important."[6] In particular, rights are bound up with a morally significant *status* that persons possess, as a person or as a self-governing agent.

This thought that rights are a matter of respecting persons as persons may help explain some of rights' most defining features, like their deontic character. Here is how Robert Nozick puts that thought: Side constraints upon action reflect the underlying Kantian principle that individuals are ends and not merely means; they may not be sacrificed or used for the achieving of other ends without their consent. Individuals are inviolable."[7] Nozick goes on to explain this violability in terms of respecting the individual lives as the loci of value: "Why may not one violate persons for the greater social good? . . . There is no *social entity* with a good that undergoes some sacrifice for its own good. There are only individual people, different individual people, with their own individual lives. . . . To use a person in this way does not sufficiently respect and take account of the fact that he is a separate person, that his is the only life he has."[8] The thought is that rights' distinctive character springs from the fact that they exist where others are under a duty *out of respect for* the rightholder as a life of their own. This is a deeply appealing idea.

There is, however, another theme that philosophers often emphasize in thinking about rights and directed duties. This is the thought that actions should be justifiable to those on whom they bear. A focus on justifiability to others has famously become the foundation for modern contractualist ethics. In T. M. Scanlon's contractualism, justifiability "provides both the normative basis of the morality of right and wrong and the most general characterization of its content."[9] Indeed, justifiability may be understood as giving content to respect and dignity. Consider Rainer Forst: "To possess human dignity means being an equal member in the realm of subjects and authorities of justification. . . . Correspondingly to act with dignity means being able to justify oneself to others."[10]

206 WRONGS AND RIGHTS COME APART

Justifiability, like respect, also offers resources to explain some of rights' distinctive features. For example, Thomas Nagel offers the following sketch of why there might be deontic constraints on action:

> [Utilitarian justifications] are really justifications to the world at large, which the victim, as a reasonable man, would be expected to appreciate. However, there seems to me something wrong with this view, for it ignores the possibility that to treat someone else horribly puts you in a special relation to him, which may have to be defended in terms of other features of your relation to him. [That] may help us to understand how there may be requirements which are absolute in the sense that there can be no justification for violating them. If the justification for what one did to another person had to be such that it could be offered to him specifically, rather than just to the world at large, that would be a significant source of restraint.[11]

The thought is that the deontic operation that is a hallmark of rights might plausibly be about acting so that our actions are justifiable to others.

Respect and justification—like interest theories and will theories, like forward-looking and backward-looking perspectives—seem to be persistent and inescapable themes in modern discussions of rights and of directedness. With each of these dualities, it would be foolhardy to think that one side completely collapses into the other—there are important differences, even if only in emphasis. And it would be equally foolhardy to dismiss one or the other side of these seemingly competing ideas as wholly misguided. Surely there is truth in each. My hope is that, by distinguishing rights and wrongs, we create conceptual space to retain both sides of each duality.

9.2 The Dual-Relation View

9.2.1 THE BASIC PICTURE: THIN RELATIONALITY AND TWO DIFFERENT KINDS OF THICK RELATIONALITY

I will now try to offer a sketch of how these ideas fit together. The picture will be recognizably Kantian in some respects, but I don't claim perfect faithfulness to that tradition and much of the sketch could probably be rendered equally well in less Kantian ways.

The first thing to observe is that all rational action relates the actor to others in a thin sense. When a person acts, she adopts a principle. She takes that principle to be one that can govern rational action. That is, she takes it to apply in a lawlike way across the community of rational agents. Put another way, in order to make her action intelligible to herself, she simultaneously makes it intelligible to another (even if just an imagined other). In this foundational but minimal way, all rational action is tethered to a community of agents. All rational action is thus relational in a thin sense: it is regarded as governed by rules that apply to other agents and other actions.[12] We might even say that there is a weak sense in which all rational action is owed to everyone, like how one might think of compliance with the rules of chess as owed to all chess players everywhere.

This minimal, general relationality is well short of the stronger form of relationality that tethers an action to a discrete other person—what Michael Thompson and Jay Wallace describe as "bipolarity." For that, there must be something more, something that relates the action to a particular individual, not merely to all agents as such in some nondescript sense. This stronger idea is what is implied by talking about one person *owing* an action to another person. Something about this action connects it with a particular person.

There is likely a connection between the thin and thick forms of relationality. The minimal relationality of rational action is perhaps a prerequisite for, perhaps presupposed by, or perhaps built into stronger relationality. It may be that I can *owe* it to you to do something only insofar as there is a sense in which your actions are subject to rules, and rules that in some sense govern both of us. The abstract relationality of all rational action would thus provide the raw material for concrete relations to individuals. Or it might be the other way around: that the thin kind of relationality depends on the fact that we inhabit a world of bipolar moral relations.[13] On this view, the idea that actions might be right or wrong simpliciter derives from the fact that people have rights and are wronged, these concepts actually being the primitives.[14] Or maybe it is a foolish quest to disentangle the ordering here at all. The important point for present purposes is that strong relationality requires something about a particular other person, not just the entire community.

My hypothesis is that there are two different ways that an action can be tethered to another individual—two different forms of bipolar relations. These two forms basically track the dualities that I laid out in the previous section. One is about ex ante respect for the life and choices of another; the other is about ex post justification to another with an affected interest (broadly construed).

Some actions are wrong because they fail to respect the status of another as an agent, living their own equally important life. Put in another familiar way, some actions are wrong because they are inconsistent with the equal freedom of others. They are impairments of—or incursions into—the life of another. The humble recognition that our own choices and actions must fit alongside everyone else's—must not exceed what is afforded to others— is a core part of membership in a normative community. One essential way to act wrongly is to arrogate to yourself power or choices that, as a matter of equal respect for all, should not be yours.

Rights are the flip side of the duties not to engage in such actions. Rights, in this way, protect a sphere for each of us as our own. That's what it is to have a claim. It is to have a piece of normative territory.[15] This is one sense in which we are cocitizens of the moral community: We each have our own normative space in which to live our lives, the boundaries of which are mutually shaping, just as my neighbors' plotlines shape the boundaries of my property. Each of us shares the normative world by, in part, recognizing that some matters are not ours. In turn, we have matters that are our own, where others have a duty to respect that it is our life to live. Rights demarcate such normative territories.

But transgressions of these boundaries—failures to respect the agency of another—are not the only way that we can act wrongly. Nor does sharing normative space constitute the only way in which we inhabit a moral community.

At a basic level, to act wrongly is to act contrary to a principle that governs the action. This idea—as already noted—involves some thin relationality. It implies that there is some other person, even just an imagined version of oneself, to whom the principle also applies. Such a relation between the action and another is basically what it means to be a reason. Thus, in this thin sense, any time one acts wrongly, one is criticizable. Someone else could point out that there is a principle that applies to the action that was not followed. This need not be anything that we would think of as moral principle, nor must the criticism sound as moral criticism. For example, if I act in a particular way because I momentarily thought that $7 \times 8 = 54$, I have acted wrongly. I have purported to use reasons—the shared currency of rational action—and I have failed. Another person can show me that I have been

RELATIONAL DUALISM

209

mistaken. And inversely, I cannot justify my action to another (though I might explain it—a simple mistake anyone might make). I have acted contrary to principles of arithmetic, and that's a fact that relates me—in the thinnest of ways—to all other arithmetic users.

Although this means that I can be criticized, such criticism would be entirely impersonal. Someone could tell me, "You did that wrong," and that would be true. We both have access to the same principles, and I did not follow them. Still, the person cannot hold me to account in any robust sense. I can reply to the criticism with, "What's it to you?" For another person to hold me to account—to criticize me in a personal way—there needs to be more than the mere fact that we both have access to the principles of arithmetic. There needs to be something tethering that person to the wrongful action. The person must have *a stake* in it.

I understand having a stake to be a sui generis concept—it includes anything that answers the question, "What's it to you?" This might include harm, normative injury, and perhaps other things too.[16] *Wrongings* are those rule or reason violations in which a discrete other has a stake.

One might think of the requirement that a person have a stake—have something that answers the question, "What's it to you?"—as a kind of anti-busybody principle. On this view, it's a gatekeeping principle, protecting us from being held to account for every error that we make. This understanding is possible because of the way in which all rational action is relational: we can conceive of being held to account for all wrong action, and we can be grateful that we are not. All rational action is, in some sense, owed to the entire rational community—it involves our shared set of principles—and this fact makes intelligible the thought that we are fortunate not to be held to account for all wrong action. On this view, the requirement that others have a stake keeps such onerous accountability out of our lives.

But gates can fence out or fence in, and I think it is better to regard the relationship of having a stake as a matter of inclusion. Having a stake operates to bring someone else into our action in a way that they would not otherwise be. Recognizing that another had a stake in my action involves a recognition that, by inhabiting the same world together, our lives become intertwined such that my actions bear on your life. This is another sense in which we are cocitizens of a community. We share not only normative space but also the physical world and the social worlds that we construct. When I act, you may be tethered to my action simply because it ended up bearing on your life. My thinking $7 \times 8 = 54$ might mean that there's no seat for you at the table or that there are more parts per million of arsenic in the river where you swim. When it does, you have an answer to the question, "What's it to you?" Harm thus functions as a kind of moral property of its own—a tie to another's actions—apart from the tie that rights provide. Simply by virtue of the way events unfold in the world, the thin impersonal criticism of any member of the rational community can take on a direct personal character. Having a stake gives someone standing that others do not have. This is a second way in which an action may be tethered to another person. It derives from the fact that we live together in community, not only in a normative way but also in a physical and social way.

Although it can often be anticipated, this form of tethering only truly arises ex post. Beforehand, the railroad can say to Mrs. Palsgraf, "What's it to you how we handle this guy's package?" Afterward, "What's it to you?" has a straightforward answer: "I am the one who ended up seriously injured." (Someone who, like Benjamin Cardozo, thinks that the railroad can still rebuff Mrs. Palsgraf afterward by saying, "What's it to you?" has mistakenly come to believe that the only way that we are tethered to each other is by having rights.) When you tell me beforehand not to break down your front door in order to save you, we might anticipate that you will have this kind of personal standing to hold me to account if I do. But as luck would have it, all may end well and you would not.[17] Unlike rights, which describe a relationship to how things *ought to unfold* going forward, what is captured here is a relationship to how things *have unfolded*.

In this picture, rights and wrongings describe different ways that a person can be normatively connected to the action of another person in more than the thin sense. But in this picture, there are common threads between them. In particular, both are related to the thinner relationality that exists in the idea of action governed by reasons (i.e., principles). Rights are part and parcel with a particular kind of duty—namely, the strict duties to respect the equal lives and agency of others. Wrongings are the combination of thin relationality with a thick connection in the world—a stake in the action. Both are, one might say, specifications of thicker relations that exist within the broader realm of action governed by reasons. Put another way, both rights and wronging describe different ways in which our action can be another person's business. But our action can be another person's business only because, in some general way, all rational action is about all of us.

9.2.2 RIGHTS, ROUGHLY DEFINED

The foregoing picture of the way that both rights and wrongings connect with the more general idea of wrong action allows for something like a rough definition of each concept.

Rights are correlates of certain duties—a description almost every theory of rights agrees on. I have suggested that the relevant duties are the duties of respect for the agency of another—or more colloquially and perhaps just as accurately, the life of another. To have a right is to be the bearer of importance in others' deliberations; this is what Stephen Darwall refers to as "recognition respect."[18] Rights are about appreciating a special normative importance of others, which shapes our deliberation. Rights thus involve a kind of authority with respect to the actions of another.

But not every instance of recognizing another entity as normatively important constitutes respect in this sense. An entity may figure within one's obligations—and thus hold normative significance—without the obligation being owed to it in the sense that matters. When driving, you ought not cross the yellow lines. The yellow lines are normatively significant, and we might even say that the yellow lines have an authority, that you should respect the yellow lines. But obviously the yellow lines don't have rights.

One might think that the issue is that your duty does not exist for the sake of the yellow lines—indeed, the yellow lines don't even have interests of their own. Mere instrumental significance is not enough. Following Joseph Raz, we might conclude that rights involve duties justified by the interests of another.[19]

The kind of respect involved in rights does seem to involve recognizing noninstrumental importance. But, to borrow a distinction from Christine Korsgaard, noninstrumental doesn't mean intrinsic significance.[20] Someone may have a status that generates respect and rights in part due to its extrinsic significance.[21] For example, the status of being a journalist may be the basis of rights in part or whole because of the role that protecting journalists plays for the autonomy of listeners or the health of civic discourse. Similarly, parental rights may be based on the significant status "parent" even though the reasons for treating parents with deference may have more to do with the importance that according that status has to children.

Even if noninstrumental normative significance captures some basic idea of respect, not every instance of this kind of respect implicates rights. We might accord a great work of art or a natural wonder its own noninstrumental normative significance. Out of respect for such an object, we would have duties that are not simply based on the human interests involved. But this respect would not mean that we are according rights to the object in question. The respect involved in rights involves more. Still, even this other kind of respect does seem to capture some form of directedness. Although we would probably not say that *Hamlet* or the great sequoia groves have rights, it is not unnatural to think that one owes it to *Hamlet* to stage the play in certain ways or to think that one owes it to the sequoias not to chop them down for toilet paper. So even here, some link exists between respect and the sense that obligations are directional. Rights, however, involve a deeper form of respect.

One might think that what is still missing are the entity's interests. The play *Hamlet* has no interests; and sequoias don't care how they're used after they are cut down. But sequoias do have interests—and being cut down is not one of them. So why not say that trees have rights? I think that this is a deeply revealing question. Raz, for his part, rules plants out with a rider about what entities can have rights—only those with interests of intrinsic value. But this is entirely ad hoc, especially in light of the fact that, for rights like a journalist's or a parent's, the rightholder's interest need not be valued intrinsically.[22] The difficulty with seeing plants (or, for that matter, other life-forms like protozoans) as rightholders is—I think—connected with an impression that they are not conscious agents, that they lack any internal perspective from which they navigate the world. Learning certain facts about plants—for example, how trees communicate through mycelial networks or how "mother" trees identify their offspring and prioritize them in distributing resources—or even just watching time-lapse videos of plant growth may shake our confidence that they do not act. When it does, the capacity for trees to have rights becomes suddenly more intelligible. To be clear, my claim is not that trees are agents or rightholders (though I think we should be taking that possibility seriously). My point is that, intuitively, rights involve respect for another's agency.[23] Rights don't safeguard interests; they safeguard spheres of action, spheres where we respect the self-determination of another.

This description is, of course, in the spirit of will theories of rights. As H. L. A. Hart put it, "In the area of conduct covered by that duty the individual who has the right is a small-scale sovereign to whom the duty is owed."[24] In the same vein, Jeremy Waldron describes the will theory as "essentially connected to a certain distribution of freedom."[25] For the will theory, rights are about distributing the control over the world around us, and I mean to be endorsing a version of that thought. But modern will theories have often inferred that rights necessarily involve control over the duties in question—the power of waiver or consent. Although such control is often present, I see no reason to believe that respect for the autonomous life of another requires they always be in control of the relevant duties. Respect for your agency may entail not killing you, even if you give me permission. It is interesting that respect for the agency of another can come apart from their having complete control over the duties. But it seems clear to me that it can and that, when it does, rights are bound up with the respect for agency, not the control per se.

If one insists on a definition, rights seem to be described by something like the following:

> X has a right that Y do φ *iff* Y has a duty to φ because φ-ing is required to respect the status of Y as another actor in the world.

Admittedly, this is still rather indeterminate. One might understandably complain that talk of "respect" is slippery and philosophically unilluminating. What I am imagining (as may be evident) are the kind of perfect duties that Immanuel Kant imagines as creating a contradiction in conception, duties that are constitutive of a world of an equal freedom for all. But the basic idea doesn't require any commitment to the Kantian details or machinery. The point is simply that there is some subset of our duties that prohibit actions because such actions would arrogate too much to ourselves, treading on what ought to belong to another. That basic idea would seem to be available to contractualists and rule utilitarians—perhaps even to act utilitarians as long as they have some epistemic humility.

Rights, then, are correlated with this special subset of our duties, the subset concerned with respecting the normative space of others.[26] I do not claim to have a test for how to derive or determine this subset of our duties. But I am confident that there is a distinctive subset. As evidence, I would point to the five characteristics described in Chapter 1. Some duties (1) can be waived or are otherwise subject to the control of another, (2) can be claimed or demanded, (3) can be coercively enforced, (4) operate as side constraints or exclusionary reasons, and (5) have a distinctive phenomenology of directedness. These are not necessary and sufficient features

WRONGS AND RIGHTS COME APART

of all duties correlated with rights, but they do all point to a cohesive package. They all capture features of another person having a kind of authority—that actions contrary to the duties would not merely be wrongful but invasions of that person's normative domain.

9.2.3 WRONGS, ROUGHLY DEFINED

My view is that wrongs, at their core, describe a kind of relationship that exists ex post and makes fitting a kind of moral repair. They are what we resent, apologize for, make reparations for, forgive, and so on.

Try to recall the most recent instance when you apologized for something. It might be that you violated someone's rights—perhaps you broke a promise, or you stepped on someone's gouty toe. But for many readers, it will not be anything like that. You expressed yourself poorly, leading another to misunderstand your meaning. Or you were clumsy or inattentive, causing someone else in your vicinity to lose some time or have to go to some extra effort. Or you just forgot to do something that you should have—acknowledge a birthday, call your mother, shovel the snow in the walkway, and so forth. Or maybe you received an undeserved benefit at someone else's expense—you were served ahead of someone who was there first, you ate the last cookie misbelieving that no one else wanted it. What unifies these examples is that, to put it colloquially, you screwed up and it mattered to someone else.

I believe that we should take this characterization basically at face value. Roughly speaking, wrongs arise when a person acts as they ought not and there is someone else who had a stake in the action. That someone else had a stake in the action tethers them to it, making the action relate to them in a personal way. The thin relationality of sharing a set of norms takes on a particularized character by virtue of how two people inhabit the world together.

But in this picture, the relational quality of sharing a set of norms should not be lost. It's not exactly the case that one commits a wrong whenever one acts wrongly and another has a stake in it. The person with the stake must also be able to appeal to the relevant norm—to regard the action in which they have a stake as wrongly performed. That is, the relevant concept is not wrongfulness per se but interpersonal justifiability. Typically, when I act wrongly, I cannot justify my action to another person—after all, I acted wrongly. But that assumes that the other person and I share a commitment to the norms that make the action wrong. If you chafe at the idea that anyone should ever have to shovel their walkway and you have never done so in your own life, then you are not wronged by the snow on your boots as you walk up to my house. I can justify *to you* why I didn't shovel the walkway, even if I can't justify it to anyone else in the neighborhood. What a wrong involves, then, is not that one person screwed up and another had a stake—rather, it is that one person cannot justify the action to another who had a stake.

Because giving justification to another is a relational concept, there is a sense in which wrongs are doubly relational. They involve one person having a stake in the action of another—which describes a kind of personal relationship between this specific person in the world and the action that was taken—and they involve an inability to justify the action to the other person, another relational concept. Put another way, wrongs involve the confluence of a material relationality in the world with a normative relationality.[27] I did something *to you* that I can't justify *to you*.

The following rough analysis thus offers a preliminary way of capturing what I understand to be the nature of wrongings:

> X wrongs Y in doing φ *iff* Y had a stake in X's doing φ and X cannot justify doing φ to Y.

This description seems to have two discrete parts, and I have been describing wrongs that way—as the confluence of the thin relation of shared norms with the personal relation of having a stake. I think there is something accurate in this image of two-part characterization. But there is perhaps also some unity here. As mentioned earlier, I take having a stake to be a sui generis concept, including within it material interests (harm and benefit), rights (normative control), and probably more—anything that answers the question, "What's it to you?" One might say that having a stake simply describes having the standing to demand justification. Insofar as that's correct, the two conjuncts of the foregoing definition are part and parcel with each other. I wrong another person when that person has the standing to demand justification and I can give none. The unifying idea is that wrongs involve the absence of justification where justification could be demanded.

Wrongs involve having a complaint. In saying that the wronged person has a complaint—could demand justification—I do not mean anything about the actual ability to complain. If the CIA ran experiments on you in your sleep, you would have a complaint, though you might never know it. If you are murdered, you obviously won't be articulating any complaints, but you still have a complaint (which, of course, is the basis for most ghost stories).

Though the actual ability to complain is not necessary, the general capacity to relate with one another in terms of justification does seem to be required. As I argued in Chapter 6, we mostly cannot relate in these ways with nonhuman animals. You cannot justify yourself to a squirrel, and though you might rebuild trust with it (maybe even lure it back to your deck), apology and forgiveness are basically inapt. It is part of what makes animals and young children so innocent that, although they can be hurt, they never really have a complaint in the way that other persons do. Talk of "wronging" is not perspicuous here. Because wronging describes a relationship where certain practices and emotions would be fitting, it requires two parties of a kind capable of engaging in those practices.

Although what is essential is the aptness of certain ex post dialogue and emotions, wrongs often come into view only through the realization of such dialogue and emotions. When a person has a stake in what another person did, she might ask for an explanation of the actor's reasons—"Why did you do that?" This might be flat-footed or it might be a sort of provisional complaint. The actor, in turn, might or might not have a good answer to the query. If it becomes clear that the actor was not, in fact, justified in what he did, then the existence of a wrong is revealed. In private law, it is no accident that wrongs are found only after a plaintiff files a complaint and the defendant files an answer—a formalized version of the same moral conversation. Of course, wrongs exist regardless of, and before, any such conversation. But on my view, wrongs basically describe the result of the moral conversation, even if hypothetical.[28]

There is an important respect in which the rough characterization given earlier is still not entirely satisfactory. Some wrongs are not best understood to *consist in* "doing φ," even where that is understood to include omissions. Wrongs that are not straightforward doings include faulty guarantees,[29] failures of attention,[30] receipt of unjustified benefits,[31] and likely others. These phenomena are deeply puzzling for theorists—all the more so the more closely one ties accountability to conscious deliberative action. The sketched view would seem not completely immune insofar as it sees rational action as the common element behind both rights and wronging.

I do not have a full answer to offer here, but the account that I have been sketching potentially has resources to understand these phenomena in ways that other theories do not. As I have emphasized, actions look different ex ante or ex post. In the ex post standpoint, actions are, in some sense, basically a kind of event. Once we draw a distinction between the ex ante and ex post, we appreciate that accountability is always for something that happened. Insofar as that's true, it should not be entirely surprising that we are sometimes answerable for things that happened that extend beyond our doing anything. That is, if we are answerable for those events that are our actions (a description that makes sense in the ex post standpoint but little sense in the ex ante), then it may seem plausible that we can be answerable for some other events too. Interpersonally, we come to own events in the world that are not our actions, strictly speaking; some events come to fall within the sphere of events that we must answer for in the way that we do for our actions.

Here is a hypothesis about one way that might come to be. Start from the thought that, in general, we call on each other to account for something that happened—that is, an event. "The scale fell on me." "You crashed into me." Normally saying, "I didn't do it," is a possible reply— it's a way of saying that this event is not one for which I must answer. But it may be that, in certain contexts, someone might be precluded from offering that reply, even though the event in question wasn't their action. If I promise you that your roof will last for ten years, I cannot answer your complaint about its subsequent collapse by saying, "I didn't do it," no matter how true that might be. If I crash into you, I may not be able to answer your complaint by saying, "I didn't do it," unless there's some extrinsic force (wind, a push, etc.) to which I can point. If we give primacy to the dialogical character of accountability—if we see accountability as about what could be said in an interpersonal conversation—then our answerability for certain events may just derive from the fact that we cannot deny our answerability for them. In this way, our accountability may bleed out beyond what we do, narrowly understood.

All of this is admittedly tentative and gestural. My primary point here is simply that an account that draws a meaningful distinction between the ex ante and ex post standpoints will be better situated to explain the way that wrongings seem to extend beyond conscious action and seem to be at least partly a matter of material occurrences in the world. If that's

218   WRONGS AND RIGHTS COME APART

correct, then perhaps a better rough gloss on wronging would be something like this:

> X wrongs Y when *e* happens *iff* (1) Y had a stake in *e*, (2) Y can call on X to justify *e*'s happening, and (3) X cannot justify *e*'s happening.

This formulation is closely related to the earlier formulation because clause (2) is regularly satisfied where *e* is something that X has done. But they may not always coincide. It is a puzzling reality that we seem to be accountable precisely for our actions but also sometimes for things that are not our actions. But I think that is less puzzling when one appreciates how actions blur into events in the ex post standpoint and how accountability is fundamentally about what we can say to one another.

9.2.4 AN ASYMMETRY

Both rights and wrongs have characteristic expressive activities that go alongside them. Rights are associated with claiming, making claims. Wrongs are associated with complaining, making complaints. And yet, in the accounts that I have offered of rights and wrongs, there is asymmetry in how the relations connect with their paradigmatic activities. Wrongs are essentially about moral dialogue in a way that rights are not.

I have suggested that wrongs are a matter of the fittingness of giving and receiving justification. To be wronged is to have a complaint—which, in turn, involves having a stake in an action and its being unjustifiable. The fittingness of a certain kind of dialogue is primary. The victim could say such and such, and the perpetrator couldn't say such and so.

A parallel account of rights would have been available. To have a right, on this view, would be to have a claim—that is, to be in a position where it would be fitting to claim. In a famous article, Joel Feinberg defends just that thought: "What is it to *have a claim* and how is this related to rights? I would like to suggest that *having a claim consists in being in a position to claim, that is, to make a claim to* or *claim that.*"[32] Rights are not passive entitlements but rather normative powers to do something—namely, make a valid claim. The activity of claiming is, for Feinberg, fundamental. In order to make his argument, Feinberg envisions a world called Nowheresville, which lacks the activity of claiming. Feinberg contends that Nowheresville might be populated by a variety of moral concepts, including wrongness and duty, but that it will not include rights as long as there is no practice of claiming. Feinberg suggests to his reader that a world without rights would be importantly lacking, and that what would be missing is not any set of duties per se but rather the interpersonal activity of making claims on one another.

I have always been enamored of Feinberg's article. It elegantly captures the way that rights seem to involve a kind of authority in the rightholder. An account of rights like Feinberg's would be pleasingly parallel to the account of wrongs. And yet, I have not offered such an account. Why?

As alluring as I find Feinberg's argument, it ultimately does not convince me. The people of Nowheresville do have rights, even though they might not know it. Insofar as there are strict deontological duties insulating their agency—insofar as it's wrong to kill them, to break promises to them, to treat them as a mere means, and so on—they have rights. There is something that cannot be done because it would trespass on their lives. It is impossible to conceptualize such duties without some idea of an entitlement. And once one admits such entitlements into Nowheresville, it seems to me that claiming follows on their heels.[33] That is, the activity of claiming derives from the existence of duties of a certain kind.

So I come back to the view that, fundamentally, rights are entitlements, correlated with duties of a certain kind. The dialogical possibility that goes with them is important, but not their essence. One advantage of this view, by my lights, is that rights can exist apart from being able to make claims. A criminal may have a right to humane treatment, even if he is in no position to claim such treatment after the heinous way he treated others. The nonhuman animal may have a right to certain treatment, even though it cannot form the thought of making a claim in Feinberg's sense.

If I am correct in seeing rights and wrongs as having asymmetrical relationships to their characteristic activities, then perhaps it is a partial explanation for the various divergences that have been found throughout this book. Some of the places where wrongs and rights come apart may be attributable to the fact that in one the dialogical activity is fundamental and in the other it is derivative.

9.3 Opening Space

Plutarch attributes to Solon, the great lawgiver, the following description of what city is best to live in: "That city in which those who are not wronged, no less than those who are wronged, exert themselves to punish the wrongdoers."[34] It is, of course, absurd to think that what makes a polity best is how much it punishes people. And yet despite that, there is still something beautiful in the description: it evokes the way being part of a moral community means that wrong action matters to everyone.

Rights are often criticized as overly individualistic, as separating us off into walled-off spheres, and as creating a zero-sum competition for control. I am not a rights skeptic by any means, but I believe that rights theorists would do well to take these criticisms more seriously. Treating rights or claims as the singular building block of interpersonal life can engender the kind of indifference that Solon warns against. And yet it would be equally erroneous to think that nothing uniquely tethers individuals to particular actions.

The view that I have tried to sketch sees two ways that the broad relation of existing in a moral community solidifies into more particular bonds between individuals. Each represents two different aspects of the ways in which we live in community with one another. On the one hand, we share a normative community, and that means sharing the normative territory. This is what rights do—they parcel up who has control over what and thereby give us some independence. On the other hand, we share a physical and social world, and that means that our actions bear on each other's lives. Wrongings reflect that interdependence.

Independence and interdependence often appear as competing ideas in normative theorizing. In many ways, they are. But to see every normative question as a forced choice between them is confining. Like Edna St. Vincent Millay's narrator in "Renascence," we would swing wildly from being confined on our own small summit to being buried in a torrent of interpersonal responsibility. Our normative concepts should afford us some space between these extremes. When wrongs and rights are tied together too tightly, we close off this space.

Throughout this book, I have offered examples of how this dynamic plays out. And in doing so, I have hopefully shown how distinguishing rights and wrongs might matter. In the law, the distinction would mean— among other things—reenvisioning our privity requirements (Chapter 2), our rights-based framework for remedies (Chapter 4), and our rights-based conceptions of guarantees (Chapter 3) and liability waivers (Chapter 7). In interpersonal ethics, it would recommend—among other things—greater attention to material consequences in accountability relations, expanding accountability in some ways (Chapter 4) and contracting it in others

RELATIONAL DUALISM

(Chapter 6); a less transactional, consent-focused picture of accountability in sexual ethics (Chapters 3 and 5), commercial contexts (Chapters 2 and 8), and other interpersonal interactions (passim); and a wariness of framing questions about what to do in terms of imagined future complaints (Chapters 3 and 6). All of these practical implications are a matter of opening up conceptual space that has otherwise been walled off. The important role of rights in ensuring normative independence need not preclude recognizing material interdependence and its associated vulnerability.

My examples throughout have been drawn primarily from private law and interpersonal relationships. There are at least two reasons for this. First, these are the places where a narrowly bipolar conception would seem to have the most plausibility, so I take myself to be engaging the conceptual claim on its advocates' strongest ground. Second, these are the areas that I know best and to which I am most prepared to speak.

But it seems to me that the conceptual point likely bears on many other contexts, including much more public-facing ones. I have neither expertise nor settled opinions in these areas. But I am struck by what seem to be similar dynamics, with independence and interdependence getting excessively set against each other by way of equating ex post claims about wrongings and ex ante claims about rights. By way of conclusion, consider three such contexts.

9.3.1 PUBLIC LAW

Perhaps the most obvious extensions are to public law. Constitutional, statutory, and regulatory disputes—as much as private law disputes—routinely raise questions about who has a right, who has a legitimate grievance when a norm is violated, and the connection between these two questions. And the dynamics are often similar. For example, if the package of Mrs. Palsgraf's fellow traveler were illegally searched by a police officer (rather than dropped on the tracks by railroad employees), then the exclusionary rule would forbid that evidence being used against him in a criminal prosecution. But if the evidence instead incriminated Mrs. Palsgraf, the law would grant her no similar right to its exclusion: the illegal search was of another's package; it violated no right of hers; and the law gives her no remedy.[35] I disagree with that outcome, for much the same reasons that I disagree with Cardozo's reasoning in *Palsgraf* itself.[36]

Perhaps the most natural intersection with public law involves the notoriously tangled rules around standing.[37] Standing doctrine poses difficult issues, and I don't purport to have the solutions. But I do suspect that recognizing the conceptual distinction between rights and wrongs might provide some assistance.

On one hand, the modern Article III standing inquiry—requiring injury in fact, causation, and redressability—seems to be primarily about wrongs in the sense developed in this book. If you're going to call someone to justify themselves before a tribunal, then there must be some way you've been hurt—there's only a "case or controversy" if there's an answer to "What's it to you?" But you need not be the primary rightholder. Being the rightholder does creep in as a "prudential" matter, but it is not strictly required.[38] Thus, in various contexts, the Supreme Court has granted standing to materially injured parties who are asserting the legal rights of their customers, clients, patients, jurors, and voters.[39] All of this reflects an appreciation that we can have a stake in what is done to others and that a real grievance requires only wrongful injury.[40]

But this orientation is not a good fit for all legal disputes. Much public litigation is not really about remedying wrongs, but rather about trying to exercise rights, to exert control. This is often true when a party seeks prospective (ex ante) relief. The Court has tried to port over the same three-factor inquiry to such cases. Consider *Warth v. Seldin.*[41] The plaintiffs claimed that a town's zoning ordinance intentionally excluded low- and moderate-income individuals in violation of the Constitution. The Court dismissed the suit for lack of standing because the plaintiffs had not sufficiently alleged an injury in fact caused by the alleged violation—they hadn't shown that, but for the exclusionary zoning, they would have been able to afford a residence in the town. This seems misguided. If a person has a right, something that they can demand—here equal treatment—then whether there is any material injury should be beside the point. The Court has all but recognized as much in other equal protection cases.[42] But it continues to try to apply the injury-in-fact test to what are better understood as attempts to exercise rights—that is, normative authority—both denying standing to purported rightholders on the basis of a lack of injury[43] and granting standing to third-party nonrightholders on the basis of material injury.[44] The test for standing to assert a wrong becomes—awkwardly and with alterations—the test to exercise a right.

These troubles in standing doctrine have not gone unnoticed. Commentators have recognized that, in practice, the standing doctrine operates differently for retrospective and prospective relief.[45] The conceptual distinction between rights and wrongings might help make sense of this difference. It would allow us to appreciate more clearly that there are two different tasks that courts face in trying to adjudicate the relation between the parties before them because there are two different possible relations between those parties. In many contexts—particularly ex post—a party is alleging they have suffered a wrong, which may stem simply from a wrongful injury in fact, in which case rightholding should be mostly irrelevant. In other contexts— particularly ex ante—a party is seeking to exercise a right, in which case injury in fact should be basically irrelevant.[46] More recognition of the divergence between complaining of a wronging and demanding something as a matter of right might thus help in public law no less than in private law.

9.3.2 MICROAGGRESSIONS

Turn now to a less legal area where the distinction might matter. Recent years have witnessed fraught debates around hurtful speech and conduct, especially in workplaces and on college campuses. Among the focal points has been the idea of microaggressions: subtle and commonplace verbal or behavioral disrespect toward members of historically marginalized groups.

The basic idea is deeply intuitive. There can be subtle forms of disrespect or hostility that take their toll through their accumulation and through their inscrutability. As Chester Pierce put it in his originating work on the subject, "The enormity of the complications they cause can be appreciated only when one considers that these subtle blows are delivered incessantly."[47] A moment's reflection should make the plausibility of this phenomenon obvious. We all know how a repetition of tiny impacts can leave a bruise, and how something normally innocuous can sting when we already bear a wound. It hardly requires any great imaginative leap to realize how significantly these dynamics might shape the experience of members of historically disadvantaged groups; and even if it did, we have ample and compelling direct accounts for anyone who cares to listen. There is nothing counterintuitive in the class of injuries that microaggressions inflict, and there should be nothing puzzling in describing such a class of wrongings, even if the precise contours remain hard to pin down.

And yet the topic has been polemical. There are many deep-seated reasons for that. But I think our conceptual apparatus contributes to the problems.

Advocates for the recognition of microaggressions have gravitated to the language of "violence" and, as the term itself includes, "aggression." These labels make sense when one is focused on the perspective of the person suffering the wrong (ex post). Indeed, Pierce's original use of the term "microaggression" was to put it in comparison and contrast with more traditional "macroaggressions"—to appreciate that, whereas racial hierarchy may have once been enacted through overt acts like lynching, it is now enacted through myriad subtle social interactions. Though the mechanism is different, the resultant injury is similar: exclusion, disrespect, and even dehumanization. But why think that the kind of injury determines the applicability of the label "violence" or "aggression"? An inchoate premise seems to be that, in order to be properly characterized as wrongings, microaggressions must have a kind of rights violation at their core. It is not enough to say that one person spoke or acted wrongly and that another person was hurt (in a socially patterned, not-one-off way). We want to be able to say that the injured person was violated.

Yet that very framing provides fuel for skeptics. For example, in their widely read essay "The Coddling of the American Mind," Greg Lukianoff and Jonathan Haidt frame their critique by saying, "There have always been some people who believe they have a right not to be offended," and they go on to say that universities are now "privileg[ing]" these "claims of a right not to be offended."[48] That way of describing the issue—which purports to carry a refutation on its sleeve—is typical and widespread among skeptics.[49] But why would one think that an apt characterization? The inference seems to be that any legitimate grievance must be unwritten by a right. If one claims to be wronged by some injury, then one must be asserting a right against that injury. But, the argument continues, there couldn't possibly be a right not to be offended because that would give practically complete control over what a person says to others. Notice the shift to the perspective of the potential perpetrator, and with that to the perspective of deliberation (ex ante). And from the standpoint of the perpetrator, microaggressions don't typically look like aggression or violence.

It seems to me that our tendency to slide between wrongings and rights is exacerbating these debates. Microaggressions are a function of interdependence—both the ways that the meaning and impact of our actions are shaped by our shared history and the ways we unavoidably depend on social recognition. There should be conceptual space to acknowledge such wrongings without immediately laying claim to, or seeing a threat to, ex ante control. Undeniably, there are hard questions about how to handle offensive speech, and I don't mean to say that improved conceptual categories will just wipe them away. But I would like to think that we can do better, appreciating that we can recognize some wrongs without thereby asserting a right to control how others speak and act.

9.3.3 ENVIRONMENTAL ETHICS

Perhaps nowhere is the clash between freedom and interdependence as starkly on display as in our relations to the natural world. For centuries, the Western tradition has regarded wild nature as the primal exemplification of freedom, and not entirely without reason. It represents space where one is subject to no normative authority but one's own.[50]

And yet, the science of ecology is all about our interconnectedness. We now know—or perhaps have relearned—that our conduct bears on all members of the ecological community. As Rachel Carson puts it, "So delicately interwoven are the relationships that when we disturb one thread of the community fabric we alter it all—perhaps almost imperceptibly, perhaps so drastically that destruction follows."[51] Dumping chemicals one place may kill the fish somewhere else; burning coal on one side of the world may change the lives of children a hemisphere away.

Our framework of individual rights is ill-equipped to handle the resulting wrongs. We appreciate that the fishermen are wronged when the fish all die; we realize that the children of the Global South have a complaint about climate change they didn't cause. But framing these grievances in terms of antecedent rights is awkward at best. What right can any person have to yet-uncaught fish or over what happens half a world away?

Among the most powerful responses from the environmentally minded has been an appeal to collective rights, to the thought that the world belongs to all of us in common. Here, for example, is how Joseph Sax puts it: "The task of protecting adequately our remaining biological patrimony demands a robust development of the idea of common heritage, of things that belong to us as members of the world community, and that are entitled to protection at our behest in whatever particular ownership patterns they are held."[52] As pragmatic legal strategy, there is much to be said for this framing. The law has long recognized that the waters and shores are held in common[53] and that the fishermen may be wronged when the fish are killed.[54] Extending those ideas may seem feasible, and as a matter of environmental ethics, seeing the earth as belonging to us all in common would be an improvement.

But we might do better still if we could jettison rights altogether in these discussions. The problem lies in thinking that the earth belongs to us—that it is our patrimony—whether individual or in common.[55] If we detach wrongs from rights, then we can understand our environmental wrongs without believing the natural world to be ours. The fishermen are wronged by the killing of the fish not because the fish belong to us all in common but because the fishermen are materially affected by what is wrongfully done to the fish. Children of the Global South are wronged by climate change not because they too own a share of the natural world but because we should never have regarded the world as ours to dispose of at will. These are not first-party wrongs but third-party wrongs—they are akin to the wrongs children suffer upon the loss of their mother.[56] They are not less grave because they are not theft of something owned by right, any more than the child's loss is less grave for that reason. We open ourselves up to committing such collateral wrongs when we tread wrongly.

Of course, we cannot avoid leaving our footprints on the earth. We are entitled to go about in the world—and, in the right places, to be free from the control or interference of others as we do so. And yet we are still responsible for the consequences of our missteps. Separating wrongs from rights may offer conceptual tools to see that. Where we are entitled to tread is a different matter from whether we are answerable for the impact of our steps.

NOTES

ACKNOWLEDGMENTS

INDEX

Notes

1. TWO WAYS OF RELATING

1. Palsgraf v. Long Island R.R. Co., 162 N.E. 99 (N.Y. 1928).

2. *Id.* at 99–101.

3. *Id.* at 100.

4. *Id.*

5. Cardozo is arguably the greatest American jurist, and one primary reason is his deep appreciation for the continuity between law and ordinary human life, especially morality. "We are not to close our eyes as judges to what we must perceive as men." People *ex rel.* Alpha Portland Cement Co. v. Knapp, 129 N.E. 202, 208 (N.Y. 1920). Though I use Cardozo as something of a stalking horse in this book, he is the opposite of a bête noire and I am loath to give that impression. It seems to me that, if one is seeking truth, it's best to spend one's scrutiny and criticism on those who are close.

6. Leo Tolstoy, *War and Peace,* trans. Louise Maude and Alymer Maude, ed. Amy Mandelker (New York: Oxford University Press, 2010), 513.

7. Tolstoy, 514.

8. Tolstoy, 643. Tolstoy describes to the reader how, in the months that followed, "she remembered Prince Andrei, prayed for him, and asked God to forgive her all the wrongs she had done him" (710). She also wonders to a friend, "Will he ever forgive me? Will he not always have a bitter feeling toward me?" (716).

9. Tolstoy, 641. Notably, this declaration follows only a moment after Andrei reiterates that "she was and is perfectly free."

10. One might argue that this only shows that we should not take Prince Andrei's grant of permission seriously—that it should be considered an empty politeness. But I think that it would be a mistake to say this. Prince Andrei firmly gave up his claim to an engagement. Natasha was not promised to him, and she does not act wrongly because she violates Prince Andrei's rights. Rather, she acts wrongly because she throws away their love in a disreputable and foolish moment of weakness and youth.

11. Tolstoy believed deeply in the wisdom of the folk, often seeing intellectualization as obscuring. In *Anna Karenina,* he writes, "Philosophical theories . . . lead[]

230   NOTES TO PAGES 4–8

man by way of thought that is strange and unnatural" along "a dubious mental path." Instead, "what I know, I do not know by reason, it is given to me, it is revealed to me, and I know it by my heart, by faith." Leo Tolstoy, *Anna Karenina,* trans. Richard Pevear and Larissa Volokhonsky (London: Penguin Books, 2003), 798–799.

12. Of course, these two stories raise many questions and answer none of them. There are many distinctions that may be drawn between them. One distinction that is likely to occur to the reader is between law and morality. Perhaps a legal wrong, which is Cardozo's subject, operates differently from a moral wrong, which is Tolstoy's. For now, notice two things: First, recall that Cardozo purports to be making a conceptual claim about human life. It would therefore be odd to interpret him as viewing the law as apart from, and radically different from, morality. Second, even if one distinguishes legal wrongs from moral wrongs, one would expect each to bear the same connection to legal rights and moral rights, respectively. It is this connection, across contexts, that is my subject.

13. Ronald Dworkin, introduction to *Taking Rights Seriously* (Cambridge, MA: Harvard University Press, 1977), xi.

14. Robert Nozick, *Anarchy, State, and Utopia* (New York: Basic Books, 1974), 29–30.

15. Joseph Raz, "On Reasons for Action," in *Practical Reason and Norms* (Oxford: Oxford University Press, 1999), 35–48.

16. This point about labeling was brought out to me by Tom Dougherty and David Owens. See David Owens, "The Roles of Rights," in *Civil Wrongs and Justice in Private Law,* ed. Paul B. Miller and John Oberdiek (Oxford: Oxford University Press, 2020), 3–17.

17. Compare R. Jay Wallace, *The Moral Nexus* (Princeton, NJ: Princeton University Press, 2019), 14: "Considerations of moral right and wrong have two very distinctive kinds of normative significance: they represent obligations of practical requirements in the first-person perspective of deliberation, and they also structure our interpersonal relations of accountability."

18. Michael Thompson, "What Is It to Wrong Someone? A Puzzle about Justice," in *Reason and Value: Themes from the Moral Philosophy of Joseph Raz,* ed. R. Jay Wallace et al. (Oxford: Oxford University Press, 2004), 34.

19. Jeremy Bentham, "A General View of a Complete Code of Laws," in *The Works of Jeremy Bentham,* ed. John Bowring, vol. 3, *1838–1843* (New York: Russell & Russell, 1962), 159.

20. G. E. M. Anscombe, "On the Source of the Authority of the State," in *Authority,* ed. Joseph Raz (New York: New York University Press, 1990), 152.

21. William Blackstone, *Commentaries on the Laws of England,* ed. Thomas P. Gallanis (Oxford: Clarendon, 2016), 3:1.

22. E. J. Bond, *Ethics and Human Well-Being: An Introduction to Moral Philosophy* (Malden, MA: Blackwell, 1996), 196.

23. Bond, *Ethics and Human Well-Being,* 200.

NOTES TO PAGES 8–13

24. Judith Jarvis Thomson, *The Realm of Rights* (Cambridge, MA: Harvard University Press, 1990), 122.

25. Alabama Power Co. v. Ickes, 302 U.S. 464, 479 (1938) (quoting Parker v. Griswold, 17 Conn. 288, 302–303 (1845)).

26. Owens, *Shaping the Normative Landscape*, 46.

27. Arthur Ripstein, *Private Wrongs* (Cambridge, MA: Harvard University Press, 2016), 29.

28. Wallace, *Moral Nexus*, 9.

29. Stephen Darwall, *The Second-Person Standpoint: Morality, Respect, and Accountability* (Cambridge, MA: Harvard University Press, 2009), 4.

30. Darwall, *The Second-Person Standpoint*, 12.

31. For another, less Strawsonian deployment of wronging as an access point to thinking about the relational character of normative relations, see Ariel Zylberman, "The Very Thought of (Wronging) You," *Philosophical Topics* 42, no. 1 (2014): 153–75.

32. I do not mean to suggest that Tolstoy held the philosophical position that I am defending. But it is noteworthy that one of the explicit themes in *War and Peace* is the interplay between "two sides to the life of every man"—the "individual" side of freedom and the "elemental hive life" of collective history. The personal side of life corresponds with the prospective orientation of action, whereas the collective side is seen from a retrospective view, in which, "as soon as [a man has done this or that action], that action performed at a certain moment in time becomes irreversible and belongs to history." Tolstoy, *War and Peace*, 536. Like Tolstoy, this book sees individual freedom as connected to an ex ante perspective and collective existence as connected to an ex post perspective.

33. To borrow the lovely description of Iris Murdoch, *The Sovereignty of Good* (New York: Routledge, 1971), 1.

34. It is deliberate that the book draws heavily on materials outside only law and philosophy, with their analytic argumentation. Here, again, Tolstoy is suggestive: "The business of art lies just in this,—to make that understood and felt which, in the form of an argument, might be incomprehensible and inaccessible." Leo Tolstoy, *What Is Art?* (Indianapolis: Hackett, 1960), 97.

35. Murdoch, *Sovereignty of Good*, 43.

36. I think that such a stipulation would be at odds with ordinary English usage. The word "wrong"—in its noun and verb forms—does not line up neatly with rights violations. See, e.g., Thomson, *Realm of Rights*, 122. The fact that our ordinary usage operates this way is mildly suggestive that we are naming different phenomena. But my argument does not turn on linguistic usage; it concerns our substantive practices.

37. One could argue that this is all that Cardozo means to say. If so, then one implicitly concedes that the celebrated opinion does not involve a reasoned argument, but rather only a stipulated definition.

38. Wesley Newcomb Hohfeld, "Some Fundamental Legal Conceptions as Applied in Judicial Reasoning," *Yale Law Journal* 23, no. 1 (1913): 16–59.

232   NOTES TO PAGES 14–17

39. I do not mean to take a stance here on whether directed duties ought to be understood simply as nondirected duties with some extra set of characteristics. For arguments that they should not be conceived in this way, see Wallace, *Moral Nexus;* and Margaret Gilbert, *Rights and Demands: A Foundational Inquiry* (Oxford: Oxford University Press, 2018). I also do not mean to take a stance on whether rights or directed duties might be more conceptually primitive than the other. For an argument that rights "enjoy justificatory or explanatory primacy," see Ariel Zylberman, "Relational Primitivism," *Philosophy and Phenomenological Research* 102, no.2 (2021), 410.

40. See, e.g., H. L. A. Hart, "Are There Any Natural Rights?," *Philosophical Review* 64, no. 2 (April 1955): 175–191.

41. For the deservedly classic discussion of claiming, see Joel Feinberg, "The Nature and Value of Rights," *Journal of Value Inquiry* 4 (December 1970): 243–260. For a theory that takes demanding as the core of rights, see Gilbert, *Rights and Demands.*

42. The idea that duties of right are enforceable, as opposed to other duties that are not, is an important theme in Kant.

43. See Dworkin, *Taking Rights Seriously;* Nozick, *Anarchy, State, and Utopia;* Raz, "On Reasons for Action"; and Wallace, *Moral Nexus.*

44. In Strawson's words, resentment is occasioned in "situations in which one person is offended or injured by the action of another." P. F. Strawson, "Freedom and Resentment," *Proceedings of the British Academy* 48 (1962): 192.

45. Strawson, "Freedom and Resentment," 199–200.

46. See Jeffrey S. Helmreich, "The Apologetic Stance," *Philosophy and Public Affairs* 43, no. 2 (2015): 75–108. Notice the parallels between stance and standing. We typically refer to "standing" only in contexts of beneficial powers, but we could say that one only has the standing to apologize if one has committed the relevant wrong. This is particularly clear when apology might come with benefits. John von Neumann allegedly responded to J. Robert Oppenheimer's expressions of guilt over the creation of the atomic bomb by remarking, "Sometimes one confesses to a sin in order to take credit for it."

47. As I will argue in Chapter 4, I consider apology to be a species of reparative action. But, for the present purpose of enumerating a list of features, I think it is clearer to flag each separately.

48. I'm thinking in particular of the work of Jules Coleman, Stephen Perry, and Andrew Gold. See, e.g., Jules L. Coleman, *Risks and Wrongs* (Cambridge: Cambridge University Press, 1992); Stephen R. Perry, "The Moral Foundations of Tort Law," *Iowa Law Review* 77 (1992); Andrew S. Gold, *The Right of Redress* (Oxford: Oxford University Press, 2022).

49. When we do talk about a "right to resent" or a "right to complain," it seems to me that we are actually talking about standing. If I say, "You have the right to resent his behavior," I mean that your resentment would be apt, not merely that you have a Hohfeldian liberty-right to resent. In the liberty sense, you have a right to resent any boulder or breadknife. We mean something else.

NOTES TO PAGES 17–21

50. On this score, it is telling that many leading theories of rights themselves invoke ideas of standing. It would be a transparently poor analysis of rights to say that they are defined by the standing to make claims if by that one simply meant the right to make claims.

51. Thompson, "What Is It to Wrong Someone?," 335.

52. See Douglas Lavin, "Other Wills: The Second-Person in Ethics," *Philosophical Explorations* 17, no. 3 (2014): 279–288.

53. See, for example, Bentham: "The fundamental idea, the idea which serves to explain all the others, is that of an offence." Bentham, "General View," 160.

54. H. L. A. Hart, "Legal Rights," in *Essays on Bentham: Studies in Jurisprudence and Political Theory* (Oxford: Clarendon, 1982), 183.

55. Statements of that assessment litter contemporary discussions of rights. See, e.g., Rowan Cruft, "Rights: Beyond Interest Theory and Will Theory?," *Law and Philosophy* 23, no. 4 (July 2004): 379: "at an impasse"; Leif Wenar, "The Nature of Rights," *Philosophy and Public Affairs* 33, no. 3 (Summer 2005): 223: "ended in a standoff"; and Gopal Sreenivasan, "A Hybrid Theory of Claim-Rights," *Oxford Journal of Legal Studies* 25, no. 2 (Summer 2005): 258: "The best objection that each theory wields against the other is unanswerable."

56. See Hart, "Any Natural Rights?"; and David Lyons, *Rights, Welfare, and Mill's Moral Theory* (New York: Oxford University Press, 1994), 36–46.

57. See Joseph Raz, *The Morality of Freedom* (Oxford: Oxford University Press, 1986), 165–186; and Matthew H. Kramer, "Rights without Trimmings," in *A Debate over Rights: Philosophical Enquiries,* by Matthew H. Kramer, N. E. Simmonds, and Hillel Steiner (Oxford: Oxford University Press, 1998), 7–112.

58. See, e.g., the criticisms in Sreenivasan, "Hybrid Theory of Claim-Rights"; and Frances M. Kamm, "Rights," in *The Oxford Handbook of Jurisprudence and Philosophy of Law,* ed. Jules Coleman and Scott Shapiro (New York: Oxford University Press, 2002), 483–487.

59. Kamm, "Rights," 485; Wenar, "Nature of Rights," 241–242.

60. Neil MacCormick, *Legal Right and Social Democracy: Essays in Legal and Political Philosophy* (Oxford: Clarendon, 1982), 154–166.

61. Feinberg, "Nature and Value," 252.

62. Karl Marx, "On the Jewish Question," in *The Marx-Engels Reader,* ed. Robert C. Tucker (New York: W. W. Norton, 1978), 42.

63. Compare Patricia J. Williams, *The Alchemy of Race and Rights* (Cambridge, MA: Harvard University Press, 1991), 153: "The Olympus of rights discourse may indeed be an appropriate height from which those on the resourced end of inequality, those already rights-empowered, may wish to jump. . . . For the historically disempowered, the conferring of rights is symbolic of all the denied aspects of their humanity: rights imply a respect that places one in the referential range of self and others, that elevates one's status from human body to social being."

64. See, e.g., Dworkin's account of competition harm, discussed in Chapter 2.2.1.

65. Marx, "On the Jewish Question," 42.

234 NOTES TO PAGES 21–31

66. Edna St. Vincent Millay, "Renascence," Poetry Foundation, https://www
.poetryfoundation.org/poems/55993/renascence

67. Millay, "Renascence."

2. THIRD PARTIES

1. Charlotte Brontë, *Jane Eyre* (New York: G. P. Putnam and Sons, 1897), 227.

2. H. L. A. Hart, "Legal Rights," in *Essays on Bentham: Studies in Jurisprudence and Political Theory* (Oxford: Clarendon, 1982), 183.

3. H. L. A. Hart, "Are There Any Natural Rights?," *Philosophical Review* 64, no. 2 (April 1955): 180.

4. Hart, "Are There Any Natural Rights?," 180.

5. For those inclined to resist this point, notice that, if the son canceled the arrangement with X, the mother could hardly insist to X on the original deal, at least absent reliance on her part. In contrast, the mother cannot waive X's contractual duty—her refusal to accept care would leave X and the son with an unresolved contract.

6. It may be tempting to wonder whether the mother might not have some kind of derivative or piggybacking right. Whatever this might mean, such a "right" would not involve the same kind of normative control. See Frances M. Kamm, "Rights," in *The Oxford Handbook of Jurisprudence and Philosophy of Law,* ed. Jules Coleman and Scott Shapiro (New York: Oxford University Press, 2002), 481–482: "What if my mother got only a derivative right contingent on my right? . . . But if she had such a right, why is she unable to singlehandedly waive the right (as I can) rather than merely set conditions for its being acted on?"

7. For a nice discussion of the standing that third parties like the mother have to forgive, see Glen Pettigrove, "The Standing to Forgive," *Monist* 92, no. 4 (2009): 583–603.

8. See Restatement (Second) of Contracts § 304. See also Nicolas Cornell, "Third Parties," in *Research Handbook on the Philosophy of Contract Law,* ed. Mindy Chen-Wishart and Prince Saprai (Cheltenham, UK: Edward Elgar, forthcoming).

9. H. R. Moch Co. v. Rensselaer Water Co., 159 N.E. 896 (N.Y. 1928).

10. *Id.* at 164.

11. *Id.* at 165.

12. See, e.g., Ogden v. Earl R. Howarth & Sons, Inc., 58 Misc. 2d 213, 215 (N.Y. Sup. Ct. 1968) (noting Cardozo's reasoning has been "subjected to severe criticism" and "only grudgingly followed").

13. See Lawrence v. Fox, 20 N.Y. 268 (1859); Contracts (Rights of Third Parties) Act 1999 (UK). Civil law jurisdictions acknowledged claims by third parties much earlier.

14. See, e.g., White v. Jones, [1995] UKHL 5; and Guy v. Liederbach, 459 A.2d 744 (Pa. 1983).

15. See, e.g., Melvin Aron Eisenberg, "Third-Party Beneficiaries," *Columbia Law Review* 92 (1992): 1429: "The classical school's rejection of the power of a third-

NOTES TO PAGES 31–34

party beneficiary to enforce a contract lacked substantial social congruence. Common-law rules that lack such congruence seldom survive."

16. See Restatement (Second) of Contracts § 311.

17. See Eisenberg, "Third-Party Beneficiaries," 1386: "The law of third-party beneficiaries is largely conceived as *remedial,* rather than substantive. The question addressed . . . is not whether the contract creates a 'right' in the third party." See also Nicolas Cornell, "The Puzzle of the Beneficiary's Bargain," *Tulane Law Review* 90, no. 1 (2015): 75–128.

18. For the importance of these boundaries, see Christopher Essert, *Property Law in the Society of Equals* (Oxford: Oxford University Press, 2024).

19. Though I have focused on contracts, similar issues arise with respect to third parties in property. For example, in *Hennigan v. Atlantic Refining Co.,* 282 F. Supp. 667 (E.D. Pa. 1967), workers on a City of Philadelphia construction site were killed by an explosion allegedly due to petroleum that had seeped into the city's property from Atlantic's property. The court refused to hold Atlantic liable to the workers because, whatever trespass of the city's property the gas might have constituted, "the invasion was not an invasion of any right of the decedents." *Id.* at 679. Even in the property context, recognition of third-party grievances has grown. This is especially so in cases where nonowner household members (including staff) are injured by a violation of the property owner's rights.

20. Hugo Grotius, *The Rights of War and Peace* (New York: M. Walter Dunne, 1901), 3.1.xi.

21. Grotius, 3.1.xiii.

22. Grotius's interest is in vindicating strategic tactics in which false communications are sent to comrades with the expectation that they will be intercepted and that the adversary will be deceived (as the Allies successfully convinced Germans that the D-Day landing would happen at Calais, not Normandy, through false communications). I accept that these cases generally do not involve wronging, but I don't take the explanation to be Grotius's. I think these cases are explained by features of war or of what it means to be not in community with another.

23. Ultramares Corp. v. Touche, Niven & Co., 174 N.E. 441 (N.Y. 1931).

24. *Id.* at 442.

25. *Id.* at 447.

26. In *Glanzer v. Shepard,* 135 N.E. 275 (N.Y. 1922), Cardozo allowed liability where a certification was prepared for a specific other third party. That is, Cardozo accepted that a certification might be addressed to an identified party other than the party paying for it and that duties would arise in that case.

27. *Ultramares Corp.,* 174 N.E. at 444.

28. *Id.* at 445. Whatever one thinks of *Ultramares,* some liability to third parties for negligent misrepresentation seems hard to avoid consistent with our moral sensibilities. Consider *Randi W. v. Muroc Joint Unified School District,* 929 P.2d 582 (Cal. 1997). A thirteen-year-old girl was sexually assaulted by her vice principal. She sued the former employer of the vice principal because the former employer had

236   NOTES TO PAGES 35–39

given unreservedly positive references for the vice principal despite knowing about prior charges of sexual misconduct and impropriety. That is, she sued alleging that the prior employer had wronged her by lying in the reference that it gave to others. The court found the former employer liable.

29. Like *Moch, Ultramares* has not be entirely followed. See Grant Thornton LLP v. Prospect High Income Fund, 314 S.W.3d 913, 918 (Tex. 2010) ("Over the ensuing decades . . . courts began to stray from *Ultramares* and expand auditors' scope of liability").

30. See Grotius, *Rights of War,* 3.1.xiii.

31. See R. Jay Wallace, *The Moral Nexus* (Princeton, NJ: Princeton University Press, 2019), 196–197: "In virtue of occupying the same public space with the speaker, those whose beliefs are apt to be influenced by the speaker's utterances are foreseeable as potential claimholders, even if they are not the immediate object of the speaker's attention at the time when the deceptive statements were put forward."

32. See Wallace, 266n7.

33. One might explain the difference by noting that negligence is a matter of avoiding unjustified risks, where justification depends partly on potential benefit. Rehearsing a play has value, whereas lying does not, so any risk imposed on others by a lie is an unjustified risk, but not so for the play. That does squeeze the phenomena back into the negligence paradigm, but it basically grants my point—namely that the wrong to the third party is not independent of, but rather derives from, the violation of the addressee's rights.

34. Immanuel Kant, "On a Supposed Right to Lie Because of Philanthropic Concerns," in *Grounding for the Metaphysics of Morals,* trans. James Ellington (Indianapolis: Hackett, 1993), 65.

35. For more on Kant's understanding of imputation, see note 116 and sources cited therein.

36. See Palsgraf v. Long Island R.R. Co., 162 N.E. 99, 100 (N.Y. 1928).

37. *Id.* at 99–100 (quoting West Virginia C. & P. R. Co. v. State, 54 A. 669, 671–672 (Md. 1903)).

38. The rescue doctrine in tort law offers another piece of support here. If a tortfeasor's conduct puts a victim in peril, the tortfeasor may be liable to rescuer who comes to the victim's aid. We can, of course, say that the risk to potential rescuers is part of the risk to be perceived. But that already puts pressure on the idea that the liability is exclusively to the direct rightholder.

39. I have—perhaps conspicuously—not yet mentioned *Palsgraf*'s dissenting opinion by Judge William Andrews. There is much that I agree with in it, including, "When injuries do result from our unlawful act we are liable for the consequences. It does not matter that they are unusual, unexpected, unforeseen and unforseeable." *Palsgraf,* 162 N.E. at 103 (Andrews, J. dissenting). But I do not wish to give the impression that I fully endorse Andrews's position. In his telling, "Every one owes to the world at large the duty of refraining from those acts that may unreasonably threaten the safety of others." This proposition involves, to my mind, the same

NOTES TO PAGES 39–41

mistake as Cardozo: that a wrong requires a duty to the wronged party to undergird it. Furthermore, while I agree with Andrews's focus on causation, I do not endorse his characterization of that inquiry as "practical politics," "public policy," and "expediency."

40. Flanders v. Cooper, 706 A.2d 589 (Me. 1998).

41. See, e.g., Althaus v. Cohen, 756 A.2d 1166, 1171 (Pa. 2000); and Bird v. W.C.W., 868 S.W.2d 767, 769 (Tex. 1994). For a thoughtful defense of the majority position, see John C. P. Goldberg and Benjamin C. Zipursky, "Triangular Torts and Fiduciary Duties," in *Contract, Status, and Fiduciary Law,* ed. Paul B. Miller and Andrew S. Gold (Oxford: Oxford University Press, 2016), 239–268.

42. "Unlike the duty to warn . . . the duty that Flanders advocates is a duty of medical treatment that goes to the core of the relationship between a patient and a health care professional. . . . Our recognition of the duty Flanders advocates . . . would intrude directly on the professional-patient relationship." *Flanders,* 706 A.2d at 591.

43. For a similar decision offering an explicit discussion of *Palsgraf,* see *Brady v. Hopper,* 570 F. Supp. 1333, 1338–1339 (D. Colo. 1983), which held that, even if the treatment offered by John Hinkley's therapist "fell below the applicable standard of care," the therapist could not be liable to those injured in Hinkley's assassination attempt. For the dependence on *Palsgraf'*s central premise, see also Goldberg and Zipursky, "Triangular Torts," 247n29.

44. "A physician's first loyalty must be to his patient. Imposing a duty on a physician to predict a patient's behavioral reaction to medication and to identify possible plaintiffs would cause a divided loyalty." Burroughs v. Magee, 111 S.W.3d 323, 334 (Tenn. 2003) (internal quotations omitted). See also Goldberg and Zipursky, "Triangular Torts," 246–247.

45. That's not to deny that medical providers can owe non-treatment-related duties—duties against defamation or reckless endangerment—to nonpatients. These duties are precisely the kind of thing that the father could demand ex ante—"you owe it to me not to do that." Such duties do not reach the treatment in *Flanders.*

46. Of course, there are practical and political questions of what moral complaints a legal system should recognize. Courts like that in *Flanders* are often partly focused on public policy concerns. In offering the argument that I have, I don't mean to imply that every moral wrong should be recognized as a legal wrong. It can be an appealing feature of privity requirements that they provide such limitations. But if they are to be maintained on these grounds, then they should be defended on substantive political arguments, not as a matter of how our normative concepts are structured.

47. William Shakespeare, *Much Ado about Nothing,* Arden edition (London: Thompson Learning, 2006), 5.1.53–66.

48. There are far too many examples to list. Modern popular culture stories range from the revenge killing in John Grisham's *A Time to Kill* (1989) to a memoir of forgiveness in Kate Grosmaire's *Forgiving My Daughter's Killer* (2016).

238 NOTES TO PAGES 41–42

49. Interestingly, Shakespeare himself may have been challenging some of these structures. For a discussion of the way that Shakespeare's *Much Ado about Nothing* varies from its predecessor sources in emphasizing the emotional aspects of the father-daughter relation, see Claire McEachern, "Fathering Herself: A Source Study of Shakespeare's Feminism," *Shakespeare Quarterly* 39, no. 3 (Autumn 1988): 276. Elsewhere, in *The Rape of Lucrece,* Shakespeare also seems to problematize the idea that the wrong in the death of a woman is based on a possessory right, where he sets the grief of the deceased's father and husband in competition with each other: "Then son and father weep with equal strife / Who should weep most, for daughter or for wife. / The one doth call her his, the other his, / Yet neither may possess the claim they lay." William Shakespeare, *Lucrece,* eds. Barbara Mowat et al. (Washington, DC: Folger Shakespeare Library, n.d.), accessed March 29, 2024, https://www.folger.edu /explore/shakespeares-works/lucrece/, 1791–1794.

50. While it seems to me that most contemporary tort theory has not grappled sufficiently with this problem, two excellent exceptions are Zoë Sinel, "Consortium as a 'Right' in the Law of Torts," *Supreme Court Law Review* 93 (2019): 229–246; and Steven Schaus, "Wrongs to Us," *Michigan Law Review* 121, no. 7 (2023): 1185–1233. Sinel considers the possibility that there is a respectable way to think that a person can have something like a property right in another person, but only with respect to third parties. Schaus tries to escape the dilemma by finding a joint agent—the marital "us"—that can be both the bearer of rights and sufferer of wrongs. Both approaches are coherent and intriguing. But for either view to be compelling, the posited rights must function ex ante in meaningful ways, not just as a kind of placeholder for the wrong, and I am not yet convinced that they do.

51. See, e.g., Sharman v. Evans, (1977) 138 CLR 563: "Actions for loss of services correctly treat [the loss of capacity to make the usual contributions of a wife and mother] as economic injury, but as a loss to the husband on the archaic view of the husband as master or owner of his wife."

52. See, e.g., Administration of Justice Act of 1982 (UK). In many American jurisdictions, actions for loss of consortium were abolished in the middle of the twentieth century, only to be reinstated a few decades later on a gender-equal basis.

53. See, e.g., Louis L. Jaffe, "Damages for Personal Injury: The Impact of Insurance," *Law and Contemporary Problems* 18 (1953): 229: "[The husband's] action is a fossil from an earlier era. It is one of a group of archaic actions based on the notion that the paterfamilias was alone competent to sue for losses suffered by the family unit. . . . Emancipation argues for the restriction or abolition of these actions rather than their extension."

54. See, e.g., Hitaffer v. Argonne Co., 183 F.2d 811 (D.C. Cir. 1950) (extending loss of consortium action to wife); and Reagan v. Vaughn, 804 S.W.2d 463 (Tex. 1990) (child's loss of parent).

55. In some versions, the plaintiff had to be fearful for their own safety, retaining a notion that one was recovering for the violation of one's own rights. But that was untenable. See *Hambrook v. Stokes Bros.,* [1925] 1 K.B. 141 (Eng. C.A. 1924), in which Lord Bankes notes that it would be odd to deny recovery to the mother who

NOTES TO PAGES 42–48

thinks in the moment of danger for her child while affording recovery to a woman "lacking in the motherly instinct" who fears instead for herself.

56. These were the facts that prompted California to reject the "zone of danger" test in *Dillon v. Legg*, 441 P.2d 912 (Cal. 1968).

57. The court in *Dillon v. Legg* describes itself as recognizing a duty of care, but that's almost certainly attributable to a Prosserian conception of "duty" as shorthand for policy considerations. Tellingly, in *Molien v. Kaiser Foundation Hospitals*, 27 Cal. 3d 916, 923 (1980), that same court would distinguish *Dillon* in a case where "plaintiff was himself a direct victim of the assertedly negligent act."

58. See John C. P. Goldberg and Benjamin C. Zipursky, *Recognizing Wrongs* (Cambridge, MA: Belknap Press of Harvard University Press, 2020), 204 ("The wrongful death statutes . . . *override* tort law's proper-plaintiff principle"); and Robert Stevens, *Torts and Rights* (Oxford: Oxford University Press, 2007), 53 (describing a "limited statutory exception").

59. Goldberg and Zipursky, *Recognizing Wrongs*, 204.

60. Van Beeck v. Sabine Towing Co., 300 U.S. 342, 350, 348 (1937).

61. Loucks v. Standard Oil Co., 224 N.Y. 99, 104 (1918).

62. Ronald Dworkin, *Justice for Hedgehogs* (Cambridge, MA: Belknap Press of Harvard University Press, 2011), 287–288. See also Arthur Ripstein, "Beyond the Harm Principle," *Philosophy and Public Affairs* 34, no. 3 (2006): 228–229.

63. For an expanded discussion of the issues on which this subsection is based, see Nicolas Cornell, "Competition Wrongs," *Yale Law Journal* 129, no. 7 (2020): 2030–2077.

64. Most notably, private suit provisions exist in the federal antitrust law by way of the Clayton Act (15 U.S.C. §15), in federal marketing law by way of the Lanham Act (15 U.S.C. § 1125), and in state unfair and deceptive practices acts.

65. For the classic discussion of games and their connection with artificial constraints, see Bernard Suits, *The Grasshopper: Games, Life and Utopia* (Toronto: University of Toronto Press, 1978).

66. An all-too-tempting idea about business is that business constitutes its own game—a game that, like poker, admits of some conduct that would be impermissible in ordinary life. See Albert Z. Carr, "Is Business Bluffing Ethical?," *Harvard Business Review,* January 1968.

67. For the idea that players' ends in games are systematically different, see the discussion of "disposable ends" in C. Thi Nguyen, "Competition as Cooperation," *Journal of the Philosophy of Sport* 44 (2017): 124–127.

68. For an illustration of the problems, see Lexmark Int'l, Inc. v. Static Control Components, Inc., 572 U.S. 118 (2014).

69. Indeed, one way of wronging another is by inappropriately regarding oneself as in competition. In the words of Fiona Apple,

> "I resent you presenting your life
> Like a fucking propaganda brochure
> And I see that you keep trying to beat me

240 NOTES TO PAGES 48–51

And I love to get up in your face
But I know if I hate you for hating me
I will have entered the endless race."

Fiona Apple, "Relay," *Fetch the Bolt Cutters,* Epic, 2020.

70. Arthur Ripstein, *Force and Freedom: Kant's Legal and Political Philosophy* (Cambridge, MA: Harvard University Press, 2009), 77–78.

71. Nor does it follow if one adds the observation that bare rights violations— mere harmless trespasses—do constitute wrongs. I will question this claim later (see Chapter 6), but for now note simply that it will not complete the argument. Ripstein often pairs these two observations, implying that because bare harm does not constitute a wrong and a bare rights violation does, wronging is a matter of rights. But that is no more valid than it would be to say that, because merely being a man doesn't make you a bachelor and because all priests are bachelors, bachelorhood is about priests and not about men.

72. My argument here mirrors the argument in David Owens, "The Role of Rights," in *Civil Wrongs and Justice in Private Law,* ed. Paul B. Miller and John Oberdiek (Oxford: Oxford University Press, 2020), 3–17, involving a disturbance in violation of a society's day of remembrance practice.

73. Compare Owens, 7: "this curbs our moral imagination."

74. In response, one might say that competitors are seeking the same ultimate prize (customers, profits, market share, etc.) so that one competitor's gain means the other's loss, whereas the same is not true of noncompetitors. That assumes an unrealistically zero-sum conception of competitive contexts. Even more problemati- cally, it implies that the competitor only has a complaint on the basis of a competi- tor's gain, not her own direct loss.

75. Restatement (Second) of Torts § 821B cmt. b, § 821C. (Am. Law Inst. 1979).

76. William Blackstone, *Commentaries on the Laws of England,* ed. Thomas P. Gallanis (Oxford: Clarendon, 2016), vol. 3, chap. 13.

77. As Blackstone recognized, public nuisance seems inconsistent with typical insistence on an individual right: "I must premise that the law gives no *private* remedy for any thing but a *private* wrong. Therefore no *action* lies for a public or common nuisance. . . . Yet this rule admits of one exception; where a private person suffers some extraordinary damage, beyond the rest of the king's subjects, by a public nuisance: in which case shall have a private satisfaction by action." Blackstone, 3:146.

78. It was reported that, when someone tried to comfort the owner by saying, "What a terrible accident," she responded, "This was not an accident. This is someone's fault."

79. Judge Andrews seems to go this far. See note 39.

80. See Wallace, *Moral Nexus,* 198.

81. Compare Siegfried Van Duffel, "The Nature of Rights Debate Rests on a Mistake," *Pacific Philosophical Quarterly* 93, no. 1 (2012): 104–123. There is

NOTES TO PAGES 51–55 241

significant affinity between my view and his assessment of the rights literature. Van Duffel concludes that interest theories and will theories describe different kinds of rights. I find it clearer to say that they describe different interpersonal relations.

82. G. E. M. Anscombe, "Who Is Wronged? Philippa Foot on Double Effect: One Point," *Oxford Review* 5 (1967): 17.

83. This locution obviously leaves open the question of what counts as a public norm. Law and morality are included. But what about other things? I believe that there can be aesthetic wrongs. Imagine the mushroom grower is foiled because the garage is being replaced by a massive glass monstrosity, completely out of place in their rural Vermont community. Or imagine a woman gives her old wedding dress to her soon-to-be daughter-in-law only to have the daughter-in-law alter it in aesthetically disastrous ways. Or imagine that an author sells the movie rights to her novel, but the studio makes a poor film that does not live up to the nuance of the novel at all. In these cases, I think that resentment, apology, and forgiveness all seem potentially apt. Such cases seem to fall somewhere in between the public nuisance examples and the imprudence examples that I discuss in the next section.

84. Charles Dickens, *Bleak House* (London: Bradbury and Evans, 1853), 228.

85. Luke 15:21 (emphasis added).

86. Sarah Orne Jewett, "A Farmer's Sorrow," in *The Complete Poems of Sarah Orne Jewett* (New York: Ironweed, 2019), 44.

87. There exists a wealth of examples of people apologizing to former teachers. In one touching instance, a man was moved to apologize thirty-nine years later for transferring out of a teacher's seventh-grade class because he was being teased for being the teacher's pet. See Tom Hallman Jr., "A Teacher, a Student and a 39-Year-Long Lesson in Forgiveness," *Oregonian*, April 21, 2012.

88. The language that Chuckie uses may sound like he is making not only a complaint but a claim, a demand—"you owe it to me." Nonetheless, in context, I think that Chuckie is not asserting a right. (Could he give Will his permission to stay? Could he force Will to leave? Should Will leave to satisfy Chuckie? I think that, even in this moment, Chuckie understands that this is Will's choice.) It's a nice example of the way that language can be ambiguous or even misleading. Chuckie's "owing" language is a reflection of the way that potential wrongings can be motivating but not justifying reasons (see Chapter 3), and the way that actions in accordance with our reasons are, in some sense, owed to everyone (see Chapter 9).

89. For a compelling defense of there being duties owed to oneself, see Paul Schofield, *Duty to Self: Moral, Political, and Legal Self-Relation* (Oxford: Oxford University Press, 2021). I consider it an advantage of this view that it explains imprudence wrongs as a subset of third-party wrongs.

90. See, e.g., Hart, "Any Natural Rights?," 181–182.

91. Tulare Irrigation Dist. v. Lindsay-Strathmore Irrigation Dist., 45 P.2d 972, 1007 (Cal. 1935). Admittedly, the example is complicated by the fact that the relevant legal rights are defined in terms of beneficial use, building the question of prudence into the right itself.

242   NOTES TO PAGES 56–61

92. Bob Dylan, "Visions of Johanna," *Blonde on Blonde,* Columbia, 1966. Literary critic Christopher Ricks notes that the words "and all" transform "acquiescent helplessness and uselessness" into the "energies of aggression and baffled anger." Christopher Ricks, *Dylan's Visions of Sin* (New York: HarperCollins, 2003), 487.

93. Joseph Raz, *The Morality of Freedom* (Oxford: Oxford University Press, 1986), 213–214.

94. Raz calls an account of morality based only on the interests of others "a partial and limited view," one that cannot capture how our own interests "exemplify universal values or values which form part of a mosaic which in its entirety makes for valuable social life." *Morality of Freedom,* 215. Compare Schofield, *Duty to Self,* 196: "We might wonder whether morality, when self-directed, would also dramatically realign one's practical orientation, or ripple through value theory in its entirety."

95. *Ultramares,* 174 N.E. at 444.

96. See Wallace, *Moral Nexus,* 9.

97. See Pamela Hieronymi, "Articulating an Uncompromising Forgiveness," *Philosophy and Phenomenological Research* 62, no. 3 (2001): 529–555.

98. Wallace, *Moral Nexus,* 11. Wallace himself concludes that one can only be wronged by a transgressor who "flouts" a directed obligation, which is to say, acts with an attitude of "knowing and even open disregard." Failing to fulfill an obligation inadvertently does not, for Wallace, constitute a wrong. I find this quite implausible. Even if one believes that a wrong requires an "attitude of indifference to or contempt for one's specific claims" (as I will argue in the text it does not), it seems to me that inadvertent transgressions often do display an attitude of indifference or contempt. Indeed, it seems to me that it can often be the worst form of disregard for another. See Seana Valentine Shiffrin, "The Moral Neglect of Negligence," in *Oxford Studies in Political Philosophy,* ed. David Sobel, Peter Vallentyne, and Steven Wall (Oxford: Oxford University Press, 2017), 3:197–228.

99. In *Sweeney Todd,* the main character kills his beloved wife, whom he has been told is dead, when he believes himself to be murdering a beggar out of misanthropic rage. It is hard to say that this was negligence with respect to his wife. Should we say that he does not wrong her? Surely not.

100. Compare Restatement (Third) of Torts: Intentional Torts to Persons §110 (American Law Institute, 2021).

101. See *id.,* cmt. b. ("the victim's presence might be neither foreseen nor very foreseeable").

102. See Ernest J. Weinrib, "Right and Advantage in Private Law," *Cardozo Law Review* 10, nos. 5–6 (1989): 1283–1310.

103. Compare Ernest J. Weinrib, "Private Law and Public Right," *University of Toronto Law Journal* 61, no. 2 (2011): 195.

104. *Moch,* 159 N.E. at 899 (emphasis added).

105. *Ultramares,* 174 N.E. at 444.

106. Compare Arthur Ripstein, *Private Wrongs* (Cambridge, MA: Harvard University Press, 2016), 57: "If I have no say about whether you do [certain] things,

NOTES TO PAGES 61–65

I have no standing to complain if you do them." The implication is that, if I were to have standing to complain, then it would mean that I have a say over whether you do certain things. For further discussion of that claim, see Chapter 5.

107. See Arthur Ripstein, "Private Authority and the Role of Rights," *Jerusalem Review of Legal Studies* 14, no. 1 (2016): 74: "Reactive attitudes are not always a reliable indicator that one person has wronged another. . . . These are not specific to interpersonal wrongs."

108. See Ripstein, "Private Authority and the Role of Rights," 75. It's not clear to me that this reflects Kant's view, as he regards freedom as involving being "beyond reproach." *Metaphysics of Morals*, 6:238.

109. There is an interesting parallel with the argument that Gabe Mendlow offers for what he calls "the enforceability constraint" in criminal law—namely that the state can only punish what it could permissibly intervene to stop. See Gabriel S. Mendlow, "Why Is It Wrong to Punish Thought?," *Yale Law Journal* 127, no. 8 (2018): 2372–2373.

110. Blame has sometimes been understood as a kind of punishment. See J. J. C. Smart, "Free-Will, Praise and Blame," *Mind* 70, no. 279 (1961): 291–306. For a different but related view, see Hanna Pickard, "Responsibility without Blame: Philosophical Reflections on Clinical Practice," in *The Oxford Handbook of Philosophy and Psychiatry*, ed. K. W. M. Fulford et al. (Oxford: Oxford University Press, 2013), 1146: "Although blame is not an action and so not a form of punishment, it is a *punishing* mental state."

111. See Chapter 4 for more on this.

112. Compare Kant: "This principle of innate freedom already involves . . . a human being's quality of . . . being a human being *beyond reproach* (*iusti*), since before he performs any act affecting rights he has done no wrong to anyone." *Metaphysics of Morals*, 6:237–238). Admitting third-party wrongs would not alter our being "beyond reproach" so long as we do nothing affecting rights.

113. George Eliot, *Adam Bede* (Chicago: Belford, Clarke, 1889), 378. For a more modern analogue, the thirteen-year-old protagonist in David Mitchell's novel *Black Swan Green* (New York: Random House, 2006), confronting the fact that his petty wrong set the stage for a series of unfortunate events, remarks, "I sometimes want to stick a javelin through my temples, just so I can stop *thinking* about how guilty I am. But then, I think, well, . . . it's [someone else's] fault too, isn't it? And if consequences of consequences of consequences of what you do're your fault *too*, you'd never leave your house, right? So [it] *isn't* my fault. But it is. But it isn't. But it is." Mitchell, 289.

114. Robert Penn Warren, *All the King's Men* (Boston: Houghton Mifflin Harcourt, 1946), 266–267.

115. Aristotle, *Poetics*, in *Aristotle: Selections,* ed. Terence Irwin and Gail Fine (Indianapolis: Hackett, 1995), 1453a8–11.

116. Immanuel Kant, *The Metaphysics of Morals,* trans. Mary Gregor (Cambridge: Cambridge University Press, 1996), 6:228. Note that Kant says only that one is accountable for the bad consequences of wrongful acts. If the point were only about

244   NOTES TO PAGES 65–68

metaphysical attribution, then the good consequences of breaking a duty should equally be attributed to the agent. For this reason, I think that the thesis should be viewed as making a substantive point about moral responsibility. To the extent that "imputation" suggests the metaphysical idea, that seems unfortunate. For further discussions of how Kant ought to be interpreted, see Thomas E. Hill, *Respect, Pluralism, and Justice: Kantian Perspectives* (Oxford: Oxford University Press, 2000), chap. 6; Andrews Reath, *Agency and Autonomy in Kant's Moral Theory* (Oxford: Clarendon, 2006), chap. 9; and Jens Timmermann, "Agency and Imputation: Comments on Reath," *Philosophical Books* 49, no. 2 (2008): 114–124.

117. G. E. M. Anscombe, "Modern Moral Philosophy," *Philosophy* 33 (1958): 12.

118. *Palsgraf,* 162 N.E. at 105 (Andrews, J., dissenting).

119. See Scott Hershovitz, "Wrongs without Rights," *JOTWELL,* January 11, 2017.

120. In legal terms, a doctrine of proximate cause never altogether eliminates questions of cause-in-fact. It may make them come up less often and with less overall at stake, succeeding therefore at mostly sweeping them under the rug. But cause-in-fact does not go away.

3. SHAPING ACTION

1. See, e.g., David Owens, "Promises and Conflicting Obligations," *Journal of Ethics and Social Philosophy* 11, no. 1 (2016): 2: "So what is distinctive of *obligation?* I will start with the following claim: it makes sense for you to do something simply because you think yourself obliged to do it." Also see Judith Jarvis Thomson, *The Realm of Rights* (Cambridge, MA: Harvard University Press, 1990), 91: "Surely the question what we ought to do itself turns on, and cannot be answered in advance of answering, what seems to be the prior question, namely what claims people have against us."

2. If the reader does not think that rights are action shaping, then this is a point to reiterate the methodological caution from Chapter 1.

3. G. E. M. Anscombe, "On the Source of the Authority of the State," in *Authority,* ed. Joseph Raz (New York: New York University Press, 1990), 152.

4. Contemporary moral philosophers often describe the fact that some act would be a wronging as itself providing a reason. For example, Terence Cuneo, *Speech and Morality: On the Metaethical Implications of Speaking* (Oxford: Oxford University Press, 2014), 236–239, suggests that the fact that some act would wrong another counts in favor of not doing it and thus "provides reasons" not to do it. Andrew Altman and Christopher Heath Wellman, *A Liberal Theory of International Justice* (Oxford: Oxford University Press, 2009), 6, explain that deontological reasons "demand a certain course of action *because* any contrary course would wrong someone" (emphasis added).

5. Arthur Schopenhauer, *The World as Will and Representation,* trans. E. F. J. Payne (New York: Dover, 1958), 1:339.

NOTES TO PAGES 68–71

6. Stephen Darwall, *The Second-Person Standpoint: Morality, Respect, and Accountability* (Cambridge, MA: Harvard University Press, 2009), 113.

7. Darwall, 12.

8. In arguing that wrongings are not action shaping, I don't mean to diminish their importance in our interpersonal lives. Compare Lisa Tessman, *Moral Failure: On the Impossible Demands of Morality* (Oxford: Oxford University Press, 2016), 159: "The approach of exclusively seeking action-guidance and its reward of moral triumph disables [people] from witnessing anything that suggests a contrary moral experience."

9. See, e.g., Mark Schroeder, *Slaves of the Passions* (Oxford: Oxford University Press, 2007), 92–97.

10. See, e.g., Hone v. Advanced Shoring & Underpinning, Inc., 291 P.3d 832 (Utah Ct. App. 2012).

11. An express warranty for a good may even be created after a contract has been completed. See U.C.C. § 2-313 cmt. 7 (Am. L. Inst. & Unif. L. Comm'n 2023).

12. Relatedly, sometimes parties guarantee the conduct of some third party. In such cases, there is nothing left to be done *by the promisor,* though there may be something left to be done.

13. Gary Watson, "Asserting and Promising," *Philosophical Studies* 117, no. 1/2 (January 2004): 66, makes a similar observation: "On this usage, promises are not confined to expressions of one's intentions. For example, 'I promise: you'll love this movie.' Or, to your incredulous children on an April morning, 'I promise: it snowed last night.'"

14. Oliver Wendell Holmes Jr., *The Common Law* (New York: Dover, 1991), 299. Holmes's observation was part of an agenda to detach the legal concept of a promise from the moral notion. See Patrick J. Kelley, "A Critical Analysis of Holmes's Theory of Contract," *Notre Dame Law Review* 75, no. 5 (2000): 1728: "Promise as redefined has the moral neutrality of a weather forecast: it is not, after all, a promise to do something, but just an accepted assurance that a certain event will happen." I do not share that agenda at all. But whereas some might resist Holmes's continuity, I see it as extending the reach of morality.

15. There is less philosophical attention to promising that some fact will obtain. Significant exceptions include Thomson, *Realm of Rights;* Watson, "Asserting and Promising"; and Jorah Dannenberg, "Promising as Doxastic Entrustment," *Ethics* 23, no. 4 (2019): 425–447.

16. One might bring these ideas closer together by understanding promises as forms of giving one's word (see Thomson, *Realm of Rights*) or as statements of intentions (see Páll S. Árdal, "And That's a Promise," *Philosophical Quarterly* 18, no. 72 [1968]: 225–237).

17. That view is most famously expressed by Learned Hand: "A warranty is an assurance by one party to a contract of the existence of a fact upon which the other party may rely. . . . It amounts to a promise to indemnify the promisee for any loss if the fact warranted proves untrue, for obviously the promisor cannot control what is

already in the past." Metro. Coal Co. v. Howard, 155 F.2d 780, 784 (2d Cir. 1946). See also Watson, "Asserting and Promising," 66: "To mean anything, a guarantee must be a commitment to respond in compensatory ways in case the 'product' is not as advertised."

18. See, e.g., Williams v. Kia Motors Am., Inc., No. 05-60018, 2005 U.S. Dist. LEXIS 40865, at *15 (E.D. Mich. Oct. 14, 2005) ("The repair or replace warranty does not promise that Plaintiff would never have a vehicle problem").

19. Contrast the issuer of a warranty with the issuer of an insurance policy.

20. Notice that this basically replicates the debate over whether all contractual commitments are just commitments to perform or pay. If one rejects this Holmesian attitude toward other contractual commitments (as one should), then one should similarly reject it here.

21. See U.C.C. § 2-313 cmt. 3 (Am. L. Inst. & Unif. L. Comm'n 2023) ("No particular reliance on such statements need be shown in order to weave them into the fabric of the agreement"); and CBS, Inc. v. Ziff-Davis Pub. Co., 553 N.W.2d 997, 1000–1001 (N.Y. 1990) ("The critical question is not whether the buyer believed in the truth of the warranted information . . . but whether it believed it was purchasing the seller's promise as to its truth"). Compare Thomson, *Realm of Rights,* 298.

22. Compare Thomson, *Realm of Rights,* 95, where she argues that it is "oversimplifying" that "a moral consideration—whether a promise or a claim or anything else—can have force for us only by way of *entailing* that a person ought to do such and such" and that promising might be thought of "as itself a 'liability-shouldering' device."

23. A. D. Woozley, "Promises, Promises," *Mind* 90, no. 358 (April 1981): 290.

24. For a defense of the idea that promising to try is not merely coherent but sometimes responsible, see Jason D'Cruz and Justin Kalef, "Promising to Try," *Ethics* 125, no. 3 (April 2015): 797–806.

25. See D'Cruz and Kalef.

26. Another possible case—though much more complicated—is illustrated by Seana Valentine Shiffrin's discussion of unscripted promises under duress. Shiffrin argues that, although such promises do not give rise to a right to performance in the promisee who has illegitimately induced them, they may nonetheless appropriately shape the choices of the promisor. Seana Valentine Shiffrin, *Speech Matters: On Lying, Morality, and the Law* (Princeton, NJ: Princeton University Press, 2014), 57.

27. Not to mention, of course, "I promise to love you forever." The literature on marriage promises offers some helpful discussions of promises to feel. See Elizabeth Brake, *Minimizing Marriage: Marriage, Morality, and the Law* (Oxford: Oxford University Press, 2011).

28. Elizabeth Porter to Mr. Moses Porter, July 17, 1801, in *Letters of Elizabeth Porter* (Loschberg, Germany: Jazzybee Verlag, 2017), 40 (emphasis added).

29. The fact that the wronging is merely potential again suggests that the wrong is not about a misrepresentation. In describing wedding vows, Marvin Gaye sings, "It shouldn't be lies because it turns out to be lies." Marvin Gaye, "When Did You Stop

NOTES TO PAGES 76-78

Loving Me, When Did I Stop Loving You," *Here, My Dear*, Motown Record Company, 1994.

30. Sheryl Crow, "Strong Enough," *Tuesday Night Music Club*, A&M, 1994.

31. Henry James, *The Wings of the Dove* (London: MacMillan & Co., 1923), 2.260–261.

32. Brake, *Minimizing Marriage*, 34, rejects the possibility of unintentional guarantees. She argues that, even if some promises can be used "to vouch for states of affairs," a promise unintentionally like that would fail for lack of uptake. I do not see why, just because a promise might have been misunderstood to involve something more than it did, it then has no effect at all. Someone offering a warranty on an already manufactured good cannot escape its effect because that warranty might have been misunderstood as a promise to manufacture the good with quality.

33. For arguments that immoral promises are not binding, see Seana Valentine Shiffrin, "Immoral, Conflicting, and Redundant Promises," in *Reasons and Recognition: Essays on the Philosophy of T. M. Scanlon*, ed. R. Jay Wallace, Rahul Kumar, and Samuel Freeman (Oxford: Oxford University Press, 2011), 155–178; and Gary Watson, "Promises, Reasons, and Normative Powers," in *Reasons for Action*, ed. David Sobel and Steven Wall (Cambridge: Cambridge University Press, 2009), 155–178. For arguments that they are binding, see Margaret Gilbert, *Joint Commitment: How We Make the Social World* (Oxford: Oxford University Press, 2011); and J. E. J. Altham, "Wicked Promises," in *Exercises in Analysis: Essays by Students of Casimir Lewy*, ed. Ian Hacking (Cambridge: Cambridge University Press, 1985), 1–21.

34. Mary Shelley, *Frankenstein*, in *Three Gothic Novels*, ed. Peter Fairclough (New York: Penguin Books, 1968), 436. The entire novel is, arguably, a study in the ways that the language of rights and justice do not fully capture the ethics of creation. For a nice explication of this reading, see Harriet Hustis, "Responsible Creativity and the 'Modernity' of Mary Shelley's Prometheus," *Studies in English Literature, 1500–1900* 43, no. 4 (Autumn 2003): 845–858.

35. Compare Shiffrin, "Immoral, Conflicting, and Redundant," 159: "Her utterance does not create any valid justificatory reason whatsoever, not even a pro tanto one, to rob the bank."

36. Shiffrin tentatively defends such an approach based on "the pseudo-promisor's fraudulent misrepresentation that the action is in that person's moral power to perform." Shiffrin, "Immoral, Conflicting, and Redundant," 160–161.

37. See Owens, "Promises and Conflicting Obligations," 12.

38. In reading the authors cited earlier, one finds that Shiffrin and Watson are primarily concerned with reasons and action, whereas Gilbert and Altham are primarily concerned with answerability.

39. Notice that, whereas a duty to do something bad is inherently problematic, there is nothing problematic with vouching that a bad event will happen. One year, I promised my uncle that the Buffalo Bills would not make the playoffs that season, so he need not watch the games. Had that been wrong, he might have complained to

248 NOTES TO PAGES 78–82

me. Though I was assuring him of something both of us considered bad, that creates no difficulty.

40. For what it is worth, the common law seems to reflect something of this duality. Illegal promises are void and unenforceable. And yet promisees may obtain equitable remedies for the breach of such promises when they are judged not to be *in pari delicto*.

41. Hallie Liberto, "The Problem with Sexual Promises," *Ethics* 127, no. 2 (January 2017): 384. As Liberto acknowledges, there are both costs and benefits associated with the stereotypical quality of this example. Liberto, 394n27. Whether I would have constructed the example in the same way or not, I have chosen to use it because I want to engage with Liberto's arguments.

42. Liberto, 385.

43. Liberto, 385. Here is another way that she puts it: "What John gains is the moral authority to determine an aspect of Jane's moral 'landscape.' John determines whether Jane will be wronging him if she fails to have sex with him. If he wants to have sex with her and she does not have sex with him, then she is guilty of breaking a promise." Liberto, 393.

44. Liberto, 387.

45. If it helps, one might imagine that John has done nothing to elicit the promise, that Jane is not inexperienced or naïve, and that Jane is advantaged in whatever power imbalances exist between her and John (all perhaps contrary to what might naturally be assumed about Liberto's vignette).

46. One might argue that the promise does operate to exclude some considerations from Jane's deliberation. Suppose that, after the game, Jane's friends are going out dancing. Jane would enjoy having sex with John that night, but she would prefer to go out with her friends. One might think that her promise does operate to exclude her desire to go out with her friends. So though her promise cannot exclude her desire to have sex or not, it can exclude certain alternatives. Thanks to Hallie Liberto for raising this argument. This does not convince me that the promise creates any kind of duty or right with respect to sex itself, and I think there is something revealing in that absence.

47. I take this example to depend on something special about sex—namely that it is something to which one cannot transfer a right. This may simply be a contingent feature of our particular social understanding of sex. While I think that Jane's promise partly misfires, it may be that in some other social world, it would not. There are probably other activities that would be similar, such as a promise to procreate. On that subject, consider the passage from *Frankenstein* quoted earlier. Or consider the alleged promise in *Perry v. Atkinson*, 240 Cal. Rptr. 402 (Cal. Ct. App. 1987).

48. Percy Bysshe Shelley, *Queen Mab: A Philosophical Poem; With Notes* (London: J. Watson, 1847), 76.

49. Frances Kamm points out that there is something perverse about deciding which life to save based on the fact that you could cure some third party's sore throat. F. M. Kamm, *Intricate Ethics: Rights, Responsibilities, and Permissible Harm*

NOTES TO PAGES 83–88

(Oxford: Oxford University Press, 2007), 61–63. One might think that the parents' case is like that: in the face of the tie between the rights of each child, the parents' claim is "an irrelevant good" relative to the children's rights. I agree with Kamm's point, but I do not think that it explains the pyrotechnics case. Kamm says that the important question is, "Would the tiebreaker have a complaint for his own sake . . . ?" (62). I believe the parent in my case would have a complaint of his own and yet should not function as a tiebreaker.

50. For a discussion of the idea that reasons must count in favor of action, at least counterfactually, see John Broome, *Weighing Lives* (Oxford: Oxford University Press, 2004).

51. Although I have used a parent-child case, the argument in this section might be developed using any of the third-party wrongs considered in Chapter 2. For example, I think a business that lowers prices by violating employee rights potentially wrongs upstanding competitor businesses, but I don't think that a business has any more reason to uphold employees' rights because it has competitors that do so—and certainly not an additional reason of the form rights involve. Or recall, again, the rescue doctrine that holds a tortfeasor liable for injuries to a victim's rescuer; you don't have more reason not to imperil a person because a high-risk rescue is likely to be attempted.

52. He would be tragically injured by *your* explosives. That's not irrelevant. Agent regret would be apt. But there's still a wronging on one side and not on the other.

53. Compare John Gardner, "What Is Tort Law For? Part 1: The Place of Corrective Justice," *Law and Philosophy* 30, no. 1 (2011): 1–50.

54. For a fuller discussion of this point, see Chapter 4.

55. Frances M. Kamm, "Rights," in *The Oxford Handbook of Jurisprudence and Philosophy of Law,* ed. Jules Coleman and Scott Shapiro (New York: Oxford University Press, 2002), 492. For a good discussion of the puzzle around the phenomenon, see Kasper Lippert-Rasmussen, "Moral Status and the Impermissibility of Minimizing Violations," *Philosophy and Public Affairs* 25, no. 4 (1996): 333–351.

56. Cass R. Sunstein et al., *Punitive Damages: How Juries Decide* (Chicago: University of Chicago Press, 2002).

57. W. Kip Viscusi, "Corporate Risk Analysis: A Reckless Act?" in *Punitive Damages: How Juries Decide,* ed. Sunstein et al. (Chicago: University of Chicago Press, 2002): 112–131.

58. Viscusi, 125.

59. The antipathy is sometimes expressed by saying that the liability-anticipating corporation treats human injuries as merely "a cost of doing business." But that framing only obscures matters. The advocate of cost-benefit analysis might respond that any risk of injury would indeed be a cost of doing business—a big cost that should be factored in rather than ignored. The problem is not believing that certain risks are a cost of doing business, but rather believing that one's legal liability is equivalent to that cost.

250   NOTES TO PAGES 88–91

60. Oliver Wendell Holmes Jr., "The Path of the Law," *Harvard Law Review* 10, no. 8 (March 1897): 461.

61. Holmes obviously knew this too: "I take it for granted that no hearer of mine will misinterpret what I have to say as the language of cynicism. The law is the witness and external deposit of our moral life." Holmes, 459.

62. "BNA Interview with AIPCA President Philip B. Chenok," *Securities Regulation and Law Report* 14 (Washington, DC: Bureau of National Affairs, 1982): 19.

63. Richard Thaler, *Quasi Rational Economics* (New York: Russell Sage Foundation, 1991), 15–16.

64. Intriguingly, this point doesn't seem to apply to agent regret. If Mr. A gets $100 and Mr. B has to be the one who faultlessly kills a child but gets $150, I think most anyone would prefer to be Mr. A. I'm not sure what to make of this, apart from concluding that agent regret is quite a different thing from ordinary regret.

65. The form of the question posed by Thaler—"Which person would you rather be?"—is quite hard to interpret. His sense that there is something irrational here depends on viewing the matter as a choice to forgo economic gain. If the question had been, "Which person do you think is likely to be more pleased?" it would not seem nearly as strange to select Mr. A. I suspect that the respondents who selected Mr. A were interpreting the question in this way.

66. The argument here has strong parallels with the argument that Elizabeth Harman makes against reasoning from the premise "I'll be glad that I did it." See Elizabeth Harman, "Harming as Causing Harm," in *Harming Future Persons: Ethics, Genetics, and the Nonidentity Problem,* ed. Melinda A. Roberts and David T. Wasserman (New York: Springer, 2009), 137–154.

67. See Victoria Husted Medvec, Scott F. Madey, and Thomas Gilovich, "When Less Is More: Counterfactual Thinking and Satisfaction among Olympic Medalists," *Journal of Personality and Social Psychology* 69, no. 4 (October 1995): 603–610; and David Matsumoto and Bob Willingham, "The Thrill of Victory and the Agony of Defeat: Spontaneous Expressions of Medal Winners of the 2004 Athens Olympic Games," *Journal of Personality and Social Psychology* 91, no. 3 (September 2006): 568–581.

68. Compare Harman, "Harming as Causing Harm."

69. Compare Richard Moran, *Authority and Estrangement: An Essay on Self-Knowledge* (Princeton, NJ: Princeton University Press, 2001), 192–193.

70. The philosophical literature on dispositions has debated and developed this point extensively. See, e.g., C. B. Martin, "Dispositions and Conditionals," *Philosophical Quarterly* 40, no. 174 (January 1994): 1–8; and Daniel Bonevac, Josh Dever, and David Sosa, "The Conditional Fallacy," *Philosophical Review* 115, no. 3 (2006): 273–316. One might put my claim by saying that whether an action would wrong someone is finkish.

71. My argument in this section is admittedly only by analogy. The concept of wronging is not simply analogous to the ideas of legal liability and regret, but often described in terms of these very ideas. Consider Erasmus: "Do not commit a wrong

now through the ignorance and thoughtlessness of youth that will gnaw at you for the rest of your life through the remorse of conscience and the bitter pangs that pleasure leaves behind in our minds as it flees from sight." Erasmus, "The Handbook of the Christian Soldier," in *The Collected Works of Erasmus: Spiritualia* (Toronto: University of Toronto Press, 1988), 117.

72. R. Jay Wallace, *The Moral Nexus* (Princeton, NJ: Princeton University Press, 2019), 86. Or again: "In respecting those claims against us, we relate to their bearers in a way . . . that ensures that there will be no basis for their resenting what we have done." Wallace, 137.

73. George Eliot, *Middlemarch* (Hertfordshire, UK: Wordsworth Editions, 1994), 205–206.

74. As Richard Moran writes of this very example, "Fred Vincy's guilty consciousness of himself blocks his attention to the actual object of his guilt: his actions and the beings who suffered the wrong." Moran, *Authority and Estrangement,* 192.

75. Sharing irrelevant personal details is what one is advised to do if ever faced with a stranger who is intending to harm you.

76. In making this argument, I am rejecting a conception of reasons according to which any evidence that something should be done counts as a reason in favor of doing it. See Stephen Kearns and Daniel Star, "Reasons: Explanations or Evidence?," *Ethics* 119, no. 1 (October 2008): 31–56, for a defense of the reasons-as-evidence view.

4. REPAIR

1. William Blackstone, *Commentaries on the Laws of England*, ed. Thomas P. Gallanis (Oxford: Clarendon, 2016), 3:78.

2. For some excellent efforts in this direction, see Linda Radzik, *Making Amends: Atonement in Morality, Law, and Politics* (Oxford: Oxford University Press, 2009); and Margaret Urban Walker, *Moral Repair: Reconstructing Moral Relations after Wrongdoing* (Cambridge: Cambridge University Press, 2006).

3. Aristotle, *Nicomachean Ethics,* trans. Robert C. Bartlett and Susan D. Collins (Chicago: University of Chicago Press, 2011), bk. 5, chap. 4.

4. See Justin D'Arms and Daniel Jacobson, "The Moralistic Fallacy: On the 'Appropriateness' of Emotions," *Philosophy and Phenomenological Research* 61, no. 1 (July 2000): 65–90. Technically, my argument requires only one or the other. If one thinks that all repair can be assimilated onto a single metric—say, holdings or welfare—then the shape might turn out to be only a matter of magnitude. My argument should also accommodate someone who is skeptical that we can assign magnitude but accepts that repair comes in different shapes.

5. For an excellent discussion of apologies as remedial acts, see Jeffrey S. Helmreich, "The Apologetic Stance," *Philosophy and Public Affairs* 43, no. 2 (2015): 75–108.

6. It would be a mistake to conclude that legal remedies are not concerned with expressive repair. See Scott Hershovitz, "Treating Wrongs as Wrongs: An Expressive Argument for Tort Law," *Journal of Tort Law* 10, no. 2 (2017): 405–447.

252   NOTES TO PAGES 97–104

7. "Comment on *Hawaii v. Office of Hawaiian Affairs*," *Harvard Law Review* 123 (2009): 302–312.

8. For the purposes of this chapter, I will assume that the *something* for which repair is being offered is a wrong. It is essential to my argument that this is sometimes the case. But nothing in this chapter depends on the claim that wrongs are the *only* things for which moral repair is apt.

John Goldberg usefully distinguishes between two different meanings of "injury." See John Goldberg, "Two Conceptions of Tort Damages: Fair v. Full Compensation," *DePaul Law Review* 55, no. 2 (2006): 435–468. Goldberg's argument is consistent with the argumentative structure of this chapter. Goldberg demonstrates the shifting meanings of "injury" by, in part, demonstrating shifting judicial approaches to awarding remedies. That is, Goldberg's argument, like mine, assumes that looking at remedies tells us something about the conception of injury at play.

9. For a nice expression of the concern about talk of "remedies" being misleading in legal contexts, see Peter Birks, "Rights, Wrongs, and Remedies," *Oxford Journal of Legal Studies* 20, no. 1 (Spring 2000): 1–37.

10. Although I have portrayed the preceding formulation as relatively uncontroversial, it does have one aspect or implication that some people might not accept. It implies that features of the parties that affect the appropriate remedial response are aspects of the wrong itself. If you step on your sister's foot, your apology might appropriately be different from if you step on a stranger's. If you lie to a well-known cheat, your remedial obligations might be different from if you tell the same lie to earnest youth. One might think these are not different wrongs—they are the same wrongs committed against different people. My own view is that these wrongs are different, as shown by the different repair that is required. But this dispute may be mostly terminological. Regardless, nothing in the chapter's argument turns on this question. One could, if one wanted, add a condition on the principle stipulating that it applies only as between the same two persons, and the argument would be the same.

11. I acknowledge the possibility of what D'Arms and Jacobson call "the moralistic fallacy," and I recognize that one must be on guard for it in arguments like the ones that I will proceed to make. Nevertheless, I persist in talking about what would be "appropriate" rather than "fitting" because the latter is a technical term and my argument depends on tapping into our intuitive understanding of ordinary human interactions.

12. *Anna Karenina*, the story of Henrietta Lacks, the life of architect Natalie de Blois, and a 2021 incident at Fordham, respectively.

13. Thomas Nagel, "Moral Luck," in *Mortal Questions* (Cambridge: Cambridge University Press, 1979), 29.

14. As an example of the strain, consider the following passage from Arthur Ripstein, which is intended to clarify the issue: "Harms and losses have a magnitude in a way that neither obligations nor wrongs consisting in the violation of those obligations do. . . . The *nature* of a wrong does not depend on its magnitude at all.

NOTES TO PAGES 107–113

The obligation is to avoid violating the rights of another. . . . Although the *obligation* makes no reference to a magnitude, a wrong in violation of that obligation will always have a magnitude, and can only be addressed by the transfer of powers of choice equivalent in magnitude." Arthur Ripstein, *Private Wrongs* (Cambridge, MA: Harvard University Press, 2016), 243–244. The first sentence says that wrongs don't have a magnitude, the final sentence says that they do, and the sentences in the middle imply that wrongs have a magnitude but one that is not part of their nature. For a theory whose elegance is certainly part of its appeal, the fumbling here is revealing.

15. In Bernard Williams's discussion of moral luck, he uses Anna Karenina in part to describe a difference between intrinsic and extrinsic failure. Williams's focus is Anna's subsequent relationship with Vronsky. The fact that it cannot bear the weight put on it is a kind of "intrinsic failure": Anna's hoped-for justification is "refuted by what happened." Bernard Williams, "Moral Luck," *Proceedings of the Aristotelian Society, Supplementary Volumes* 50 (1976), 122–123. I am focused on the subsequent relationship of the other party, but there is perhaps an interesting parallel. We might say that whether a betrayed lover forever pines or comes to move on without regrets is also of "intrinsic" significance to the wrong itself.

16. Ernest J. Weinrib, *Corrective Justice* (Oxford: Oxford University Press, 2012), 131. For an insightful discussion of the inadequacy of explaining disgorgement of profits as merely reinstating the victim's rights, see Nicholas W. Sage, "Disgorgement: From Property to Contract," *University of Toronto Law Journal* 66, no. 2 (Spring 2016): 244–272.

17. See Wendy Brown, *States of Injury* (Princeton, NJ: Princeton University Press, 1995), chap. 3. I consider my position to be compatible with Brown's influential concerns about political organizing around "wounded identities."

18. For a fuller defense of the legal point, see Nicolas Cornell, "What Do We Remedy?," in *Civil Wrongs and Justice in Private Law,* ed. Paul B. Miller and John Oberdiek (Oxford: Oxford University Press, 2019), 209–230.

19. See, e.g., Weinrib, *Corrective Justice.*

20. See, e.g., John Gardner, "What Is Tort Law For? Part 1: The Place of Corrective Justice," *Law and Philosophy* 30, no. 1 (2011): 1–50.

21. This is particularly clear in Gregory C. Keating, *Reasonableness and Risk: Right and Responsibility in the Law of Torts* (New York: Oxford University Press 2022). Keating criticizes corrective justice for focusing so much on tort law's remedial aspect, rather than emphasizing primary duties. I am sympathetic with his rejection of the continuity thesis and with his omnilateralism about primary duties. But I am less aligned with his characterization of the institution of tort law as creating primary duties; here, I am with the corrective justice theories in their remedial orientation.

22. Goldberg and Zipursky have developed civil recourse theory over a number of excellent articles, but their recent book, *Recognizing Wrongs,* is the most developed articulation of the theory. John C. P. Goldberg and Benjamin C. Zipursky, *Recognizing Wrongs* (Cambridge, MA: Harvard University Press, 2020).

254   NOTES TO PAGES 113–118

23. This feature of civil recourse theory creates some ambiguity, which has been the source of criticism. Ripstein, for example, argues that civil recourse faces a dilemma: either the recourse available is shaped by the nature of the obligation that gives rise to the action, in which case the theory collapses into corrective justice, or the recourse is not shaped by the obligation, in which case the theory defends mere revenge or instrumentalism. See Ripstein, *Private Wrongs,* 203.

5. THE UNCLAIMABLE

1. This form of argument is slightly perilous, as it is essential that the wrongs *consist in* the denial of the good, not merely arise associated with it. There is nothing, in general, surprising about a wrong springing from the denial of a good to which the person was not entitled. Consider a minority job applicant. They may not have a right to the job in question, but they will be wronged if they are denied the position on the basis of their race. That's straightforwardly explicable in terms of a right—the right to equal opportunity, a right against discrimination. The wrong arises out of the denial of the job, but it doesn't consist in it; it consists in the discrimination. I believe the examples described in this chapter are not like that. They are wrongs that consist in the denial of the relational good, but there is no right to which one can point. I am grateful to Gabe Mendlow for pressing me on this point.

2. See Immanuel Kant, *The Metaphysics of Morals,* trans. Mary Gregor (Cambridge: Cambridge University Press, 1996), 6:452.

3. John Stuart Mill, *Utilitarianism* (New York: Humboldt, 1890), 45.

4. Adam Smith, *The Theory of Moral Sentiments* (Los Angeles: Logos Books, 2018), 2.2.1.

5. The classic example is Peter Singer, "Famine, Affluence, and Morality," *Philosophy and Public Affairs* 1, no. 3 (Spring 1972): 229–243.

6. See Chapter 2.2.2.

7. G. E. M. Anscombe, "Who Is Wronged? Philippa Foot on Double Effect: One Point," *Oxford Review* 5 (1967): 17.

8. For an excellent discussion of the structure of requests, see Micha Gläser, "The Normative Structure of Request," in *Oxford Studies in Normative Ethics,* ed. Mark Timmons (Oxford: Oxford University Press, 2019), 9:29–49. As Gläser makes clear, one can be wronged both by declined requests and by improperly issued requests. These too may be wrongs that are not correlative to any right. Gläser's crucial insight is that requests, like testimony, should be transparent to the existing reasons. That fits with the point that I am making here: it is the reasons of the actor (the doctor, you with your apple)—and the disregard of them—that generate the wrongings. The request only serves to tether the would-be recipient to the action, much as a third-party beneficiary is tethered to a promised contractual performance.

9. Anscombe, "Who Is Wronged?," 17. I have deliberately offered a mundane, low-stakes example in the hope that it may have familiar resonances. Although it is always guilt inducing to decline a panhandler, my sense is that it is qualitatively

NOTES TO PAGES 118–121

different when one is engaged in a transparently frivolous, self-indulgent, or wasteful activity. But if the example does not stir your intuitions, I will dial it up a notch. Imagine the billionaire who stockpiles large quantities of malaria drugs, only to burn them in pyres for amusement. Couldn't those in need of malaria drugs around the world resent such conduct?

10. Hollywood Silver Fox Farm Ltd. v. Emmett [1936] 2 Eng. Rep. 408 (KB).

11. Burke v. Smith, 37 N.W. 838 (Mich. 1888).

12. Fortune v. National Cash Register Co., 364 N.E.2d 1251 (Mass. 1977).

13. Joseph Perillo, "Abuse of Rights: A Pervasive Legal Concept," *Pacific Law Journal* 27 (1995): 47.

14. Frederick Schauer, "Can Rights Be Abused?," *Philosophical Quarterly* 31, no. 124 (1981): 227.

15. A subsequent settlement among the estate and heirs reduced the dog's trust to $2 million and did provide sums to grandchildren not provided for in the will.

16. See, e.g., "Ruff Inju$tice," *New York Post*, August 30, 2007.

17. Smith, *Theory of Moral Sentiments*, 2.2.1.

18. Claudia Card, "Gratitude and Obligation," *American Philosophical Quarterly* 25, no. 2 (April 1988): 120. Emphasis in original.

19. Barbara Herman, *The Moral Habitat* (Oxford: Oxford University Press, 2021), 13.

20. In Act 1, Scene 4, the Knight speaks up about Goneril's treatment of her father, proclaiming, "My duty cannot be silent when I think your Highness wronged." William Shakespeare, *King Lear,* eds. Barbara Mowat et al. (Washington, DC: Folger Shakespeare Library, n.d.), 1.4.65–66. accessed March 31, 2024 https://www.folger.edu/explore/shakespeares-works/king-lear/

21. I quite like the way that Herman puts it: "Ingratitude is a refusal to admit the new relationship, denying that the benefactor is worthy of one's attention. It is as if the benefactor is not regarded as person, just a happenstance source of a good, or a sucker. There is in ingratitude an active insult to the benefactor." Herman, *Moral Habitat,* 20.

22. Jonathan Swift satirizes the potentially tyrannical nature of duties of gratitude in his description of the laws of Lilliput: "Ingratitude is among them a capital Crime . . . for they reason thus; that whoever makes ill Returns to his Benefactor, must needs be a common Enemy to the rest of Mankind, from whom they have received no Obligation; and therefore such a Man is not fit to live." Jonathan Swift, *Gulliver's Travels* (London: Collector's Library, 2004), 68.

23. In civil law jurisdictions, ingratitude can sometimes be grounds for revoking a gift. But, interestingly, this legal argument is understood as personal. For example, one's heirs cannot argue ingratitude to reverse a gift. See, e.g., Grandchampt v. Administrator of Succession of Billis, 49 So. 998 (La. 1909). This structures seems to me (correctly) to regard ingratitude as a wrong to a beneficiary, but gratitude as not any kind of *in rem* right.

24. See Fred Berger, "Gratitude," *Ethics* 85, no. 4 (1975): 300.

256 NOTES TO PAGES 121–123

25. Herman makes the related point that this is why debts of gratitude cannot be released: "Release would amount to a rejection by the benefactor of the equality of agency that comes with taking the duty of gratitude seriously." Herman, *Moral Habitat,* 20.

26. Judith Jarvis Thomson, *The Realm of Rights* (Cambridge, MA: Harvard University Press, 1990), 122.

27. David Owens, *Shaping the Normative Landscape* (Oxford: Oxford University Press, 2012), 62.

28. For a more recent and extended defense of such wrongings, see Rima Basu and Mark Schroeder, "Doxastic Wronging," in *Pragmatic Encroachment in Epistemology,* ed. Brian Kim and Matthew McGrath (New York: Routledge, 2018), 181–205.

29. Consider Julius Caesar, Act 4, Scene 3:

> That you have wronged me doth appear in this:
> You have condemned and noted Lucius Pella
> For taking bribes here of the Sardinians,
> Wherein my letters, praying on his side,
> Because they knew the man, was slighted off.

William Shakespeare, *Julius Caesar,* eds. Barbara Mowat et al. (Washington, DC: Folger Shakespeare Library, n.d.), 4.3.1–5. accessed March 31, 2024 https://www.folger.edu/explore/shakespeares-works/julius-caesar/

30. Miranda Fricker, *Epistemic Injustice: Power and the Ethics of Knowing* (Oxford: Oxford University Press, 2007), 20.

31. Fricker, 2.

32. That is not to say that we are only responsible for the activity of directing our attention. It seems to me that we can be responsible for the failure to see, not just the failure to look. See Nicolas Cornell, "Looking and Seeing," in *Conversations in Philosophy, Law, and Politics,* ed. Ruth Chang and Amia Srinivasan (Oxford: Oxford University Press, forthcoming).

33. Iris Murdoch, *The Sovereignty of Good* (New York: Routledge, 1971), 17–18.

34. Exod. 20:17.

35. Hilkhot Gezeila Va-aveida 1:9.

36. Thomas Aquinas, *The Summa Theologica* (Notre Dame, IN: Christian Classics, 1948), Q.71, art. 5.

37. Jimmy Carter, interview, *Playboy,* November 1976, 66.

38. See Gerald Gardner, *Campaign Comedy: Political Humor from Clinton to Kennedy* (Detroit: Wayne State University Press, 1994), 181.

39. In his final interview before being executed, Ted Bundy described how he harbored fantasies of sexual violence before acting on them: "I knew it was wrong to think about it." James Dobson, *Fatal Addiction: Ted Bundy's Final Interview* (Pomona, CA: Focus on the Family Films, January 24, 1989).

40. For a nice defense of a moral principle "requiring us to have basic attitudes of respect and goodwill toward others," see Angela M. Smith, "Guilty Thoughts," in

NOTES TO PAGES 124–129

Morality and the Emotions, ed. Carla Bagnoli (Oxford: Oxford University Press, 2011), 235–256. Smith's focus is on what morality requires of us, not whether we wrong others by transgressing.

41. Jewish families were outraged to learn that Mormons, who believe that ancestors can be brought into the church through posthumous baptism, had been giving these proxy baptisms to victims of the Holocaust. A policy in Israel permits Jews to enter the Temple Mount / Haram al-Sharif as tourists but not to pray there, which would be taken as an offense to Muslims.

42. Very much in this vein, consider the following example from Frances Kamm, used to argue against Joseph Raz's account of rights: "If I have a duty to help you by praying to God for your recovery, you still might not have a right that I relate to God in this particular way." Frances M. Kamm, "Rights," in *The Oxford Handbook of Jurisprudence and Philosophy of Law,* ed. Jules Coleman and Scott Shapiro (New York: Oxford University Press, 2002), 483.

43. As George Sher provocatively puts it, "each person's subjectivity is a limitless, lawless wild west in which absolutely everything is permitted," for otherwise we could experience "neither the exhilaration that accompanies the frictionless free play of the imagination nor the solace of a redoubt that is ours and ours alone." George Sher, *A Wild West of the Mind* (Oxford: Oxford University Press, 2021), 1, 16. I quite disagree with Sher's thesis that no thoughts are ever morally impermissible. But note that his whole focus is on permissibility and the need for freedom; it all operates ex ante, not ex post.

44. Anthony Trollope, *The Eustace Diamonds* (New York: Penguin Books, 2004), 97.

45. Taylor Swift, "All Too Well," *Red,* Apollo A-1, 2012.

46. In the quoted lyrics from Swift (unlike the Trollope), it is not explicit that she is describing a grievance, as opposed to merely harm and sadness. If you have that thought, ask any Swiftie whether Jake Gyllenhaal wronged her.

47. Compare (or contrast) Alanis Morrisette: "You told me / You'd hold me until you died / 'Til you died, but you're still alive." Alanis Morrisette, "You Oughta Know," *Jagged Little Pill,* Maverick Recording Company, 1995. As I argue in the text, even Morrisette's grievance is probably not about the breach of this promise as such. It's about "the mess you left when you went away" and "the cross I bear that you gave to me."

48. Amia Srinivasan, *The Right to Sex: Feminism in the Twenty-First Century* (New York: Farrar, Straus and Giroux, 2021), 73.

49. Srinivasan, 90. Srinivasan's primary point is to see the formation of desire as "political." This focus allows us to avoid censuring individuals for their desires while still critiquing the social structures at play beneath. Although I fully agree that there are political questions here, I believe that they also ramify to the individual interpersonal interactions.

50. Srinivasan. For her part, Srinivasan ends her essay by gesturing toward the ways that desire is malleable and sometimes surprising. This is an important point

258   NOTES TO PAGES 129–135

that is worth making, but it is, to my mind, not the crucial point and too much of a concession to the liberal worldview. I think that even completely intransigent desires can potentially wrong when they are unjustifiable.

51. Leo Tolstoy, *Anna Karenina,* trans. Richard Pevear and Larissa Volokhonsky (London: Penguin Books, 2003), 84.

52. See Simon Căbulea May, "Directed Duties," *Philosophy Compass* 10, no. 8 (August 2015): 523: "Directed duties are duties that an agent owes to some party—a party who would be wronged if the duty were violated. They therefore comprise a three-place relation between the agent (or *subject*), the required action (or *content*) and the party (or *object*) who stands to be wronged."

53. Tony Manela, "Obligations of Gratitude and Correlative Rights," in *Oxford Studies in Normative Ethics,* ed. Mark Timmons (Oxford: Oxford University Press, 2015), 5:162.

54. Manela, 162.

55. Compare Jonas Vandieken, "Bipolar Obligations, Recognition Respect, and Second-Personal Morality," *Ethics* 23 (2019), 310: "the post-obligation view cannot account for the principle of bipolar recognition respect, a principle that calls for the ex ante recognition of another person's valid claim"

56. Adrienne M. Martin, *How We Hope: A Moral Psychology* (Princeton, NJ: Princeton University Press, 2014), 74.

57. Compare Wallace's explanation that the duty of gratitude is directed but not a right because it "lacks the determinacy characteristic of cases involving standard moral rights." R. Jay Wallace, *The Moral Nexus* (Princeton, NJ: Princeton University Press, 2019), 204. Like Manela, the only manifestation that Wallace offers of the directed duty is the wronging: "This [i.e. the relational claim] shows itself . . . in the fact that a failure to discharge the debt of gratitude that is held by the beneficiary would not merely be wrong, but something that wrongs the benefactor in particular." Wallace, 204.

58. Martin, 76.

6. THE COMPLAINTLESS

1. Jeffrie G. Murphy, "Moral Death: A Kantian Essay on Psychopathy," *Ethics* 82, no. 4 (July 1972): 291–293.

2. Peter Jones, "Group Rights and Group Oppression," *Journal of Political Philosophy* 7, no. 4 (1999): 361–362.

3. Imagine, perhaps, the lone person on a world without others. They would be "the sort of thing to which duties can be owed and which is capable of being wronged," but they would have no standing to claim or complain against anyone.

4. Stephen Darwall, *The Second-Person Standpoint: Morality, Respect, and Accountability* (Cambridge, MA: Harvard University Press, 2009), 3.

5. "When someone attempts to give another a second-personal reason, she purports to stand in a relevant authority relation to her addressee." Darwall, 4.

NOTES TO PAGES 135–137

6. Darwall, 13.

7. R. Jay Wallace, "Reasons, Relations, and Commands: Reflections on Darwall," *Ethics* 188, no. 1 (October 2007): 26.

8. For Wallace, this fact calls into question the "voluntarist" element of Darwall's account—that is, Darwall's view that second-personal reasons are "claims on the will of an agent that are grounded in another agent's authority to issue claims of the relevant kind." Wallace, 27. Of course, it is not as though it had not occurred to Darwall that the reasons are there all along. In fact, he writes, "Moral obligations involve implicit demands that are 'in force' . . . even when actual individuals have not explicitly made them." Darwall, *Second-Person Standpoint,* 290n22. The puzzle is how to fit these ideas together.

9. In what follows, I simplify and put my own gloss on things, to avoid getting lost in the nuances and technical terminology. For those interested in the details, I recommend reading both Wallace, "Reasons, Relations, and Commands"; and Stephen Darwall, "Bipolar Obligations," in *Oxford Studies in Metaethics,* ed. Russ Shafer-Landau (Oxford: Oxford University Press, 2012), 7:333–358.

10. Wallace labels Darwall's account "voluntarist" and argues that any voluntarist account cannot do justice to the inherent relationality of morality.

11. Wallace, "Reasons, Relations, and Commands," 26.

12. See Darwall, "Bipolar Obligations," 357.

13. Here is an inchoate mapping (about which I feel substantial uncertainty): Darwall's relational normativity is voluntarist, but that operates at the level of the moral community; bipolar normativity is only a subset thereof. Wallace's relational normativity is nonvoluntarist and at the level of individuals; it just is bipolar normativity. By distinguishing rights and wrongs, my view allows for something like voluntarism at the individual level with respect to wronging, while retaining a kind of nonvoluntarist or collective perspective with respect to the ex ante.

14. Trained lawyers might be confused by the use of the word "standing" in this context. In law, "standing" typically has a narrow meaning, referring to whether parties have a relevant interest in the disputed controversy. But as I highlight later, there are legal principles—especially drawn from equity—that govern when a party may make particular arguments, and we might just as well think of these as rules of standing. In general, to challenge the opposing party's standing is, essentially, to pose the question, "What is it to you?" That challenge can be used either to demand what interest the other party has at stake or to question the other party's appeal to the relevant norm. To my mind, doctrines from unclean hands and estoppel to unconscionability, mitigation, duress, and more should all be understood as rules of standing.

15. John Rawls, *A Theory of Justice* (Cambridge, MA: Harvard University Press, 1999), 190–191.

16. For useful discussions of this idea, see G. A. Cohen, "Casting the First Stone: Who Can, and Who Can't, Condemn the Terrorists?" and "Ways of Silencing Critics," in *Finding Oneself in the Other,* ed. Michael Otsuka (Princeton, NJ: Princeton University Press, 2013), 115–133, 134–142.

260 NOTES TO PAGES 137–139

17. The following draws on Nicolas Cornell, "A Complainant-Oriented Approach to Unconscionability and Contract Law," *University of Pennsylvania Law Review* 164, no. 5 (2016): 1131–1176.

18. This is not self-defense. If the context of a physical altercation raises questions about self-defense for you, then consider a different retaliatory example—e.g., a spouse who cheats after having been cheated on, a coworker who belittles after having been belittled.

19. For a more literary but brutal example, consider the story of Hermotimus the eunuch, as told by Herodotus. Hermotimus finds the man who castrated him and forces him to castrate his children and then be castrated by his children. Hermotimus then exclaims, "You have acted vilely, and . . . you cannot complain of the vengeance that will come to you from me." Herodotus, *The History,* trans. David Greene (Chicago: University of Chicago Press, 1987), 595. We might agree that the man "cannot complain" about being castrated after having inflicted that very fate on Hermotimus, while still concluding it is very wrong.

20. Compare Immanuel Kant, *The Metaphysics of Morals,* trans. Mary Gregor (Cambridge: Cambridge University Press, 1996), 6:307. Emphasis in original. "Human beings do *one another* no wrong at all when they feud among themselves; for what holds for one holds also in turn for the other, as if by mutual consent." I think that the "as if" is important here—we should not say that the transgressor did consent, for they surely did not. See also Cohen, "Casting the First Stone," 119.

21. The existence of truly identical violations is certainly too strong a requirement. The guy at the bar could not rationalize his complaint by saying, "I acknowledge a principle that retaliation is wrong—one should always turn the other cheek—and you did not. But I didn't violate *that* principle. I acknowledge no principle against defending the honor of one's soccer club by violence."

22. Cohen, "Casting the First Stone," 123.

23. For a discussion of provoking, see Kimberly Kessler Ferzan, "Provocateurs," *Criminal Law and Philosophy* 7 (2013): 597. Because her topic is criminal liability, Ferzan is focused mainly on the forfeiture of defensive rights, not the forfeiture of one's complaint—though these ideas are related.

24. Waiver, often described as the voluntary relinquishment of a right, may seem like it doesn't belong on this list, as it might seem to be about shifting rights themselves. But as it operates in the law, waiver is often a sibling of estoppel—waiving a complaint without waiving first-order rights. For one example, see the final section of Chapter 7.

25. For a full treatment of the doctrine, see T. Leigh Anenson, *Judging Equity: The Fusion of Unclean Hands* (Cambridge: Cambridge University Press, 2018).

26. See Ori J. Herstein, "A Normative Theory of the Clean Hands Defense," *Legal Theory* 17, no. 3 (2011): 171, noting that both unclean hands and *tu quoque* "are doctrines of standing that deflate the illocutionary force (and not the truth-value) of normative speech acts directed against wrongdoers by those guilty of similar or connected wrongdoing."

NOTES TO PAGES 139-142

27. Answer and Affirmative Defenses of Plaintiffs and Counterclaim Defendants, Fairey et al. v. Associated Press, No.09-01123 (S.D.N.Y. April 14, 2009).

28. For a comprehensive account of the dispute, including Fairey's own remarks, see William W. Fisher et al., "Reflections on the Hope Poster Case," *Harvard Journal of Law and Technology* 25, no. 2 (2012): 243–338. Incidentally, the AP also attempted to use the "unclean hands" argument against Fairey because he had concealed and destroyed relevant documents. The case ultimately settled with Fairey and the AP agreeing to share rights to the image.

29. Saul Smilansky, "The Paradox of Moral Complaint," *Utilitas* 18, no. 3 (2006): 285.

30. Smilansky, 285.

31. Smilansky, 290.

32. Smilansky, 289.

33. These cases, I will note, seem to provide problems for a demand theory of rights. The transgressor lacks, as far as I can tell, the individual standing to demand proper treatment, but I would still say that he has rights.

34. It seems to me that the norm transgressor may still be entitled to something akin to impersonal indignation if his rights are violated.

35. Smilansky suggests this thought in a footnote. He says that "when we forbid stealing from our thief, we do so not out of concern for his rights" but instead out of "the conventional nature of property relations, and the thought that we cannot permit lawlessness." Smilansky, "Paradox of Moral Complaint," 28n2.

36. As evidence, notice two things. First, the reason would seem to have a deontological character in the sense that it would not permit interpersonal aggregation. If we thought that the reason not to do violence to one who has done us violence were not rights-like, then it would seem like one could do such violence against the person as long as there were a good enough reason. If our reason for not violating the bodily integrity of rapists is not a distinctly rights-based reason, then it becomes harder to see why we could not subject them to medical experimentation if the potential benefits would be sufficiently large. Second, the reason is still a matter of some control by the transgressor. If the reasons not to subject the rapist to medical experimentation have nothing to do with their rights, then their consent to the experimentation would be irrelevant. But such consent may not be irrelevant.

37. There are interesting parallels between Ripstein's argument from harmless trespass and David Owens's argument from "bare wrongings," See David Owens, *Shaping the Normative Landscape* (Oxford: Oxford University Press, 2012), 127. Despite focusing on similar phenomena, Ripstein and Owens come to quite different conclusions. Whereas Ripstein concludes that wrongs are not about interests as such, Owens concludes that there must be a kind of interest (a normative interest) that underwrites bare wrongings.

38. Arthur Ripstein, "Beyond the Harm Principle," *Philosophy and Public Affairs* 34, no. 3 (2006): 218.

262 NOTES TO PAGES 142–145

39. For an equally fun but creepy story about a rogue fluoridating dentist, see Arthur Ripstein, *Force and Freedom: Kant's Legal and Political Philosophy* (Cambridge, MA: Harvard University Press, 2009), 44.

40. If you asked someone to think of a harmless trespass, I doubt that they would conjure cases like Ripstein's. Far more likely, they would give you a recollection of that time they walked across a neighbor's field because it was getting late and they wanted to get home. And I doubt they would think that they thereby wronged the neighbor. Ripstein has deliberately constructed the examples to pump the intuition that there is a wronging—after all, his purpose is to show the existence of wrongings without harm. It's another matter to show that all harmless trespasses are wrongs.

41. See Meir Dan-Cohen, *Harmful Thoughts: Essays on Law, Self, and Morality* (Princeton, NJ: Princeton University Press, 2009), chap. 6, for an idea of how this might proceed.

42. In the words of Benjamin Cardozo, "It is ancient learning that one who assumes to act, even though gratuitously, may thereby become subject to the duty of acting carefully, if he acts at all." Glanzer v. Shepard, 135 N.E. 275, 276 (N.Y. 1922). Due to its perceived harshness, the common law position has been widely amended by Good Samaritan statutes, which often limit liability to reckless or willful failures or immunize professional responders.

43. Two clarifications: First, one might think that you had no right against my doing whatever was necessary to save you, because this was an emergency. But assume that this was not that level of life-saving emergency—the kind that would make even unwanted assistance permissible. Second, one might contend that, given that the back door was locked, kicking down the door actually was justified as a matter of necessity, and thus I had a right to do it—it was just unbeknownst to you or me at the time. But it is not necessary that the back door was locked all along. Suppose that it was unlocked at the time when I disregarded your instruction, but that moments later (less time than it would have taken me to get around the house) your security firm remotely deadbolted the door.

44. See Seana Valentine Shiffrin, "Wrongful Life, Procreative Responsibility, and the Significance of Harm," *Legal Theory* 5, no. 2 (1999): 117–148.

45. I'm grateful to Frances Kamm for raising this issue. I am open to the thought that one can lack standing to complain because of one's debt of gratitude, though it can be hard to disentangle whether one lacks standing (complaint is inapt) or one simply ought not complain (impermissible ingratitude). Regardless, I do not think that it is the operative feature of this case.

46. One might point to nominal damages in the law as evidence that parties do have a complaint despite suffering nothing apart from the rights violation per se. But actually, the law uses nominal damages in two different ways, a division that supports my view. Nominal damages can be used expressively to vindicate rights, especially where they are what the plaintiff seeks and where there might be nonmonetizable injuries (and they may also open the door to punitive damages or recovery of legal fees). But nominal damages can also be used to express contempt for the

NOTES TO PAGES 145–147

plaintiff's case, where a plaintiff is judged to be pressing a right without any real complaint. English law explicitly distinguishes such "contemptuous damages," awards for them "the smallest coin in the realm," and will not award attorney's fees alongside them. Put simply, if you have a real but nonmonetizable injury, then we will award you a symbolic one dollar and let you recover your litigation costs and perhaps punitive damages too; if you are suing for a bare rights violation when you have nothing truly to complain of, then we will award you a penny and send you home to pay your own attorney. In American law, another point of reference here might be de minimis rules. Consider *Harris v. Time, Inc.*, 237 Cal. Rptr. 584, 590 (Ct. App. 1987), in which the court dismissed the plaintiff's "technically valid" lawsuit over allegedly having been tricked into opening a junk mail envelope. Thanks to Steve Schaus for helpful pointers here.

47. E. P. Evans, *The Criminal Prosecution and Capital Punishment of Animals* (London: W. Heinemann, 1906), 18.

48. "It was the product of a social state, in which dense ignorance was governed by brute force, and . . . tended to foster [club law] by making a travesty of the administration of justice and thus turning it into ridicule." Evans, 41.

49. For the view that animals can be plaintiffs, see Cass R. Sunstein, "Standing for Animals," *UCLA Law Review* 47 (2000): 1333–1368. I am sympathetic with animal standing where it involves prospective rights enforcement, less so for any kind of corrective justice.

50. For the importance of shared concepts to wronging, see Michael Thompson, "What Is It to Wrong Someone? A Puzzle about Justice," in *Reason and Value: Themes from the Moral Philosophy of Joseph Raz,* ed. R. Jay Wallace et al. (Oxford: Oxford University Press, 2004), 333–384.

51. Christine M. Korsgaard, *Fellow Creatures: Our Obligations to the Other Animals* (Oxford: Oxford University Press, 2018), 37. I mean very much to be following this same approach (although I might not accept every detail), including the acknowledgment that "which creatures actually *have* those forms of cognition, if any do, is an empirical question that cannot be answered by philosophy alone."

52. See Korsgaard, 43.

53. Christine M. Korsgaard, "Getting Animals in View," *Point*, December 23, 2012.

54. The distinction Korsgaard draws is not exactly the same as the contrast Percy Bysshe Shelley draws with the skylark (see Chapter 9). But there is a similarity. I cannot help but think that the capacity to step back and evaluate reasons (normative self-government) is deeply connected with the retrospective imaginative capacity to see different counterfactual histories—to "pine for what is not."

55. See, e.g., Frans de Waal, *Mama's Last Hug: Animal Emotions and What They Tell Us about Ourselves* (New York: W. W. Norton, 2019).

56. One might wonder how this claim fits with Oliver Wendell Holmes Jr.'s quip, "Even a dog distinguishes between being stumbled over and being kicked." Holmes's point is that the dog can distinguish action (intentional) from accident. That's a different matter from evaluating why the action has been performed.

264 NOTES TO PAGES 147-150

57. Both compare and contrast Ludwig Wittgenstein's well-known remark, "If a lion could talk, we wouldn't be able to understand it." Ludwig Wittgenstein, *Philosophical Investigations,* trans. G. E. M. Anscombe, P. M. S. Hacker, and Joachim Schulte (Malden, MA: Wiley-Blackwell, 2009), §327. The famously mysterious comment seems to be about the way in which understanding requires more than mere linguistic competence, requires a kind of shared set of experiences. But, in some contexts, animals do speak and we do understand them. We share enough to understand what it is to want, to be in pain, to play. My claim is that, if a lion could talk, he could not make complaints—because he does not share the right sort of things with us for that in particular.

58. It's a peculiar thing that many of us—though we certainly do not think an animal life more important than a human life—nonetheless find ourselves shedding far more tears at the movie scene in which a horse or a dog dies.

59. See Raimond Gaita, *The Philosopher's Dog: Friendships with Animals* (New York: Random House, 2005), 176: "Animals lack almost entirely [rationality]. That is one reason why we cannot wrong them when we are cruel to them as we would wrong a fellow human being to whom we are cruel. It is why we cannot wrong them when we kill them as we would wrong a human being if we murdered him."

60. Implicit here may be an assumption that, in order to be wronged, something must be the sort of thing capable of understanding what it means to be wronged. I mean to be relying on the related (but perhaps slightly weaker) idea that, to be wronged, one must be capable of receiving justification (and thus of appreciating a lack of justification). The key point is that wronging is a two-place relation that requires an entity of a special sort on both sides. See Thompson, "What Is It?"

61. T. M. Scanlon, *What We Owe to Each Other* (Cambridge, MA: Harvard University Press, 1998), 182.

62. See Darwall, *Second-Person Standpoint,* 28; and Scanlon, *What We Owe,* 181.

63. This question is basically the same question pressed throughout Chapter 3.

64. There is a real condition vaguely like this called anterograde amnesia, which reached popular awareness after the film *Memento.* What I am imagining would be far more extreme than any real case.

65. Recall the discussion in Chapter 1.6. In a paper that exemplifies many of the conceptual problems discussed in this book, Lawrence Haworth attempts to argue that animals can have rights because they can be wronged. See Lawrence Haworth, "Rights, Wrongs, and Animals," *Ethics* 88, no. 2 (1978): 95–105. But what Haworth is focused on is the fact that animals are not indifferent to our treatment of them, not that they can hold us to account.

66. Compare Jacques Derrida, *The Animal That Therefore I Am* (New York: Fordham University Press, 2008).

67. Marc Bekoff, *The Emotional Lives of Animals* (Novato, CA: New World Library, 2007), 51.

68. Aldo Leopold, *A Sand County Almanac* (New York: Random House, 1986), 138.

NOTES TO PAGES 151–153

69. Compare Scanlon, *What We Owe,* 182: "But torturing an animal may seem wrong in a sense that goes beyond the idea that its pain is a bad thing: it is something for which we should feel guilty to the animal itself, just as we can feel guilt to a human being."

70. Gaita, *Philosopher's Dog,* 35–36.

71. Gaita, *Philosopher's Dog,* 37.

72. Compare Darwall, *Second-Person Standpoint,* 29: "To the extent that we find the thought that we owe obligations to nonrational beings a natural thing to think, it seems likely that we also impute to them a proto- or quasi-second-personality, for example, as when we see an animal's or an infant's cry as a form of complaint." Notice that Darwall is almost certainly using "complaint" here to mean prospective demand. Something is amiss if you hear your baby's cry as a kind of proto-resentment.

73. If it's not obvious, I am speaking of our moral duties toward animals, not our legal ones, which could desperately use a little more strictness. As Saskia Stucki puts it, where statutes do afford animals basic rights, "the substantive guarantee of these facially fundamental rights is, to a great extent, eroded by a conspicuously low threshold for permissible infringements." Saskia Stucki, "Towards a Theory of Legal Animal Rights: Simple and Fundamental Rights," *Oxford Journal of Legal Studies* 40, no. 3 (2020): 550.

74. Apparently, not everyone shares this intuition. Ralph Wedgwood wrote in a blog post, "Surely you *could* permissibly kill one bear if that is the only way for you to save five other bears from being killed by someone else." Ralph Wedgewood, "Scheffler's Paradox: Persons vs. Animals," *PEA Soup* (blog), January 25, 2010, https://peasoup.typepad.com/peasoup/2010/01/schefflers-paradox-persons-vs-animals .html. More needs to be filled in before we can fully judge the case, but I reject any serious asymmetry between bears and people. Supposing one can permissibly switch the trolley with people on the tracks, the same goes if there are bears on the tracks. One cannot slaughter people as a source of ready organs for others, and I think the same about bears. The interesting question isn't whether there is a case in which saving the greater number is permissible, but whether there is a case in which it is not.

75. There are interesting legal cases in which people have attempted to invoke the defense of others or the necessity defense in criminal trials concerning private attempts to prevent harms to animals. I discuss this topic in Nicolas Cornell, "In Defense of Animals," *Penn Undergraduate Law Journal* 2, no. 1 (2014): 1–11. This argument has generally been unsuccessful, though I attribute that primarily to the fact that the issue is typically raised when animal liberation groups attempt to circumvent the existing legal regime concerning animal treatment by directly pro-viding aid or escape. See, e.g., Hawaii v. LeVasseur, 613 P.2d 1328 (Haw. Ct. App. 1980); and United States v. O'Dowd, 2022 U.S. Dist. LEXIS 173264 (D. Utah). I hold out hope that a court might allow the defense where a private citizen trespasses to save an imperiled animal, at least outside the agricultural or research animal context.

266   NOTES TO PAGES 153–159

76. See Rebecca F. Wisch, "Table of State Laws That Protect Animals Left in Parked Vehicles" Michigan State University Animal Legal and Historical Center, 2023, http://www.animallaw.info/topic/table-state-laws-protect-animals-left-parked -vehicles. Of course, these laws do not apply to farm animals, who make up the overwhelming number of animals being mistreated and neglected.

77. Scanlon, *What We Owe*, 183.

78. Darwall, *Second-Person Standpoint*, 29.

79. David Favre, "Equitable Self-Ownership for Animals," *Duke Law Journal* 50, no. 2 (November 2000): 473–502.

80. To his credit, Scanlon accepts that an appeal to trustees' complaints must add something—something like an individual perspective on the world. For this reason, Scanlon explicitly rejects the idea that we could incorporate objects like trees, which have a good but which lack consciousness or action. As he puts it, "Nothing would be added by bringing in the idea of what a trustee for these objects would have reason to reject." Scanlon, *What We Owe*, 183. As Darwall's own example suggests, in contrast, he thinks that our obligations with regard to trees might be rendered second-personal as long as there were someone who could, like the Lorax, "speak for the trees." But given that, for Darwall, the addressor can just be our own conscience, one does wonder how much work the trustee idea is doing at this point.

81. Thinking about nonhuman animals suggest to me that recognition of another life might matter ethically without requiring, as Doug Lavin puts it, "mutually recognitive relation to the subject reflecting." Douglas Lavin, "Other Wills: The Second-Person in Ethics," *Philosophical Explorations* 17, no. 3 (2014): 287. I am inclined to see such mutual recognition as more essential to wronging.

82. Murphy, "Moral Death," 293. Emphasis in original.

7. PREEMPTIVE FORGIVING

1. H. J. N. Horsbrugh, "Forgiveness," *Canadian Journal of Philosophy* 4, no. 2 (1974): 269.

2. David Londey, "Can God Forgive Us Our Trespasses?," *Sophia* 25, no. 2 (1986): 4.

3. For an applied example of this argument, consider the following discussion of presidential pardons: "A pardon can only forgive past actions. A president cannot use the pardon power to preapprove an offense, because that is suspension of the law and not a pardon. This is just inherent in the word 'pardon,' and it limits the president even though the Pardon Clause says nothing more explicit about it." Brian C. Kalt, *Constitutional Cliffhangers* (New Haven, CT: Yale University Press, 2012), 44.

4. J. L. Austin never lists "I forgive" as a performative, though he does countenance similar utterances like "I accept your apology" and "I pardon." See J. L. Austin, *How to Do Things with Words* (Oxford: Clarendon, 1962). The claim that forgiving can be a performative has been defended by several authors. See Glen Pettigrove, *Forgiveness and Love* (Oxford: Oxford University Press, 2012); Kathryn

Norlock, *Forgiveness from a Feminist Perspective* (Lanham, MD: Lexington Books, 2009); Glen Pettigrove, "The Forgiveness We Speak: The Illocutionary Force of Forgiving," *Southern Journal of Philosophy* 42, no. 3 (2004): 371–392; and Joram Graf Haber, *Forgiveness* (Lanham, MD: Rowman and Littlefield, 1991).

5. Something roughly like this idea is found in Bishop Butler's *Fifteen Sermons* (1726). The scholarly literature interpreting Butler can be read as largely a debate over what, precisely, must be given up in forgiveness. On a standard reading of Butler, forgiving involves giving up one's resentment and revenge. But this may be too strong. See Ernesto V. Garcia, "Bishop Butler on Forgiveness and Resentment," *Philosophers' Imprint* 11, no. 10 (2011): 1–19; and Andrea Westlund, "Anger, Faith, and Forgiveness," *Monist* 92, no. 4 (2009): 507–536. Regardless, the point of consensus is that forgiving involves giving up some form of holding another accountable.

6. Pamela Hieronymi, "Articulating an Uncompromising Forgiveness," *Philosophy and Phenomenological Research* 62, no. 3 (2001): 529–555.

7. One challenge for Hieronymi's account is to explain who it is that has the standing to resent and thus to forgive. See Kevin Zaragoza, "Forgiveness and Standing," *Philosophy and Phenomenological Research* 84, no. 3 (2012): 604–621. I believe that any adequate account of forgiving should face precisely this challenge.

8. See David Owens, *Shaping the Normative Landscape* (Oxford: Oxford University Press, 2012).

9. This thought might be bolstered by pointing out that, analogously, granting permission after the fact is impossible because all that one can do is forgive. See Quynh Truong v. Allstate Ins. Co., 147 N.M. 583, 599 (N.M. 2010): "Allstate essentially argues for a retroactive grant of permission. This approach is contrary to the plain meaning of 'permitted' and ignores the important distinctions between obtaining permission and seeking forgiveness."

10. Piers Benn, "Forgiveness and Loyalty," *Philosophy* 71, no. 277 (1996): 380.

11. Widely attributed to Rear Admiral Grace Hopper.

12. See TransCore, LP v. Elec. Transaction Consultants Corp., 563 F.3d 1271, 1276 (Fed. Cir. 2009) (stating that "a non-exclusive patent license is equivalent to a covenant not to sue" and collecting citations for this proposition).

13. This fact is part of what Kolnai labeled "the Paradox of Forgiveness." See Aurel Kolnai, "Forgiveness," *Proceedings of the Aristotelian Society* 74 (1974): 97–98.

14. Seana Valentine Shiffrin, "The Divergence of Contract and Promise," *Harvard Law Review* 120 (2007): 729.

15. See, e.g., R. S. Downie, "Forgiveness," *Philosophical Quarterly* 15, no. 59 (1965): 131.

16. Jeffrie G. Murphy and Jean Hampton, *Forgiveness and Mercy* (Cambridge: Cambridge University Press, 1988), 167.

17. Trudy Govier and Wilhelm Verwoerd, "Forgiveness: The Victim's Prerogative," *South African Journal of Philosophy* 21, no. 2 (2002), 98–99.

18. Owens rejects the claim that forgiving is a performative, but he recognizes that "forgiveness changes the normative situation by ensuring that guilt and blame for that wrong are no longer apt." Owens, *Shaping the Normative Landscape*, 52.

19. This can be obscured by the way that the example is described. Perhaps "nagging" and attempting to "score points" are always wrong. But not all complaints or expressions of resentment are inappropriate if one has yet to forgive.

20. "It may be thought that to say 'I forgive you' without experiencing the relevant emotions is empty. But that is false. The request for and granting of forgiveness has behavioral consequences. If V says 'I forgive you,' V cannot continue to express a desire to see O suffer, or to demand additional apologies." Albert W. Dzur and Alan Wertheimer, "Forgiveness and Public Deliberation: The Practice of Restorative Justice," *Criminal Justice Ethics* 21, no. 1 (2012): 12.

21. One might describe forgiving in terms of what Jeff Helmreich has described as "stance-taking." See Jeffrey S. Helmreich, "The Apologetic Stance," *Philosophy and Public Affairs* 43, no. 2 (2015): 75–108.

22. P. E. Digeser, *Political Forgiveness* (Ithaca, NY: Cornell University Press, 2001), 71. As Norlock notes, "a negotiation rather than a unilateral promise" may sometimes be a better metaphor. Norlock, *Forgiveness from a Feminist Perspective*, 101.

23. Margaret R. Holmgren, *Forgiveness and Retribution: Responding to Wrongdoing* (Cambridge: Cambridge University Press, 2012), 44–45.

24. Norlock, *Forgiveness from a Feminist Perspective*, 97.

25. Kazuo Ishiguro, *The Buried Giant* (New York: Random House, 2015), 139–140.

26. Stendahl, *The Red and the Black: A Chronicle of 1830* (London: Kegan Paul, 1916), 127.

27. Preemptive forgiving is, in some sense, necessarily conditional. It takes the form, "I forgive you *if* you ϕ." This raises questions about how to understand what has happened if you do not ϕ. There appear to be two possibilities. First, we might say that no forgiving occurred, interpreting it as "[I forgive you] if [you ϕ]." Alternatively, we might say that I forgave something nonactual, interpreting it as "I forgive [you if you ϕ]." (If forgiving something nonactual sounds mysterious, consider forgiving a transgression that one mistakenly believes to have been committed.) I will remain neutral between these views. What is essential to my argument is that, if the wrong is committed, it has *already* been forgiven.

28. John 13:21–29.

29. Owens argues that forgiving makes it the case that even third parties should relinquish reactive attitudes. See Owens, *Shaping the Normative Landscape*; and David Owens, "The Role of Rights," in *Civil Wrongs and Justice in Private Law*, ed. Paul B. Miller and John Oberdiek (Oxford: Oxford University Press, 2020), 3–17. As a categorical or essential claim, this strikes me as implausible.

30. Compare the discussion in Chapter 3.1 about how some promises might have no effect on one's duties but an effect on complaints.

NOTES TO PAGES 169–173

31. Herbert Morris, "Persons and Punishment," in *On Guilt and Innocence: Essays in Legal Philosophy and Moral Psychology* (Berkeley: University of California Press, 1976), 53.

32. Recall Chapter 2. The standard response in the forgiving literature is that parents are victims in their own right when their children are harmed. See Horsbrugh, "Forgiveness," 276; Murphy and Hampton, *Forgiveness and Mercy,* 56n16; and Haber, *Forgiveness,* 49. For a compelling rejection of this claim as an explanation of third-party forgiving, see Glen Pettigrove, "The Standing to Forgive," *Monist* 92, no. 4 (2009): 583–603.

33. Forgiving one's own killing seems to be a good place to find preemptive forgiving. In 2004, the last words of a prisoner executed by the State of Virginia were, "I forgive you for what you're doing." In the Hollywood film *Faster* (2010), Dwayne Johnson's character is about to execute an evangelist who wronged him when the preacher says, "That's all right. . . . Because I forgive you for what you're about to do."

34. In a rare discussion of forward-looking forgiveness, Robin Dillon describes as "preservative self-forgiveness" a disposition not to form negative evaluations and emotions that would need to be overcome. See Robin Dillon, "Self-Forgiveness and Self-Respect," *Ethics* 112, no. 1 (2001): 72.

35. Madalen Edgar, *Stories of the Earthly Paradise: Retold from William Morris* (London: George G. Harrap, 1907), 178.

36. Notice that, even in compassion, it may be important to maintain that the action is still wrong—something that forgiving accomplishes but excusing does not. Indeed, affirming the wrongness may be important to transgressors themselves, as Martha Minow's discussion of child soldiers brings out powerfully. See Martha Minow, *When Should the Law Forgive?* (New York: W. W. Norton, 2019), 33–67.

37. This example is loosely based on my experience as an unconvincing Ferdinand in a high school production of *The Tempest*. If it adds texture, imagine one actor as an awkward teenage boy and the other as a seasoned drama club mainstay.

38. For psychological evidence that it might be, see Julie Juola Exline et al., "Not So Innocent: Does Seeing One's Own Capability for Wrongdoing Predict Forgiveness?," *Journal of Personality and Social Psychology* 94, no. 3 (2008): 495–515. For a rich philosophical account along these lines, see Eve Garrard and David McNaughton, "In Defense of Unconditional Forgiveness," *Proceedings of the Aristotelian Society* 103 (2002): 39–60. This may be one way to cultivate the compassion that can underwrite forgiveness. See David Novitz, "Forgiveness and Self-Respect," *Philosophy and Phenomenological Research* 58, no. 2 (1998): 299–315.

39. One might object here that what one cares about is what the wounded soldier thought and felt, not whether he performed the act of forgiving per se. But I don't think that's entirely accurate. Norlock discusses a case in which Simon Wiesenthal was asked by a Nazi soldier to forgive him. She uses the example to show how we often care about the performative, not an internal emotional state: "The soldier who asked Simon Wiesenthal for forgiveness didn't seem to be asking for a report of how

270 NOTES TO PAGES 173–181

Wiesenthal felt. It was critical to him that someone express something like forgiveness to him for his war crimes before he died." Norlock, *Forgiveness from a Feminist Perspective,* 105.

40. Compare Helmreich on the meaningfulness of deathbed apologies. See Helmreich, "Apologetic Stance," 85, 102.

41. This is a bit quick. It seems plausible to say, "I promise to forgive you next week, but right now I cannot." But it is important, in that case, that there is a temporal gap. It preserves some role for the complaint or resentment to play. Similarly, one might say, preemptively, "If you do that, I promise to forgive you within a week." But it seems much more odd to say, "If you do that, I promise to forgive you that very instant."

42. Compare the following: (1) "I promise you that tomorrow, if my wife agrees, I will promise you that I will take you to the airport the following day." (2) "I promise you that tomorrow I will promise you that, if it is raining, I will take you to the airport." In (1), the condition is a condition on making the second promise and the two-layer structure makes some sense. In (2), the condition is on the action being promised and the two-layer structure is essentially pointless.

43. Samuel Williston and Richard A. Lord, *Williston on Contracts,* 4th ed. (Eagan, MN: Thomson/West, 1990), 677–678.

44. On the expressive value of obtaining a legal judgment, see Scott Hershovitz, "Treating Wrongs as Wrongs: An Expressive Argument for Tort Law," *Journal of Tort Law* 10, no. 2 (2017): 405–447.

45. See, e.g., Divine Tower Int'l Corp. v. Kegler, Brown, Hill & Ritter Co., L.P.A., 2008 U.S. Dist. LEXIS 85246, 9–10 (S.D. Ohio Sept. 24, 2008).

46. See, e.g., Colton v. New York Hospital, 53 A.D.2d 588, 589 (N.Y. App. Div. 1976): "A covenant not to sue is . . . merely an agreement not to enforce an existing cause of action. . . . Thus, the party possessing the right of action is not precluded thereby from thereafter bringing suit; however, he may be compelled to respond in damages for breach of the covenant."

47. Morgan v. Butterfield, 3 Mich. 615, 624–625 (1855) (affirming Robinson v. Godfrey, 2 Mich. 408 (1852)).

48. Staver & Walker v. Missimer, 6 Wash. 173, 175–176 (1893).

49. Artvale, Inc. v. Rugby Fabrics Corp., 363 F.2d 1002, 1008 (2d Cir. 1966).

50. See Bukuras v. Mueller Group, LLC, 592 F.3d 255, 266 (1st Cir. 2010) (collecting cases).

51. Cheshire Calhoun also describes forgiving as giving up one's second-personal address: "Aspirational forgiveness is the choice not to demand that [the wrongdoer] improve." Cheshire Calhoun, "Changing One's Heart," *Ethics* 103 (1992): 95.

8. EXPLOITATION

1. Not, at least, if the permission is genuine, rather than mere politeness. There may be social contexts in which we express a grant of permission that is not truly meant and not intended to be taken as such. A host might say, "Stay as long as you

NOTES TO PAGES 181–188

like," never meaning the guest could move in. But related examples do present a bit of a problem for the strictly rights-based view. If the host says, "Have as many cookies as you like," must we say that the permission was not genuine or implicitly restricted in scope if we are to explain the wrong in taking a few too many? I think not. This relates to the issues raised in Chapter 5.

2. Joel Feinberg, *Harm to Others* (Oxford: Oxford University Press, 1984), 35.

3. See Karl Marx, *Capital*, vol. 1, in *The Marx-Engels Reader,* ed. Robert C. Tucker (New York: W. W. Norton, 1978), 362–363.

4. For a helpful survey of the various ways that "exploitation" is used and for the distinction between "harmful exploitation" and "mutually advantageous exploitation," see Alan Wertheimer, *Exploitation* (Princeton, NJ: Princeton University Press, 1999), chap. 1.

5. For an extended argument to this effect, see Chris Meyers, "Wrongful Beneficence: Exploitation and Third World Sweatshops," *Journal of Social Philosophy* 35, no. 3 (2004): 319–333.

6. Robert E. Goodin, "Exploiting a Situation and Exploiting a Person," in *Modern Theories of Exploitation,* ed. Andrew Reeve (London: Sage, 1987), 182.

7. John Miller, "Why Economists Are Wrong about Sweatshops and the Anti-sweatshop Movement," *Challenge* 46, no. 1 (2003): 97.

8. Vernon v. Bethell, 2 Eden 110, 113.

9. See, e.g., Paul Krugman, "In Praise of Cheap Labor," *Slate,* March 21, 1997; and Ian Maitland, "The Great Non-debate over International Sweatshops," in *Ethics at Work: Basic Readings in Business Ethics,* ed. William H. Shaw (Oxford: Oxford University Press, 2003), 49–66.

10. Krugman, "In Praise."

11. Joel Feinberg, *Harmless Wrongdoing* (New York: Oxford University Press, 1988), 176.

12. Feinberg, 18, 20.

13. See Matt Zwolinski, "Sweatshops, Choice, and Exploitation," *Business Ethics Quarterly* 17, no. 4 (2007): 689–727.

14. Andrew Morgan, dir., *The True Cost* (Untold Creative, 2015).

15. Gethin Chamberlain, "India's Clothing Workers: 'They Slap Us and Call Us Dogs and Donkeys,'" *Guardian,* November 24, 2012.

16. Ermine Saner, "'You're Consenting to Being Raped for Money,'" *Guardian,* December 10, 2007.

17. Madelaine Hanson, "The Real Pretty Woman: An Interview with a Sex Worker," *Medium,* August 30, 2018.

18. For a compelling and perhaps more representative account of prostitution, I recommend Rachel Moran, *Paid For: My Journey through Prostitution* (New York: W. W. Norton, 2015). On consent, she writes, "a woman's compliance in prostitution is a response to circumstances beyond her control. . . . There is a difference between consent and reluctant submission" (160).

19. See Catharine A. MacKinnon, "Prostitution and Civil Rights," in *Women's Lives, Men's Laws* (Cambridge, MA: Harvard University Press, 2007), 151–161.

272   NOTES TO PAGES 188–190

20. See Denise Brennan, "Selling Sex for Visas: Sex Tourism as a Stepping-Stone to International Migration," in *Global Woman: Nannies, Maids, and Sex Workers in the New Economy,* ed. Barbara Ehrenreich and Arlie Russell Hochschild (New York: Henry Holt, 2002), 155: "I have been particularly alarmed at the media's monolithic portrayal of sex workers in sex-tourist destinations, such as Cuba, as passive victims easily lured by the glitter of consumer goods. These overly simplistic and implicitly moralizing stories deny that poor women are capable of making their own labor choices."

21. See Catharine A. MacKinnon, "Liberalism and the Death of Feminism," in *Women's Lives, Men's Laws,* 259–260.

22. One can imagine characterizing this right not to be exploited in various ways. It might, for example, be procedural or substantive. According to a procedural account, the exploiter violates a duty to be appropriately generous or fair-minded in the negotiation process. The exploitation occurs in how the terms of the agreement come to be; thus, the consent of the exploited party to those terms does not obviate the violation. According to a substantive account, the exploiter violates a right of the exploited party against the substance of the transaction. This might be a right to a fair share of what is produced or it might be a right against ever being used in the way that the transaction contemplates. The exploitation thus occurs in the overall shape of the transaction, and the consent within the transaction does not obviate that. I won't dwell on the differences; my arguments should largely apply regardless. But for what it's worth, I find a substantive right to be the more plausible. First, it seems that exploitative agreements can arise without the exploiter acting badly in the formation process. An employer might hire a worker through a third-party broker, neither knowing nor having reason to know that the worker is vulnerable. A person might even initiate her own exploitation—such as a woman who, gripped by false consciousness or oppressive social norms, seeks out traditional and excessive domestic work. Second, a procedural account will locate the wrong in the process creating the transaction, not in how the transaction actually unfolds. An employer that negotiates unfair contractual terms but then leaves the terms to languish does not seem to engage in exploitation, even though they were unfair in the negotiating process. Third, more generally, a procedural account will not reflect the apparent moral luck involved in exploitation. If a filmmaker gets an impoverished person to play a role on-screen for a pittance, whether and to what extent it is exploitative seems to depend in part on whether the film makes millions or never makes a dime.

23. Whether inalienable or not, there is something odd here. It's hard to see the complaint of the exploited party as neatly circumscribed by the violation of the right against exploitation. Suppose a sweatshop worker agrees to work eighteen-hour days. It would be artificial, I think, to say that the sweatshop worker can complain about being exploited but (having consented) cannot complain about eighteen-hour days. They seem to be part and parcel. The thing agreed to is the source of injury and resentment.

NOTES TO PAGES 190–192   273

24. See Ruth J. Sample, *Exploitation: What It Is and Why It's Wrong* (Oxford: Rowman and Littlefield, 2003). I accept that there are inalienable rights against certain kinds of degrading or dehumanizing treatment. And it might, interestingly, be the case that some treatment is degrading or dehumanizing in part because it occurs in a transactional form. But I am skeptical that this can explain all exploitation.

25. A reader might have a concern that our intuitions here are skewed by the example's use of foreign, culturally "other" persons—that it is contaminated in a way similar to Bernard Williams's problematic example of Jim and the Indians. I share the general concern about the construction of philosophical examples, so let me say two things. First, we should be concerned about philosophical examples that might subtly distance readers from the persons within them and thereby elicit permissibility judgments that we might not accept for cases closer to home— something one might worry happens in the Williams example. In contrast, I have chosen to use the indigenous villagers for the sake of eliciting the reader's sympathy, both for their collectivist request and for the judgment that exploitation is present. My view is that we intuitively recognize the phenomenon of exploitation in the interactions of the affluent with the global poor, and I have deliberately constructed the example with that dynamic. Second, if one remains troubled by this element, then here is an alternative case: You operate a small pet store. As you have gotten older, you've found the intensive labor involved—especially for the birds—is catching up with you, so you advertise for a part-time employee, to be paid a living wage, though you can barely afford it. A week later, you have received no inquiries yet, and a nine-year-old boy comes into the shop and asks about the job. You explain that child labor laws prohibit hiring a kid. Disappointed, he asks if he can nonetheless spend some time with the birds that afternoon. Having no customers presently, you take the kid into the bird enclosure and let him feed them with you. He ends up staying the whole afternoon. He returns the next day, and the next. You come to learn that he is a neglected latchkey kid, desperate for something to do after school other than watch TV alone. He also displays a deep love for birds and an intuitive skill for it. After two weeks, he has a new spring in his step when he enters the shop each day. And he is doing most of the care for the birds, relieving you of significant work and making the day-to-day feel quite manageable again. Then, one day, a woman enters the shop inquiring about the job advertisement. Because fire and health codes sharply limit the number of people allowed inside the bird enclosure at one time, if you hire the woman, you will have to tell the boy that he can no longer come to the shop. I suggest that it may be permissible to turn the woman away, take down the advertisement, and carry on with the boy, but that this also involves a kind of exploitation—reflected in a moral residue—in a way that hiring the woman would not.

26. If the constructed example does not elicit that intuition for the reader, then imagine the work to be even more unpleasant (your research will involve handpicking through rancid insect larvae) or hazardous (handling poisonous snakes) and imagine the pay to be even less per villager.

274   NOTES TO PAGES 193-198

27. But see Aditi Bagchi, "Lying and Cheating, or Self-Help and Civil Disobedience?," *Brooklyn Law Review* 85, no. 2 (2020): 355–392.

28. See, e.g., Cowin Equip. Co., Inc., v. General Motors Corp., 734 F.2d 1581, 1582 (11th Cir. 1984).

29. See Nicolas Cornell, "A Complainant-Oriented Approach to Unconscionability and Contract Law," *University of Pennsylvania Law Review* 164, no. 5 (2016): 1131–1176; and Seana Valentine Shiffrin, "Paternalism, Unconscionability Doctrine, and Accommodation," *Philosophy and Public Affairs* 29, no. 3 (2000): 205–250.

30. Some scholars have questioned whether unconscionability should be constrained in these ways. There have been, over the years, various calls to let unconscionability serve as an affirmative cause of action for damages. See, e.g., H. G. Prince, "Unconscionability in California: A Need for Restraint and Consistency," *Hastings Law Journal* 46 (1995): 548. But on most such reformist proposals, unconscionability would still basically be a shield, simply paving the way for an action in restitution. See, e.g., Prince Saprai, "Unconscionable Enrichment?," in *Philosophical Foundations of the Law of Unjust Enrichment,* ed. Robert Chambers, Charles Mitchell, and James Penner (Oxford: Oxford University Press, 2009), 417–436; and In re Checking Overdraft Litig., 694 F. Supp. 2d 1302 (S.D. Fla. 2010).

31. Indeed, Zwolinski argues that exploited parties have a right not to have their options constrained in these ways. See Zwolinski, "Sweatshops, Choice, and Exploitation."

32. Consider, for example, the experience of haggling in a bazaar. To pay the first price offered may be regarded as disrespectful—an expression of superiority—but to squeeze tiny sums from a poor merchant seems also problematic.

33. This is put roughly and requires qualification. For one, it need not be the actor who benefits directly; one can exploit in order to benefit some third party. Second, exploitation may not require true all-things-considered benefit but only perceived benefiting. A man who exploits a prostitute may not actually be better off, only debasing himself.

34. See, e.g., Hillel Steiner, "A Liberal Theory of Exploitation," *Ethics* 94, no. 2 (1984): 225–241; and Wertheimer, *Exploitation.*

35. Or, to put it slightly differently, one might say that the exploiter acts wrongly by offering the transaction only in this form *if* they are offering the transaction at all. In pursuing this strategy, one might fruitfully draw comparisons to blackmail. Like exploitation, blackmail seems to involve an impermissible offer, even though the offeror is free to engage (or not) in the conduct subject to the offered transaction. See Mitchell N. Berman, "Blackmail," in *The Oxford Handbook of Philosophy of Criminal Law*, ed. John Deigh & David Dolinko (Oxford: Oxford University Press, 2011): 37–106. It might seem that the puzzle in both cases can be resolved by distinguishing wide- and narrow-scope obligations. In both cases, the relevant norm should be understood to have the structure, "If you are going to X (hire worker, conceal information), then you ought do Y (fair terms, not take money)." Even if such a strategy can explain the problem of blackmail (about which I am unsure), I do

NOTES TO PAGES 198–200   275

not believe the problems to be analogous. For one, blackmail seems to be distinctively about making a threat—it's not blackmail if the transaction is wholly initiated by the other party—but a transaction can still be exploitation if initiated and driven by the exploited party. Second, at an intuitive level, the phenomena strike me distinct. The blackmail offer naturally registers as coercion and be met with hostility—the philosophical puzzle is in explaining why. The offer of new sweatshop employment to a region does not register in the same way. Indeed, it might even be received with gratitude. Whereas the blackmailer does seem to be coercively imposing an illegitimate option set onto the victim, that explanation of exploitation seems less fitting.

36. The main problem is explaining why it is wrong for the exploiter to refuse to offer a particular better option (e.g., paying a living wage) if the exploiter was not obligated to offer any option in the first place (one is free not to employ anyone). This problem, faced by any theory of interpersonal exploitation, is not merely a matter of the greater power automatically including the lesser, which is not always true (as in the case of blackmail; see note 35). Nor must seeing this as a problem deny the general point about consent to an option not being the same as consent to the set of options. Where offering no option is impossible (the basic structure) or morally impermissible (affirmative obligation), then the point has more bite. See, e.g., Kristi Olson, "Our Choices, Our Wage Gap?," *Philosophical Topics* 40, no. 1 (2012): 45–61. The problem is that, whereas the blackmailer or the basic structure are plausibly understood as setting or constraining our options, the individual offering an exploitative transaction is not so naturally understood this way and, even if they might be, that seems not to capture the nature of the wrong.

37. In referring to "benefiting," I do not mean to imply that we are simply interested in the end results. Benefiting may be better understood as describing a process than simply in terms of outcome. See Tommie Shelby, "Parasites, Pimps, and Capitalists: A Naturalistic Conception of Exploitation," *Social Theory and Practice* 28, no. 3 (2002): 381–418.

38. Jonathan Wolff, "Marx and Exploitation," *Journal of Ethics* 3, no. 2 (1999): 119–120.

39. Compare Wendell Berry's remark: "This is what is wrong with the conservation movement. It has a clear conscience. The guilty are always other people, and the wrong is always somewhere else. . . . The history of the exploitation of the Appalachian coal fields is long, and it is available to readers. I do not see how anyone can read it and plug in any appliance with a clear conscience." Wendell Berry, "Why I Am Not Going to Buy a Computer," in *The World-Ending Fire: The Essential Wendell Berry,* ed. Paul Kingsnorth (Berkeley: Counterpoint, 2017), 240.

40. See Shelby, "Parasites, Pimps, and Capitalists."

41. In defense of the view that the Marxist concept of exploitation is at least in part moral, see G. A. Cohen, "The Labor Theory of Value and the Concept of Exploitation," *Philosophy and Public Affairs* 8, no. 4 (1979): 338–360; Richard J. Arneson, "What's Wrong with Exploitation?," *Ethics* 91, no. 2 (1981): 202–227; and Wolff, "Marx and Exploitation." For defenses of the nonmoral view of exploitation,

276 NOTES TO PAGES 200–207

see Shelby, "Parasites, Pimps, and Capitalists"; and Allen W. Wood, "Exploitation," *Social Philosophy and Policy* 12, no. 2 (1995): 135–158.

42. See Arneson, "What's Wrong with Exploitation?"

9. RELATIONAL DUALISM

1. "The application of temporal physics is in ethics. . . . Seeing the difference between now and not now . . . there morality enters in." Ursula K. Le Guin, *The Dispossessed* (New York: Avon Books, 1974), 181.

2. T. S. Eliot, "Burnt Norton," in *Four Quartets* (New York: Harcourt, 1943), 3.

3. Percy Bysshe Shelley, "To a Skylark," Poetry Foundation, accessed February 22, 2024, https://www.poetryfoundation.org/poems/45146/to-a-skylark.

4. Immanuel Kant, *The Metaphysics of Morals,* trans. Mary Gregor (Cambridge: Cambridge University Press, 1996), 6:434–435.

5. Warren Quinn, *Morality and Action* (Cambridge: Cambridge University Press, 1993), 170, 173. See also Joel Feinberg, "The Nature and Value of Rights," *Journal of Value Inquiry* 4 (December 1970): 252: "Respect for persons . . . may simply be respect for their rights, so that there cannot be the one without the other; and what is called 'human dignity' may simply be the recognizable capacity to assert claims."

6. Frances M. Kamm, "Rights," in *The Oxford Handbook of Jurisprudence and Philosophy of Law,* ed. Jules Coleman and Scott Shapiro (New York: Oxford University Press, 2002), 487.

7. Robert Nozick, *Anarchy, State, and Utopia* (New York: Basic Books, 1974), 30–31.

8. Nozick, 32–33.

9. T. M. Scanlon, *What We Owe to Each Other* (Cambridge, MA: Harvard University Press, 1998), 189.

10. Rainer Forst, *Justification and Critique: Towards a Critical Theory of Politics,* trans. Ciaran Cronin (Cambridge, UK: Polity, 2014), 101.

11. Thomas Nagel, "War and Massacre," *Philosophy and Public Affairs* 1, no. 2 (1972): 137.

12. Ideas in this vein have been developed well by others. See especially Christine M. Korsgaard, *Self-Constitution: Agency, Identity, and Integrity* (Oxford: Oxford University Press, 2009), and Thomas Nagel, The Possibility of Altruism (Princeton, NJ: Princeton University Press, 1970). While I am obviously drawing on this tradition, I should not be understood as committing to any kind of Kantian constructivism here. All that I mean to be claiming is that rationality involves principles that apply across a community, nothing about their source of normative force. I mean for the picture I'm sketching to be as metaethically agnostic as possible.

13. See R. Jay Wallace, *The Moral Nexus* (Princeton, NJ: Princeton University Press, 2019).

14. See Ariel Zylberman, "Relational Primitivism," Philosophy and Phenomenological Research 102, no.2 (2021): 401–422.

NOTES TO PAGES 208–212

15. Compare H. L. A. Hart, "Are There Any Natural Rights?," *Philosophical Review* 64, no. 2 (April 1955): 182: "Rights are typically conceived of as *possessed* or *owned by* or *belonging to* individuals, and these expressions reflect the conception of moral rules as not only prescribing conduct but as forming a kind of moral property of individuals to which they are as individuals entitled." Emphasis in the original.

16. Although I sometimes focus on harm, I should not be misread as saying that material harm is the only way that one can have a stake in an action. As Arthur Ripstein's examples of harmless trespasses show, one can have a stake in an action simply because it is a trespass on one's sphere of normative control, material harm aside. I have a stake in whether you sleep in my bed. I think there are still other ways to have a stake. For example, where my thoughts or fantasies concern you, it seems that I might wrong you. (See Chapter 5.) That's not necessarily because you are harmed (you might not be), nor because you have a right (my thoughts are mine to control). But there is a straightforward answer to the question, "What's it to you?"—namely, the thoughts are about you. For another example, the exploited party might not be harmed and yet it hardly seems that the exploiter can say, "What's it to you that I'm making millions here?" The fact of the interaction—the fact that it's *my* labor—seems to be sufficient to tether the person to the action. (See Chapter 8.)

17. See Chapter 6.

18. Stephen Darwall, *The Second-Person Standpoint: Morality, Respect, and Accountability* (Cambridge, MA: Harvard University Press, 2009), 122–123.

19. Joseph Raz, *The Morality of Freedom* (Oxford: Oxford University Press, 1986), 166.

20. Christine M. Korsgaard, "Two Distinctions in Goodness," *Philosophical Review* 92, no. 2 (1983): 169–195.

21. It is a crucial feature of Raz's theory, as I understand it, that he distinguishes between an interest and what gives the interest its importance. This distinction purports to allow Raz to accommodate the apparent mismatch between the value of some interests and the protections that they are afforded. See Joseph Raz, "Rights and Individual Well-Being," *Ratio Juris* 5, no. 2 (1992): 138; and Raz, *Morality of Freedom*, 178. I am not convinced that this crucial move is successful, but I will not pursue the point here. For an excellent discussion of this feature of Raz's account, see Kamm, "Rights."

22. This is, on my view, a major problem with Raz's account. There's no connection between the capacity to have rights and what it means to have rights. The former requires interests of ultimate value, the latter does not. Raz acknowledges that it "seems plausible" that these ideas should be symmetrical, but he rejects such symmetry because "there are plenty of counter-examples." Raz, *Morality of Freedom*, 178. That is, to my mind, an admission that the capacity condition is simply ad hoc. One thing that should be essential to a theory of rights is that what it means to have a right is connected deeply with the capacity to have rights.

NOTES TO PAGES 212–219

23. Compare Zylberman, "Relational Primitivism," 409: "Moral personhood, as I think of it, is itself a *relational* property: it represents the agent who bears relational incidents, the *agent-as-rights-bearer*, as it were."

24. H. L. A. Hart, "Legal Rights," in *Essays on Bentham: Studies in Jurisprudence and Political Theory* (Oxford: Clarendon, 1982), 183.

25. Jeremy Waldron, *The Right to Private Property* (Oxford: Clarendon, 1988), 128.

26. While I describe rights and directed duties as a subset, that might be misleading. I am open to the possibility that they are primitive and the essence of all moral oughts. See Zylberman, "Relational Primitivism," and Jonas Vandieken, "Bipolar Obligations, Recognition Respect, and Second-Personal Morality," *Ethics* 23 (2019): 291–315. What is important to me is that there are two ways that we can relate to another's duty, as the correlative rightholder or as a plain member of the moral community, and that the latter is a form of normatively significant relation.

27. The significance of the two elements can be illustrated by contrasting with cases in which each is absent. We sometimes witness another person acting wrongly, who could not justify his or her behavior to us if called on to do so. But the action may not concern us. In such circumstances, we are not wronged. Still, some lesser analogue exists. P. F. Strawson describes the negative reaction arising in such cases as "moral indignation"—"the vicarious analogue of resentment." P. F. Strawson, "Freedom and Resentment," *Proceedings of the British Academy* 48 (1962): 70–71. Another lesser analogue of wronging arises when the requirements for standing to demand justification are met—when a person had a special stake—and yet there is no one from whom one can demand justification. This happens when one feels a sense of injustice at misfortune. The victims of a hurricane, for example, may feel some analogue to resentment. The similarity makes sense: the hurricane has caused them harm for which no justification can be given.

28. Rowan Cruft has recently defended an "addressive" theory of rights and directed duties, in which an addressive character is (at least paradigmatically) constitutive of directedness. See Rowan Cruft, *Human Rights, Ownership, and the Individual* (Oxford: Oxford University Press, 2019). One might say that I am endorsing an "addressive" theory of wronging, but not (as will become clear in the next section) an addressive theory of rights.

29. See Chapter 3.

30. See Nicolas Cornell, "Looking and Seeing," in *New Conversations in Philosophy, Law, and Politics,* ed. Ruth Chang and Amia Srinivasan (Oxford: Oxford University Press, 2024), 277–298.

31. See Zoë Sinel, "Through Thick and Thin: The Place of Corrective Justice in Unjust Enrichment," *Oxford Journal of Legal Studies* 31, no. 3 (2011): 551–564.

32. Feinberg, "Nature and Value," 253. Emphasis in original.

33. This problem becomes most evident in Feinberg's discussion of desert. Insofar as Feinberg admits into Nowheresville the concept of duty and the concept of desert, then there should be no reason why the two should not combine. And this starts to look like a right, even though we have said nothing about claiming. This is basically

the criticism that Jan Narveson raised in his commentary after Feinberg's original article. Jan Narveson, "Commentary," *Journal of Value Inquiry* 4, no. 4 (1970): 258. Feinberg says, "The propriety involved [in Nowheresville desert] is a much weaker kind than that which derives . . . from his having qualified for it by satisfying the well-advertised conditions of some public rule. In the latter case he could be said not merely to deserve the good thing but also to have a *right* to it." Feinberg, "Nature and Value," 245. That seems basically correct to me, but I don't see why Feinberg should believe it. In Nowheresville, satisfying the conditions of a public rule should be like deliberately becoming the beneficiary of someone else's promise. There's performance owed, but not to you. And yet Feinberg concedes that satisfying the conditions of a public rule would count as a having a right.

34. Plutarch, *Plutarch's Lives,* ed. Bernadotte Perrin (London: Heinemann, 1914), 1:455.

35. See, e.g., Rakas v. Illinois, 439 U.S. 128 (1978).

36. Ostensibly, the legal reasoning is different here, as the exclusionary rule is supposedly justified on more instrumentalist grounds—as a prophylactic deterrent on police misconduct. But if the purpose is to remove any police benefit from illegal searches and thus any incentive to conduct them, then the inapplicability of the exclusionary rule to third parties is hard to justify, as it leaves in place a potential benefit. See, e.g., United States v. Payner, 447 U.S. 727 (1980). I suspect that Cardozo's reasoning is operating here, even if courts don't acknowledge it.

37. For the widespread agreement on the muddled nature of the doctrine, see Richard H. Fallon Jr., "The Fragmentation of Standing," *Texas Law Review* 93 (2015): 1062n3 (collecting sources).

38. See June Med. Servs. LLC v. Russo, 140 S. Ct. 2103 (2020). The reluctance to grant third parties standing seems related to private law privity concepts, on which early standing jurisprudence drew significantly. See, e.g., Tennessee Elec. Power Co. v. Tennessee Valley Auth., 306 U.S. 118, 137–138 (1939). But the Court has distanced itself from those ideas, or at least treated them as merely prudential. See Bond v. United States, 564 U.S. 211, 219 (2011) (explaining that relevant portions of *Tennessee Electric* "should be deemed neither controlling nor instructive on the issue of standing as that term is now defined and applied").

39. See, e.g., Craig v. Boren, 429 U.S. 190 (1976); U.S. Dep't of Labor v. Triplett, 494 U.S. 715 (1990); Griswold v. Connecticut, 381 U.S. 479, 481 (1965); Powers v. Ohio, 499 U.S. 400 (1991); and Bush v. Gore, 531 U.S. 98 (2000).

40. Compare Baker v. Carr, 369 U.S. 186, 204 (1962) ("Have the appellants alleged such a personal stake in the outcome of the controversy as to assure that concrete adverseness . . . ? This is the gist of the question of standing.").

41. Warth v. Seldin, 422 U.S. 490 (1975).

42. See Heckler v. Mathews, 465 U.S. 728 (1984) (granting standing for equal protection challenge even though plaintiffs stood to gain nothing material from the lawsuit).

43. See Clapper v. Amnesty Int'l USA, 568 U.S. 398 (2013) (denying standing to plaintiffs seeking to challenge the Foreign Intelligence Surveillance Act surveillance

NOTES TO PAGES 222–226

program on the grounds that they could not show that their being surveilled was "certainly impending"). *Clapper* has been a source of confusion, generating a circuit split over how to apply it in consumer deception cases. Even the leading standing decision, *Lujan v. Defenders of Wildlife*, 504 U.S. 555 (1992), strikes me as a mistaken demand that plaintiffs show themselves to have been wronged, when they were actually seeking to exercise a kind of normative authority granted to them under the Endangered Species Act.

44. See Biden v. Nebraska, 600 U.S. 477 (2023).

45. See, e.g., Fallon, "Fragmentation of Standing," 1110–1111.

46. For discussion of how this difference plays out with public duties in the private law sphere, see Nicolas Cornell, "Public Duties," in *Interstitial Private Law*, ed. Paul B. Miller et al. (Oxford: Oxford University Press, forthcoming).

47. Chester Pierce, "Offensive Mechanisms," in *The Black Seventies*, ed. Floyd B. Barbour (Boston: Porter Sargent, 1970), 265.

48. Greg Lukianoff and Jonathan Haidt, "The Coddling of the American Mind," *Atlantic*, September 2015.

49. See, e.g., Ben Shapiro, "What Right Not to Be Offended?," *National Review*, January 24, 2018.

50. "We cannot have freedom without wilderness, we cannot have freedom without leagues of open space beyond the cities where boys and girls, men and women, can live at least part of their lives under no control but their own desires and abilities, free from any and all direct administration by their fellow men." Edward Abbey, *The Journey Home* (New York: Plume, 1991), 235.

51. Rachel Carson, "Essay on the Biological Sciences," *Good Reading*, 1958.

52. Joseph Sax, "The Unfinished Agenda of Environmental Law," *Hastings West Northwest Journal of Environmental Law and Policy* 14 (2008): 6.

53. See Illinois Central Railroad v. Illinois, 146 U.S. 387 (1892).

54. See, e.g., Columbia River Fishermen's Protective Union v. City of St. Helens, 87 P.2d 195 (Or. 1939); and Burgess v. M/V Tamano, 370 F. Supp. 247 (D. Me. 1973).

55. "We abuse land because we regard it as a commodity belonging to us. When we see land as a community to which we belong, we may begin to use it with love and respect." Aldo Leopold, *A Sand County Almanac* (New York: Random House, 1986), viii.

56. Consider Smohalla, a spiritual leader of the Wanapum people: "You ask me to plow the ground. Shall I take a knife and tear my mother's breast? . . . You ask me to dig for stone. Shall I dig under her skin for her bones?" T. C. McLuhan, *Touch the Earth: A Self-Portrait of Indian Existence* (New York: Outerbridge and Dienstrey, 1971), 56. See also Robin Wall Kimmerer, *Braiding Sweetgrass: Indigenous Wisdom, Scientific Knowledge, and the Teachings of Plants* (Minneapolis: Milkweed Editions, 2020), 100: "We spill over into the world and the world spills over into us. The earth, that first among good mothers, gives us the gift that we cannot provide ourselves. . . . She gives what we need without being asked."

Acknowledgments

This book is the culmination of a project that I have been working on for basically my entire adult life. It draws on prior work. Chapter 1 builds on ideas presented in and Chapter 2 includes text first published in "Wrongs, Rights, and Third Parties," *Philosophy and Public Affairs*, 43, no. 2 (2015), 109–143. Chapter 4 expands on concepts introduced in "What Do We Remedy?" my chapter in *Civil Wrongs and Justice in Private Law*, edited by John Oberdiek and Paul Miller and published by Oxford University Press in 2020. Much of Chapter 7 was first published as "The Possibility of Preemptive Forgiving," *The Philosophical Review*, vol. 126, no. 2 (2017), 241–272.

With this being such a long-standing project, I have failed to keep a list of all the people who have given me feedback and help along the way. It would be very long. I regret that, in trying to offer acknowledgments, I am bound to leave out very many.

I have been immensely fortunate to have had outstanding teachers— starting from the public schools in Brunswick, Maine, and lasting all the way through my years at Harvard—and this book would not exist without them. First and foremost, Chris Korsgaard was unsparingly generous as a mentor and model, and this project owes so much to her. Tim Scanlon and Frances Kamm also shaped me immensely as a philosopher, in addition to helping shape and support this project. Others in Emerson Hall played important roles in the beginning stages of this work, especially Niko Kolodny, Doug Lavin, and Dick Moran. And my law teachers—especially John Goldberg, Charles Fried, Anne Alstott, and Justice John Dooley— defined the way that I think about legal doctrine and its connection with moral philosophy.

ACKNOWLEDGMENTS

Some people have been particularly valuable, valued, and repeated interlocutors over the years and have seen many different iterations of these ideas. They include Tom Dougherty, Chris Essert, Micha Gläser, John Goldberg, Scott Hershovitz, Rob Hughes, Gabe Mendlow, Sarah Moss, Jen Nadler, David Owens, David Plunkett, Arthur Ripstein, Nick Sage, Zoë Sinel, Becca Stone, Jean Thomas, Sabine Tsuruda, and Ariel Zylberman. And I have also been greatly enriched by all my colleagues, first in the Legal Studies and Business Ethics Department at Wharton, and now at the University of Michigan. Emily Dupraz supported this project over many years, not only intellectually through reading and discussing ideas, but also with care and emotional support.

The book has benefited immensely from written comments on the entire manuscript by four people: Christa Cornell, Don Herzog, Micha Gläser, and Amy Sepinwall. Their contributions are throughout the book.

I also received valuable comments on particular ideas or chapters from many people: Cheryl Abbate, Sarah Amighetti, Mitch Berman, Monika Betzler, James Brandt, Suzanne Buri, Sarah Buss, Sherman Clark, Rowan Cruft, Simon Ewers, Giulio Fornaroli, Scott Hershovitz, Nien-hê Hsieh, Felix Koch, Ishani Maitra, Gabe Mendlow, Sarah Moss, Jen Nadler, Anne Peters, Kristi Olson, David Owens, Sanjukta Paul, Anni Raty, Peter Schaber, Steve Schaus, Will Thomas, Salomé Viljoen, Jonas Vandieken, Fred Wilmot-Smith, Ariel Zylberman, and two referees for Harvard University Press.

The book benefited from two workshops on the entire manuscript, one through University of Zurich and the other at the University of Michigan; I am grateful to all the participants in those workshops. Discrete chapters have benefited from audiences at Albany, Binghamton, Cornell, Penn, Notre Dame, Toronto, Vermont, the Normative Powers Workshop, the LMU-Zürich Early Career Conference on Relational Normativity, the Canadian Private Law Workshop, MANCEPT, the Philosophy Desert Workshop, and the Normative Foundations of the Market Conference.

I have been fortunate to work with two excellent editors at Harvard University Press. James Brandt played a pivotal early role in assembling the book, helping to frame the project and providing detailed and thoughtful feedback on early chapters. Grigory Tovbis has patiently ushered the book to completion, helping at every step to make it more accessible and enjoyable to read. I am also grateful to Nolan Altvater for creating the cover image.

ACKNOWLEDGMENTS

Christa Cornell has read more of my words and corrected more of my mistakes than anyone ever will, but that only scratches the surface of how she has tirelessly supported me in all things.

Amy Sepinwall is my partner in all work as well as play—the two often blurring—and her contributions are everywhere.

This book is dedicated to my father, who had the questing heart of a philosopher and the creative mind of an artist.

Index

abuse of rights, 118–119

accountability: and animals, 145–147, 155, 204; and authority, 134–137; for consequences, 36, 63–66, 102–104; and directedness, 18, 129–132, 141, 203; as ex post, 6, 17, 93; and forgiving, 160, 163–164, 173–174; and freedom, 45, 60–63, 118; and harmless trespasses, 142–145; for imprudence, 52–56; to the moral community, 20–21, 25, 51, 141, 209–210; and moral status, 134–137, 149, 156; and negligence, 36–40; for nonactions, 73, 216–218; and second-personal reasons, 9, 68, 136; and standing, 134–137, 140–141; and wrongs, 5–6, 9, 15–17, 84

accountant liability, 33–34

action: as events, 217–218; rational, 146–147, 206–210; shaping, 37–40, 67–69, 82–84, 87, 191–195; spheres of, 20–21, 44–45, 62–63, 132, 208, 212–213, 225–226; and time, 203–204

addressees, 31–37, 147

aesthetic wrongs, 241n83

agent regret, 38, 249n52, 250n64

aggregation, 14, 152, 192, 261n36, 265n74

all's well that ends well, 133–134, 142–145, 210

All the King's Men (Warren) example, 64, 65

Andrei and Natasha example. See *War and Peace* example

Andrews, William, 63, 65, 236n39, 240n79, 244n118

animals, 19, 134, 145–156, 196, 216, 219

Anna Karenina (Tolstoy), 129, 252n12, 253n15

Anscombe, Elizabeth, 8, 51, 65, 68, 117–119

answerability, 36, 39, 54–56, 61, 70, 182, 217. *See also* accountability; "what's it to you?,"

apology: aptness as a feature of wrongs, 6, 12, 16, 94, 106, 132, 138, 192; to former teachers, 241n87; having size and shape, 96, 102–103; for imprudence, 53, 55, 118, 241n83; public, 97, 107–108; as reparative act, 97, 106; to third parties, 27, 31–33, 40, 49, 58, 82

Apple, Fiona, 239n69

Aquinas, Thomas, 123

Aristotle, 64, 95–96, 98, 104, 111–112

art, 139, 150, 152–153, 211–212, 231n34

Article III, 221–223

Austin, J. L., 266n4

286 INDEX

authority: of claiming, 14–15, 152; and
normative injury, 58–60, 144; rights
as, 5, 15, 19, 125, 134–137, 140,
211–214, 219
autonomy, 20–21, 206–210. *See also*
freedom

barista example, 198–199
Bekoff, Mark, 150–151
beliefs, 76, 121–123
beneficence, 116–119
benefiting, 105, 107, 144, 197–201, 216,
275n37, 275n39
betrayal, 126, 167–168
bipolar normativity, 18, 136, 207–208
blackmail, 274n35
Blackstone, William, 8, 50, 94, 98–99,
111, 240n77
blame, 15–16, 58, 157, 161. *See also*
reactive attitudes; resentment
Brake, Elizabeth, 246n27, 247n32
Burke v. Smith, 118
business ethics, 44–48, 249n51, 249n59

Card, Claudia, 119
Cardozo, Benjamin: axiom of, 2, 7, 10,
28–29, 68; on duties of rescuers,
262n42; *Moch* opinion, 29–30, 60–61,
63; moral vision of, 229n5; *Palsgraf*
opinion, 1–2, 10, 37–40, 210, 221,
231n37; *Ultramares* opinion, 33–34,
57, 61, 63; on wrongful death
statutes, 43
Carson, Rachel, 225
Carter, Jimmy, 123
causation, 63–66, 222–223, 244n120
children, 41–42, 52–53, 81–83, 148,
169
civil recourse theory, 113–114, 254n23
claiming: authority of, 9; and beneficence,
116–118; and directed duties, 130–132;
and exploitation, 194–195; and
gratitude, 119–121, 131–132; and

rights, 14, 130, 213, 218–219; and
thoughts, 124–125
claim-rights, 13, 54, 119, 160
claims: and claiming, 14, 218–219; and
complaints, 7, 9–10, 160; to love,
127–128; promissory, 28; and
rights, 5–7, 18–20; standing to make,
134–137; to thoughts, 121–125
"Coddling of the American Mind, The,"
(Lukianoff and Haidt), 224
coercive enforcement, 14, 61–62,
152–153, 193–194
Cohen, G. A., 137–139
community. *See* moral community
compensation: aptness as feature of
wrongs, 6, 12–13, 16, 29, 94–95;
rescue as, 85; size and shape, 96–97,
102, 105
competition, 44–48, 49
complaints: and ability to complain,
154–155, 215–216; and abuse of
rights, 118–119; of animals, 145–148;
of exploited, 184–188; as ex post, 6,
9, 132; and freedom, 61–63; giving up,
157, 161, 178; hypocritical, 137–142,
172, 214–215; legal, 175–177, 216;
and love, 127–129; nature of, 35–36,
58–59, 127; potential as reasons,
91–93; resentment as, 161–162,
178; and stakes, 49, 129, 142–145;
standing to make, 19, 38, 51, 137–142,
180–181; of third parties, 27–40,
45–51; of transgressors, 137–142;
trustee, 153–155; and wrongs, 6,
12–13, 16, 142, 144, 214–219
consent, 6, 13, 124, 181–190, 198, 201.
See also permission; waiver
continuity thesis, 112–114
contract law, 27–31, 72–73, 175–177,
193–194
corrective justice, 95–100, 109, 112–114
cost-benefit analysis, 88–89
Crow, Sheryl, 76

INDEX

damages, 41–42, 46, 88, 111, 175–176

D'Arms, Justin, and Daniel Jacobson, 251n4, 252n11

Darwall, Stephen, 9–10, 68, 135–137, 154, 265n72

De Blois, Natalie, 252n12

deception. *See* lying

defense of others, 62, 152–153, 265n75

deliberation, 6, 13, 80–91, 140–141, 203, 211, 224

demands: of animals, 152–154; authority of, 13–14, 134–135; and belief, 122; and gratitude, 121, 131–132; for respect, 125; standing to, 134–137, 194–195. *See also* claiming

dialogue, 62, 214–219

directed duties: ambiguity in, 130–132; correlation with claim-rights, 13–14; not to exploit, 189–197; phenomenology of, 15, 67, 150–152, 195–197; promissory, 70–81; relation to non-directed duties, 67, 232n39; threat of omnilateralism to, 50–51

doctors, 39–40, 51, 85, 117–119

duties: imperfect, 116, 130–132; non-directed, 67, 232n39; public, 48–51; to self, 54, 241n89; unwaivable, 168–170, 190. *See also* directed duties, owing

Dworkin, Ronald, 44–45, 48–49

Dylan, Bob, 56, 242n92

economic duress, 183–188

Eliot, George, 64, 92

environmental ethics, 225–226

epistemic injustice, 122

equity, 139

Erasmus, 250n71

estoppel, 100, 139

Evans, E. P., 145, 263n48

ex ante and ex post, 4–7, 61–63, 87, 129–132, 136–137, 170, 180, 217–218

exclusionary reasons, 5, 67, 203, 213

excuses, 179–180

exploitation, 181–201

Fairey, Shepard, 139, 141

"Farmer's Sorrow, A" (Jewett), 52–53

Feinberg, Joel, 20, 181, 184, 218–219, 278n33

fishermen, 225–226

fittingness, 99–100, 108, 174, 214–216, 218

Flanders v. Cooper, 39–40

forgiving: aptness as a feature of wrongs, 16–17; performative, 163–165, 177–178; preemptive, 157–180; promises to, 172–174; as release, 160–161; and resentment, 162–165, 178; third party, 29, 32, 40–41, 52, 58, 234n7, 237n48

Fortune v. National Cash Register Co., 118

foxhole example, 166–168, 173

Frankenstein (Shelley), 77–78, 247n34

freedom, 11, 20–21, 60–63, 130, 212–213

Fricker, Miranda, 122

Friendly, Henry, 176–177

Gaita, Raimond, 151

game show example, 55

garage example (Ripstein), 48–49

Goldberg, John, 113–114, 237n41, 252n8

Good Will Hunting, 53–54

gophers, 55–56

Govier, Trudy, 162–163

gratitude, 119–121, 125, 130–132, 144

Grotius, Hugo, 32–33, 35–37

guarantees, 70–74, 216

guilt, 16–17, 38, 136, 171

harm, 44–45, 48–50, 102–104, 142–145, 209–210, 222–223

Harman, Elizabeth, 250n66

harmless trespass, 142–143, 262n40

INDEX

Hart, H. L. A., 18, 27–28, 212, 277n15

Helmreich, Jeffrey, 232n46, 251n5, 268n21, 270n40

Helmsley, Leona, 119, 125

Herman, Barbara, 120–121, 255n21, 256n25

Hershovitz, Scott, 244n119, 251n6, 270n44

Hieronymi, Pamela, 160, 178

Hohfeld, Wesley Newcomb, 13–14, 17–18, 168

Hollywood Silver Fox Farm v. Emmett, 118

Holmes, Oliver Wendell, Jr., 70–71, 73, 88–89, 245n14, 263n56

Holmgren, Margaret, 163–164

Horsburgh (Horsbrugh), H. J. N., 158, 163

hypocrisy, 137–142, 172, 214–215

imprudence, 52–56, 207–210

ingratitude, 119–121, 255nn21–23

interdependence, 21, 65, 209–210, 219–220, 224–226

interest theory, 18–20, 203, 211–212, 240n81

intuitions, 12–13, 25, 27, 86, 273n25

inviolability, 5, 14–15, 190, 205

Ishiguro, Kazuo, 164–165

James, Henry, 76–77

Jane Eyre (Brontë), 26–27

Jesus, 167–168

Jewett, Sarah Orne, 52–53

Judas, 167–168

justification, 147–150, 200–201, 205–206, 214–218

Kamm, Frances, 86, 205, 248n49, 257n42

Kant, Immanuel: on beneficence, 116, 130; duties of right and duties of virtue, 130; equal freedom, 213; on

feuds, 260n20; on imputation, 36–37, 65, 243n116; on lying, 36–37; on reproach, 243n108, 243n112; on respect, 204–205

Keating, Gregory, 253n21

King Lear (Shakespeare), 120

Korsgaard, Christine, 146–147, 211, 276n12

Lacks, Henrietta, 100–102, 104–106, 109

legal liability: avoiding as reason, 87–89; release of, 175–177. *See also* damages, legal remedies

legal remedies: election of, 109–110; and liability waivers, 175–177; theories of, 111–114

Leopold, Aldo, 150, 280n55

liability waivers, 171, 175–177

Liberto, Hallie, 78–80, 248nn41–46

limbo, 80–81, 85–87, 103

lived experience, 108–110

Londey, David, 158–159

loss of consortium, 42, 238n50

lottery example, 30–31

love: right to, 3–4, 128–129; withdrawal of, 102, 106–107, 125–129, 165

"Lovers of Gudrun, The," 170

lying, 5, 26, 31–37, 65, 76

Maimonides, 123

making amends, 95–100

Manela, Tony, 131

markets, 47

Martin, Adrienne, 131–132

Marx, Karl, 21, 182, 198–201

medical providers. *See* doctors

memory, 149–150, 203–204

methodology, 11–13, 27, 202

microaggressions, 101, 103, 223–225

Mill, John Stuart, 116

Millay, Edna St. Vincent, 21–22, 220

Moch v. Rensselaer Water Co., 29–30, 60–61, 63

INDEX

289

mom-and-pop store, 45
moral community, 20–22, 50–51,
134–137, 140–141, 154–155,
207–210, 219–220
moral luck, 40, 63, 102–104, 253n15
Morris, Herbert, 169
Much Ado About Nothing, 40–41, 44
Murdoch, Iris, 11, 122–123
Murphy, Jeffrie, 133, 155–156
mutual reinforcement of arguments, 23,
25, 220–221

Nagel, Thomas, 103, 206
nature of rights debate, 18–20, 203,
240n81
negligence: common wrongs of, 214,
216; as explanation for transferred
intent, 58–59; in *Palsgraf*, 2, 37–40;
and preemptively forgiving, 171; in
pyrotechnics case, 84–86; in spreading
falsehoods, 31–37
nominal damages, 262n46
nonhuman animals. *See* animals
normative injury, 57–60, 144–145
Nozick, Robert, 205

Olympic medals, 90–91
ornithologist example, 191–193, 195,
196, 198
overheard lies, 31–37
Owens, David: on bare wronging,
261n37; connection between rights and
wronging, 9; on forgiving, 268n18,
268n29; terminology of "wrong," 4;
wronging attitudes, 121–122
owing, 13–14, 50–51, 130–132, 149–150,
207. *See also* directed duties

pajamas, 142–143
Palsgraf v. Long Island Railroad, 1–2,
10, 26, 37–40, 63, 65–66, 210,
221
pardons, 266n3

parents, 28–29, 40–44, 52–53, 81–84,
169–170, 211, 226, 269n32, 280n56
permission, 159–162, 165–166, 181,
267n9, 270n1
pet shop example, 273n25
Pierce, Chester, 223–224
placeholder rights, 13, 124, 131–132,
189, 197
plants, 154, 212
price gouging, 193
privity, 2, 8, 34. *See also* Cardozo,
Benjamin: axiom
prodigal son, 52
promises: to believe, 76–77; to care for
mother (Hart), 28–29; conflicting,
172; to feel, 74–76, 127–128; to
forgive, 172–174; to go camping,
168–169; implied, 127–128; to
promise, 173–174, 270nn41–42;
marriage, 80, 173, 246n27, 246n29;
not to sue, 175–177; promising to vs.
promising that, 71, 245n13; sexual,
78–81, 248nn41–47; third-party
beneficiaries of, 27–31; wicked,
77–78
property, 31, 41, 225–226, 235n19
prostitution, 186–188, 271n18,
272n20
psychopaths, 133, 155–156
public nuisance, 49–50
public policy, 237n46
pyrotechnics examples, 81–87

Quinn, Warren, 204–205

*Randi W. v. Muroc Joint Unified School
District*, 235n28
rational action, 206–210
Rawls, John, 137
Raz, Joseph, 18, 56, 211, 257n42,
277nn21–22
reactive attitudes, 15, 61–62, 135–137,
162–165, 178, 203

290 INDEX

reasons, 69, 75, 82–84, 244n4, 251n76;
conscious reflection on, 146–148;
moral, 140–141, 261n36; motivating
versus justifying, 92–93; and relationality, 206–210; second-personal,
135–137; to act vs. of fit, 174; to love,
128
reassurance, 76–77
regret, 89–93, 147, 250nn64–65
relational goods, 115–116, 254n1
relationality, 18, 67–69, 92, 95–96,
120–121, 206–210, 214–215
reliance, 32–37
repair: aptness as a feature of wrongs,
4–5, 16, 33, 214; and ex post considerations, 100–110; in exploitation,
192, 197–201; nature of, 94–100,
111; responsiveness, 97–100
requests, 117, 254n8
rescue doctrine, 236n38, 249n51
resentment, 15–16; anticipatory,
164–165; and forgiving, 162–165
respect: normative injury and, 57–60;
rights and, 204–205, 211–214
responsibility, and loss of standing,
138–139
retaliation, 137–139, 260nn18–21
rights: analysis of, 211–214; of animals,
149–155; and claims, 5, 218–219;
correlativity with duties, 13–14; of
criminals, 137–142, 219; and equality,
20, 233n63; fetishization, 145; five
features of, 13–15, 213–214; initial
description of, 5; minimizing violations of, 86; not to be exploited,
188–197, 272n22; not to be offended,
224; in Nowheresville, 219, 278n33;
primary and secondary, 17, 51,
232n49; shaping action, 37–40,
67–69; skepticism of, 21, 220;
theories of, 18–20, 203; of trees,
212; unwaivable, 168–170, 190

Ripstein, Arthur: connection between
rights and wronging, 9; criticism of
civil recourse theory, 254n23; freedom
and complaints, 242n106, 243n108;
harm and magnitude of wrongs,
252n14; on harmless trespass, 142–143,
277n16; insignificance of bare harm,
48–49

Sax, Joseph, 225
Scanlon, T. M., 149, 153–155, 205,
266n80
Schopenhauer, Arthur, 68
second-personal reasons, 9, 68, 135–137,
259n8
semantics, 4, 12–13, 231n36
sex: promises of, 78–81; right to,
128–129; work, 186–188
Shakespeare, William, 40–41, 120,
238n49, 256n29
Shelley, Mary, 77–78, 247n34
Shelley, Percy Bysshe, 204, 263n54
Shiffrin, Seana Valentine, 161,
247nn35–36, 262n44
side constraints, 5, 14, 190, 205
Smilansky, Saul, 140–141, 261n35
Smith, Adam, 116–117, 119
soldiers, 166–168, 173, 269n39
Solon, 219–220
Southgate, Eliza, 74–76
sovereignty, 18, 27, 31, 62, 182, 208,
212, 220
spite fence, 118
Srinivasan, Amia, 128–129, 257nn49–50
stakes: and harm, 51, 277n16; lack of,
144–145; in others, 21, 43–44, 47,
52–56; and relationality, 137, 209–210;
and wrongs, 19, 214–218. *See also*
"what's it to you?,"
standing: and capacity to complain,
154–155, 174; to claim, 7, 13–14,
194–195; to complain, 7, 16–17,

61–62, 133, 161–163, 178–180, 232n49; to demand justification, 118, 214–218; and fittingness, 174; to forgive, 169; and injury, 51, 142–145, 210; legal, 29, 221–223, 259n14; loss of, 137–142, 144; and rightholding, 13–14, 134–137, 172–173; and stakes, 210, 215

Stendahl, 165

Strawson, P. F., 15, 137, 278n27

subjunctive conditionals, 91

surrogacy, 183

sweatshop labor, 183, 185–186, 198–200

Swift, Taylor, 126–127

swimming lanes (Dworkin), 44–48

temporal perspectives, 4–7, 85–87, 180, 203–204, 276n1

testimony, 76

Thaler, Richard, 89–90, 250n65

third-party beneficiaries, 27–31

Thompson, Michael, 7–8, 18, 207

Thomson, Judith Jarvis, 8, 121, 244n1, 245nn15–16, 246nn21–22

thoughts, 121–125

tiebreaking, 81–87

Tolstoy, Leo, 2–4, 115, 129, 201, 229n11, 231n32, 252n12

transferred intent, 59

Trollope, Anthony, 126

True Cost, The, 185–186

tu quoque, 137–142

Ultramares Corp. v. Touche Niven & Co, 33–34, 57, 61, 63

unclean hands, 139, 141

unconscionability, 193–194, 274n30

Verwoerd, Wilhelm, 162–163

waiver, 14, 28, 157, 160, 166–169, 172–174, 190

Waldron, Jeremy, 212–213

Wallace, R. Jay: bipolarity, 207; connection between rights and wronging, 9; on Darwall and second–personal address, 135–137, 259n8, 259n13; different perspectives, 230n17; interpersonal recognition, 92; normative injury, 58, 242n98

War and Peace example, 2–5, 11, 13, 115, 125, 128, 201, 229n10

warranties, 70–74, 86

Warren, Robert Penn, 64–65

Warth v. Seldin, 222

Weinrib, Ernest, 109

"what's it to you?," 145, 209–210, 222

will theory, 18–20, 203, 212–214, 240n81

Wings of the Dove (James) example, 76–77

Wittgenstein, Ludwig, 264n57

wrong (adjective), 4, 68, 148, 207–210

wronging. *See* wrongs

wrongs: analysis of, 214–218; to animals, 148; and consent, 181–188; and directed duties, 79–80; environmental, 225–226; of exploitation, 182–188; harmless, 142–147; initial description of, 5–6; interest theory of, 18–20; of microaggressions, 103, 223–225; as morphing void, 111; normative injury and, 57–60; phenomenology of, 15–16; as placeholders, 13; and repair, 4–5, 16, 214; six features of, 15–17; supposed connection with rights, 7–10; terminology of, 4; to transgressors, 137–142; will theory of, 18–20; and wronging, 4

Zipursky, Benjamin, 113–114, 237n41